THE PROCLAMATIONS OF THE TUDOR KINGS

THE PROCLAMATIONS
OF THE
TUDOR KINGS

R. W. HEINZE
ASSOCIATE PROFESSOR OF HISTORY
CONCORDIA TEACHERS COLLEGE, RIVER FOREST, ILLINOIS

CAMBRIDGE UNIVERSITY PRESS
CAMBRIDGE
LONDON · NEW YORK · MELBOURNE

CAMBRIDGE UNIVERSITY PRESS
Cambridge, New York, Melbourne, Madrid, Cape Town, Singapore, São Paulo, Delhi

Cambridge University Press
The Edinburgh Building, Cambridge CB2 8RU, UK

Published in the United States of America by Cambridge University Press, New York

www.cambridge.org
Information on this title: www.cambridge.org/9780521209380

© Cambridge University Press 1976

This publication is in copyright. Subject to statutory exception
and to the provisions of relevant collective licensing agreements,
no reproduction of any part may take place without the written
permission of Cambridge University Press.

First published 1976
This digitally printed version 2008

A catalogue record for this publication is available from the British Library

Library of Congress Cataloguing in Publication data
Heinze, Rudolph W.
The proclamations of the Tudor kings.
Includes index.
1. Great Britain – Proclamations. 2. Great Britain – History – Tudors, 1485–1603.
I. Title.
KD4435.H44   342'.42'02   75-22983

ISBN 978-0-521-20938-0 hardback
ISBN 978-0-521-08554-0 paperback

CONTENTS

		page
Preface		vii
Abbreviations		x
1	The early Tudor royal proclamations	1
	Definition and number	1
	Formulation	6
	Promulgation	20
2	The authority of royal proclamations	30
3	The use of royal proclamations: an overview	55
4	The use of royal proclamations: Henry VII	65
5	The use of royal proclamations: Henry VIII – the first stage	85
	Wolsey (1509–29)	86
	Cromwell (1529–39)	109
6	The Statute of Proclamations	153
	Previous interpretations	153
	A new look	165
7	The use of royal proclamations: Henry VIII – the second stage	178
8	The use of royal proclamations: Edward VI	200
	Somerset (1547–9)	201
	Northumberland (1549–53)	223
9	The enforcement of royal proclamations	250
	Administrative enforcement	252
	Judicial enforcement	262
10	Conclusions	293

CONTENTS

Appendix A	Texts of proclamations not included in Hughes and Larkin	296
Appendix B	Proclamations for which no text has been found	302
Index of Statutes cited		305
Index		308

PREFACE

New monographs are generally justified by the contention that the subject has either been neglected or misinterpreted. To some degree both arguments apply to this study. The existence of a continuing historical controversy suggests that at least some historians have not interpreted correctly the role of royal proclamations in early Tudor government. Unfortunately, this controversy has not stimulated any serious effort to investigate in depth the actual use and purpose of royal proclamations in the early Tudor period. G. R. Elton wrote in 1961: 'Proclamations remain a subject to be studied; we do not even yet possess a complete list... nor has anyone yet attempted a systematic analysis of their content, enforcement, and general significance.'[1] Almost a decade and a half later we are still lacking a 'systematic analysis.' However, Paul L. Hughes and James F. Larkin made a major contribution when they published the long awaited scholarly edition of the texts of the early Tudor royal proclamations in 1964.[2] It is in large measure due to their work that this study has been made possible.

Royal proclamations were used extensively by the Tudor monarchs to announce their decisions and to administer the realm. They also made an impact on early Tudor legislation. Most of the controversy has centered on this question. Some historians have interpreted the Crown's use of royal proclamations as a real or potential threat to the legislative supremacy of Parliament. Others have argued that the Tudor monarchs used royal proclamations to complement and to uphold statutory legislation rather than to compete with Parliament's authority. The Statute of Proclamations of 1539[3] has served as the focal point for much of this discussion, but there is little agreement on its true significance. In the long and often heated debate over the

---

[1] G. R. Elton, 'State Planning in Early Tudor England,' *ECHR*, XIII (1961), 434.
[2] Paul L. Hughes and James F. Larkin eds., *Tudor Royal Proclamations*, Vol. 1: *The Early Tudors (1485-1553)* (New Haven, 1964).
[3] 31 Henry VIII c. 8.

meaning and intent of this enigmatic statute, it has been both denounced as the high point of 'Tudor Despotism' and heralded as a striking documentation of respect for statutory legislation. Although the Statute of Proclamations has probably received more attention than it deserves, the question at issue is a legitimate one. This study attempts to provide evidence for dealing with the legislative role of royal proclamations in a more convincing way than has been offered in the past, but its objectives range further than this.

The major concern of this monograph is to delineate the role of royal proclamations in early Tudor government and to evaluate how effectively they served that function. The plan of the book alternates between a chronological and topical approach. The study begins with an effort to establish a more accurate count of the royal proclamations issued during the period. A description of their formulation and promulgation follows. Chapter 2 investigates the authority of royal proclamations as defined by Parliament and the role and power attributed to them by Tudor judges and legal writers. Chapters 4 to 8 are the center of the study and employ a chronological organization. They trace the actual use of royal proclamations as well as their relationship to statutory legislation and common law. The discussion of the use of royal proclamations is interrupted by a chapter on the meaning and significance of the Statute of Proclamations. Since this act has received so much attention in the past, previous interpretations are first reviewed. The reign of Henry VIII is subdivided into a first stage, ending with the enactment of the Statute of Proclamations, and a second stage covering the period when the statute was in effect. The first stage is further divided into periods roughly corresponding to the age of Wolsey's dominance and Cromwell's ministry.[4] Edward VI's reign is also subdivided for the purpose of more meaningful analysis. The royal proclamations issued before October 1549 reflect Edward Seymour's policy; those issued afterwards must have been heavily influenced by the ideas of John Dudley, the dominant figure on the council during the remainder of the reign. A major concern of these chapters is to determine whether the role of royal proclamations was modified or if there was an attempt at change by the successive monarchs or their ministers between 1485 and 1553. Chapter 7 finally takes up the question of

[4] Wolsey was Chancellor from 1515 to 1529. Cromwell was the King's chief minister from 1532 to 1540. The Statute of Proclamations was enacted in the Parliament which began to meet in April 1539. It was repealed by 1 Edward VI c. 12.

PREFACE

effectiveness by investigating the long neglected matter of enforcement both on the national and local levels.

This study is the result of ten years of research liberally supported by grants from the Folger Shakespeare Library in Washington D.C., the American Endowment for the Arts and Humanities, and the American Philosophical Society. I am also indebted to the skill and courtesy of the staffs of the British Museum, the Public Record Office, the Corporation of London Records Office, the Institute of Historical Research and local record offices throughout England. I am grateful to the many teachers and scholars who encouraged this work and who willingly lent their assistance and advice. I wish to thank especially Professor Paul L. Hughes, who first stimulated my interest in royal proclamations, Professor Robert Kingdon, who supervised my doctoral dissertation, and Professor Merle Radke, who made many valuable suggestions for improving the prose and readability of the manuscript. I owe major debts to Professor James F. Larkin, whose friendship and kind but frank criticism have been indispensable, and to Professor Frederic Youngs, who has worked in close cooperation with me since we first met in 1967, and whose knowledge of Marian and Elizabethan royal proclamations has helped me immeasurably. Finally, Professor G. R. Elton deserves special mention for his patience, encouragement and aid for over a decade.

River Forest, Illinois R. W. Heinze
December 1975

ABBREVIATIONS

AgHR	*Agricultural History Review*
Antiq	Society of Antiquaries
BCR	Borough of Colchester Records
BIHR	*Bulletin of the Institute of Historical Research*
BM	British Museum
CCRO	Chester City Record Office
CJ	*Journals of the House of Commons*
CLRO	Corporation of London Records Office
CPR	*Calendar of Patent Rolls*
CSPSp	*Calendar of State Papers Spanish*
CSPV	*Calendar of State Papers Venetian*
Dasent	Acts of the Privy Council of England 1452–1628, J. R. Dasent ed., 32 vols. (1890–1907)
DNB	*Dictionary of National Biography*
EcHR	*Economic History Review*
EHR	*English Historical Review*
Foxe	John Foxe, *Acts and Monuments*, G. Townsend ed., 8 vols. (1843–9)
GCA	Grimsby City Archives
HHL	Henry Huntington Library
HJ	*Historical Journal*
HMCR	Historical Manuscript Commission Reports
IESRO	Ipswich and East Suffolk Record Office
KRO	Kent Record Office
LCRO	Lincolnshire County Record Office
LJ	*Journals of the House of Lords*
LP	Letters and Papers, Foreign and Domestic of the Reign of Henry VIII, J. S. Brewer, J. Gairdner, R. H. Brodie eds., 36 vols. (1862–1932)
Nicolas	Proceedings and Ordinances of the Privy Council of England, N. H. Nicolas ed., 7 vols. (1834–7)
NNRO	Norfolk and Norwich Record Office

ABBREVIATIONS

SCRO   Shrewsbury Corporation Record Office
Steele   Robert Steele, *A Bibliography of Royal Proclamations of the Tudor and Stuart Sovereigns...with an Historical Essay on their Origin and Use*, Vol. v, *Bibliotheca Lindesiana* (Oxford, 1910)
Strype   *Ecclesiastical Memorials*, John Strype ed., 3 vols (London, 1721)
TRHS   *Transactions Royal Historical Society*
TRP   *Tudor Royal Proclamations*, Paul L. Hughes and James F. Larkin eds., 3 vols. (New Haven 1964–9)
YCRO   York City Record Office

Manuscripts cited without location are from the Public Record Office in London: the following classes have been used.

C 66   Chancery, Patent Rolls
C 82   Chancery, Warrants for the Great Seal, Series II
C 193   Chancery, Miscellaneous Books, Crown Office
Dur 3   Palatinate of Durham, Cursitor's Records
E 36   Exchequer, Treasury of Receipt, Miscellaneous Books
E 40   Exchequer, Treasury of Receipt, Ancient Deeds, Series A
E 101   Exchequer, King's Remembrancer, Various Accounts
E 111   Exchequer, King's Remembrancer, Bills, Answers and Depositions
E 122   Exchequer, King's Remembrancer, Customs Accounts
E 159   Exchequer, King's Remembrancer, Memoranda Rolls
E 163   Exchequer, King's Remembrancer, Miscellanea of the Exchequer
E 198   Exchequer, King's Remembrancer, Documents Relating to Serjeanties, Knights' Fees etc.
KB 9   King's Bench, Ancient Indictments
SP 1   State Papers, Henry VIII
SP 2   State Papers, Henry VIII, folio volumes
SP 3   State Papers, Henry VIII, Lisle Papers
SP 6   State Papers, Henry VIII, Theological Tracts
SP 7   State Papers, Henry VIII, Wriothesley Papers
SP 10   State Papers, Edward VI
SP 46   State Papers, Supplementary
St Ch 1   Star Chamber Proceedings, Henry VII
St Ch 2   Star Chamber Proceedings, Henry VIII
St Ch 3   Star Chamber Proceedings, Edward VI

ABBREVIATIONS

I have modernized the spelling and punctuation of all quotations with the exception of the newly found proclamations included in Appendix A. Although I feel that documents should be submitted in their original form, I see no reason to burden the reader with archaic and idiosyncratic spellings and punctuation in the analytical portion of the book. Though I have included the *LP* references in footnotes for the convenience of the reader I have, as the citations indicate, relied on the manuscript source rather than the calendar in almost every case.

I

THE EARLY TUDOR ROYAL PROCLAMATIONS

Definition and Number

Proclamation is a notice publicly given of anything whereof the King thinketh good to advertise his subjects.[1]

It would be simple to identify royal proclamations if John Rastell's facile definition could be accepted as the starting point for this study. Unfortunately, it would make the task of collecting and analyzing them impossibly massive.[2] Neither of the two modern compilers of royal proclamations accepted such a broad definition. Robert Steele, whose bibliography served as the basis for most comments on proclamations before 1964, defined them according to certain characteristics:

They have been proclaimed, they have passed (potentially or actually) under the great seal, and they have been made by the advice and consent of the Council. Of these characteristics the first two are invariable, while as to the third we can only affirm it to be true in every case of which we know the facts...[the essential characteristic is] a schedule to a chancery writ validated by the sign manual as superscription.[3]

Steele, however, did not limit his bibliography by that definition, because he included in his list statutes and other non-royal proclamations.[4] Paul Hughes and James Larkin, the editors of the first printed edition of early Tudor royal proclamations, improved on Steele's work by rejecting many items which were clearly not royal proclamations and including a number of proclamations not listed

---

[1] John Rastell, *Les Termes de la Ley* (London, 1629), 260.
[2] G. R. Elton in his review of the first volume of *Tudor Royal Proclamations* commented: 'Technically, a proclamation was no more than any announcement of a royal order: the bulk of them covered such technicalities as outlawries proclaimed in the shire court or forfeited goods. These are naturally and rightly excluded here.' G. R. Elton, 'Government by Edict,' *HJ*, VIII, 2 (1965), 268. [3] Steele, ix, xx.
[4] Statutes were printed and proclaimed in the same fashion as proclamations during Henry VIII's reign. The printed copies look very similar to the printed copies of proclamations and it is not unusual for collections of printed proclamations to include a number of statutes. The New Romney collection, for example, has thirty-two early Tudor broadsides, but seventeen of these are statutes. KRO NPZPr 1-33.

by Steele. They also recognized the difficulty of establishing a definitive definition. For the purpose of determining what documents to include in their volume, they tentatively defined a royal proclamation as 'a public ordinance issued by the King, in virtue of his royal prerogative with the advice of his council, under the Great Seal, and by royal writ.'[5] Even that definition was not entirely satisfactory. In his study of Marian and Elizabethan proclamations Frederic Youngs accepted the essentials of the earlier definitions, but questioned whether the statements on conciliar advice or consent added 'any distinguishing characteristics.' He also felt the need to construct a more 'descriptive' definition in order to distinguish royal proclamations from other types of documents. He placed his emphasis on the 'distinctive format' found in the printed proclamations of the Tudor queens:

They were headed 'By the Queen' and occasionally had a title, and they concluded with the place of issue preceded by the phrase 'Given at...,' with the invocation 'God save the Queen,' and with the identification of the royal printer. Even though none of those points was unique to proclamations, the combination was.[6]

Unfortunately, none of these definitions provides an infallible guide. If the printed copy of the proclamation, the validating seal and the writ were always available, it would be relatively easy to establish a canon of royal proclamations. Needless to say survivals have not been that complete, and culling non-royal proclamations from the earlier collections remains a formidable task. It has already been mentioned that Steele included statutes and other documents which were not royal proclamations. Hughes and Larkin recognized the problem, but in doubtful cases they preferred to err on the side of broadness 'in the interests of completeness.'[7] This was probably

[5] *TRP*, xxiii.

[6] Frederic A. Youngs, *The Proclamations of the Tudor Queens* (Cambridge, 1976), 9. His complete definition reads: 'a royal command, normally cast in a distinctive format, validated by the royal sign manual, issued under a special chancery writ sealed with the Great Seal, which was publicly proclaimed.'

[7] 'A vexing problem in this edition has been that of deciding whether to include texts that are questionable on grounds of literary form or lack of chancery protocol. Examples of texts lacking conformity with one or more of the criteria established at the outset of this edition for a working definition of a Tudor royal proclamation...are certain letters patent, injunctions, Privy Council orders, statutory provisions, and other public utterances made in the name and by the authority of the sovereign. On balance we have been inclined to include such texts (drafts, coronation pardons, injunctions for religion, alms placards, patents of monopoly) in the interests of completeness and because of the probability, at least in some cases, that probative evidence will be forthcoming at a later date.' *TRP*, II, xvi-xvii.

Table 1. *Items rejected as royal proclamations*

(1) Purely local orders		(5) Duplicates[e]
Nos. 8	78	Nos. 103–102
15	98	132–131
41	99	180–179
(2) Church Briefs[a]		232–231
Nos. 32	84	(6) Signet letters
82	185	Nos. 14
(3) Letters patent		351
Nos. 145[b]	210	(7) Miscellaneous
192	251	Nos. 65 – Statute[f]
(4) Circular letters		191 – Draft: no evidence of issue
Nos. 85[c]	285	277.5 – Heraldic proclamation
158[d]	353	287 – Religious injunctions[g]
		338 – Instructions to commissioners

[a] A church brief was 'A royal warrant authorizing a collection in places of worship, and sometimes from house to house for a special charitable object.' Wyndham A. Bewes, *Church Briefs or Royal Warrants for Collections for Charitable Objects* (London, 1896), 82.

[b] The preamble to a bill in parliament refers to this item as 'the said letters patent' while it called no. 153 dealing with the same subject 'a proclamation'. SP 1/105/213–15 (*LP* xi no. 204).

[c] Foxe calls this the 'King's letter for to aid of John Longland, Bishop of Lincoln against heretics.' Foxe, iv, 241.

[d] See G. R. Elton, *Policy and Police* (Cambridge, 1972), 238 n. 5 for an explanation of why this circular was printed.

[e] None of these are exact duplicates. Proclamation no. 103 is worded slightly differently from no. 102, but this may be a copyist's error and the dating is so close that they must be the same proclamation. No. 132 seems to be an order to the sheriffs of London to proclaim no. 131. No. 180 is exactly the same as no. 178, but it is dated four months later. This may be an error in dating by the compiler of the London Letter Books or it could be an example of the same proclamation being proclaimed several times in the same year. No. 232 is exactly the same as no. 231 except that it includes a section on pricing fowl meant specifically for London.

[f] This is a portion of 4 Henry VIII c. 19.

[g] This was issued in quarto rather than broadside as was normal for proclamations. It is always referred to as an 'injunction' rather than a proclamation.

a wise decision, but they were too generous. G. R. Elton noted this in his review essay. He listed twenty-seven items included by Hughes and Larkin in their first volume which he did not consider royal proclamations.[8] Operating with the benefit of his observations, it is considerably easier to make judgments on a number of questionable documents in that volume. Table 1 contains a list of twenty-one items which I have rejected as royal proclamations together with brief explanations of why they were rejected.[9]

[8] Elton, *HJ*, viii, 268.

[9] I have rejected all the items rejected by Professor Elton in his review article with five exceptions. Proclamations nos. 109, 113, 114, and 119 were not accepted by him because they were proclaimed only in chancery and were not 'of general import'. While

Despite impressive labors in a variety of archives, Hughes and Larkin did not locate all the surviving proclamation texts. Nine more proclamations can be added to those in Volume I and the appendix to Volume III of *Tudor Royal Proclamations*.[10] These proclamations are included in Appendix A. There are also references to unfound proclamations in a number of sources. A careful analysis of these references makes it possible to establish with some degree of certainty that at least forty-four additional proclamations whose texts have not been found were issued. Appendix B contains a list of these proclamations together with the source of the reference.[11] Even with these additions it is obvious that we do not have a complete count of all the royal proclamations issued between 1485 and 1553. Gaps in our present list raise suspicions. Unless we assume that there were no proclamations for periods which at times exceeded two years, it seems likely that a good number of proclamations have

accepting them as doubtful, I have retained them, because there is no clear evidence that they were proclaimed only in the chancery and the texts certainly have wider implications than the proclamations of commissions of oyer and terminer to which Professor Elton compares them. He also classified nos. 76 and 79 as duplicates. This is not accurate. The first proclamation announced the original treaty between England and France sealed by the marriage alliance between Mary and Louis XII on 7 August 1514. Louis died on 31 December 1514 and the treaty was renegotiated with Francis I. This was proclaimed in the second proclamation on 16 April 1515. There are a number of doubtful cases among the proclamations I have accepted, but in cases where some uncertainty prevailed I have preferred to err on the side of caution, respecting Hughes' and Larkin's judgments whenever there was no positive evidence that they were mistaken.

[10] The appendix to Volume III contains early Tudor royal proclamations discovered after the publication of Volume I. Hughes and Larkin were able to draw on a number of earlier collections as starting points. The earliest collection was made by Richard Grafton in 1550 (Richard Grafton ed., *All Suche Proclamations as Have Been Sette Furth by the Kynges Maiestie from the Last of January in the First Year of His Highnesses Reign unto the Last Day of Januarri Beeying in the IIII Yere of His Reigne*, London, 1550). The Society of Antiquaries has an impressive collection which was the result of the efforts of the eighteenth century antiquarian, Peter Le Neve. Harleian 422 in the British Museum contains copies of many early Tudor proclamations including writs and notes where the proclamations were proclaimed. Some local archives have useful collections. One of the best is in the Kent Record Office. Unfortunately, none of these collections is complete. Even Grafton, despite his ambitious title, failed to include all the proclamations issued during the brief period he covered. Much of the work of finding new proclamations texts depended on a tedious page for page search of the records of the Corporation of London. These are the richest local record source of proclamations texts.

[11] Many of these proclamations were listed by Steele. Steele also included many documents which were not proclamations under his listing 'not found'. A careful reading of the reference reveals that some of these were mayoral proclamations (Steele, nos. 188, 412c, 414), statutes (nos. 20a, 412a, 412b) or royal letters (no. 275). A good number of the texts of others were found by Hughes and Larkin and included in their volume. The list in Appendix B accepts twenty-four of the items listed by Steele as authentic proclamations and adds twenty additional ones. There are numerous other references to proclamations, but either the reference is not clear enough to establish that it was actually a royal proclamation or there is not enough information to determine the subject matter.

Table 2. *Average number of proclamations issued per month (1485–1553)*

Period	Proclamations texts	Evidence of issue	Total	Number of months	Average per month
Henry VII					
(1) 25 Aug. 1485 to 21 April 1509	58	9	67	284	0.24
Henry VIII					
(2) 22 April 1509 to 31 Dec. 1529	71	4	75	248	0.30
(3) 1 Jan. 1530 to 31 June 1539	64	13	77	114	0.68
(4) 1 July 1539 to 30 Jan. 1547	85	6	91	92	0.99
Edward VI					
(5) 31 Jan. 1547 to 8 Oct. 1549	76	1	77	32	2.41
(6) 9 Oct. 1549 to 6 July 1553	39	11	50	45	1.11
Total	393	44	437	815	0.54

disappeared without trace especially for the reign of Henry VII and the early part of Henry VIII's reign.[12]

After one takes deletions and additions into consideration there remain at least 437 royal proclamations that were issued in the sixty-eight year period during which the Tudor monarchs reigned. The texts of 393 of them have survived. Table 2 gives a chronological breakdown of the number of proclamations during each subdivision of the period and a computation of the average number per month. The table reveals a vast increase in the number of proclamations during the latter part of the period. The increase was gradual until the enactment of the Statute of Proclamations, but after 1539 the

[12] There is a four-year period between April 1505 and April 1509 during which there is no evidence of the issue of any proclamations and a gap of almost two and a half years between September 1493 and February 1496. Gaps of a year or more are found between June 1486–June 1487; December 1487–January 1489; November 1509–July 1511; April 1515–June 1516; July 1519–August 1520; October 1520–December 1521; October 1523–October 1524; June 1530–June 1531; and October 1531–October 1532. After October 1532 there are no more periods of this length without either surviving proclamations or evidence of their issue.

incidence of use rose significantly. The peak period of use came after the repeal of the Statute of Proclamations. While Somerset was in power the average number of proclamations issued per month was more than double that of the previous period. Only nineteen of these were issued before the Statute of Proclamations was repealed. The final period witnessed a decline in use, but the incidence of use was still higher than while the Statute of Proclamations was in effect. Although these figures are affected by the chances of survival, it seems likely that most undiscovered proclamations belong to the first two periods, and it is unlikely that the sharp differences noted in the last four periods would be radically altered by the discovery of new proclamations.

Formulation

The first stage in the making of a royal proclamation was obviously the detection of a need. This could occur either as the result of information received by the King or council from a variety of sources or more directly through a petition for action from a private party, a group of individuals, or a local governing body. Although evidence of originating factors is not available for most of the early Tudor proclamations, cases where evidence survives reveal that a surprising number of them resulted from the initiative of parties other than the central government. The motivating force behind specific proclamations will be discussed in greater detail in later chapters, but at this point a few examples may be offered to document this contention.

The government was especially responsive to the needs of the London city government. A significant number of proclamations originated in petitions from the mayor and aldermen of London. Although this widespread evidence of London's influence may in part be due to the excellent records which have survived, certainly, considering the size, importance and proximity of London, it should not be surprising that the central government responded to the city's needs. Some of these proclamations were related to the vital question of the supply of food for London, a constant problem for a city of that size. It can be documented that one of the proclamations designed to provide victual for London was the result of a specific request from the city government, and it is likely that others originated from the same source.[13] A number of the proclamations which imposed

---

[13] *TRP* no. 70; CLRO Rep 2/150d. The mayor and aldermen appointed six people to go to the King's council 'for wheat that cometh to the city that it be not taken by the King's taker.'

restraints on export can also be traced to the shortage of grain and the resulting high price of food in London. In the two cases where a definite relationship can be established, the central government reacted with surprising speed to the request of the city officials. On 17 April 1548 the Court of Aldermen agreed that the mayor, on his next visit to the King's council, would ask 'for the staying of butter, cheese and tallow here within the realm.' On 24 April a proclamation imposed a restraint.[14] On 18 September 1548 a messenger from the Court of Aldermen was commissioned to ride to the Lord Chancellor 'desiring his lordship in my lord mayor's name and my masters' the aldermen' to intercede with Somerset 'that a restraint may be had with expedition by proclamation.' Eight days later a proclamation forbade unlicensed export of victuals.[15] Some of the price control proclamations were also influenced primarily by the high price of food in London. A number of the meat price proclamations during the 1530s, including several which suspended statutes, can be traced to the needs of London. The prices set in a proclamation of 21 May 1544 were exactly the same as those set by the mayor and aldermen of London on 10 May which were to be 'delivered upon Monday next in the afternoon unto the King's most honorable council.'[16] The same connection between the prices set in a royal proclamation and those requested by the London officials can be documented in one of the wine price proclamations. On 8 June 1546 the Court of Aldermen set prices on wine and asked the King's council 'to have the King's proclamation for the establishment thereof within this city.' On 11 June a proclamation ordering compliance with those prices was issued.[17]

The city at times asked for royal proclamations to arbitrate internal disputes or to defend the city's rights of jurisdiction. The intervention of the central government in the dispute over tithes between the citizens and clergy of London was urged by the Court of Aldermen. The royal proclamation which reaffirmed the authority of the mayor and aldermen to set prices on fish and to regulate fishing in the Thames was issued in reply to an appeal from a special committee set up by the Court of Aldermen to go to the Lord Privy Seal 'for the

[14] CLRO Rep. 11/426; *TRP* no. 304.
[15] CLRO Rep. 11/490d; *TRP* no. 313.5.
[16] CLRO Rep. 11/66d; *TRP* no. 231. Other meat-price proclamations which can be traced to a request of London authorities are nos. 139, 144, 148. See R. W. Heinze, 'The Pricing of Meat: A Study in the Use of Royal Proclamations in the Reign of Henry VIII,' *HJ*, XII, 4 (1969), 583–95.
[17] CLRO Rep. 11/226d; *TRP* no. 267.

matter of the Thames and the prices of fresh fish lately assessed.'[18] At times the city solicited the central government's aid in local law enforcement. London authorities prohibited plays and interludes long before the central government intervened in October 1544. A second proclamation on that subject in August 1549 may have been the direct result of a petition from the mayor to the Lord Chancellor in July 1549 for 'aid and advice for the staying of all common interludes and plays within the city.'[19] One of the few proclamations which ordered the death penalty could have been inspired by the needs of London. On 18 April 1538 a proclamation threatened subjects with forfeiture of lands, goods and chattels as well as 'perpetual imprisonment' for hurting or maiming 'mayors, sheriffs, bailiffs, sergeants' and other of the King's officers in the performance of their duties, and with death 'without remission or pardon' or 'privilege of sanctuary or clergy' for killing them. The motivation for the initial proclamation cannot be established, but on 7 December 1549 the recorder of the city reported 'that he had moved the right honorable Lord Admiral for the renewing of the King's most gracious proclamation for the surety of the officers of this city in doing of their arrests and other offices within this city.'[20]

In sharp contrast to the numerous proclamations that can be traced to appeals from London, the influence of other cities can seldom be documented. One of the few examples is a proclamation of 30 May 1542 which revised 33 Henry VIII c. 15. The statute had provided that the city of Chester would be a sanctuary town. It included a clause that allowed the King to alter the statute by royal proclamation if information was received that Chester was 'not meet to be sanctuary nor place of privilege.' It is hardly surprising that this information came from the city government of Chester which appealed for removal of the sanctuary because of the 'intolerable inconveniences which were like to have ensued to this city being a port town and standing so nigh Wales.' The reaction to the petition was a royal proclamation which moved the sanctuary to Stafford.[21]

Private individuals and groups also petitioned for proclamations. If the need could be established, the government tended to be quite

[18] CLRO Rep. 8/275d; *TRP* no. 153; CLRO Rep. 10/314d; *TRP* no. 214.
[19] CLRO Rep. 10/322d; Journals 14/319; *TRP* no. 240; CLRO Rep. 13(1)/100; *TRP* no. 344.
[20] CLRO Rep. 10/185; *TRP* no. 179. The request seems to have been motivated by the injury done to one of the sheriffs of the city. Whether or not the central government responded cannot be documented since the proclamation has not survived.
[21] CCRO A/B/1/75; *TRP* no. 212.

8

receptive. The statute on wool cloth manufacture was reluctantly suspended a number of times as a result of the petitions of the clothiers. Each proclamation mentioned specifically the 'most humble petition of the cloth makers.' In the case of the later suspensions the government acted only after convincing evidence was submitted that the action was essential for the economic survival of the cloth makers.[22] In some cases the petition of a single individual resulted in a royal proclamation. For example, the proclamation of 6 May 1541, which ordered that every parish have a copy of the Great Bible by a set date, can be traced directly to a petition by the printer, Anthony Marler.[23] At times the government solicited the advice of experts before acting. The proclamations in 1537 and 1538, which permitted free exchanges, seem to have originated from the petition of concerned groups and upon the advice of Richard Gresham.[24] In at least one case the King seems to have issued a royal proclamation because of the plea of a foreign ambassador. On 3 September 1540 the French ambassador wrote to Francis I that he had asked the King of England to provide that strangers leaving the realm be not molested since some had complained of robberies and beatings. In response to that request 'this King, three days ago proclaimed that no stranger should be outraged by deed or word.'[25]

A series of proclamations, which cannot be attributed to direct petitions, may reflect the influence of complaints and advice received from both private individuals and government officials. The government often received advice that a proclamation might aid in resolving a particular problem. While it cannot always be established that there is a direct relationship between that advice and the issuance of a proclamation, in many cases a connection seems likely. In 1517 Richard Fox, bishop of Winchester, wrote to Wolsey that there was great confusion 'about the taking and refusing of pennies.' He suggested that Wolsey 'command proclamations to be made in every shire like to the proclamations that were last made for that matter.'[26] In the same year Fox also advised Wolsey that proclamations be

---

[22] BM Titus B v/187. The statute, 27 Henry VIII c. 12, was suspended at least five times. The texts of four of these proclamations have survived (*TRP* nos. 175, 198, 202, 207). A fifth suspension, probably in September 1538, can be inferred from the petition of the wool cloth manufacturers for the repeal of the statute. St Ch 2/23/115.

[23] Nicolas, VII, 185; *TRP* no. 200.

[24] *TRP* nos. 181, 182; SP 1/123/240 (*LP* 12[2] no. 464); SP 1/124/24-9 (*LP* 12[2] no. 509); BM Ortho E x/45 (*LP* 13[1] no. 1453); SP 1/135/7-8 (*LP* 13[2] no. 13).

[25] *LP* 16 no. 11. The proclamation text is not extant. It is included in Appendix B as item no. 27.

[26] SP 1/232/27 (*LP* App. 1[1] no. 188).

made 'that clothiers shall have their liberty in buying of wool' and that artificers and journeymen be paid 'in ready money and not in wares according to the statutes.' He warned of local unrest if this were not done.[27] It is quite possible that proclamations were issued as a result of this advice, but since they have not survived, we have no way of being certain. Cromwell also received advice suggesting the use of royal proclamations. In late 1532 and early 1533 he received two letters warning him that grain hoarding was causing shortages and driving up prices. The first, written by Robert Corson on 20 December 1532, warned of a shortage in East Anglia and suggested that justices of the peace be ordered to search for grain and command that it be brought to market. The second, from the Treasurer of Berwick, George Lawson, dated 18 January 1533, specifically recommended a proclamation. He maintained that there was grain hoarding in Northumberland and that 'if proclamation be made throughout the county to thresh out their corn reasonably and at a reasonable price there would be enough and sufficient.'[28] How Cromwell reacted that winter cannot be determined because no proclamation has survived, but two years later under similar economic conditions a proclamation forbade grain hoarding and ordered that grain be brought to market.[29]

Information received on abuses seems to have influenced the drafting of a number of proclamations even when none was directly recommended. George Whelplay, the professional informer, made a series of accusations of corruption among port officials to the council in October and November of 1540. A proclamation of 16 February 1541 with severe penalties for corrupt officials followed.[30] On 6 May 1542 William Boys, justice of the peace in Kent, wrote to Edward Ringley, Comptroller of Calais, that after visiting his parishes he found that people could not get bows and arrows, 'but at excessive price wherefore if there could a remedy be provided in that behalf no doubt there would be as great a number of archers in our parts as hath been in many years before.' At the end of August in the same year the government issued a proclamation setting prices on bows and arrows on the grounds that this was necessary because subjects were unable to acquire them 'at reasonable and convenient prices to

---

[27] SP 1/232/23 (*LP* App. 1[1] no. 185).
[28] SP 1/72/165 (*LP* 5 no. 1650); SP 1/74/62 (*LP* 6 no. 51).
[29] *TRP* no. 151.
[30] *TRP* no. 197.6; SP 1/243/196-7 (*LP* App. 1 no. 1490[3]).

serve his majesty and the realm.'[31] A proclamation of 18 September 1547 concerning religious pensioners must have been influenced by information the council received in June 1547. It would seem that some English monks had devised a clever way of obtaining support from the English government while continuing as monks. According to the report they had gone to Flanders 'where they have again received their monk's habit and profession, and, nevertheless, procured with their friends here to have payment of the pensions to them allotted.' Acting on this information as well as the shocking report that others were planning the same action, the council decided that pensioners would be required to present themselves in person at the next payment date in Michaelmas 'to be viewed whether they were the same persons to whom such pensions were assigned.' The proclamation, which was issued shortly before the payment was due, gave as its justification the vague phrase 'for divers causes and considerations.' It ordered that pensioners formerly paid by the Receivers of the Court of Augmentations should be paid by the Treasurer or his deputies and that they should appear before the deputy of the Treasurer at a specified date to show their patents and grants for the pensions.[32]

Finally, a number of proclamations seem to have resulted from the personal concerns of the King. The King obviously had an interest in the proclamations dealing with hunting and hawking. Over half of the surviving proclamations on these subjects were issued in the last years of the reign of Henry VIII. The King, who was becoming physically less able to pursue the sport with his former vigor, was obviously vitally concerned about the preservation of his favorite pastime. These proclamations inevitably gave as their justification the preservation of the King's 'pleasure and pastime' or words to that effect.[33] The King was also interested in the religious proclamations. He corrected the drafts of some with his own hand.[34] Shortly before a proclamation exiling Anabaptists was issued in November 1538, the King sat at the trial of an Anabaptist and tried to 'convert the miserable man.' At the same time Cromwell informs us 'the King's highness caused some proclamations to be made.'[35] A proclamation of feast and fast days on 22 July 1541 was directly

[31] *TRP* no. 213; SP 1/170/100 (*LP* 17 no. 303).
[32] *TRP* no. 289; Dasent, II, 97–8.
[33] *TRP* nos. 205, 211, 217, 222, 247, 254.
[34] *TRP* nos. 186, 191.
[35] BM Harl. 282/217d (*LP* 13[2] no. 924).

ordered by the King.[36] The King's personal concern can also be established shortly before the promulgation of a proclamation of 8 July 1546 prohibiting heretical books. On 20 June 1546 he had written to Mary of Hungary complaining that books written by 'heretical and wicked men both in Latin and English are sent over.' The proclamation which followed prohibited the importation of any religious books printed abroad without special license by the King.[37]

These examples serve to illustrate the diversity of the motivating factors. Although in most cases it is not possible to determine specifically how the government detected the need for a proclamation, it is clear that the information came from many sources and that early Tudor governments used proclamations as a method of responding in a relatively rapid fashion to expressed needs and problems that demanded swift temporary solutions. The group which most often received the petitions for proclamations and the information on problems was the council. The second step in the making of a royal proclamation often involved its advice and even consent; however, the degree of the council's involvement has been a matter of some debate. Steele stated that proclamations were 'made by the advice and consent of the council,' while admitting that 'we can only affirm it to be true in every case of which we know the facts.' In his discussion of Henry VIII's proclamations he commented that due to a lack of records 'the part taken by the privy council is not very clear.'[38] Hughes and Larkin included only 'advice of council' in their definition, stating that 'the early Tudor proclamation involves, at least in principle, the advice of the King's council.' Except for noting the number of Henry VIII's proclamations that recorded the advice of council and a brief paragraph on the council's role, they avoided any detailed consideration of the question.[39]

Perhaps the ambiguity of the council's role results from the difficulty of ascertaining how often it was actually involved in pro-

[36] *TRP* no. 203; SP 1/166/114 (*LP* 16 no. 978).
[37] *TRP* no. 272; SP 1/220/172 (*LP* 21[1] no. 1098).
[38] Steele, ix, lxxix.
[39] *TRP*, xxiv. 'In his own royal proclamations Henry VIII records his council's advice 44 times and its consent three times,' *TRP*, xxiv n. 11. This must refer to the period when the Statute of Proclamations was in effect, because the remainder of the footnote is devoted to the question of advice during that period. Unfortunately, the figure 44 is a puzzle. It may be a printer's error, or what may have been meant is that 44 proclamations during the period do not record the advice of council since considering only the proclamations in the first volume this would have been correct. On the question of advice and consent, no. 249, which uses the word 'assent' rather than 'consent', seems to have been overlooked in their count.

Table 3. *Types of advice mentioned in early Tudor royal proclamations*

Period[a]	None	Council[b]	Somerset and council	Advice and consent	Other	Total	Total advice	Total council	Percentage advice
Henry VII									
1485–1509	51	6	0	0	1[c]	58	7	7	12
Henry VIII									
1509–29	39	31	0	0	1[d]	71	32	32	45
1530–9	41	21[e]	0	0	2[f]	64	23	22	36
1539–47	43	36[g]	0	4	2[h]	85	42	40	49
Edward VI									
1547–9	11	4	37	21	3[i]	76	65	62	86
1549–53	11	25	0	3	0	39	28	28	72
Total	196	123	37	28	9	393	197	191	50

[a] These periods correspond exactly to the periods in Table 2. Months have not been included for the sake of brevity.

[b] This includes also proclamations which have advice stated only in the title and those which do not specifically state advice but strongly imply it.

[c] *TRP* no. 54: 'lords spiritual and temporal and others of the council.'

[d] *TRP* no. 72: 'lords of his blood, captains of his army, and other folk as be of his council.'

[e] *TRP* no. 128 has advice stated in title but not in text.

[f] *TRP* no. 129: 'Primates and other substantial learned personages of both universities and by the assent of his nobles and others of his most honorable council.' *TRP* no. 163: 'lords spiritual and temporal and commons in this present Parliament assembled.'

[g] *TRP* nos. 200, 203, 224, 272 have advice stated in title but not in text.

[h] *TRP* no. 270: 'advice of the Lord Chancellor of England and the justices of both benches.' *TRP* no. 268: 'deliberate advice and consideration.'

[i] *TRP* nos. 298, 316, 347 advice of Somerset only.

[j] *TRP* no. 368 has advice stated in title but not in text.

viding advice or consent for proclamations. Council records are lacking for most of the period; therefore, one is forced to rely heavily on the texts of the proclamations. That elusive phrase 'advice of council' occurs in approximately half of the early Tudor royal proclamations, but it is extremely difficult to determine how much this really reveals. Table 3 contains a summary of the number of proclamations stating various kinds of advice. It seems to reveal that the council was more actively involved in the making of proclamations in some periods than in others. As might be expected, the largest number of proclamations which mentioned the advice of council were issued during the reign of Edward VI, when over seventy-five percent contained the phrase on advice, compared to only twelve percent during the reign of Henry VII. However, the phrase is not as revealing as one might hope. Proclamations did not always mention advice even when other sources establish that the council dealt with them. Eleven of the proclamations issued during Somerset's protectorate said nothing about advice even though, during the minority of the King, one would expect that all of the proclamations were the product of some advice. Henry VII seemingly felt no need to include the statement on advice even when the council was involved. It can be documented that a number of the proclamations which came before the council did not contain the phrase.[40] It is, furthermore, difficult to find any correlation between the inclusion of a statement on advice and the subject matter of the proclamation during most periods. Henry VII's more controversial proclamations did not specify advice, while the proclamation which contained one of the more elaborate statements on advice – advice of 'lords spiritual temporal and others of the council' – was simply an effort to clear up certain ambiguities in a recently enacted statute on coinage.[41]

The same observations apply to the reign of Henry VIII. If one were to assume that the phrase 'advice of council' was included in the text whenever the council was really involved and only then, we should have to conclude that Wolsey, who is normally accused of neglecting the council, used it more extensively than Cromwell.[42] Over half of the proclamations issued when the Statute of Proclamations was in effect did not specify the advice of council even though the Statute stated that the 'King with the advice of his most honorable council or the advice of the most part of them may set forth at all times by authority of this act his proclamations...'[43] Furthermore, council records reveal that not all of the proclamations on which the council acted contained the phrase. At least one of the meat price proclamations which was the result of a petition of the mayor and aldermen of London to the council does not mention its advice.[44] In addition there does not seem to be any correlation between the subject matter of the proclamation and the statement on

[40] *TRP* nos. 5, 6, 7, 19, 52. Charles G. Bayne and William H. Dunham Jr eds., *Select Cases in the Council of Henry VII* (London, 1958), 3–4, 8, 13, 22, 42.

[41] *TRP* no. 54; 19 Henry VII c. 5.

[42] In 1515–29, when Wolsey was dominant, forty-five percent of the proclamations mentioned advice. Only thirty-six percent of the proclamations issued in the period 1532–July 1540, when Cromwell was the King's chief minister, claimed advice.

[43] 31 Henry VIII c. 8. Even one of the proclamations which specifically mentioned in its text that it was based on the authority of the Statute of Proclamations and quoted directly the clause on advice did not state that the order was given with the advice of council: *TRP* no. 205.

[44] CLRO Journals 13/378; *TRP* no. 139. The council records reveal that in at least three cases the council was involved in the formulation of a proclamation when no mention was made of advice in the text: *TRP* nos. 212.5, 219, 254; Dasent, I, 23, 156, 201.

advice. Proclamations dealing with the same subject sometimes mentioned advice and sometimes did not.[45] Even the phrase 'advice and consent' of council, which appears for the first time in the period 1539–47, seems to reveal very little. Four proclamations used that terminology in the period. One was based on the Statute of Proclamations but simply revised an earlier proclamation to allow for the victualing of Calais. Two set prices on weapons and armor. The fourth simply adjourned Trinity term, a matter dealt with in two other proclamations of the period which did not even record the advice of the council.[46] One is led to conclude that at least during the reigns of the first two Tudor monarchs the phrases 'advice' of council or 'advice and consent' of council reveal very little about the degree of its involvement in the formulation of the proclamation. Exclusion or inclusion of those phrases cannot be explained on the basis of the available evidence by any external factor except possibly the idiosyncrasies of the individual drafting the proclamation.

During the reign of the last Tudor King the statement on advice seems at first to have more significance. In his study of the Edwardian council Dale Hoak has, in fact, found some correlation between that claim and the subject matter of the proclamation during Somerset's protectorate. However, it does not reveal a great deal about what actually happened. Only eleven of Somerset's proclamations did not mention advice and none of them involved a controversial matter. The more important proclamations often even included a statement of consent. During the period of Northumberland's dominance and especially after 1551 there was a decline in the number of proclamations citing advice or consent; thus, it would seem that if the phrase really reveals the degree of involvement of the council, Somerset relied on the council more than Northumberland. Hoak, however, offers evidence to prove that the opposite was true. Somerset tended to ignore the council and to make decisions, including those on proclamations, on his own authority, while Northumberland, who used the council more, may have deliberately omitted the statement on advice in his later proclamations to give the

---

[45] Only two of the proclamations which suspended the meat-price statute, 25 Henry VIII, specified advice of council (*TRP* nos. 144, 159). Two of the proclamations permitting exchanges listed advice of the council (*TRP* nos. 181, 182), but the first proclamation on that subject did not (*TRP* no. 174.5).

[46] *TRP* no. 201 revised no. 197.6. This was probably the least controversial of the proclamations specifically based on the authority of the Statute of Proclamations. None of the others mentioned consent. *TRP* nos. 213 and 235 priced armor. No. 249 adjourned Trinity term. Nos. 223 and 256 also adjourned law terms without recording even the advice of council.

impression that Edward VI was actually ruling. 'Northumberland's proclamations therefore conceal what Somerset's orders usually falsely proclaim, a power wielded with the council's consent.'[47] All this suggests that the proclamations texts are not reliable guides for evaluating the role of the council. Although the council was certainly actively involved in the formulation of many, if not most, royal proclamations, it is impossible to determine on the basis of the statements in the text how often it actually gave 'advice' or 'consent.'

The actual process of formulating royal proclamations and the role of the council in that work can be described to some extent by examining the few surviving council records. In some cases they disclose very little except that the council sent a letter to the chancellor ordering that a proclamation be made. Sometimes the entries in the council minute book state that the council 'devised' the proclamation.[48] The more important information on the decision making process is more difficult to obtain, but it is at least sometimes possible to describe it in more detail. A brief entry in the council records for 16 March 1542 sheds a good deal of light on the procedure that was followed in determining whether to repeal a now lost proclamation:

Certain men of the town of York appearing before the council sued unto the same for the repealing of the proclamation made in Hull by the King's commandment touching foreign bought and foreign sold; and after sundry allegations and reasons declared by them how noyful the said proclamation was to the whole country, the council resolved to declare the same to the King's highness thereupon and to make thereof at a convenient leisure a resolute answer.[49]

The process here is interesting. The petition for repeal came from a concerned group. The council heard the arguments and then

[47] Dale Hoak, 'The Council of Edward VI' (unpublished PhD dissertation, University of Cambridge, 1971), 215. Hoak also noted that four proclamations which did not include Somerset's name were made when Somerset was not present. *Ibid.* 213. The statistics in Professor Hoak's dissertation differ somewhat from those found in Table 3 largely because of the discovery of new proclamations texts and my rejection of one of the items which he accepts as a proclamation (*TRP* no. 287). In addition I have listed three price-control proclamations as having advice of council because they state that the prices were set by members of the council even though there is no specific statement on advice (*TRP* nos. 366, 380, 383).

[48] *TRP* no. 254; Dasent, I, 201. *TRP* no. 219; Dasent, I, 156. The entry in the council minute book for 13 October 1551 reveals that the council both devised *TRP* no. 382 and sent 'a letter to the Lord Chancellor to put [the proclamation] to the print with all speed.' Dasent, III, 387.

[49] Nicolas, VII, 326–37. I have not included this proclamation in the list of unfound proclamations in the Appendix, for one cannot be certain from the reference in council records that it was a royal proclamation. It may have been a local proclamation made at the King's command.

reported the information to the King who in this case seems to have made the final decision. Whether or not the proclamation was repealed cannot be determined because neither it nor evidence of its revocation has survived. At times the council served as a forum where the issues involved in making a decision on a proclamation could be debated by concerned parties. For example, before suspending the cloth manufacturing statute in 1541, the council ordered both the kersey manufacturers and the 'setters forth of the said act' to appear before them to defend their positions. In another case the council went so far as to establish a committee to study a problem before taking action. Before moving the sanctuary from Chester a committee that included the mayor of Norfolk was appointed to investigate the question and to make recommendations.[50]

After the need for a remedy to a specific problem had been discussed, the council had a number of alternative methods for dealing with the matter. Royal proclamations were only one of those options. The council often issued direct orders to administrative officials or ordered local officials to make proclamations in the King's name. It also issued proclamations on its own authority. Although detailed considerations of these alternative means is beyond the scope of this work, some examples might be cited. The council often issued orders to local authorities to make regulations or proclamations. Elaborate articles dealing with vagabonds were formulated by the city government of London in April 1518 'at the commandment of the King's most honorable council.' In July 1532 articles 'concerning ale brewers and beer brewers' in London were 'made by the King's council.' In October 1516 the 'chancellor and other lords of the King's most honorable council gave in commandment to the mayor and diverse of his brethren the aldermen articles for gauging vessels for ale and beer.'[51] Restraints on export were often imposed by methods other than royal proclamation. An example of this procedure is found in the New Romney records. A Latin writ was sent to the Warden of the Cinque Ports to prohibit the export of grain. The warden then sent a mandate to the Cinque Port officials commanding them 'in the King's behalf and by virtue of my office...' not to allow unlicensed export of grain.[52]

[50] *Ibid.* 156; NNRO Mayors Court Book 1534–40, 152.
[51] CLRO Letter Book N/74; *ibid.* O/252; *ibid.* N/25.
[52] KRO NR/CP/W. In the reign of Elizabeth this became the most common method of imposing restraints. 'There is only one example of a general restraint made by the Queen or royal proclamation, and this was for a duration of one and a half months only.' Frederic A. Youngs, 'The Proclamations of Elizabeth I' (unpublished PhD dissertation, University of Cambridge, 1969), 103.

Proclamations by local governments were commonly made 'on our sovereign lord the King's behalf.'[53] Sometimes the council began by ordering a local proclamation and later used a royal proclamation, possibly because it commanded more authority. The price controls imposed on sugar between 1541 and 1543 provide an example of this. On 2 January 1541 the council sent a letter to the mayor of London ordering him to call 'five or six merchants of experience' and to ask them how sugar and spices were sold on the continent. They were to inform the council 'to the intent order might be taken for the setting of prices of certain sugar and spices' brought to London. On 12 January the council sent another letter to the mayor ordering him 'in the King's name to make a proclamation in London' that sugar should not be sold above 8d a pound. In May of 1543 a royal proclamation based on the Statute of Proclamations maintained that sugar was being sold at excessive prices and set the price at 7d a pound.[54]

Once the council decided to use a royal proclamation, the text of the document had to be formulated. At times direct help was sought from those most closely affected. The proclamation of 15 January 1505, which set up a free market at Calais and contained detailed regulations for that market, was probably originally drawn up by the Merchant Adventurers. The vintners were consulted on the prices to be set in the wine price proclamations.[55] We do not know who actually drew up the first draft, but corrections in the few draft proclamations that have survived reveal that in some cases Henry VIII took an active part in correcting and revising the draft although this was probably unusual. It is likely that corrections were more often made by the King's chief minister or the principal secretary. At least one draft shows corrections in Cromwell's hand and another was revised by Wriothesley's when he was the King's secretary.[56]

---

[53] CLRO Journals 13/279d; 14/253, 271, 272 are examples. Ten percent of the proclamations issued by the London city government during Elizabeth's reign were issued at the command of the Queen or the council. Youngs, 'Proclamations of Elizabeth,' 172.

[54] Nicolas, VII, 104-5, 113; *TRP* no. 218.

[55] *TRP* no. 56; Bayne, *Select Cases*, 43; Nicolas, VII, 276.

[56] Drafts corrected by the King are BM Cleo E v/357-84 (*TRP* no. 186) and *ibid.* 311-26 (*TRP* no. 191). Professor Elton speculates that another of Henry VIII's proclamations may have been his 'own composition.' Elton, *Policy and Police*, 252 (*TRP* no. 168). A draft corrected by Cromwell is found in SP 6/4/262-80. This is probably a draft of *TRP* no. 188, but it is worded in a very different fashion. Wriothesley corrected a draft of a proclamation of July 1546 that forbade heretical books (*TRP* no. 272), but the draft seems to have been drawn up while Wriothesley was still one of the Principal Secretaries of State before March 1544. It is somewhat different from the final proclamation, and it may have been issued as a separate proclamation in 1543 or 1544. SP 1/169/116-26 (*LP* 17 no. 177).

Earlier proclamations were often used as guides for the actual wording. When Robert Beale drew up his Instructions for a Principal Secretary in 1592, he recommended that Grafton's collection be consulted for examples of previous proclamations on the same subject.[57] The formulators of the text sometimes copied verbatim from earlier proclamations. The proclamations which dispensed the Lenten fast from white meats always had the same text as the first one discovered on that subject. A proclamation of April 1543 prohibiting hawking had precisely the same text as one issued a year earlier. The proclamations decreeing severe penalties for assaulting the King's officers were issued at least twice with exactly the same wording. A proclamation on wool export issued late in Henry VIII's reign was repeated almost verbatim in the first year of Edward VI's reign.[58] The proclamations suspending the meat price and wool cloth manufacturing statutes and those pricing wines were always worded in a very similar fashion with the obvious exception of necessary changes in prices and dates. In one case heavy reliance for wording on earlier proclamations may have been the reason for a significant oversight in the first proclamation to set retail prices of wine. Earlier ones had only set wholesale prices, citing 23 Henry VIII c. 7 as their authority. The new proclamation also cited that statute, even though it only empowered the council to set wholesale prices and provided that local officials were to set retail prices. The statute that should have been cited was 34 and 35 Henry VIII, c. 7, which did grant the council authority to set retail prices.[59]

Although the council seems to have payed an important role in devising many royal proclamations, the final authority was inevitably the King. Even if he played no role in deciding to employ a proclamation or in drafting and revising the texts, proclamations obviously had to be signed by him and approved. This could lead to some delays when the King was absent from London. An example is a proclamation of 22 July 1541 revising feast and fast days which had been originally ordered by the King and probably devised by Cranmer. The draft proclamation was sent by the council in London to the

---

[57] R. B. Beale, 'A Treatise of the Office of a Councilor and Principal Secretary' in Conyers Read, *Mr. Secretary Walsingham and the Policy of Queen Elizabeth*, 1 (Oxford, 1925), 439.

[58] *TRP* nos. 177, 197.7, 209, 214 are the surviving proclamations on the Lenten fast. There were probably other proclamations on this subject whose texts have not been found. *TRP* nos. 211, 217 prohibited hawking; *TRP* nos. 179, 228, 288 dealt with assault on the King's officers. The wool export proclamations were *TRP* nos. 264 and 278. The second added a clause not in the first proclamation.

[59] *TRP* no. 267.

council with the King who was on his way north for his planned meeting with James V of Scotland. They were instructed 'to advertise us of the King's majesty's pleasure touching the same.' The King seemingly approved of the text since almost two weeks later the draft was returned with an order that the chancellor should take steps to have the matter proclaimed. The final draft was then drawn up and three days later copies were sent to the council.[60]

Promulgation

Once the text of a proclamation had been agreed upon it passed through a number of stages before it was promulgated in local areas. It was engrossed on parchment, signed by the King, and often printed. At some point in the process it was delivered to the chancery where a writ under the great seal ordering local officials to proclaim the accompanying text was issued. Finally it was delivered to local areas where the proclamation was proclaimed and posted. How all this took place and in what order is not entirely clear for the early Tudor period.[61] The normal procedure seems to have been for the schedule to be engrossed on parchment, signed by the King, and then sent to the chancery with an accompanying letter which ordered the chancellor to issue writs under the great seal for the publication of the proclamation. The engrossed proclamation with the King's sign manual served as a warrant for the issuance of the writ under the great seal, while the letter must have informed the chancellor where the writs were to be sent.[62] The chancery warrants at times also included the signatures of the councilors. Two of the surviving warrants from the reign of Henry VIII and all the surviving warrants from the reign of Edward VI are signed by members of the council.[63] On two occasions proclamations also passed under the privy

[60] SP 1/166/114, 142–6, 150–1 (*LP* 16 nos. 978, 1019, 1028); *TRP* no. 203.

[61] Professor Youngs has been able to describe the process for the Elizabethan period in some detail since more evidence has survived. See Youngs, *Proclamations of the Tudor Queens*, 18–26. Hughes and Larkin have only outlined the procedure in general terms for the early Tudor period, and Steele's comments, though helpful, are fragmentary and not entirely accurate. *TRP* xxiiiff; Steele, ixff.

[62] The warrant for *TRP* no. 308 specifically stated that 'this bill signed with your most gracious hand may be sufficient and immediate warrant unto the Lord Chancellor for the issuance of writs under the great seal' (C 82/884). Examples of proclamations sent to the chancellor with 'letters for the sending forth of the same proclamation' are found in Nicolas, VII, 33; Dasent, I, 201.

[63] *TRP* nos. 60.5; 61(C 82/342). The number of councilors who signed warrants in Edward VI's reign varied. No. 308 (C 82/884) was signed by six, no. 311 (C 82/885) was signed by nine, no. 378 was signed by eight, nos. 375, 377, 379 were signed by ten and no. 376 was signed by twelve (C 82/935).

seal. Although there is no evidence that Hughes and Larkin were correct in their assumption that the sign manual served normally 'as a warrant for the privy seal,'[64] two proclamations specifically state that the proclamation was 'given under our privy seal...'[65] This may have been an archaic form used only occasionally early in the period. The only two proclamations which mention the privy seal were issued early in the reign of Henry VIII, and Professor Youngs has not been able to find any Marian or Elizabethan proclamations which passed the privy seal.[66]

Normally proclamations were sent to the printer after the authenticated parchment had been delivered to the chancery. The council minutes for 20 November 1551 reveal what was probably the general practice. The proclamation was sent with an accompanying letter to the chancellor ordering him 'to cause the proclamation signed by the King for reformation of the former proclamation and for bringing victuals to markets to pass the seal, to be put to print and published.'[67] The most detailed description of the process of sending out a proclamation occurs in a letter from Cromwell to chancellor Audley on 11 November 1534. However, the procedure followed here seems to have been somewhat unusual. The letter reads:

Forasmuch as it shall be very necessary to have some copies of the proclamation also printed this night to the intent that the same may be sent into sundry parts with the books of answer, these shall be to desire and pray your lordship to send me by this bearer a true copy of the same, and I shall send for Berthelet, the printer, and first swear him and then cause him to attend this night to the printing of the copies thereof accordingly... I require your lordship to cause the proclamations to be written and sealed with such expedition as you may take the pain to be here with them

[64] They believed that the slits in the chancery warrants were 'originally made in the folded document for closure by the privy seal,' *TRP*, xxiv. Professor Elton questioned 'the improbable assertion that warrants for the issue of proclamations carried both the sign manual and the privy seal'; Elton, *HJ*, VIII, 267. Professor Youngs has suggested that since the slits are 'irregular in number and spacing' they do not provide evidence of sealing with the privy seal since these slits 'were always regular and straight'; Youngs, 'Proclamations of Elizabeth,' 31 n. 111.

[65] *TRP* nos. 61.5, 87. Both dealt with uncontroversial matters. The first ordered enforcement of certain statutes for the sale and manufacture of wool. The second requisitioned empty wine casks. Hughes and Larkin do not note the privy seal warranty in their head notes for either proclamation, but the manuscript copies of both clearly end with the phrase 'given under our privy seal...' (NNRO Liber Albus, 176v; BM Harl. 442/18).

[66] Youngs, *Proclamations of the Tudor Queens*, 19 n. 38. Proclamations occasionally mentioned the signet, but this was relatively rare. Only twelve Elizabethan proclamations closed with the words 'Given under our Signet...' (*ibid.*). Five early Tudor proclamations contained that phrase (*TRP* nos. 20.5, 20.6, 23.5, 116, 146).

[67] Dasent, III, 420; *TRP* no. 382.3.

tomorrow by ten of the clock when my lord of Norfolk and I with others will tarry there till your coming.

Audley did not follow the instructions exactly. Rather than sending the proclamation with the messenger he appended a note to the bottom of the letter:

My lord there shall be good diligence in the writing of the proclamations to the number of xx according to your request, and I have also an aid Croke to deliver our true original of the proclamation to the intent he should put in print the number of ccc and charged Croke to command him to set the print himself this night and to make speed thereof. I will not fail God willing but be with you tomorrow at the hour appointed.[68]

Cromwell may have felt it necessary to proceed quickly because of the nature of the proclamation being sent out which was probably that directed against the Lincolnshire rebels in the autumn of 1536, so that it is understandable why speed was vital.[69] The need for rapid publication may have resulted in a somewhat unusual procedure, but obviously the proclamation was in the hands of the chancellor before Cromwell decided to act so quickly. The chancellor would probably have sent it to the printer later. The unusual part was that the proclamations were to be written and sealed at the same time that printing was taking place. The number of copies ordered is interesting. Twenty proclamations were to be written and sealed. These were the manuscript copies which were sent to local officials with the great seal attached for proclamation while the three hundred printed proclamations would probably be posted.

Not all proclamations were printed. A description of the publication of proclamations in the city of Exeter during the reign of Elizabeth states that after proclamations were proclaimed they were posted 'if they be imprinted.'[70] Henry VIII's proclamation ordering the surrender of John Fisher's books and sermons may not have been printed until the city officials in London ordered it. The proclamation must have been proclaimed in London on or before 13 December 1535 because Chapuys mentioned it in a letter to Charles V on that date. The following day the mayor and aldermen

---

[68] BM Vesp. F XIII, 191 (*LP* 7 no. 1415).

[69] *TRP* no. 168. I am indebted to Professor Elton for his aid in identifying the proclamation. I was originally misled by the 1534 dating in the *LP* entry. However the letter must have been written after July 1536 since Audley addressed Cromwell as 'Lord,' and the reference to 'books of answer' suggests that the proclamation in question was probably no. 168.

[70] John Vowell alias Hooker, *The Description of the City of Excester*, Walter J. Harte, J. W. Schopp, H. Tapley-Soper eds. (Exeter, 1947), III, 846.

of London ordered 'that the proclamation last made concerning a sermon made by John Fisher, late bishop of Rochester, in derogation and diminution of the royal estate of the King's majesty should be printed and openly published by the curates in the pulpit upon Sunday next and then to be affixed in tables and set upon their several churches.' The date on the printed proclamations used for the text in *Tudor Royal Proclamations* is 1 January 1536.[71] Sometimes it is evident from a comparison of different copies of the same proclamation that it was not printed. Rather written copies were altered slightly to apply to a specific area. A proclamation of 24 October 1522 ordered the citizens of Kent to keep watches. It spoke specifically of 'dwellers and inhabitants within... the county of Kent.' The chancery warrant records that writs were also sent to a series of other counties. Obviously the same wording did not apply to those areas. The manuscript copy surviving in the Palatinate of Durham records reveals that the proclamation sent to that area was worded specifically to apply to Durham since it read 'dwellers and inhabitants within... the said county Palatine.'[72] A number of other early Tudor proclamations were also worded to apply specifically to one area even though the chancery warrants indicate that writs were sent to other localities. This was particularly true of muster proclamations. One, in fact, survives with a blank where the name of the county should have been written. The chancery clerk would fill in the name of the specific county as he prepared the writs to accompany the manuscript copies of the proclamation to be sent out.[73] We shall probably never know how many early Tudor proclamations were printed. Although it is likely that most of the later proclamations were printed, less than one third of the texts of the surviving proclamations are based on printed copies.[74]

The number of proclamations that were printed depended on the subject matter. Only twenty copies of the proclamation which added two manors to Hatfield Chase were printed, probably because it needed to be posted only in select areas of Yorkshire and Lincolnshire. On the other hand, 600 copies of the proclamation dated

---

[71] *TRP* no. 161; CLRO Rep. 9/145.

[72] C 82/524. This is the copy included in *TRP* as no. 92; Dur 3/70/36.

[73] C 193/3/2; *TRP* no. 90. Other examples are *TRP* no. 28 (C 66/572/31d), no. 37 (C 66/581/6d), no. 61 (C 82/342), no. 67 (C 66/619/9d), no. 94 (C 82/524), no. 97 (BM Harl. 422/25). None of these proclamations has survived in printed form, probably because they were never printed.

[74] Approximately twenty-eight percent (109 proclamations) of the items accepted by me as royal proclamations are based on printed texts. The vast majority of these proclamations (eighty-four) were issued after 1539.

23 January 1542 on the royal style and that of 3 February 1542 dispensing the Lenten fast from white meats were printed, because they would have to be posted throughout the country. In some cases several printings of the same proclamation occurred. The Stationers' Register lists three deliveries of printed copies for the proclamation of 16 April 1542 prohibiting hawking. On 11 April 400 copies were delivered to the chancellor, on 16 April another 400 copies were delivered, and on an unspecified date the register lists another 400 'new made.'[75]

During the early Tudor period writs were normally separate from the proclamations which contained the exact words that the local officials were to proclaim. The only exceptions to that rule were the distraint of knighthood proclamations. These, which ordered individuals having £40 or more income a year to appear before the King to become knights, followed an earlier form in which the matter to be proclaimed was included as part of the writ. In contrast to all the other surviving proclamations they are in Latin rather than English, and the exact words to be proclaimed are not specified.[76] In other cases only the writ was in Latin. The writ most commonly used simply ordered the person or persons to whom it was addressed to make public proclamation of the accompanying schedule 'in hec verba.' The writ ended with a formal threat to officials who failed to carry out these instructions together with the date and place of issue: 'et hoc sub periculo incumbendo nullatenus omittatis. Teste me ipso apud Westmonasterium quinto die Julii anno regni nostri decimonono.'[77] Occasionally the form varied. Sometimes a statement that the proclamation had been made 'de avisamento consilii nostri pro bono publico' was included. Another writ contained an order that certification be made in chancery immediately after the proclamation had been made.[78]

In addition to the Latin writ under the great seal, proclamations were at times also sent out with accompanying letters. Twenty-nine copies of the same signet letter sent with one of Henry VIII's

[75] Edward Arber ed., *A Transcript of the Registers of the Company of Stationers in London* (London and Birmingham, 1875–94), II, 51 (*TRP* nos. 205, 208), 52 (no. 209), 54 (no. 211).

[76] There are five surviving proclamations on this subject: *TRP* nos. 9, 48, 49, 53 and Dur 3/78/3d (App. A no. 138.5). There is evidence that at least seven others were issued during the early Tudor period (App. B items 5, 7, 10, 17, 21, 32, 33). See Steele, xi, for a discussion of the earlier form of royal proclamations.

[77] This is taken from the writ for *TRP* no. 54 (Antiq 1:9). Most surviving writs have a similar wording. See Steele, xiiff, for examples of early Tudor writs.

[78] BM Harl. 442/47 (*TRP* no. 112), 62 (no. 118), 73 (no. 123). For an unusually long writ directed to the justices of assize, jailers and justices of the peace see BM Harl. 442/42 (no. 110).

proclamations have survived in the state papers. The proclamation placed an embargo on all ships in English ports. The accompanying letter provided a brief explanation of why the proclamation was issued and ordered that the 'enclosed' proclamation be proclaimed and enforced:

Trusty and well beloved we greet you well, and for sundry causes and considerations as well concerning the avoidance of piracy and robbery upon the seas, where it is of late reported unto us that sundry pirates shortly intend to resort, as also for the preservation of our true subjects and the commonwealth of them with other special reason of importance to be declared afterward, we will and straightly charge and command you and every of you that with all possible diligence, after the receipt thereof, you shall not only cause the proclamation here enclosed to be made everywhere within our port and haven there and within all the creeks and places within the precinct of your limits, but also to see the effect thereof to be put in use so that no man as well English as of any other nation whatsoever he or they be shall depart or have passage beyond the sea without our special license dated after this date, to be signified unto you by our own letters or by the letters of our right trusty and well beloved councilor, the lord privy seal, or of some other of our Privy Council, and that otherwise ye shall do your duties therein as appertaineth, as we trust you and as for your negligences therein ye will answer at your extreme perils. Given under our signet at our palace of Westminster the first day March the xxxth year of our reign.[79]

We cannot be sure if the sending of an additional letter with the proclamation and the writ was common policy or if it was only used in exceptional cases. The above letter served some purpose in that it added a justification and information not in the proclamation. It also informed enforcement officials that the King was extremely serious about seeing that his proclamation was enforced.[80] Other surviving letters sent with proclamations also had a clear purpose. The proclamations issued in the summer of 1551 which changed the value of a shilling were sent out with letters ordering local officials not to break the seal on the writ until a specified date and then to keep the contents secret 'until the very time of publication thereof.' Since it was vitally important that the contents of the proclamation be kept secret until the moment of publication in order not to

[79] SP 1/143/210-38 (*LP* 14[1] no. 1408); *TRP* no. 190. The proclamation had a regular Latin writ dated 27 February 1539; BM Harl. 442/121.

[80] The proclamation contained only a general justification – 'for divers respects and considerations,' and did not specify that the license must be signed by Cromwell or members of the council. *TRP* no. 190.

create economic chaos, these additional instructions were clearly necessary.[81] However, not all the surviving letters sent with proclamations clearly served a purpose. A letter signed by Somerset and Richard Rich on 13 August 1549 was sent with a proclamation that limited the export of wool. It contained the same instructions included in the writ. It simply ordered local officials to be sure that the enclosed proclamation was 'openly published and proclaimed in all places requisite.'[82]

One of Edward VI's proclamations, which has been preserved in the Public Record Office with the seal still attached, may reveal how proclamations looked when they were sent out from the chancery in the early Tudor period. The parchment document is in manuscript. It begins with the normal Latin writ which takes up the first line of the document and extends eight words into the second line. The writ is addressed to the sheriff of Northamptonshire and is followed immediately by the proclamation text in English. After the last line of the schedule the normal ending of this type of writ – 'et hoc sub periculo incumbendo nullatenus omittatis' follows. In the center bottom the phrase 'per ipsum Regem & Consilium' is written. The name of the county to which the proclamation was sent is noted on the lower left. In the lower right-hand corner the name of the chancery clerk who wrote the document is written. The seal is affixed in the method described by Maxwell-Lyte as 'sur simple queue.' A cut halfway across the bottom of the parchment creates a large strip and the seal is attached to this. A second narrower strip used as a tie is no longer attached, but a ragged edge on the lower left reveals that it was probably torn off.[83] If this is a typical example, it suggests that the Elizabethan practice of sending out proclamations together with a writ on a strip of parchment separate from the proclamation schedule was not followed.[84] This, however, was

---

[81] NNRO Mayors Court Book 1549–55, 125; *TRP* no. 376. The instructions were followed exactly, and the Mayors Court Book records that on 9 July between 7 and 8 a.m. the seal was broken by the mayor and sheriffs of the city in the presence of nine witnesses, NNRO Mayors Court Book, 126. A similar letter was sent with no. 379, *ibid.* 140–1.

[82] R. C. Anderson, *Letters of the Fifteenth and Sixteenth Centuries from the Archives of Southampton* (Southampton, 1921), 73; *TRP* no. 345.

[83] SP 13/Case H/2; *TRP* no. 359. Steele maintained that this was not a typical example but that it was 'probably only an exemplification authenticated for production in some legal proceedings' (Steele, xx). This is not a very convincing explanation since it seems unlikely that an exemplification for legal purposes would include the writ and various other notations on the document. See H. C. Maxwell-Lyte, *Historical Notes on the Use of the Great Seal* (London, 1926), 300 for a description of the 'sur simple queue' method of sealing.

[84] Youngs, *Proclamations of the Tudor Queens*, 19. A copy of an Elizabethan proclamation in the collection of J. Eliot Hodgkin is described as having attached to it 'by

certainly not the only method. The proclamations lowering the value of the shilling in the summer of 1551 must have been dispatched in a manner guaranteeing that the text would remain secret until the seal was broken. The 'sur simple queue' method, which made it possible to open and close the document without breaking the seal, could not have been used.[85] When the proclamation text was also printed, the printed copies must have been sent together with the manuscript copy for purposes of posting.

The time it took to deliver a proclamation depended on the distance the messengers had to travel. Proclamations were often proclaimed in London within a day or two after the date on the writ; travel to a more distant city could take considerably longer. This could prove a bit awkward, because, although statutes became law immediately after enactment, proclamations did not take effect until they were proclaimed.[86] In cases where it was extremely important that the proclamation went into effect in all parts of the country simultaneously the government took special precautions. For example, the instructions sent with the proclamations changing the value of a shilling in the summer of 1551 were intended to assure that they were proclaimed throughout the country on the same date. In some cases the difference between the dates of proclamation in various localities was so great that it must indicate a second proclaiming. The proclamation forbidding unlicensed export, issued on 16 February 1541, was proclaimed in Kent on 18 March, in Lynn on 28 March, and in Pembrokeshire on 5 November.[87] Some procla-

the original sewing two MS instructions to the Sheriff of Southampton – one in Latin on a strip of vellum, and the other in English, on a larger piece of paper – for the proclaiming of the proclamation and the fastening the same "in one publique place" in some market town.' I have not been able to locate this document but Hodgkin calls it 'perhaps the sole surviving exemplification of the way in which broadside proclamations were at the time disseminated.' Eliot Hodgkin, *Rariora* (London, 1902), III, 7, x. The Latin instructions were obviously the writ under the great seal and the English letter may have been the accompanying signet letter.

[85] *TRP* nos. 376, 379. Wriothesley's description of the proclaiming of no. 379 in London indicates that the seal had to be broken to read the text: 'Proclamation was made in Cheap by the common cryer for the abatement of the coin, he first showing the proclamation to the audience under the King's seal that it was whole and not opened to witness the same.' Charles Wriothesley, *A Chronicle of England During the Reigns of the Tudors*, William D. Hamilton ed. (London, 1875), 54.

[86] Steele, ix. For an example of a defendant accused of a violation of a proclamation who based his defense on the claim that the offense took place before the proclamation had been proclaimed in his area even though the proclamation had been issued considerably before the alleged offense see St Ch 2/29/175.

[87] *TRP* no. 198 was proclaimed in London on 21 March 1541 (CLRO Journals 14/248). No. 208 was proclaimed in London on 6 February 1541 (CLRO LB Q 300d). Both were proclaimed in Norwich five days after their proclamation in London (NNRO Mayors Court

mations were clearly proclaimed several times, often as much as a year later. One, regulating plays and interludes, was first proclaimed in London in October 1544. On 5 February 1545 the mayor and aldermen ordered a second proclamation and in February of the following year it was decided that the proclamation 'heretofore made against the common players of interludes within the city shall tomorrow be proclaimed again.'[88]

The final step in making an early Tudor proclamation was the actual proclaiming. We are fortunate in having a number of descriptions of how this was done. The place of proclamation was chosen to attract the widest audience. In Colchester one of Henry VII's proclamations was proclaimed by the bailiffs of the city 'in the King's highway in front of St James Church near to east gate, because on that day the parishioners of the parish of St James procured certain musters and memorials to be displayed there.'[89] One of Henry VIII's proclamations permitting the eating of white meat in Lent was to be 'published in churches' throughout the diocese and 'in markets within the head places of this diocese where great recourse of people resorted.'[90] The actual proclamation often took place with a great deal of ceremony. A description of the method of proclaiming in the city of Exeter reads as follows:

> The mayor or in his absence his lieutenant...is to make his repair into the open and full market place associated with his brethren and aldermen and his officers and then the swordbearer standing before with the sword holden up and the four sergeants. One of the said sergeants is to make three oyezs and to command every man to keep silence. Then one of them is to pronounce openly and with a loud voice the proclamation then and there by the clerk to be read to him. Which done, the said proclamations if they be imprinted are to be set up upon the gates of the city and in such order upon places as have been accustomed.[91]

When a particularly dramatic event was proclaimed, such as the conclusion of a peace treaty, the ceremony was considerably more elaborate. The proclamation of the peace treaty with Scotland in August 1534 included a procession by the sheriffs of London 'in their

Book 1540–9, 48, 85). The dates for the proclaiming of the proclamation of 16 February 1541 (*TRP* no. 197.6) are based on the dates given in litigation involving this proclamation (St Ch 1/1/153, 29/175, 23/208, 1/22).

[88] *TRP* no. 240; CLRO Journals 15/241d; Rep. 11/142, 11/244d.

[89] W. Gurney Benham, *The Red Paper Book at Colchester* (Colchester, 1902), 109; *TRP* no. 21.

[90] SP 1/117/41(*LP* 12[1] no. 679). The text of this proclamation has not been found. It is listed in App. B as item no. 22.

[91] Hooker, *Description of Excester*, III, 846.

scarlet gowns,' the sergeants at arms and the heralds with trumpeters through the streets of the city. Proclamation was made with trumpet fanfares at London Bridge, Leadenhall, Cheapside and in Fleet Street.[92] The proclamation of the peace treaty with France in June 1546 was even more impressive. Wriothesley, the herald, describes it as taking place on 13 June beginning with a high mass in St Paul's cathedral where the mayor and aldermen and 'all the citizens in their best liveries' were assembled. A procession through the city followed and then the heralds and sheriffs of London with four trumpeters made the first proclamation at St Magnus in Fish Street. This was followed by proclamations at Leadenhall, Cheapside and Fleet Street with trumpet fanfares in each case. Bonfires and a banquet with enough wine 'for all comers by to drink as long as it lasted' followed in the evening.[93] A similar ceremony took place in York on 6 July at the order of the King that the proclamation be made 'with sound of trumpeters, procession, making of bonfires and other ceremonies.' York, however, was not as fortunate as London. They surprisingly were unable to find any trumpeters in that whole city and they were forced to agree 'in default of a trumpet to have a drum before them.'[94]

[92] BM Harl. 442/92 (*TRP* no. 147).
[93] Wriothesley, *Chronicle*, I, 163–5 (*TRP* no. 268).
[94] YCRO House Books 18/45d.

2

THE AUTHORITY OF ROYAL PROCLAMATIONS

Proclamacion serra a confirmer et ratefier un ley ou statute, et ney a chaunger un ley ou de faire un novel ley.[1]

The Lord Chancellor said he had learned a rule that the prerogative meddles not with meum et tuum; the King can not take my lands or goods and give it to another but where the common state or wealth of the people or kingdom require it, the King's proclamation binds as a law and need not stay a Parliament.[2]

Both of these statements were made after the end of the early Tudor period. They reveal the disparity of opinion on proclamations that still existed among judges during the reigns of the Tudor Queens. Medieval practice and constitutional theory had delineated the broad limits of the power and authority of royal proclamations. However, it was not until the Stuart period that Coke's decision set a precedent for later legal writers to deny the Crown an independent legislative prerogative even in emergency situations.[3] Although differing points of view continued into the reign of James I, the early Tudor period was one of formative importance in the development of the theory of royal proclamations. As the result of a series of statutes, enacted

[1] BM Harl. 5141/31.
[2] John Hawarde, *Les Reportes del Cases in Camera Stella*, William P. Baildon, ed. (London, 1894), 329.
[3] 'The King cannot create any offense by his prohibition or proclamation which was not an offense before for that was to change the law and to make an offense which was not.' Edward Coke, *The Reports of Sir Edward Coke* (London, 1929), VI, 299. The opinion was not published until 1656. Curiously it had very little impact at the time and was not cited in the great debates about proclamations in the 1620s. Esther Cope, 'Sir Edward Coke and Proclamations, 1610,' *American Journal of Legal History*, XV (1971), 221. Later legal authorities, however, consistently cited it: Matthew Bacon, *A New Abridgement of the Law* (Philadelphia, 1876), VIII, 79–81; John Comyns, *A Digest of the Laws of England* (London, 1800), VI, 34–5; Giles Jacob and T. E. Tomlins, *Law Dictionary* (New York, 1811), VI, 33–5; Henry Rolle, *Un Abridgement Des Plusiers Cases et Resolutions Del Common Ley* (London, 1688), 209–10; Charles Viner, *A General Abridgement of Law and Equity* (London, 1873), XVII, 197–9; T. Cunningham, *A New and Complete Law Dictionary or General Abridgment of the Law* (London, 1765), II, 117. In the reign of Elizabeth, Coke had allowed a much larger prerogative to the King's proclamations: 'If anything be hurtful or prejudicial to the commonwealth or the state, albeit the same be not prohibited by laws her majesty may prohibit the same for the good of the people': SP 12/276/81.

largely in the 1530s, the vague and relatively undefined legislative powers of the medieval monarchs were circumscribed. Even though the most significant of these statutes, the Statute of Proclamations, was repealed at the beginning of the reign of Edward VI, the limitations on the proclaiming power stated in that act and the precedents set by the other early Tudor statutes had a major impact in determining the future role of royal proclamations in English government.

Although he never mentioned royal proclamations, Sir John Fortescue outlined the general boundaries of the Crown's legislative powers at the beginning of the Tudor period. Throughout his works he advocated a strong monarchy based on the royal prerogative, but he insisted that the King of England must be and was limited by Parliament both in legislation and taxation:

> For the King of England is not able to change the laws of his kingdom at pleasure, for he rules his people with a government not only regal but also political. If he were to preside over them with a power entirely regal, he would be able to change the laws of his realm, and also impose on them tallages and other burdens, without consulting them; this is the sort of dominion which the civil laws indicate when they state that what pleases the prince has the force of law. But the case is far otherwise with the King ruling his people politically, because he is not able himself to change the laws without the assent of his subjects nor to burden an unwilling people with strange imposts, so that, ruled by laws that they themselves desire, they freely enjoy their properties, and are despoiled neither by their own King nor any other.[4]

Statutes could be made only by Parliament and 'do not emanate from the will of the prince alone, as do laws in kingdoms which are governed entirely regally.'[5] But since Parliament was an exceptional rather than a regular part of English government, Fortescue also allowed wide discretionary powers to the council:

> The councilors may continually at such hours as shall be assigned to them commune and deliberate upon matters of difficulty that fall to the King, and then upon the matters of the policy of the realm; as how the going out of money may be restrained, how bullion may be brought into the land, how also plate, jewels, and money late borne out, may be gotten again, of which right wise men may soon find the means. And also how the prices of merchandise growing in this realm may be held up and increased, and how the prices of merchandise brought into this land abated. How the navy may be maintained and augmented and upon such other points of policy to the greatest profit and increase that ever come to this land. How

[4] Stanley B. Chrimes ed., *Sir John Fortescue De Laudibus Legum Angliae* (Cambridge, 1942), 25.   [5] *Ibid.* 41.

also the laws may be amended in such things as they need reformation in; where through the Parliaments shall be able to do more good in a month to the mending of the law than they shall be able to do in a year if the amending thereof be not debated by such council ripened to their hands.[6]

Thus Fortescue envisioned a strong monarchy based on the royal prerogative, but limited in its powers. The limits of the prerogative were clear: the King could not change the common law, impose new taxes, or make a statute without the consent of Parliament. However, within those limits the King and council had large independent powers, the range and extent of which were not clearly defined.[7]

Tudor political theorists added little to the general statements made by Fortescue. Christopher St Germain, who wrote his major work in 1535, reiterated Fortescue's statements. Whenever he spoke of legislation he consistently referred to the King in Parliament rather than the King in council. He distinguished between a 'jus regale' where the King made the law without his subjects' consent, and a 'jus regale politicum' where the King made the law with the 'assent of his lords spiritual and temporal; and of his commons gathered together by his commandment in his Parliament.' Since English government followed the latter model, the King could not change the common law, the customs of the realm, or statutes without the consent of Parliament.[8] St Germain simply ignored the King's independent legislative powers. Even in ecclesiastical affairs he emphasized that changes in the religious settlement should be made through Parliament. He maintained that the King 'is especially bound to prohibit all things as nigh as he can whereby his subjects spiritual and temporal might have occasion to break the laws of God.' Therefore the King could prohibit preaching which caused 'unquietness among his subjects.' If the King, however, intended to make new

---

[6] John Fortescue, *The Governance of England*, Charles Plummer ed. (London, 1926), 147–8.

[7] Holdsworth, who has a useful discussion of the use of royal proclamations in the Middle Ages, states: 'The large vague powers of legislation possessed by the medieval King had never been expressly defined or curtailed. Parliament, it is true, had become a partner with the King in the exercise of legislative authority; and, from the end of the thirteenth century, it was clear that a law which was made by the authority of Parliament could only be changed by the same authority; and the same authority was needed for changes in the old established rules of the common law. This involved in practice a limitation upon the King's power to legislate; but it was an indirect and therefore a vague limitation.' William Holdsworth, *A History of English Law*, 3rd ed. (London, 1923), IV, 101. The best account of royal proclamations in the Middle Ages is still found in Steele, who also includes a list of medieval proclamations. Steele, lff, clviiff.

[8] Christopher St Germain, *An Answer to a Letter* (London, 1535), Gvi-Gvid. *The Doctor and Student or Dialogues between a Doctor of Divinity and a Student in the Laws of England*, William Muchall ed. (Cincinnati, 1874), 18–19.

laws for the Church or establish new doctrine, he should do this with the advice and consent of Parliament.⁹ St Germain's failure to mention the King's legislative prerogative is difficult to explain. Baumer maintains that he deliberately chose to ignore it: 'St Germain knew perfectly well that the King possessed a legislative prerogative, but the fact remains that he ignored it altogether in his discussion.'¹⁰ As in Fortescue, it is clear that certain actions such as taxation, alteration of the common laws, or making of statutes demanded Parliamentary consent. But within these general limitations there is a large area for which St Germain's treatises offer little guidance.

That uncertainty prevailed about the authority and sphere of royal proclamations in the early Tudor period is suggested by one of the earliest Elizabethan treatises mentioning them. The work was probably written by Thomas Egerton. It briefly discussed proclamations when summarizing the methods of legislation in the kingdom:

All that law which is positive consisteth either in proclamations or in acts of Parliament. In proclamations as if the prince by his council have thought good and expedient to publish anything as a law. But therein hath been doubted of what effect such proclamations have been, and what pain he that breaketh them should have. And some said that the pain is the loss of his allegiance. As for the authority of them an act of Parliament was made in 31 H. 8 which is now repealed. Howbeit it is certain that the readers affirm that by the common law if the ordinance that was made had been in supplement or declaration of a law, that that had been good being ordained by the lords and never consented to by the commons... but for anything that is in alteration or abridgement they have no power.¹¹

He seems to be saying that proclamations can only be used 'in supplement or declaration of a law' and not to make new laws or change old ones.¹² But he also says they are 'positive' laws and that the Statute of Proclamations defined their authority. Since its repeal, that authority may again have been in doubt. What 'is certain' is

⁹ St Germain, *Answer to a Letter*, Gii, Giv.
¹⁰ Franklin L. Baumer, *Early Tudor Theory of Kingship* (New Haven, 1940), 149. Baumer states that although St Germain believed that the royal supremacy was Parliamentary and 'must be interpreted to mean the rule of the Church by the King in Parliament' this represented only one line of thought on the question: 'It is obvious that the Henrician political writers were not all of one mind in deciding whether the Royal Supremacy applied to the King alone or the King in Parliament.' *Ibid.* 62.
¹¹ Samuel E. Thorne ed., *A Discourse upon the Exposition and Understanding of Statutes with Sir Thomas Egerton's Additions* (San Marino, California, 1942), 103–7.
¹² This is the way Professor Elton interpreted the statement: 'There is no prerogative power of making new laws and abrogating old.' G. R. Elton, 'The Rule of Law in Sixteenth-Century England,' *Tudor Men and Institutions*, A. J. Slavin ed. (Baton Rouge, 1972), 278. However, he quoted only the last sentence in the selection, and unless it is understood in the context of Egerton's other comments this can be misleading.

that 'the readers' believed that their authority did not extend to the 'alteration or abridgement' of existing law.[13]

Legal and constitutional writers may have hesitated to discuss the authority of royal proclamations because the judges and courts had also said little about them during either the Middle Ages or the early Tudor period. By the time of the Stuart period there were abundant judgments concerning proclamations, but one searches in vain for anything in the medieval or early Tudor legal records which provides the same kind of information. This is possibly easiest to document by comparing law abridgments. The early abridgments, Brookes, Stantham, and Fitzherbert, differ markedly from the later abridgements in their coverage of royal proclamations. Although a separate listing is accorded the topic 'proclamations' in each of the early abridgements, the cases listed under that heading deal with practically every type of public announcement known to the law of England except royal proclamations.[14] The closest reference to a royal proclamation is found in Brooke. It involved an incident in the 1530s. Sir Edmund Knightly, executor of the will of Sir William Spencer, was fined and imprisoned for proclaiming 'in markette villes in nome le roy' that Spencer's creditors should come on a specific day and prove their debts. Coke later cited this reference to establish that subjects could not make proclamations 'without authority from the King or lawful custom.'[15] Holdsworth drew some sweeping implications from the decision:

> The fact that Brooke could class together cases relating to the by-laws of these communities [manors, hundreds, boroughs, parishes] and cases relating to royal proclamations, is very significant of the effect which the rise of Parliament had upon the King's once extensive power to legislate.

---

[13] The same writer in a speech before the Exchequer in 1607 attributed considerably greater powers to royal proclamations, possibly as a result of his experience in Elizabethan government. He reminded his audience that in the Middle Ages the King possessed wide powers to legislate outside of Parliament: 'Of the strength of Proclamations, being made by the King, by the advice of his council and judges, I will not discourse, yet I will admonish those that be learned and studious in the laws and by their profession are to give counsel, and to direct themselves and others to take heed that they do not condemn or lightly regard such proclamations. And to induce them thereunto, I desire them to look upon and consider advisedly these few proclamations, provisions or ordinances, which I will point out unto them, and if what validity and force they have been holden to be in construction of law, albeit they be neither statutes nor acts of Parliament.' Thomes Egerton, *The Speech of the Lord Chancellor of England in The Eschequer Chamber Touching the Post-nati* (London, 1609), 13–15.

[14] Robert Brooke, *La Grande Abridgement* (London, 1576); Margaret C. Kligelsmith ed., *Stantham's Abridgement of the Law* (Boston, 1915); Anthony Fitzherbert, *La Graunde Abridgement* (London, 1565).

[15] Brooke, *Abridgement*, 160; Coke, *Reports*, IV, 297.

It is clear proof that in this period the royal proclamation was regarded as being like a by-law in this essential respect that it was subordinate to the statute or common law.[16]

Holdsworth was certainly right. Proclamations were 'subordinate to the statute or common law.' But he based this conclusion on an extremely questionable source. The case Brooke cited had no connection with royal proclamations. Cromwell described the incident in detail in a letter to Henry VIII. The judgment was given by Cromwell, William Paulet, Thomas More and members of the council. Knightly and his brother were intending to defraud their sister, Lady Spencer, and the King of William Spencer's inheritance. Knightly tried 'to set pike between the said lady and the executors and to defeat your grace of your title to the heir of the said Spencer,' but 'it was openly proved that your grace had good title.' Whereupon Knightly 'to the intent to slander your grace's title' had proclamation made in Warwickshire, Leicestershire, Northamptonshire and a number of cities 'to the high contempt of your grace and your laws. For it hath not been seen nor heard that any subjects within this realm should presume to make proclamation within this realm but only in your grace's name.'[17] Although it is an interesting case, Holdsworth's inference that the result indicates contemporary opinion about the authority of royal proclamations is unwarranted by the evidence. Another heading in the abridgements which might have included a reference to judicial judgments on proclamations is 'prerogative le Roy.' Once again the search is in vain. Brooke cited a case that established that the King could not alter or change a law by his grant, but again this case did not deal specifically with royal proclamations.[18]

When these early abridgements are compared with later abridgements there is a striking contrast. Charles Viner devoted three pages under the title 'prerogative of the King' to royal proclamations. Rolle's coverage is similar in length. The legal limits of royal proclamations were carefully defined and supported by numerous precedents; however, it is significant that the earliest judicial decision cited occurred in the reign of Mary.[19] Even Coke found it difficult to

[16] Holdsworth, *History of English Law*, IV, 100.
[17] Roger B. Merriman, *Life and Letters of Thomas Cromwell* (Oxford, 1902), I, 349.
[18] Brooke, *Abridgement*, 60.
[19] Viner, *Abridgement*, XVII, 197–9; Rolle, *Abridgement*, 209–11. Rolle's abridgement was written shortly before 1656, while Viner's was first published between 1742 and 1753. Stantham's was published around 1495; Fitzherbert's was first published in 1516, and Brooke's in 1568.

locate early precedents in support of his statements in 1610. He used some extremely questionable references and may have invented others. Two medieval Year Book references were cited in support of his statement that 'the King by his proclamation or other ways, cannot change any part of the common law, or statute law, or the customs of the realm.'[20] I have not been able to find the second (18 Henry IV 35, 36) in any extant copy of the Year Books, but the first (11 Henry IV 37) certainly did not deal with the authority of royal proclamations. The case involved was initiated by a writ of *Quare Impedit* against the Bishop of Salisbury. The Pope had granted him the right to retain his former benefice, but the King sued for the right to present, because he considered it a vacant benefice, arguing that the Pope could not lawfully make such a grant. Justice Hill, deciding for the King, maintained that the grant violated the law of the land, and that the Pope could not change the law of England any more than could the King. Even if the monarch had granted a man the right to keep his lands after he had entered religion, such a grant would be void because it was contrary to the common law and reason.[21] The decision had nothing to do with proclamations although it did state that neither the Pope nor the King could change the law by a Bull of dispensation or a grant. Coke also cited Knightly's case, although it did not apply. Finally, he listed an example of an illegal proclamation in the Middle Ages, using it to show that proclamations suspending statutes were illegal. Once again his evidence cannot be traced.[22]

A final possible source for judicial decisions are the law reporters. Again I have not been able to find any judgments on royal proclamations recorded by the early law reporters for the period 1485–53.[23] The earliest judicial decision on proclamations mentioned by the law reporters occurred in the reign of Mary. It is included in the reports

[20] Coke, *Reports*, VI, 299. Coke's other references were to Fortescue, *De Laudibus Legum Angliae*.
[21] Year Books: Henry IV (London, 1852), 11 Henry IV 37.
[22] Steele, I, xcii–xciii: 'The precedents of illegal proclamation cited by Coke cannot be verified. There is no such proclamation as he quotes on the Close Roll of 8 Henry IV and no such act in 9 Henry IV.'
[23] I have checked the following printed reports: Gulieme Bendloes, 'Les Reports de Gulieme Bendloes Serjeant de la Ley,' *English Reports*, Vol. 73 (London, 1900–39), 931–1063; Robert Brooke, 'Some New Cases of the Years and Times of King Henry VIII, Edward VI and Mary,' *ibid.* 847–930; Robert Keilway, 'Reports d'Ascuns Cases,' *ibid.* Vol. 73, 153–396; Francis Moore, 'Cases Collected and Reported per Sir Fra More,' *ibid.* Vol. 145, 397–997. In addition I have sampled manuscript reports of John Carrell, Sr (BM Landsown 1084), John Spelman and John Pollard (BM Hargrave 388), Edmund Anderson (BM Harl. 4817).

of William Dalison, a justice of the King's Bench from 1554 to 1559, and is dated Easter term 2 and 3 Philip and Mary. It seems to have been expressed at a meeting between justices and serjeants at law at Serjeants Inn rather than in open court. Because of its importance, it is worth quoting in full:

> Nota auxi agree per tonte q le roy poet fair un proclamacon a lour subiects quoad terrore populi de mitter eux en feare de son displeasure et indignacon, mes nei sur auter payne certein come a forfeyture tres ou beins ou de faire fine, ou de suffer imprisonment, ou auters paynes quel nul proclamacon en soy mesme poet faire un ley quel ne fuit adepart, mes proclamacon serra de confirmer et ratefier un ley ou statute, et ney a chaunger un ley ou de faire un novel ley et uncore divers presidentes fuer traves et mines hors del Exchequer a le contrary mes a cest les justices ment par regard qil nota bein et per justice Stamfort de roy poet faire proclamacon a lyer subiects de augmenter le coyne le realme a pluis haute quel ceo est per le benefitt ses subiects, mes dadiminisher ou imbasser le dit coyne de meynder valewe per proclamacon cest per loy ne estoit ove ley, quia est al prejudice les subiects comit quel anterint fiut mise en use per proclamacon en le temps E6 per John duke le Northumberland le graund traytor et malement ut medo.[24]

This must have been the 'reader's' opinion mentioned by Egerton, but it certainly reveals that there was some disagreement on the authority of royal proclamations in the early Tudor period. Even among those discussing the questions precedents 'a le contrary' from the Exchequer were offered. True, 'a cest les justices ment par regard'; but it is clear from the recorded decision that there were other opinions on the subject.

In contrast to the vagueness about royal proclamations characteristic of the Middle Ages and the early Tudor period, writers and judges made very specific statements on the authority of royal proclamations after 1553. Numerous decisions on proclamations were rendered in the courts especially during the reigns of Elizabeth and James I. Hobart reported a case in the Star Chamber in the

---

[24] BM Harl. 5141/31. The printed version does not include the last section dealing with coinage proclamations, but it does list references to three statutes not mentioned in the manuscript version. It ends: 'vide anno 31 H 8 cap 8 and anno 35 Hen 8 cap 23, inde and 25 Hen 8 cap 2.' Guilieme Dalison, *Les Reports Des Divers Special Cases Adjudged en le Court del Common Bank en les Reignes de les Tre Hault & Excellent Princes Henry VIII, Edward VI et Les Reignes Mary and Elizabeth* (London, 1689), 241. 25 Henry VIII c. 2 gave the council the right to set prices on food and forbade unlicensed exports. 31 Henry VIII c. 8 is the Statute of Proclamations, and 35 Henry VIII c. 23 is probably a reference to 34 and 35 Henry VIII c. 23, the statute which amended the Statute of Proclamations. I am indebted to Professor L. W. Abbott for pointing out to me that this was not a judicial decision in open court. His recent work, *Law Reporting in the Sixteenth Century* (London, 1973) was an important aid for locating manuscript copies of law reports.

reign of James I in which the justices held that proclamations against the increase of building in London were valid since they were made 'pro bono publico.'[25] The King's right to alter the coinage by proclamation was upheld several times.[26] Coke also reported a case in the reign of Mary when a proclamation forbidding the importation of French wines without license was declared illegal because the two countries were not at war.[27] In addition Sir Thomas Smith and James Morrice, writing early in the reign of Elizabeth, described the role and authority of royal proclamations in some detail.

The earlier of the two treatises was Smith's *De Republica Anglorum*. He probably wrote the work as early as 1562, but it was not published until 1582. He was active in both the Edwardian and Elizabethan governments and well versed in the law; therefore, his work is an extremely useful source.[28] Although Smith held that the legislative power in England was vested in the King acting through Parliament, the King also had powers to act without Parliament. He could declare war or make peace or enter into alliances 'at his pleasure or the advice only of his privy council.' He also had absolute power in diplomatic negotiations and in dealing with internal rebellions. In addition the King had 'absolute power in crying and decreeing the money of the realm by his proclamations only,' and 'the form, fashion, manner, weight, fineness and baseness thereof is at the discretion of the prince.'[29]

The second of the treatises went considerably further in defining the limits of the King's legislative powers. Written by James Morrice, an able and successful Tudor lawyer, it was first presented as a reading at the Middle Temple in May 1578.[30] Morrice maintained that there were three ways in which the King could legislate:

[25] Henry Hobart, 'The Reports of that Reverend and Learned Judge the Honorable Sir Henry Hobart,' *English Reports*, Vol. 80, 398.

[26] John Davis, 'Les Reports des Cases & Matters en Ley Resolved & Adjudged en les Courts del Roy en Ireland,' *English Reports*, Vol. 88, 509; Edward Coke, *Coke Upon Littleton* (London, 1830), 207; Coke, *Reports*, III, 234.

[27] Edward Coke, *The Second Part of the Institute of the Laws of England* (London, 1671), 62–3. See T. Cunningham, *Law Dictionary*, II, under listing 'proclamation' for a series of references to other judicial decisions on proclamations.

[28] Thomas Smith was a clerk of the privy council during the reign of Edward VI. In 1548 he became one of the Secretaries of State, so that he had practical experience dealing with royal proclamations. Although he wrote *De Republica Anglorum* early in the reign of Elizabeth, it was not published until six years after his death. Thomas Smith, *De Republica Anglorum*, Leonard Alston ed. (Cambridge, 1906), vii–xi.   [29] *Ibid.* 58–60.

[30] BM Add. 36081/229ff. The work was presented to Lord Burghley and may have been one of the reasons for Morrice's appointment as Attorney of the Courts of Wards and Liveries in 1579. He later served in a number of Elizabethan Parliaments and was a mem-

Three manner of ways I find the King is said to make and give laws unto his subjects, that is in and by his high and great court of Parliament, by his letters patent under the great seal of England, and by his princely and royal commandment.[31]

In Parliament the King was in fact the legislator, because although he needed the advice and consent of the Lords and Commons, the matter did not become law until the King gave assent. This advice and consent was needed

to make any new law or ordinances touching the life, land, goods or inheritance of his subjects, to impose on them for the defense of the realm and maintenance of the state any subsidy, tax, or payment of money, to alter or declare the sense of any former statute, acts of Parliament, to decide and determine the doubtful case of the common law or custom of the realm, to abridge any part of them.[32]

Even though the King was bound by laws made in Parliament, under certain circumstances he could 'surmount the force and authority of the law.' He could, for example, grant pardons, issue licenses, and in matters 'that touch the common profit and wealth of the realm' he had 'a pre-eminence above the law.' For this reason he had the power to apply or suspend 'all acts of Parliament forbidding the transporting of victual and other commodities of the realm into foreign countries.'[33]

A second means of legislation was by letters patent under the great seal. By this method the King could make grants of liberties and franchises, but these grants could not violate the common law or common right. He could also restrain the general liberty of his subjects by granting to one of them or a group of them a monopoly in some trade. But there were certain limitations on this power since he could not 'erect a monopoly depriving the merchants of his realm of their trade and traffic,' nor could he 'make any kind of mystery or occupation used within his kingdom to be altogether private to few.'[34] The third method of legislation was by the King's commandment. It was under this category that Morrice discussed royal proclamations. The King could declare war and peace by proclamation. Although he could call upon the full assistance of his subjects for the defense of the realm, he could not command his subjects

ber of the Puritan opposition. Edward T. Lampson, 'The Royal Prerogative 1485–1603' (unpublished PhD dissertation, Dept. of History, Harvard University, 1938), Appendix, ii. Lampson edited Morrice's treatise and included it in an appendix to his doctoral dissertation. He calls the treatise: 'The first treatise I know of which considers the public power of the King.' Ibid. v.   [31] BM Add. 35081/237–237d.
[32] Ibid. 238.   [33] Ibid. 241, 248d.
[34] Ibid. 251.

to provide soldiers or supplies for the invasion of foreign countries unless they were so bound 'by the tenure of their lands.' He also could not compel his subjects to provide more assistance in war than they owed the King as service 'except it be by common assent and grant made in Parliament.'[35] Although the King could not compel men to leave the land to fight in a foreign war, he could keep his subjects from leaving the land in time of war, because certain restrictions on the subjects' liberties might be necessary in wartime for the good of the commonwealth. The King could also command individuals to return from a foreign country, and if they refused to obey, he could seize their lands and goods. He could use proclamations to alter the coinage of the realm and 'enhance or abase the same at his good pleasure,' or he could make proclamations for his 'princely pleasure disports and pastime.'[36] Finally, he could even afforest lands by proclamations as long as they were his own lands. However, he could not order that his subjects' lands be 'subject to the laws of the forest' since this was 'a matter of greater importance and tendeth to the disinheritance of the subject wherein the King can have no prerogative at all.'[37] Offenses against proclamations were contempts of the King's commandment. They could be punished like other contempts by imprisonment and fine. He summed up his comments on the powers of proclamations in a way which indicated that although he accepted the ancient limits on the King's prerogative, he believed that proclamations were positive law and that within those limits they had the force of law.

But to conclude concerning the King's commandments either by writing or proclamation. They are all so far the binding laws unto the people as the same are agreeable to the word of God, not repugnant to the laws of the realm, impossible to be performed or not injurious to the subject.[38]

Morrice's treatise is by far the most useful of the Tudor legal treatises mentioning royal proclamations because of the detail he provides.[39]

[35] *Ibid.* 254.
[36] *Ibid.* 255.
[37] *Ibid.* 255d.
[38] *Ibid.* 257.
[39] In addition to Morrice and Smith an anonymous tract entitled 'The Force and Strength and Practice of Royal Proclamations' probably written in the reign of Elizabeth also attributed a good deal of authority to royal proclamations: 'Proclamations or edicts (even by the common laws of the realm) in certain criminal or penal offenses not touching the lives of subjects or their freedoms in blood or the charging or changing their lands in nature and quality of term or exposing them to forfeiture, they not only have legis vigorem as being declaratory of the King's pleasure upon some sudden urgency or necessity of state not curiously by ordinary subjects to be entered into but that many of them have been observed as statutefull laws in such cases especially as tend to the performance of the regal office touching the defense of holy church, the preservation of

It is also an accurate description of how proclamations were generally used in the early Tudor period. It clearly describes the way in which we can speak of the King 'legislating' by proclamation. Although it was a limited sphere, it was, nevertheless, considerably broader than Coke would later allow. However, it was only in the Elizabethan period that such a specific description of the role and authority of royal proclamations was written.

The uncertainty about royal proclamations in the early Tudor period created problems for someone as concerned about legality as Thomas Cromwell. This is graphically illustrated by an incident which took place in 1531. Cromwell described it in a letter he wrote to the Duke of Norfolk, probably on 15 July 1531.[40] Cromwell informed Norfolk of a discussion on the validity of royal proclamations which arose in connection with an effort of the council to prevent the export of coin. There seems to have been some concern about the authority upon which the council could act. Cromwell related the discussion in the following manner.

Mr Attorney and I both did intimate and declare the King's pleasure unto my lord chancellor who immediately sent for my lord chief justice of the King's Bench, the chief justice of the Common Pleas, the chief baron and Mr Fitzherbert – Mr Attorney, Mr Solicitor and I being present; and the case by my said lord chancellor opened, divers opinions there were, but finally it was concluded that all the statutes should be searched to see whether there were any statute or law able to serve for the purpose. And if there were, it was thought good that, if it should happen any accident to be whereby there might be any occasion that the money should be conveyed out of the realm, that then proclamation should be made grounded upon the said statute adding thereunto politically certain things for the putting the King's subjects and other in more terror and fear.

the rights of the crown, the upholding of the common law, right and justice of the realm, the peace and concord between the kingdom and the priesthood, the establishment and reviving of good laws and the abrogation or denunciation of bad and evil laws derogative to Magna Carta or the points aforesaid for to this the King is solemnly sworn.' The tract cited Fitzherbert and Stanford in support of the author's statement that the King could fine and imprison those who broke his proclamations and it cited precedents from the Middle Ages where laws were made 'even in weighty matters albeit they had no other foundation than upon the same edict, proclamations, grants, writs or mandate.' BM Hargrave 29/136-7.

[40] The letter is dated 15 July 1535 by *LP* VII 8 no. 1042 and Merriman, *Letters of Cromwell*, I, 409; however, the manuscript is dated only 15 July (BM Titus B I/311-12). Professor Elton has recently maintained that the letter must have been written in 1531: 'This is proved not only by the extraordinarily deferential tone, very different from that which by 1535 he was using to the duke, but also by its contents. It is concerned with preventing the export of coin from the realm, and the committee of legal advisers wished to rest the necessary proclamation on an act of Richard II. The proclamation which resulted was published on July 18, 1531...There was no proclamation on the subject in 1535.' Elton, *Tudor Men and Institutions*, 282 n. 35.

41

Upon which device search was made and a good statute found which was made in the fifth year of King Richard the Second. The copy whereof translated into English I do send unto your grace drawn in manner of a proclamation by the advice of the King's learned council.[41]

Interestingly the most important legal officers in the land were not clear on the power of royal proclamations. The fact that questions arose concerning the authority by which the council could act in this matter, and that there were divers opinions, surely suggests that the limits of the King's power to act by proclamations were not at all clearly defined. Cromwell was concerned about this and sought a clearer statement on what could be done by proclamations. He asked the justices, if no statute were available, 'what might the King's highness by the advice of his council do to withstand so great a danger.' The lord chief justice responded:

The King's highness by the advice of his council might make proclamations and use all other policies at his pleasure as well in this case as in any other like for the avoiding of any such dangers, and that the said proclamations and policies so devised by the King and his council for any such purpose should be of as good effect as any law made by Parliament or otherwise.[42]

If we can believe Cromwell's report, then at least in the opinion of the lord chief justice the authority and sphere of royal proclamations were extremely wide in emergency situations. The limits stated by the judges in Mary's reign did not seem to apply in these situations. However, the decision may not have reflected the unanimous opinion of the officials present. After all, 'divers opinions' had been expressed, and it was finally decided to base the proclamation on an existing statute.

Three years later Anthony Fitzherbert in his *La Novel Natura Brevium* commented on the King's right to restrict his subjects' departure from the realm in a way that may reflect the influence of the earlier decision. He maintained that although 'per course del comen ley' a subject could leave the realm without the King's permission, the King, because of the need to defend the realm, could by his writ prohibit a subject from leaving without license. That command might be given under the great, privy, or signet seal. It could also be issued in the form of a general command by royal proclamation:

---

[41] BM Titus B 1/311–311d; Merriman, *Letters of Cromwell*, 1, 409–10.
[42] *Ibid*. The proclamation which followed was based on 5 Richard II st. 1, c. 2; *TRP* no. 133.

Le roy per son proclamation poet inhibit son subjiecte q̄ il ne aler oustl le meer ou hors de son roialme sauns son lincence, et ceo sans maunder ascum briefe ou auter commaundment a son subjiecte: quar per cas il ne poet trover son subjiecte, ou conustr lou il est, et pur ceo cause le proclamation le roy est sufficient. Et si le subjiect fair encont cell ceo est yn contempt, et il fra fyn pur cell al roy.[43]

Fitzherbert's opinion was later cited by Morrice in support of his statements on proclamations and by a conference of justices in the first year of Elizabeth's reign. Merchants in Mary's reign had complained about new duties on cloth which had been imposed without Parliamentary approval. The justices met to discuss the complaint, and during their deliberations someone questioned whether a subject could leave the realm or export goods without the license of the King. In response the justices referred to Fitzherbert who agreed 'that the King by his general proclamation or special prohibition by writ may restrain his subjects from going out without his special licence, and if anyone attempt to do so it is a contempt.'[44]

A second judicial decision in the 1530s also suggests that questions arose over the authority of royal proclamations. It was reported in a letter Stephen Gardiner wrote to Somerset in 1547. It is not described in detail nor is its meaning easily explained. The letter was written to protest that the injunctions of 31 July 1547 were illegal because they violated an earlier statute. In the course of his argument Gardiner cited the following decision:

Since that time, being of the council, when many proclamations were devised against the carriers out of corn, at such time as the transgressors should be punished, the judges would answer – it might not be by the laws. Whereupon ensued the Act of Proclamations, in the passing of which act many liberal words were spoken, and a plain promise that, by authority of the Act of Proclamations, nothing should be made contrary to an act of Parliament or common law.[45]

Gardiner was trying to prove to Somerset that proclamations which violated statutes had been declared illegal by the judges, and that the Statute of Proclamations had confirmed that decision. An earlier draft of the letter said this more specifically, but inaccurately, so when Gardiner revised the letter he may have been describing the real

[43] Anthony Fitzherbert, *La Novel Natura Brevium* (London, 1534), 89d.
[44] John Vaillant ed., *Reports of Cases in the Reigns of Henry VIII, Edward VI, Queen Mary, and Queen Elizabeth Taken and Collected by Sir James Dyer Knt* (London, 1794), II, 165d.
[45] James Muller ed., *The Letters of Stephen Gardiner* (Cambridge, 1933), 391; BM Harl. 417/84–9.

decision even though it did not fit his polemic purpose as well.[46] Thus, it would seem that offenders against certain proclamations involving the export of corn were not punished by the judges perhaps because the court did not have jurisdiction or the penalty was illegal. The letter touches upon the reasons for making the Statute of Proclamations, and since a proper understanding of its meaning demands a more detailed explanation, a full discussion has been saved for a later chapter.

The decisions reported by Cromwell and Gardiner reveal a good deal of uncertainty about the sphere and authority of royal proclamations in the early Tudor period and a general lack of definition. This may explain why Thomas Cromwell turned to Parliament. One of the unique aspects of the 1530s was the sudden appearance of an impressive number of statutes which delegated power to royal proclamations or defined their authority. Of course, the most famous was the Statute of Proclamations, but there was also a series of other less well-known acts. The phrase that so shocked eighteenth and nineteenth century historians was, in fact, not unique to the Statute of Proclamations. A number of earlier acts included clauses that stated in essence that proclamations made by the authority of the statute were to be obeyed as though they had been made by act of Parliament.

The use of statutes to delegate powers to the King's council or other officials was not entirely new. Medieval statutes at times also delegated powers, even though they did not specifically mention royal proclamations. One of Edward III's acts, which was enacted to correct abuses in the herring trade at the fair of Great Yarmouth, empowered the chancellor, treasurer, justices and other councilors to regulate the buying and selling of fish and wines at specific fairs.[47] A series of statutes during the reign of Henry VI also delegated authority. The first of these contained a phrase similar to the one found in the Statute of Proclamations, but it dealt with proclamations by justices of the peace. Justices of the peace were to make proclamations in sessions once a year setting wages for laborers, and 'every proclamation so to be made be holden as thing ordained by statute.'[48] Three statutes in the 1430s provided that the King and the council could change statutes when needed. Two of them regulated the

[46] In his first draft Gardiner reported that the judges said 'it might not be by the law, because the act of Parliament gave liberty wheat being under a price.' *Ibid*. Since 25 Henry VIII c. 2 forbade unlicensed export of corn, a proclamation forbidding export would not have been in violation of a statue. See below p. 171–2 for a full explanation.
[47] 31 Edward III st. 2, c. 3.   [48] 6 Henry VI c. 3.

Staple at Calais. The first, 11 Henry VI c. 13, continued an earlier statute, 8 Henry VI c. 17, for three years. It also added that the King with the advice of council could 'modify the same statute' when it seemed necessary 'for the profit of him and his realm.' This was followed two years later by another act which recited the earlier two and added that licenses should not be granted to ship wools to Calais contrary to those statutes. However, once again the King and the council were empowered to modify the statute 'according as to him best shall seem for the profit of him and of his realm of England.'[49] A final statute enacted exactly a century before the Statute of Proclamations allowed the export of butter and cheese without license, but included a provision 'that the King may restrain the same when it shall please him.'[50]

The statutes of the 1530s differed from their medieval predecessors in that they specifically mentioned royal proclamations. They all assumed that in certain emergency situations it might be necessary either for the King to have a discretionary power to act without Parliament, or that certain matters like price setting, which needed to be adjusted to economic changes, could be handled more efficiently through delegated authority. The earliest of these statutes coincided perfectly with Thomas Cromwell's rise to power. The same Parliamentary session which Professor Elton maintains revealed that 'a new temper had taken hold of the government' in the struggle with Rome,[51] also gave the council power to set prices by royal proclamation. The statute forbade the importation of French wines between Michaelmas and Candlemas and allowed a conciliar committee to set wholesale prices on wine by proclamation. The next session of Parliament passed a second act which set new penalties and elaborated on the enforcement procedure. In 1536 another statute repeated the provisions of the first.[52] More sweeping price-control legislation was enacted in the 1533 Parliament. The action was justified by the assertions that 'cheese, butter, capons, hens, chickens and other victuals necessary of men's subsistence' were subject to variations in price due to 'dearth, scarcity, good cheap and plenty' and therefore 'it is very hard and difficult to put any certain prices to any such things.' Since the prices of these items were often enhanced more than was warranted 'upon any reasonable or just

---

[49] 14 Henry VI c. 2.
[50] 18 Henry VI c. 3.
[51] G. R. Elton, *England under the Tudors* (London, 1955), 130.
[52] 23 Henry VIII c. 7; 24 Henry VIII c. 6; 28 Henry VIII c. 14.

ground,' upon 'every complaint made of any enhancing of prices of such victuals without ground or cause reasonable,' the council (or at least seven of them) was empowered to set prices both 'in gross or by retail' and 'after such prices set and taxes in form aforesaid, proclamation shall be made in the King's name under the great seal of said prices.' Victuallers were ordered to sell at these prices or to suffer the penalties which would be stated in the proclamations. The statute also included a proviso protecting the authority of local governments to continue setting prices as they had in the past.[53]

Another power granted to the King by the statutes of the 1530s was the authority to use proclamations to suspend statutes when emergency situations warranted such action. The earliest of these again involved price controls. In the previous session of Parliament, 24 Henry VIII c. 3 had ordered that meat be sold by weight and had set maximum prices per pound. Since seasonal fluctuations resulted in a scarcity of meat at certain times of the year, these prices could not be kept because 'the graziers and butchers in such a dear time shall not be able to afford the same at such prices and rates as when they be in more plenty.' Therefore, the King was empowered to suspend the earlier statute as he saw fit and to set new prices by royal proclamation.[54] More sweeping authority to suspend statutes was granted the following year. This act began by summarizing the provisions of 23 Henry VIII c. 7 which forbade the importation of French wines at certain times of the year. It went on to argue that acts such as this, restricting importation of foreign commodities or others restricting export, might prove harmful to the King's foreign policy or be in violation of treaties when the foreign situation changed. The King was therefore granted power until the end of his reign to repeal the recited act or other acts of Parliament made since the beginning of that session which regulated exports or imports by royal proclamation. These proclamations were to be

of the same quality, force, strength, condition effect to all intents and purposes, as it had been done with all due circumstances by authority of Parliament; any thing or things contained in any such acts, or any usage or custom of this realm to the contrary hereof notwithstanding.[55]

Another statute granted the King power to suspend or alter a statute setting rules for the governing of Wales. It authorized the chancellor to send out commissioners to study the laws of Wales and to divide the area into hundreds. The King and the council were empowered

---

[53] 25 Henry VIII c. 2.   [54] 25 Henry VIII c. 1.
[55] 26 Henry VIII c. 10.

to act on the findings of the commission. The sovereign was granted the right for three years to repeal, suspend or alter the statute by royal proclamation and to set up courts and appoint officials. These proclamations were to 'be as good and effectual to all intents and purposes as if the same had been done by authority of this present Parliament.' Two additional statutes of Wales also gave the King power to act without Parliament. In 1536 the King was allowed to allot divisions in shires and to choose shire towns for the next three years. When that statute expired it was extended for three more years. Once again the statutes stated that the King's actions carried out by authority of those acts were to be 'as good and effectual to all intents and purposes as though it had been done and made plainly and particularly by authority of Parliament.'[56]

Another statute simply ordered obedience to proclamations dealing with Calais. In 1535, when a series of detailed ordinances involving the governing of Calais was under consideration, Sir William Fitzwilliam wrote to Lord Lisle that it was not yet resolved whether the ordinances drawn up for Calais by Fitzwilliam and the royal commission established to study the problems at Calais 'shall be passed by act of Parliament or by council from the King's highness.'[57] The enactment of 27 Henry VIII c. 63 reveals that it was decided to proceed by statute; however, the statute included a clause ordering the officers and subjects of Calais to 'diligently duly and truly observe and keep as to him or them it shall be, belong or appertain,' all proclamations 'yet standing in their force and not repealed as here before have been made, ordained and devised by the King's highness or his council or by his right noble progenitors.'

The most far-reaching statute dealing with proclamations was the Statute of Proclamations. Whereas earlier statutes had granted authority to proclamations in limited areas, the Statute of Proclamations provided a general definition of both their powers and

[56] 27 Henry VIII c. 26; 28 Henry VIII c. 3; 31 Henry VIII c. 11. Dr Roberts maintains in his study of the union of England and Wales: 'It was clear that Cromwell as architect of union did not mean to return to Parliament with the business of Wales, and saw to it that the King's powers to execute the settlement were defined beforehand. In that it was an attempt to ground upon statute the King's right to issue proclamations, this was an instance of the legalism of Cromwell which was to find a more striking illustration in the more ambitious act of proclamations.' Peter R. Roberts, 'The Acts of Union and the Tudor Settlement of Wales' (Cambridge PhD dissertation, 1966), 165-6.

[57] SP 3/3/69 (*LP* 9 no. 766). The initial report of the commission stated that they could not 'at this present time reform all the things which is out of order here for some things there is that cannot be perfected without an act of Parliament.' BM Caligula E 11/213-14 (*LP* 9 no. 192). However, upon their return to England it was seemingly seriously debated in the council whether or not a statute was needed.

limitations. It was enacted by the Parliament which began to meet in April of 1539, and was in effect for approximately eight years. A later chapter of this study is devoted to a detailed discussion of the significance and purpose of the statute, but at this point it is necessary briefly to review its provisions. The act consisted of ten sections. It was entitled 'An Act that Proclamations made by the King Shall Be Obeyed.' The preamble began by stating the justification for the statute. The King had made numerous proclamations on 'divers and sundry articles of Christ's religion' and for the 'unity and concord' of the realm as well as for 'the advancement of his commonwealth and good quiet of his people.' These proclamations had been disobeyed by 'willful and obstinate persons' who did not consider 'what a King by his royal power may do, and for lack of a direct statute and law to cohort offenders to obey the said proclamation.' The second stated need for the statute was that sudden emergencies often arose 'which do require speedy remedies, and that by abiding for a Parliament in the meantime might happen great prejudice to ensue to the realm.' Finally, the statute was necessary so that 'his majesty (which by the kingly and regal power given him by God may do many things in such cases)' would not be forced 'to extend the liberty and supremacy of his regal power and dignity by willfulness of froward subjects.' The most controversial section of the statute followed:

Be it therefore enacted by the authority of this present Parliament, with the King's majesty, the lord's spiritual and temporal and the commons' assent, that always the King for the time being, with the advice of his honorable council, whose names hereafter followeth (or with the advice of the more part of them), may set forth at all times by (authority of this act his) proclamations under such penalties and pains and of such sort as to his highness and his said honorable council (or the more part of them) shall seem necessary and requisite; and that those same shall be obeyed, observed, and kept as though they were made by act of Parliament for the time in them limited, unless the King's highness dispense with them or any of them under his Great Seal.[58]

Section II imposed significant limitations on the power and authority of royal proclamations. It barred them from imposing the death penalty and exempted freehold of all kinds from the operation of proclamations:

Provided always that the words, meaning and intent of this act be not understood, interpreted, construed, or extended, that by virtue of it any of the King's liege people, of what estate, degree, or condition soever he or

[58] 31 Henry VIII c. 8. Sections in parentheses are the amendments added to the bill by the House of Lords.

they be, bodies politic or corporate, their heirs or successors, should have any of his or their inheritances, lawful possessions, offices, liberties, privileges, franchises, goods, or chattels taken from them or any of them, nor by virtue of the said act suffer any pains of death, other than shall be hereafter in this act declared.

The only exception was in cases of persons who offended against proclamations 'concerning any kind of heresies against Christian religion.' This section further barred proclamations from infringing, breaking or subverting 'any acts, common laws standing at this present time in strength and force, nor yet any lawful or laudable customs of this realm.'[59]

Section III was intended to make certain that the King's officers gave proclamations full publicity. It ordered them to make proclamation within fourteen days in at least four market towns or at least six other towns or villages in the area of their authority, and to post the proclamation in a place where all could see it. They were threatened with both fines and imprisonment 'as shall be contained in the said proclamation or proclamations' if they failed to obey. Sections IV and V set up the machinery of enforcement. The first created a statutory court consisting of twenty-six judges, thirteen of whom were necessary for a quorum, to try offenses against proclamations. It also provided that those convicted before that court could be punished by fines, forfeiture or imprisonment as stated in the proclamation. Section V authorized either the chancellor or the lord privy seal, with the assent of six members of the court, to begin process upon information 'by writs under the King's great seal or under his grace's privy seal.'

The remaining sections of the statute can be quickly summarized. Section VI decreed the penalties of treason for those who left the realm to avoid punishment under the act. Section VII stated that those who concealed themselves within the realm for eighteen months to avoid a summons were to stand convicted. Section VIII provided that proclamations issued during the minority of Henry's successor must be signed by the counselors who devised them, or the 'more part of

---

[59] Professor Elton has pointed out that 'the drafting of this clause leaves something to be desired. As it stands, it does not protect subsequent legislation from infringement by proclamations which could have been a serious matter if the act had lasted.' G. R. Elton, 'Henry VIII's Act of Proclamation,' *EHR* (April 1960), 211. The government, however, did not interpret the act in this fashion since a series of statutes enacted while the statute was in effect specifically contained clauses allowing the King to alter them by proclamation. If the government had believed that the Statute of Proclamations did not protect subsequent statutes from infringement by proclamation, these clauses would not have been necessary.

them,' or the proclamation would be of no effect. Section IX ordered justices of the peace to enforce the proclamations directed to them and threatened them with 'every penalty or pain limited and appointed by the same proclamation' if they were negligent in their duties. Section X gave the tribunal, set up by the statute, power to reduce the penalties specified in the proclamation with the consent of the King.

In 1543 it was found necessary to revise the Statute of Proclamations because the statutory tribunal set up by the act was too unwieldy to operate effectively. The quorum, it was stated in the revising act, proved too large to enable the court to be readily constituted; hence the new statute lowered the quorum from thirteen to nine members. The act was to endure only for the lifetime of Henry VIII; however, the first Parliament of Edward VI repealed both the Statute of Proclamations and the 1543 act.[60]

A series of new statutes defining the powers of proclamations was enacted in the closing years of Henry VIII's reign. The majority of these statutes were necessitated by the restrictions in the Statute of Proclamations which prohibited royal proclamations from conflicting with or negating existing statutes. A 1540 act concerning aliens contained a proviso that protected earlier proclamations in case they might be interpreted as being in conflict with the statute:

That this act nor anything therein contained shall be hurtful or prejudicial to such proclamations as by the King's majesty hath published or proclaimed for and concerning the payment of custom for strangers granted by the goodness of his majesty to endure for certain years, but that the same proclamation shall abide by and remain in the same plight and strength that it is, as if this act had never been made.[61]

A statute which declared Chester a sanctuary town in 1541 contained a clause which empowered the King to alter the place of sanctuary by proclamation if Chester should not prove a good place for the sanctuary 'anything in this act contained to the contrary notwithstanding.'[62]

A series of statutes involving ecclesiastical legislation empowered the King to legislate on these questions. The first seemingly added

[60] 34 and 35 Henry VIII c. 23; 1 Edward VI c. 12.
[61] 32 Henry VIII c. 16. The proclamation, *TRP* no. 189, granted alien merchants the same customs as English merchants for seven years. There was nothing in the statute which really conflicted with the proclamation, therefore the proviso was not really necessary. Its inclusion may indicate that a year after the enactment of the Statute of Proclamations the council was acutely sensitive to the limitations imposed by that statute, and therefore was especially cautious to make sure that there was no conflict between statutes and proclamations.
[62] 33 Henry VIII c. 15.

nothing to the power already confirmed in the Statute of Proclamations since it simply gave the King power to appoint a committee of theologians to review the principal articles of the faith and the rites and ceremonies of the Church. After confirmation by the King the decisions of this committee were to be as valid as if they had been stated in the statute provided that nothing contained in them was 'repugnant or contrary to the laws and statutes of this realm.'[63] A second statute which forbade books that taught contrary to the doctrines set forth since 1540 contained a provision that previous proclamations were not to 'be comprehended in the prohibitions of this act unless the King's said majesty shall hereafter make special proclamation for the condemnation and reproving of the same.' In addition the King was granted the right to 'change and alter' the statute during his lifetime as he saw fit.[64] Another statute enacted the following year also protected proclamations which might conflict with previous ecclesiastical legislation. The King was empowered to appoint a committee to examine and reform the canon law. The ordinances and laws made by that committee would be 'established and declared by the King's majesty's proclamations under his highness' great seal.' These proclamations were to be 'taken reputed and used for the King's laws ecclesiastical of this realm, any act to the contrary of this statute notwithstanding.' A final statute on religious matters in 1545 simply ordered that the decision of the committee appointed to give final determination on a dispute over tithes between the citizens and clergy of London was to be as valid as if it had been done by statute.[65]

The King was also given additional powers to set wine prices by proclamation and to legislate for Wales. The earlier wine price statutes had set definite retail prices while empowering a conciliar committee to set wholesale prices by royal proclamation. However, the government found it impossible to keep wholesale prices low enough to enable the vintners to sell at the statutory retail prices; therefore, the new legislation empowered the same conciliar committee also to set retail prices by royal proclamation. Since these proclamations might violate the earlier statutes, the new act provided specifically for that possibility. The committee was empowered to set prices 'anything in the said former act contained to the

[63] 32 Henry VIII c. 26.
[64] 34 and 35 Henry VIII c. 1. This statute was probably designed to give statutory authority to the King's Book, *A Necessary Doctrine and Erudition for any Christian Man*, which had been passed by Convocation in April 1543.
[65] 35 Henry VIII c. 16; 37 Henry VIII c. 12.

contrary thereof notwithstanding.' The new prices 'after proclamation made' were 'to be observed and kept upon pain or penalty in the same proclamation contained.' The act was made to endure until the next Parliament when it was renewed by a second statute which added that prices were to be set between 20 November and 31 December each year.[66] The most sweeping powers granted to proclamations at any time during the period were contained in a 1543 statute completing the union of Wales with England. The King seemingly was granted unlimited authority to legislate for Wales. The statute empowered the King 'to make laws and ordinances for the commonwealth and good quiet' of Wales anything contained in any previous statutes 'to the contrary thereof... notwithstanding' and 'change, add, alter, order, minish and reform' anything in the statute as he saw fit. The alterations, laws and ordinances 'devised and published by authority of this act by the King's majesty in writing under his highness' great seal' were to be considered 'of as good strength virtue and effect as if they had been had and made by authority of Parliament.'[67]

The use of statutes to delegate authority to royal proclamations ceased abruptly with Somerset's rise to power. Edward VI's first Parliament repealed the Statute of Proclamations, and no new statutes granting specific powers to proclamations were enacted until after Somerset's fall. A statute on unlawful assemblies in the first Parliament after his fall included the words of a proclamation to be made by local officials 'in the King's name' ordering unlawful assemblies to disperse. It was to be made when groups of people assembled unlawfully. If they prevented the proclamation from being made and posted they were still to be punished as if the proclamation had been made.[68] In the next Parliament a statute regulating the buying and selling of wool allowed the King 'by his proclamation at any time hereafter to be made and set forth to repeal this statute and all and every article clause sentence and other thing or things therein contained.' Another act in the same session ordered subjects not to take or receive more in value for coins than 'is or shall be declared by the King's majesty his proclamation to be current for within this his highness' realm.' It threatened offenders with

[66] 34 and 35 Henry VIII c. 7; 37 Henry VIII c. 23.
[67] 34 and 35 Henry VIII c. 26. Dr Roberts comments: 'in that it affected a whole area of the realm, this discretionary authority vested in the crown was a far greater concession by Parliament than that of the Statute of Proclamations, yet no one has suggested that by it the King assumed despotic powers.' Roberts, 'The Acts of Union,' 226.
[68] 3 and 4 Edward VI c. 5. The statute was renewed by 7 Edward VI c. 11.

imprisonment and fine and allowed informers to sue for a portion of the fine in 'any court of record.'[69]

Although these acts at the end of Edward's reign could be interpreted as the beginning of a new trend to use statutes to grant authority to proclamations,[70] the total impact of the legislation in Edward's reign was to reverse the process of definition. The repeal of the Statute of Proclamations eliminated both the restrictions on the proclaiming power as well as the positive statements which insisted on respect for royal proclamations in their legitimate sphere and provided for enforcement. Therefore, this left their position almost as vague as it had been at the beginning of the Tudor period. However, at least some progress had been made. Although it had been clearly established by 1485 that the King could neither tax nor change statute or common law without the consent of Parliament, there was room within those boundaries for expanding the powers of royal proclamations which might have produced a constitution considerably different from the one which finally emerged. The authority of royal proclamations was further defined during the reigns of the Tudor Kings primarily by statutory enactments, especially during the 1530s. The numerous statutes passed in the eight years of Cromwell's dominance, climaxed by the Statute of Proclamations, set major precedents. Even though the Statute of Proclamations was repealed, the consistent utilization of statutes to grant powers to proclamations must have pushed the definition of their authority more and more in the direction of denying them a legislative power independent of statute rather than emphasizing the legislative potential in the undefined areas of the royal prerogative. Two years after the end of the early Tudor period the judges in the decision recorded by Dalison maintained that proclamations could not be used to change the law or to make new laws. This was a remarkably different view from that of the justices at the beginning of Cromwell's ministry two decades earlier. We do not know what arguments they advanced in support of that statement; and clearly, judges and lawyers in the reign of Elizabeth attributed more authority to royal proclamations. However, the decision that finally triumphed was the one which reserved law making to the King in Parliament and made all extra-Parliamentary legislation dependent on powers delegated

[69] 5 and 6 Edward VI c. 7; 5 and 6 Edward VI c. 19.
[70] The Spanish ambassador thought that Northumberland was contemplating a new Statute of Proclamations: 'The King of England's council are trying to pass an act giving all orders of the council the same force as acts of Parliament' (*CSPSp*, x, 468).

by statutes. The statutes of the 1530s were a major step in that direction. Without them Mary's judges would have been hard pressed to find any clear precedents for their judgment.[71]

[71] It is interesting that when Dalison's report was printed the editor listed three statutes which delegated powers to proclamations. Two of them were enacted in the 1530s. See above, n. 24.

3

THE USE OF ROYAL PROCLAMATIONS: AN OVERVIEW

A proclamation of any period may call attention to and enforce the observation of some existing law, make some new regulation or prohibition in virtue of a recognized prerogative of the Crown, formally announce some executive act, or (before the Great Civil War) enforce the rights of the Crown as the feudal chief of the kingdom.[1]

Robert Steele's concise summary has long served as the standard explanation of the role of royal proclamations in Tudor government. Although there is little doubt that a large number of proclamations were used to serve the functions described by Steele, his view has recently been questioned.[2] His discussion also leaves many problems unresolved. In addition, it is clear that different monarchs and their ministers used proclamations in varying ways. Since we can find no evidence that their role and power had been clearly defined, it is logical to ask whether some of the monarchs or their ministers sought to expand the powers of royal proclamations or used them in a way that indicated they held a more exalted view of their legislative function. The tables on the following pages attempt to begin the investigation of these concerns by providing some basic statistics. Three are based on a simple tabulation of statements in the texts of the proclamations. One involves a more difficult and certainly less objective judgment requiring comparisons with other types of legislation. They seek to provide initial evidence for answering four fundamental questions: (1) To which subjects were proclamations

---

[1] Steele, ix.
[2] Holdsworth, *History of English Law*, IV, 99ff, 296ff, has one of the more extensive discussions of the use of royal proclamations. He agrees with Steele. Professors Hughes and Larkin cite Steele and Holdsworth in their introduction but suggest that this traditional view may no longer be entirely adequate in view of the evidence in the proclamations. *TRP*, xxv–xxvi. Professor Jordan feels that the 'traditional view' is not adequate for explaining the use of royal proclamations in the reign of Edward VI: 'Only about a tenth of the proclamations issued had as their purpose the enforcement of existing statutes and not more than a third laid any claim to authority from statute law. The great majority of, them, then, created law, at least for the time specified, and possessed a kind of legislative character which appears in this reign to have been questioned neither by Parliament nor by the courts.' W. K. Jordan, *Edward VI: The Young King* (Cambridge, Mass., 1969), 349.

Table 4. *Subject matter of early Tudor royal proclamations*

Period	Royal person and administration	Religion	Economic	Social	Foreign relations	Military	Total
(1) Henry VII (1485–1509)	14	0	23	10	13	7	67
(2) Henry VIII (1509–29)	7	0	36	17	12	8	80
(3) Henry VIII (1529–39)	15	8	39	16	4	2	84
(4) Henry VIII (1539–47)	12	3	40	21	3	7	86
(5) Edward VI (1547–9)	22	9	31	13	3	8	86
(6) Edward VI (1549–53)	7	2	30	9	2	5	55
Total	77	22	199	86	37	37	458

addressed? (2) What did they actually do? (3) What penalties did they threaten for disobedience? (4) What provisions were made for enforcing these orders and exacting these penalties?

Table 4, 'Subject matter of early Tudor royal proclamations,' summarizes under six general categories the number of proclamations issued during each subdivision of the period. It is the only table which includes the 'unfound proclamations' listed in Appendix B, because their subject matter can easily be determined from the contemporary references to them, but these comments are seldom detailed enough to glean other information. The number in the table exceeds the total number of proclamations in the period, because many of them dealt with more than one subject. The table involves grouping some sixty-four different subject classifications under general categories; therefore, I have made some judgments which may be questioned. The first category, 'royal person and administration,' is especially subject to criticism. It includes a variety of different types of proclamations which did not conveniently fit other groups, such as those dealing with court regulations, law matters, the King's feudal rights, riots and rebellions as well as those specifically concerned with administrative matters and the King's title. Other categories are self-explanatory.

In some cases a judgment had to be made to decide which category best suited a particular type of proclamation. Proclamations dealing with the Lenten fast, for example, seem at first glance to fit under 'religion'; however, since their motivation was primarily economic they have been included under that grouping.

The table does not reveal anything particularly unusual. As might be expected in a period of economic changes and growing inflation, almost fifty percent of the proclamations in the period dealt with economic questions. In fact, the preponderance of economic proclamations can be noted in each of the subdivisions of the period. What might be a bit surprising is the small number of religious proclamations. The first surviving dates from the early years of the English Reformation. Even then such proclamations were not exceptionally numerous. Despite statements in the preamble of the Statute of Proclamations justifying its need because it said that religious proclamations were not being obeyed, only four percent of the proclamations issued while the statute was in effect in the last years of Henry VIII's reign dealt with religious questions. The largest number of religious proclamations were issued under Somerset and most of them date from the period after the Statute of Proclamations was repealed.[3] A large percentage of Henry VII's proclamations and those issued in the first years of his son's reign were concerned with foreign affairs or military matters. Foreign affairs proclamations became considerably less numerous after 1529, but with the glaring exception of period 3, military ones were fairly common. This was obviously because the 1530s were the only period when England was not engaged in a major war. What is probably more interesting than the differences are the similarities. Throughout the early Tudor period most royal proclamations dealt with economic and social questions. With only slight variations the subject matter remained fairly consistent.

Subject matter has little to do with the broader questions of what proclamations actually did and whether or not they were used in a way that indicated that some of the Tudor monarchs or their ministers had a broader concept of the power of royal proclamations than others. The answers to these questions are sought in the remaining tables. Table 5 is certainly the most revealing on these matters. It was the most difficult to construct, because it involved a series of judgments which demanded knowledge of other legislation. One might also debate on whether a proclamation belongs in one category or another. Those dealing with more than one subject often had to be placed in separate categories for each subject. Therefore,

[3] Only two of the nine proclamations came before the repeal (*TRP* nos. 289, 292).

Table 5. *Analysis of the function and role of early Tudor royal proclamations*

	Period						Total
	1	2	3	4	5	6	
(1) Enforce King's feudal rights	5	0	1	0	0	0	6
(2) Deal with matters related to military, war, rebellion and foreign policy	25	25	8	25	17	5	105
Foreign policy	(15)	(8)	(4)	(2)	(1)	(2)	
Military and war	(6)	(16)	(2)	(23)	(8)	(3)	
Rebellion	(4)	(1)	(2)	(0)	(8)	(0)	
(3) Make new regulations or prohibitions not based on statutory authority	5	7	5	8	12	7	44
Coinage	(4)	(5)	(2)	(2)	(5)	(6)	
Religion	(0)	(0)	(3)	(2)	(2)	(0)	
Other	(1)	(2)	(0)	(4)	(5)	(1)	
(4) Regulations concerning the King's court	0	1	1	0	2	0	4
(5) Enforce existing law	11	26	16	14	18	15	100
Enforce statute without change	(3)	(10)	(2)	(1)	(4)	(2)	
Explain, revive or apply statute	(5)	(2)	(7)	(2)	(4)	(3)	
Enforce statute some changes	(2)	(5)	(3)	(9)	(4)	(9)	
Deal with negligent officials	(1)	(4)	(2)	(1)	(1)	(1)	
General law enforcement	(0)	(2)	(1)	(0)	(5)	(0)	
Explain, revise or enforce	(0)	(3)	(1)	(1)	(0)	(0)	
(6) Provide temporary or emergency solutions	7	9	12	14	14	6	62
New regulation or change in statute followed by statute	(6)	(1)	(4)	(1)	(0)	(1)	
Economic	(1)	(7)	(3)	(4)	(9)	(4)	
Plague	(0)	(1)	(3)	(2)	(2)	(0)	
Suspend statute	(0)	(0)	(2)	(6)	(0)	(0)	
Other	(0)	(0)	(0)	(1)	(3)	(1)	
(7) Announce executive act or deal with administrative matter	5	7	6	8	11	3	40
(8) Dispense from statute or custom	0	0	5	4	0	1	10
(9) Carry out provision of statute which allows for or demands use of proclamations	2	0	13	8	1	4	28
(10) Terminate previous proclamation	0	0	0	4	3	2	9
Total	60	75	67	85	78	43	408

the total number listed in the table again exceeds the total number that actually survive. The categories in the table are based on Steele's analysis (presented at the beginning of this chapter), though Steele overlooked a number of other uses which were common in the early Tudor period. An obvious oversight was the use of proclamations to provide temporary or emergency solutions. Almost fifteen percent of the early Tudor proclamations performed this function. Other uses not mentioned by Steele are listed in the last three categories.

AN OVERVIEW

The most striking revelation of the table is that early Tudor proclamations seldom made new law. It was not always easy to determine when a proclamation was actually introducing a new regulation or prohibition which was intended to have at least some degree of permanence. However, if no previous legislation on that topic still in effect could be found, and if the proclamation was not closely followed by a statute which restated it, I assumed that these proclamations were introducing new regulations of a more permanent nature on the authority of the royal prerogative alone. Doubtful cases were included under this category in order to test generously the assumption that proclamations made new law. After including a number of proclamations which might just as easily have been placed elsewhere, and even allowing for some mistakes in judgment, it is still clear that early Tudor monarchs seldom used royal proclamations to introduce new legislation.

Approximately eleven percent of the total number of proclamations surviving from the early Tudor period could be interpreted as imposing new long-term regulations or prohibitions on the authority of the prerogative alone. The vast majority of these dealt with coinage matters, an area reserved to the royal prerogative even by later legal writers. Proclamations often did introduce new prohibitions or regulations. However, they were either temporary measures designed to meet an emergency situation or the next session of Parliament enacted a statute which incorporated the changes introduced by the proclamation. Over one quarter of the proclamations were related to war, rebellion or foreign policy and had no connection with legislation. Almost the same number were used to enforce existing legislation. In a number of cases proclamations changed earlier statutes in an effort to improve enforcement either by increasing penalties or altering enforcement procedures. This was most common under Northumberland and least common under Cromwell and Henry VII. In some cases these alterations were quite significant. Wolsey, for example, seldom used proclamations to modify statutes, but the changes he did introduce, largely in enforcement, were major ones.

Despite obvious similarities in the use of royal proclamations throughout the early Tudor period, there were also some striking differences. The most notable was in the use of royal proclamations as delegated legislation (category no. 9). With the exception of two highly questionable cases in the reign of Henry VII,[4] the use of

---

[4] Henry VII's two proclamations included in this category were *TRP* nos. 17 and 27. The first was included because 4 Henry VII c. 12 ordered that this proclamation be made four times a year in quarter sessions; however, it is certainly not a definite case of

proclamations in this way did not begin until the 1530s, when it became very common. During Cromwell's ministry twenty percent of the proclamations served this function. Although proclamations based on the legislation of the 1530s continued to be issued throughout the early Tudor period, the percentage in this grouping never exceeded ten percent after Cromwell's fall.[5] The table also reveals Cromwell's respect for statutory authority in a number of other ways. Less than eight percent of the proclamations in the 1530s introduced new regulations or prohibitions without specific statutory authority. This percentage was exceeded in every other period. Another revealing figure is the number of proclamations introducing new regulations or altering statutes which were then followed by new statutes incorporating these changes. This practice was common during only two periods. Of Henry VII's seven proclamations providing temporary or emergency solutions, six were followed by statutes. However, the figure is not as impressive as the bare statistics might seem to indicate. Four of them involved the same statute which was not enacted until six years after the first proclamation on the subject.[6] In contrast, three proclamations issued during period no. 3 were followed by statutes passed in the next session of Parliament which incorporated the changes introduced by the proclamations.[7]

Table 5 is based on a number of subjective judgments. Therefore any conclusions drawn from it may be open to valid criticism. Less subjective but equally interesting are the remaining tables. Table 6 records the penalties stated in early Tudor proclamations. It shows that they seldom threatened extremely severe penalties. Approxi-

delegated legislative authority since it deals only with enforcing existing law. The second established a Staple of Mines at Southampton. It was included because 14 Henry VI c. 2 gave the King the right to modify 8 Henry VI c. 17 which had provided that tin was to be exported only to the Staple at Calais.

[5] While the Statute of Proclamations was in effect, proclamations based on it might have been included here, but since they did not involve specific delegated legislative authority, as in the wine and meat price proclamations, they were not included. There were ten proclamations based on the Statute of Proclamations. If they were added to the other eight issued in 1539–47 which were based on specific statutory authority, the total percentage for this type of proclamation would still not exceed the percentage under Cromwell.

[6] *TRP* nos. 38, 42, 43, 44 all ordered subjects not to refuse the King's coinage even if it were clipped. 19 Henry VII c. 5 introduced considerably more detailed legislation on the topic revising the earlier proclamations.

[7] *TRP* no. 134 prohibited unlicensed export on 7 September 1531. This policy was made statutory by 25 Henry VIII c. 2. Nos. 139 and 142 introduced changes in the meat price legislation which were incorporated in 25 Henry VIII c. 1. The final proclamation, no. 128, was issued in June 1530, before Cromwell came to power. It changed penalties in the vagabond legislation. These changes were included in 22 Henry VIII c. 12 which was enacted in the next Parliament.

Table 6. *Penalties stated in early Tudor royal proclamations*

	Period						
	1	2	3	4	5	6	Total
(1) None	13	13	13	18	15	6	78
(2) Vaguely worded	13	21	21	17	16	4	92
(3) Statutory penalties	5	15	20	17	11	14	82
(4) Fine, imprisonment, forfeiture	23	20	10	30	29	23	135
(5) Punishment for negligent officials	6	11	18	11	12	10	68
(6) Severe penalties	5	4	8	9	14	3	43
Death	(4)	(3)	(5)	(1)	(9)	(0)	
Large fine or forfeiture	(1)	(1)	(2)	(5)	(3)	(2)	
Mutilation or whipping	(0)	(0)	(1)	(0)	(0)	(1)	
Slavery in galleys	(0)	(0)	(0)	(3)	(1)	(0)	
Other	(0)	(0)	(0)	(0)	(1)	(0)	
(7) Other	2	4	3	0	2	1	12
Total	67	88	93	102	99	61	510

mately eleven percent included penalties which could be classified as 'severe.'[8] Death, for example, was very uncommon. As will be shown later, in most cases the death penalty was applied only to offenses which carried the same penalty in the common law. A large number of proclamations either mentioned no penalty or stated it in terms of a vague threat like 'indignation,' 'displeasure,' 'extreme perils,' 'uttermost peril,' or 'answer to the contrary at peril.' As might be expected, the most common penalty was fine, imprisonment or forfeiture. Quite often statutory penalties were specified and additional threats or penalties were added. In those cases the proclamation was listed both under the grouping 'statutory penalties' and under whatever other categories applied. Although contrasts are not as dramatic as in the previous table, some differences between periods are apparent. Severe penalties were most common under Somerset, but they were also comparatively common not only in the 1530s but also while the Statute of Proclamations was in effect. But none of the proclamations issued in 1539–47 violated the limitations on penalties set in that statute. Proclamations tended to become more specific about penalties as the period progressed. Failure to include any penalty statement or one that was vaguely worded was common in the first three periods. After the enactment of the Statute of Proclamations there was a steady decrease in the percentage of

---

[8] Percentages are naturally based on the total number of proclamations issued. Since many proclamations threatened more than one penalty, the total under penalties is considerably larger than the actual number of surviving proclamations.

Table 7. *Enforcement procedures mentioned in early Tudor royal proclamations*

	Period						
	1	2	3	4	5	6	Total
(1) None mentioned	36	40	27	51	34	17	205
Individuals or groups ordered to enforce proclamations							
(1) None mentioned	37	42	30	55	37	18	219
(2) Local officials	10	11	26	20	23	16	106
(3) Ecclesiastical officials	0	0	3	2	1	0	6
(4) Port officials	3	6	4	6	7	3	29
(5) Commissions	1	4	1	0	1	1	8
(6) Conciliar personnel	4	0	1	4	0	0	9
(7) Subjects in general	5	6	12	5	8	6	42
(8) Reward offered to informers or enforcement officials	4	0	4	7	7	9	31
(9) Other	3	5	2	2	5	0	17
Courts ordered to try offenders or exact penalties							
(1) None mentioned	53	59	53	71	56	25	317
(2) Council	1	3	6	5	15	6	36
(3) Star Chamber	0	2	0	0	0	1	3
(4) Court set up by Statute of Proclamations	0	0	0	9	0	0	9
(5) Chancery	0	4	0	0	0	0	4
(6) Exchequer	1	0	3	2	0	4	10
(7) King's Bench	0	0	0	2	0	1	3
(8) Common pleas	0	0	0	2	0	1	3
(9) Assizes	1	1	1	0	0	0	3
(10) J.P. sessions	0	0	0	0	0	3	3
(11) 'Any court of record' or common law courts in general	0	1	0	1	3	2	7
(12) Local courts	0	3	1	0	2	2	8
(13) Ecclesiastical courts	0	0	2	0	1	1	4
(14) Other	2	2	0	0	2	0	6

proclamations not stating specific penalties. Under Northumberland only ten proclamations failed to do so. Statutory penalties were most common under Cromwell, obviously because a high percentage of his proclamations were either based on statutes or were designed to enforce existing legislation. The proclamations ordering enforcement of statutes often added a punishment for negligent officials not in the original statute. Twenty-eight percent of the proclamations issued in period no. 3 included a clause threatening negligent officials. With the exception of period no. 5, when twenty-five percent of the proclamations included similar clauses, this was almost double the percentage of any other period.

AN OVERVIEW

To be effective law must be enforced. Penalties remain only vague threats unless some machinery for exacting them is set up. As revealed in Table 7 early Tudor royal proclamations were often vague on enforcement. While over half said nothing about both penalties and enforcement, procedures became more specific after the Statute of Proclamations was enacted, and especially during the reign of Edward VI. Over half of the proclamations issued during his reign directed certain individuals or groups to see that the proclamation was carried out, and over one third mentioned or implied a specific court or courts. Without specific enforcement procedures and penalties, proclamations surely could not have been equated with statute law. It is only in the reign of Edward VI, when proclamations texts became more precise on these matters, that one can more easily see their resemblance to statutes.

A final interesting aspect of Table 7 is found in its second half, which notes the courts that were mentioned or implied in the texts of the proclamations. Although it was once commonly believed that proclamations were normally enforced in the Court of Star Chamber and not in common law courts,[9] their texts do not substantiate this. Only three mentioned the Star Chamber.[10] Even Common Law Courts were cited more frequently than this. Three proclamations even decreed that offenders could be tried in the Court of King's Bench or the Court of Common Pleas. The council was also not commonly used until 1539. During the period when the Statute of Proclamations was in effect, six proclamations provided that the council would determine penalties, and nine specifically mentioned or implied that trial would take place in the conciliar court set up by the Statute of Proclamations.[11] Under Somerset the use of the council peaked, and although there was a significant drop under Northumberland the total percentage of proclamations using the council for enforcement remained high in comparison with other periods.

A good deal more could be said about the evidence in these tables and the conclusions suggested by this. But beyond the rough generalizations offered above, further use of the tables is dangerous. It is, for example, clear that many of the proclamations issued by

[9] Steele, xxx–xxxi; see below Chapter 9 n. 40.
[10] *TRP* nos. 118, 118.5 ordered that offenders be reported to the 'council in Star Chamber.' No. 365 is the only proclamation which mentions the 'court of Star Chamber.'
[11] Not all of these proclamations refer to the court specifically, but I have assumed that all those based on the Statute of Proclamations implied enforcement by that court. The one exception is *TRP* no. 225.5, which simply dispensed from earlier legislation and therefore did not involve any judicial enforcement.

Henry VII have not survived; therefore, inferences drawn from the statistics for his reign must be heavily qualified. Statistics can also be misleading because they are often too dependent on the compiler's judgments. Quantifiable information tends to give the impression of a mathematical precision, and this can be deceptive. Consequently, it seldom does more than suggest or indicate possible areas for more detailed investigation. The tables and the cursory comments based on them are intended as an introduction to a consideration of the purpose and role of royal proclamations in the early Tudor period. The chapters which follow utilize more traditional historical methods and materials to elucidate that role in a more complete and accurate fashion.

4

THE USE OF ROYAL PROCLAMATIONS: HENRY VII

> He would like to govern England in the French fashion, but he cannot. He is subject to his council, but has already shaken off some and got rid of part of this subjection.[1]

Governing 'in the French fashion' inevitably conjures up images of Renaissance monarchies and government by decree.[2] There were but seven Parliaments during the twenty-four years Henry VII ruled England. After the Spanish Ambassador, Don Pedro de Ayala, recorded his suspicions about Henry's philosophy of rule in 1498, Parliament would meet only two more times during the remaining decade of the reign. Thus there are reasons to suspect that Henry VII preferred to rule without Parliament, and that he may have tried to find a method of legislating that was independent of Parliament. Since royal proclamations provided a potential instrument for independent law making by the monarch, one must seriously ask whether there is any evidence of an attempt to use them to replace statutes during Henry VII's reign.

Most of Henry VII's surviving proclamations do not help in answering that question because over sixty percent of them were concerned with matters unrelated to new legislation. As might be expected, a large number of them, especially during the early part of the reign, dealt with problems associated with his accession. His first proclamation not only announced the death of Richard III, and thereby his own accession to the throne, but it also tried to curb the ensuing unrest and attempts at personal revenge which might be expected to follow upon a transfer of the crown by violent means. It threatened with death those who utilized the situation to 'rob' or 'spoil' or to pursue 'quarrels for old or new matters.'[3] Other

---

[1] *CSPSp*, I, 178.
[2] Lawrence Stone, *The Causes of the English Revolution 1529-1642* (New York, 1972), 58, cited the Spanish ambassador's comment to suggest that Henry VII as well as his son 'were only too anxious to acquire those powers upon which were founded the strong Renaissance monarchies of Europe.'
[3] *TRP* no. 1. The editors' title 'Announcing the Death of Richard III' is somewhat misleading since the proclamation is primarily concerned with the resulting internal unrest.

proclamations offered pardon to those who had fought against the King, dismissed forces mustered to deal with the rebellion in the North, and publicized the Bull of Pope Innocent VIII recognizing Henry VII as the legitimate King of England.[4]

Henry VII's difficulties with internal unrest did not end with his initial victories. Proclamations throughout the early part of the reign testify to the continuing need to deal with rebellion. In 1487 the threat from Lambert Simnel's supporters was the occasion for two proclamations. They were issued on successive days in early June as Henry gathered forces to move north to meet the rebel force led by John de la Pole, Earl of Lincoln. The first utilized the Crown's right of purveyance to supply the army. Victuallers and other subjects along the route were ordered 'to provide and make ready plenty of bread and ale and of other victuals as well for horse as for men at reasonable price.'[5] The second was designed to assure that the host moving north did not alienate the population by behaving as was not unusual for armies in the midst of civil war. Plundering, theft, rape and a variety of other offenses against the local population were forbidden under strict penalties including death for those offenses which carried that penalty at common law. Additional regulations to assure an orderly and well-disciplined army were also included in the proclamation.[6] Two other proclamations related to rebellion were issued later in the reign. The first reveals something of the uneasiness that prevailed after Henry Percy, Earl of Northumberland, was killed by an angry mob while trying to suppress the rebellion in the North brought about by an effort to collect the subsidy voted by Parliament for the war in Brittany. Obviously worried about unrest in the South while he went north with an army, Henry issued a proclamation in May 1489 ordering local officials and subjects to 'repress, subdue and make to cease all matter of insurrections, riots, routs, unlawful assemblies, and other misdoers.' The second proclamation eight years later simply pardoned the Cornish rebels who had been defeated at Blackheath in June 1497.[7]

[4] *TRP* nos. 2, 4, 5.
[5] *TRP* no. 12. Two other proclamations were also related to purveyance. One provided for payments to subjects for victual taken by purveyance since the first year of the reign (no. 20.5). A second, on 19 August 1504, announced that subjects claiming that the King owed them money 'for anything that he had bought or that had been delivered to the use of his honorable house or wardrobe' were to present their claims to a special committee set up to deal with the matter (no. 55). C. G. Cruickshank, *Army Royal: Henry VIII's Invasion of France 1513* (Oxford, 1969) contains a good discussion of the right and utilization of purveyance.
[6] *TRP* no. 13. These included orders banning vagabonds and prostitutes from following the King's host.   [7] *TRP* nos. 19, 35.

Proclamations were also used to enforce the King's feudal rights. A series of them ordered persons with an income of £40 or more a year to become knights. Proclamations of this type were common throughout the early Tudor period, but with one exception texts are available only for Henry VII's reign.[8] Four proclamations survive and at least two others were issued during the reign. They tended to become more detailed as the reign progressed. The first, in 1486, simply ordered all persons who were not knights but who had the required income to appear before the King by 4 February to receive the order of knighthood under threat of 'uttermost perils.' Sheriffs were to seek out people with these qualifications and to certify their names to the chancery by that date. A second, in March 1500, repeated the first and threatened sheriffs who neglected their duties with 'peril of penalties they may incur.' The third, late in 1500, stated that some individuals having the necessary income were not yet knights. The King, 'wishing to know more exactly the names of all and singular such persons,' ordered sheriffs to summon those individuals so that they could prepare themselves to receive the order of knighthood. The final proclamation added an extremely severe fine of £200 for individuals who failed to appear by a specific date.[9] Another proclamation devoted to enforcing the King's feudal and prerogative rights was issued in the last year of the reign. In accordance with the King's prerogative right to shipwrecks, it ordered that no one was to carry away any part of a wreck at Calais except people designated by the officials at Calais. The penalties were forfeiture and imprisonment.[10]

The largest percentage of Henry VII's proclamations dealt with foreign affairs and military matters. They announced peace treaties or truces, declared war, announced alliances, mustered forces, and gave instructions for the treatment of allies and friends.[11] Since some

[8] The exception is a proclamation issued 26 April 1533. The text is found in Dur 3/78/3d. It repeats verbatim *TRP* no. 48. See Appendix A no. 174.5. An excellent discussion of this question with an appendix listing unfound proclamations on the subject is included in Henry Leonard, 'Knights and Knighthood in Tudor England' (University of London PhD Thesis, 1970), 325ff. Leonard regards these proclamations primarily as a device for exacting money, especially when their issue did not coincide with a ceremonial occasion like a coronation. *Ibid.* 79.

[9] *TRP* nos. 9, 48, 49, 53. See Appendix B items 7 and 10 for unfound proclamations.

[10] *TRP* no. 58. The King's prerogative to wrecks of the sea is stated in 3 Edward I c. 4 (Westminster I). People who violated these rights could be punished with fine and imprisonment. Although included in the statute book, the so-called 'Prerogativa Regis' is not a statute but simply a statement of the King's common law prerogatives.

[11] *TRP* nos. 3, 21, 29, 40, 51 announced peace treaties and truces. No. 34 declared war, nos. 23 and 52 announced alliances, nos. 6, 20, 28, 36 and 37 dealt with musters and defense, no. 7 ordered that the Emperor's armies be allowed to victual and rest in English

of these proclamations were only public announcements of a completed event, they sometimes contained neither orders nor penalties.[12] Normally an order that subjects keep the terms of the treaty or alliance was included. This was followed by threats of punishment for those who failed to heed it. In one case a proclamation announcing an alliance with Maximilian against the Turks commanded anyone who was a 'rebel or traitor to the King of Romans' to depart the realm immediately 'upon pain to be executed and put to death immediately after he be taken.' It concluded with a reference to its function as a device for making the terms of the alliance known to the realm so that no one would incur the penalties of treason through ignorance: 'and that this proclamation be sufficient advertisement, notice and publication to every person it toucheth, to the intent that from henceforth no person have cause to pretend ignorance in the same.'[13] Elaborate justifications were often included as part of the propaganda effort to convince Englishmen of the justice of the King's action. The proclamation of 25 September 1496 declaring war on Scotland described the perfidy of the King of Scotland which forced Henry to resort to war:

> The said King of Scots, of his wilful headiness, and without cause or occasion given by our said soverign lord, hath entered with his person and with the power he could make, and with his banner displayed, some four miles within this realm, contrary to the truce and his sign manual, and contrary also to his seal and promise aforesaid, directly and expressly to his reproach and dishonor in that part.[14]

Other proclamations included orders on how Englishmen were to treat new enemies or friends. The announcement of the peace treaty with Denmark on 15 April 1490 ordered all subjects not only to cease hostility but also to allow Danes driven into English ports for any reason 'peaceable to arrive, sojourn and depart at their liberties.'[15] Since foreign affairs were clearly prerogative matters, one would not expect Parliamentary actions on these subjects; however, at least one treaty was also confirmed by Parliament. The Treaty of Etaples with France in November 1492 was ratified by the next Parliament in 1495. This seems to have been done because agreement by the estates of both realms was specified in the treaty.[16]

---

ports, no. 23.5 provided for protection of French fishermen, and no. 24 ordered the punishment of pirates who sold prizes taken from England's allies in English ports.

[12] *TRP* no. 29.
[13] *TRP* no. 52. In contrast the announcement of the alliance with the Empire and Spain against France in 1490 simply threatened 'displeasure of our said sovereign lord, his body to be committed to prison and further to be punished according to his demerits.' No. 23.   [14] *TRP* no. 34.   [15] *TRP* no. 21.   [16] 11 Henry VII c. 65.

Proclamations were often used for musters of troops, either to hire mercenary troops or to raise the ancient shire levy. Henry VII's efforts to raise an army for his invasion of Brittany in 1489 was preceded by an effort to hire troops for the venture. All subjects who would 'take upon them to go in any of the said armies for their competent wages to them to be paid in that behalf' were ordered to go to the King's deputy, Charles Somerset, who had been appointed to take musters for the raising of the army.[17] When troops were mustered for the defense of the realm, the King could rely on the shire levy or fyrd. The threatened Scottish invasion in 1497 resulted in the exercise of this prerogative right. The sheriffs of the northern counties were directed in June and again in August to proclaim that all able bodied subjects between the ages of sixteen and sixty arm themselves and prepare to serve the King in the war against Scotland. The second proclamation specifically mentioned the need to guard against an expected invasion, stating that the King wished 'the said marches to be defended against the said Scots according to the ancient custom used there.'[18]

Throughout his reign Henry used trade as a weapon of diplomacy. Therefore, regulations on trade were often directly connected with foreign policy. The first four years of the reign were a period of strained relations with Burgundy as a result of the Yorkist intrigues in that area. In response, trade with Burgundy was partially restricted by a proclamation in 1487.[19] On 14 February 1489 the outstanding problems between the two countries were resolved and an alliance of mutual defense was signed with Maximilian. This was made public in April when the earlier proclamation was rescinded and trade relations with Austria and Burgundy were restored.[20] The peace treaty with France in 1492 brought another period of strained relations with the Emperor. Shortly after the Peace of Etaples, Perkin Warbeck, the pretender to the English throne, was given refuge in Burgundy. Henry tried at first to negotiate the issue, but

---

[17] *TRP* no. 20.

[18] *TRP* nos. 36, 37. A final muster proclamation which gave as its justification 'the defense of this his realm of England' sought to raise an army in the south of England for the French war in 1492 (no. 28). See Cruickshank, *Army Royal*, 195ff for a discussion of military obligations. The shire levy or fyrd was primarily a defensive levy and 'it was statutorily exempt from serving outside the county boundary, although in practice this exemption was usually ignored.' *Ibid.* 196.

[19] C 82/34 (Appendix B item 3). The proclamation text has not been found but a license of 29 January 1487 refers to it as 'a proclamation that no manner of merchants denizens or strangers should bring into this realm and utter and sell any merchandise shipped or carry out any to any parts under the obeisance of the King of Romans without specific license under the great seal.'   [20] *TRP* no. 18.

when this proved unsuccessful he turned again to economic pressure. In 1493 he issued a proclamation prohibiting unlicensed trade with Burgundy. In the same year the mart for English cloth in Antwerp was moved to Calais.[21] The obvious intention of these moves was to use trade as a weapon of foreign policy, but, since Maximilian found it difficult to forgive Henry for the Treaty of Etaples, trade relations were not renewed until the Intercursus Magnus was negotiated in 1496. This trade treaty was followed by a proclamation announcing the treaty and revoking the earlier prohibition on trade. Shortly afterwards problems arose over a new duty imposed on English cloth which Henry maintained was contrary to the treaty. In retaliation the English mart was again moved to Calais. This forced withdrawal of the duty in July 1497. Although English merchants returned to Antwerp, the remaining differences were not settled until a second treaty in May 1499. Again a proclamation announced the terms of the treaty and ordered subjects to keep the treaty 'upon pain of forfeiture of all that he may forfeit, and further to be punished at the pleasure of our sovereign lord.'[22]

When further troubles developed between England and Burgundy in 1504, the two countries returned to economic warfare. Burgundy opened the fray by imposing new customs duties. Henry responded on 15 January 1505 with a proclamation that moved the mart from Antwerp to Calais for a third time. A market with quarterly fairs was to be held in Calais for merchants who had formerly traded at Antwerp. This proclamation, one of the longest issued by Henry VII, cited the new duties imposed on English merchants as the reason for the action. Merchants were ordered not to buy any goods in the 'Archduke's countries' or ship or convey any goods to any place but Calais upon pain of forfeiture of those goods, one third of which was to go to the King, another third to the Merchant Adventurers, and the final third to the 'finder.'[23]

The authority for these proclamations was the King's prerogative right to deal with foreign affairs. Although they imposed restrictions on trade, these measures were directly related to foreign policy problems and did not resemble the legislation regulating trade normally enacted by Parliamentary statutes in the Middle Ages.

[21] *TRP* no. 31; Wilhelm Busch, *England under the Tudors* (London, 1895), I, 88.
[22] *TRP* no. 33, 45, p. 52.
[23] *TRP* no. 56, pp. 63, 68. The first two changes in the mart were probably also announced by royal proclamations, but they have not survived. The third change was also temporary since the outstanding differences were negotiated and finally settled by a new treaty in 1507.

However, two of Henry VII's proclamations which regulated foreign trade were not as clearly connected with foreign policy. Furthermore, they dealt with matters often governed in the past by statutory legislation. One of them violated at least the spirit of a medieval statute; the second encroached on an area normally reserved to statute. The first prohibited unlicensed grain export in September 1491. The justification given for the restriction was 'the great dearth and scarcity of grain' and that the King 'intendeth with an army royal to pass in his person over seas to resist the malice of his great enemy of France.' It was therefore explained as a temporary measure related to foreign policy. However, the proclamation not only altered a policy set by a statute of Henry VI, but there is also some question whether it was really only a temporary measure.[24]

Although earlier legislation had recognized the King's right to limit export for the benefit of the realm, by the reign of Henry VII it was not at all clear if this prerogative was free from the restrictions imposed by later statutes. In the fourteenth century the power to limit export was considered one of the King's prerogatives. A statute in 1361 specifically stated this.[25] In 1394 the commons petitioned for a change. Richard II assented to the petition in a new statute which granted 'license to all his liege people of this realm of England to ship and carry corn out of the said realm, to what parts that please them except to his enemies.' Richard, however, continued to claim the prerogative to limit export without the consent of Parliament: 'nevertheless he will that his council may restrain the said passage when they shall think best for the profit of the realm.'[26] By 1437 a policy of demanding licenses for grain export seems to have developed. In that year a new statute interpreted the earlier legislation in that fashion: 'forasmuch as by law it was ordained that no man might carry nor bring corn out of the realm without the King's license.'[27] However, there were complaints that because of this practice corn could not be sold 'but of a bare price to the great damage of the realm'; consequently, the statute allowed free export as long as the price of wheat was not above 6s 8d a quarter and barley not above 3s a quarter. The statute was to endure until the next Parliament which renewed the act for ten years. Before the period elapsed a third statute made it 'perpetual and to stand in his force forever.'[28] This regulation was, therefore, still in effect when

[24] TRP no. 26. [25] 34 Edward III c. 20.
[26] 17 Richard II c. 7.
[27] 15 Henry VI c. 2. Norman S. B. Gras, *The Evolution of the English Corn Market* (Cambridge, 1915), 137. [28] 20 Henry VI c. 6; 23 Henry VI c. 5.

Henry VII issued his proclamation prohibiting all unlicensed grain export, but technically the earlier statutes which allowed the King this prerogative had never been rescinded. Consequently, it would seem that as long as the price levels were higher than the statutory levels the prerogative applied, but if they were lower any effort to limit export without Parliamentary consent would be in violation of the statutory policy.

Since price levels varied so rapidly, the restrictions on this prerogative could be somewhat ambiguous. Even if Henry VII was aware of the earlier statutes, he may have felt well within his rights to introduce a temporary restriction at least indirectly connected with foreign policy. However, historians have not generally accepted that it was intended only as a temporary measure. Schanz, who felt that Henry VII would not allow his prerogative to be inhibited by statutory prohibitions, believed that the proclamation introduced a regular policy of forbidding unlicensed export.[29] Busch thought much the same. Although he was surprised that this policy was adopted by a government which 'aimed at encouragement of agriculture,' he maintained that a request from the Pope in 1504 and 1505 for permission to have corn exported from England to the papal states demonstrated that the policy of restricting export still existed over a decade after the proclamation.[30] Gras rejected these earlier explanations, maintaining that export of corn flourished to a greater extent in Henry VII's reign than it had in the Yorkist period and that the license system was not established until 1516. He believed that Henry VII's restriction was a temporary expedient, but he was unable to offer any convincing evidence in support of this assertion.[31] Leadam disagreed with Gras and the earlier writers. He considered the proclamation 'an invasion of statute by the prerogative,' probably following precedents set by the Yorkist Kings.[32] Although Leadam did not offer evidence for his assumption that the policy had begun before Henry VII, he was clearly correct. Edward IV issued at least four proclamations forbidding unlicensed export of grain in 1481 and 1482.[33] However, they may have been intended as

[29] 'Noch weniger als ihre Vorgänger waren Heinrich VII. und VIII. geneigt, in den Gesetzen unübersteigbare Schranken zu sehen. An der Prärogative, durch Proklamationen und Licenzen über die Statuten sich hinwegzusetzen, hielten sie fest.' Georg Schanz, *Englische Handelspolitik gegen Ende des Mittelalters* (Leipzig, 1881), I, 641.

[30] Busch, *England under Tudors*, 261; Tawney also believed that a permanent policy had been introduced. R. H. Tawney, *The Agrarian Problem in the Sixteenth Century* (London, 1912), 197.   [31] Gras, *Corn Market*, 221.

[32] I. S. Leadam, *Select Cases before the King's Council in Star Chamber (1509-44)* (London, 1911), I, xxvii.   [33] Steele, clxxvii-clxxviii.

temporary measures, because they were issued during years of bad harvests when the average price of grain was considerably higher than it had been in previous years. Henry VII's proclamation, on the other hand, does not seem to have had a similar justification nor was it a temporary policy. It was issued in a year when there was an 'average' harvest, and the price of grain was lower than it had been either in the previous year or would be in the following year.[34] Furthermore, it is evident that, although this is the only surviving proclamation, it either was in effect for some time or other grain restraints must have been issued throughout the reign. Licenses to export grain were not uncommon even in times of relatively low grain prices not exceeding the statutory level. More significantly, port records suggest that two and a half years after the proclamation the restrictive policy on grain exports was still being maintained.[35] In light of this evidence it is difficult to accept Gras' conclusions or the justification in the proclamation. Henry VII may well have simply been following the precedents of his Yorkist predecessors; nevertheless, he seems to have adopted a policy on grain export which emphasized the prerogative right to limit export and ignored the statute allowing free export when grain was below the stated price.

A second economic proclamation which intruded on an area normally regulated by statute established a Staple at Southampton for metals mined in England. It was issued in June 1492 and was justified by the contention that mining was being neglected in England. It stated that the King had 'granted and licensed an incorporation to be had of a mayor and a certain fellowship of merchants of the Staple of all manner metals' at Southampton. The Staple was to see that the 'mines be occupied and much idle people to be set over in work' and also that the metals mined 'be uttered for a reasonable price.' The proclamation included a series of

[34] The prices in Edward IV's reign were higher than they would be again for forty years. W. G. Hoskins, 'Harvest Fluctuations and English Economic History 1480–1619,' *AgHR*, 12 (1964), 44. Peter Bowden, 'Statistical Appendix,' *Agrarian History of England and Wales*, Joan Thirsk ed. (Cambridge, 1967), II, 846–7 has a table listing average grain prices. Although 1490 had been a year of a 'deficient' harvest and relatively high grain prices, the proclamation was issued in September 1491, so that it is unlikely that it was motivated by the grain problems of the previous year.

[35] Borough of Harwich Muniments, Bundle 39, contains at least five bonds made in February and March of 1495. This was the normal method of enforcing grain restraints. Shippers claiming to be exporting to Calais or English ports bonded themselves not to ship to other ports upon pain of forfeiture of the bond. They were required to bring back a certificate from the port to which the grain had been delivered certifying that delivery had been made. *CSPSp*, I, nos. 7, 10, p. 2 lists licenses to export grain in February 1486 when the price of grain was below the statutory level so there must have been a restraint early in the reign.

regulations for the Staple. No tin or lead was to be exported unless it were 'brought and stapled at one of the said staples.' No one was to smelt tin unless he was a member of the Staple. Four tinnages were to be held each year, and merchants of the Staple were to buy tin there at specific prices set in the proclamation. The Staple also was to regulate the mining of other metals, especially gold and silver. Every merchant of the Staple was to spend at least £10 a year on silver mines and all lead ores bearing silver were to be smelted at a place provided by the Staple. Violations of the regulations were to be punished by forfeiture for most clauses and imprisonment for others. The Staple was granted power to punish offenders and all subjects and local officials were commanded to assist the officers of the Staple in enforcing the regulations concerning export and the smelting of tin by a promise of one half of the forfeiture.[36]

Fortunately, a good deal more information has survived to assist in analyzing the purpose and intent of the proclamation. The patent incorporating the Staple is found on the patent rolls, dated 1 April 1492. It contains additional regulations on mining and marketing of metals as well as ordinances on the organization of the Staple. The first clause adds information on the reasons for the action. Earlier regulations setting the Staple for lead and tin at Calais were not being observed, and merchants of the Staple were exporting only wool to Calais. Therefore it was necessary to establish a new Staple in England.[37] A second document, entitled 'The Copy of the King's Commission,' reveals more about the government's motivation. This curious manuscript is not what the title leads one to believe – another copy of the patent setting up the Staple. Rather, it seems to be a memorandum noting the advantages of the policy, drawn up after the proclamation was issued. It reveals that although the major concern of the government was the revival of tin and lead mining, it was also hoped that the move would stimulate the mining of gold and silver, thereby increasing England's supply of precious metals.[38]

Although the King's right to grant monopolies of trade was recognized as part of his prerogative,[39] previous legislation on the

---

[36] *TRP* no. 27.

[37] C 66/572/29-30. The Staple was not limited to Southampton since lead mined in Derbyshire could be carried to York as well as Southampton.

[38] *HMCR* (Hereford, 1911), 'Report on the Manuscripts of Lord Middleton Preserved at Wollaton Hall Nottinghamshire,' 614-17. The document spoke of the Staple benefiting the realm by the great increase in silver that would come and that 'the continual working of the said mines shall be daily renewed as well as gold and silver out of the same as lead, tin and copper and thereby shall be brought into the realm both gold, silver or ware to the value.' *Ibid.* 614.   [39] BM Add. 36081/251.

Staple had normally been included in statutes. A series of acts during the Middle Ages regulated the wool Staples and at times also the tin Staple. The Staple for tin was at Calais from 1376 to 1390 when it was moved to Dartmouth by 14 Richard II c. 7. However, this statute was repealed by 15 Richard II c. 7 and the Staple was returned to Calais. A series of new statutes in the late Middle Ages also included regulations on the tin Staple. The major act, 8 Henry VI c. 17, forbade the export of tin or lead except to the Staple at Calais, and it was confirmed by 11 Henry VI c. 13 and 14 Henry VI c. 2 both of which contained a clause allowing the King and council to modify the statute for the benefit of the realm: 'Saving always to our sovereign Lord the King power and authority to modify the same statute when it shall please him by authority of his council, according as to him best shall seem for the profit of him and of his realm of England.'[40] The proclamation never cited this authority, and it is possible that Henry VII was not even aware of it. It would seem that Henry VII felt that his prerogative gave him the right to act in this matter without Parliamentary approval. Therefore, he did not feel it necessary to cite a statutory basis for his action nor did he seek Parliamentary confirmation of the proclamation.[41]

The largest percentage of Henry VII's economic proclamations were concerned with questions involving the coinage. Although the right to make regulations for this was a recognized part of the prerogative, in curious contrast with his readiness to regulate export and the Staple by proclamation, Henry VII used Parliament a good deal more than other Tudor monarchs to legislate on such matters. The proclamations dealt with both the quality and the quantity of money, a subject of constant anxiety throughout the reign. Exchanges were controlled by three proclamations. The earliest was probably issued in 1485. Although the text has not been found, the subject matter is described by a reference on the patent rolls. An indenture between the King and the keepers of exchanges in the Tower of London recorded on 4 November 1485 includes a promise by the King to issue a proclamation forbidding exchanges, based on a statute of 25 Edward III.[42] The proclamation probably was similar to

[40] 14 Henry VI c. 2.
[41] Later in the reign a new statute on the wool Staple, 19 Henry VII c. 27, failed to include any mention of the Staple for metals. George R. Lewis, *The Stannaries* (New York, 1908), 63 n. 1 does not believe that the Staple for tin remained at Southampton for much over a decade. 'In 1492 the place [Southampton] became the legal staple for tin and lead, but this could not have been for long, as in 1506 we find Fowey exporting twice as much of the former metal.'
[42] C 66/562/10–11. The statute must have been 25 Edward III st. 5 c. 12.

a second one issued on 15 June 1486 which forbade both unlicensed money exchange and the export of 'any gold or silver in money, bullion, plate, vessel nor for exchange to make, nor otherwise.' It stated that this was contrary both to the King's 'prerogative royal' and to a number of statutes which were cited in the proclamation.[43] It followed the statutes in ordaining the forfeiture of the sum illegally exported or exchanged. One of Edward IV's statutes had made unlicensed export of coin a felony, but it had expired by 1486. When Henry desired to restore that severe penalty in 1488, he turned to Parliament and obtained the authority in a new statute.[44]

Parliament was also used to change enforcement procedures. A new statute passed by the Parliament immediately following the proclamation on exchange repeated the proclamation and outlined the method of enforcement in detail. The proclamation had said nothing about enforcement although one of the statutes cited stated that informers were to report violators to the council or the treasurer. The new statute utilized the method common in many penal statutes. Informers were allowed to sue by action of debt at the common law, 'and the defendant in the same action be not admitted to his law, nor essoin nor protection for the same defendant allowed.'[45] It is interesting that in this case the King not only did not use a proclamation to introduce the penalty of felony, but he also turned to Parliament for common law methods of enforcement.[46]

The other proclamations on money matters attempted to correct the increasingly severe problem brought about by the debased coin that remained in circulation. This was caused by counterfeiting and clipping of English coins as well as by introducing base foreign coins. Statutes as well as proclamations were used to deal with the problem. Counterfeiting was made high treason by 4 Henry VII c. 18, and a proclamation of 4 March 1490 ordered the enforcement of the legislation against it.[47] Clipping, which debased the coin by removing small amounts of precious metal in a variety of ways, was an even

[43] *TRP* no. 10. The statutes cited were: 25 Edward III st. 5 c. 12; 5 Richard II st. 1 c. 2; 2 Henry IV c. 5; 4 Henry V c. 6; 2 Henry VI c. 9.
[44] 17 Edward IV c. 1 made coin export a felony. It was made to endure for seven years and was not renewed. 4 Henry VII c. 23 restored that penalty.
[45] 3 Henry VII c. 6. The earlier statute was 2 Henry VI c. 6.
[46] A final proclamation on the exchange set exchange rates at Calais early in the reign. The rates had previously been set by Edward IV's council but the proclamation maintained they were now 'broken and discontinued and all manner of coins have course within the said town and marches at over great and exceeding value and price.' This proclamation also failed to mention any court but it did provide that informers would receive half of the forfeiture decreed in the proclamation. *TRP* no. 14a.
[47] *TRP* no. 20.6.

more widespread practice. Coins subject to successive clipping quickly became seriously underweight. In some cases coins in circulation had been diminished to almost half their standard weight by this practice. This had been a serious problem for some time. Numerous statutes and proclamations had attempted to control it, often with extremely severe penalties including that of death.[48] Henry VII's legislation did not add additional penalties or prohibitions to those already in effect, but rather tried to correct the confusion caused by the large number of debased coins in circulation. Understandably, people were refusing to accepted clipped coins at their normal value. The proclamations and statutes, therefore, attempted to define what coins should be accepted and at what values. In December 1498 the King tried to enforce acceptance of pennies by simply ordering that subjects 'take and receive in payment all manner of pennies of our said sovereign lord's coinage so that they be silver and whole' on pain of imprisonment and fine.[49] Apparently this was unrealistic, for many pennies were seriously underweight. Three months later a second proclamation admitted the need to lower the value of some pennies. Subjects were ordered to accept all pennies at full value except those 'bearing divers spurs or the mullet betwixt the bars of the cross.' These were also to be accepted 'but only for an half-penny.'[50] The problem, however, was too complex to be dealt with in a piecemeal fashion, and major legislation was enacted in the 1504 Parliament. The new statute attempted to define current coin in a comprehensive manner and to make it possible to detect clipped coin easily. Although gold coins were to be accepted only if they were of full weight, silver coins stamped in England were to be accepted even when they were imperfect as long as they bore the royal stamp. Clipped pieces were to be refused, and new coins would be stamped with a circle around the edge to prevent clipping. The statute also mentioned foreign coins. Groats, whether English or foreign, were declared current. They were to be accepted at full value even if they were 'cracked or worn' as long as they were not clipped.[51]

The statute was followed by two more proclamations. On 5 July 1504 a proclamation attempted to clear up some of the ambiguities

---

[48] Albert Feaveryear, *The Pound Sterling: A History of English Money* (Oxford, 1931), 5. 25 Edward III st. 5 c. 13, 4 Henry V c. 6 made clipping treason. Steele, clvii (13 August 1247 and 26 November 1247); clix (1 March 1289 and 23 September 1291); clxi (10 January 1317 and 2 February 1319) are examples of medieval proclamations.

[49] *TRP* no. 42. The editorial title 'Declaring Clipped Pence Legal Tender' is misleading.   [50] *TRP* no. 44.

[51] 19 Henry VII c. 5.

in the statutes. Englishmen seemingly found it difficult to distinguish between clipped and worn coins; so a standard was set for differentiation and the order in the statute that worn coins were to be accepted and clipped coins refused was repeated. Clipped money could be exchanged for 3s 2d an ounce, but it should be 'cut in sunder' immediately in the presence of the seller.[52] Neither the statute nor the proclamation provided an adequate solution to the problem. The following year another proclamation complained that individuals were still refusing worn coin. It added more explanation and mentioned coins not in the earlier legislation. It also repeated the statutory prohibitions against clipping. Individuals continuing to 'clip, mash, batter, boil, or otherwise minish or impair any coin' were threatened with death. Although the proclamation did not cite any statutory authority for the penalty, it was not a new penalty for the crime since it could have been based on 4 Henry V c. 6.[53]

A final problem was the importation of debased foreign coin. Once again Henry VII used both statutes and proclamations in an effort to control the practice. March 1490 saw the first of a series of proclamations. It ordered that placks from the Empire and Burgundy, which were being brought into the realm in large quantities and valued far above their real value in precious metal, should not be accepted. They could, however, be brought to the King's mint to be coined into English coins without any charge to the bringer. Irish coins posed an even more difficult problem. Three proclamations ordered the refusal of Irish pence. They were followed by a statute restricting the exchange of coins between Ireland and England and providing that Irish coins found in England could be seized. A final proclamation was concerned with Imperial groats and two penny pieces. Since many of these coins had been counterfeited, no one was to receive these coins in payment unless they were approved by the King and council.[54]

Most of Henry VII's remaining proclamations follow the same patterns discussed above. They do not reveal any large scale reliance on the prerogative, and at least in some cases the King later sought Parliamentary approval for changes introduced by proclamations. Most of them dealt with matters which could be classified in a general

---

[52] *TRP* no. 54.
[53] *TRP* no. 57, p. 71. Gladys Temperley, *Henry VII* (New York, 1915), 191 gives a false impression and leads one to believe that the penalty was introduced by the proclamation: 'a proclamation of the following year [1505] made the clipping of coin punishable by death and a false coiner was hanged at Tyburn as a warning.'
[54] *TRP* nos. 20.7, 25, 38, 43, 39; 19 Henry VII c. 5.

way as social questions. One simply carried out the provisions of 4 Henry VII c. 12 which attempted to improve general law enforcement. That statute ordered that a proclamation be made at quarter sessions four times a year and specified the wording. The proclamation ordered justices of the peace to enforce existing laws according to their commission and threatened them with penalties for failure to comply. Individuals who did not receive justice from the justices were instructed to complain to another justice of the peace; and if they still failed to receive a 'remedy,' they could bring their complaint to the justices of assize, or if the wait was too long, to the King or his chancellor.[55]

Two proclamations regulated foreign travel. The first, in August 1499, forbade the carrying of passengers in ships leaving the realm unless the passenger had a license from the King or was 'of such substance and truth that the township where he passeth will be chargeable for his demanding against the King, his realm, and his subjects.' In addition no one was to be allowed into the realm 'but such as shall think of true disposition toward the King.'[56] This action, which was probably motivated by the flight of Edmund de la Pole, Earl of Suffolk, to the continent in the summer of 1499, must have been designed to discourage others from joining him to plot against the King. However, it seems to have also restricted legitimate merchants, for less than a fortnight afterwards a second proclamation repeated the order to port officials that 'suspect' persons be not allowed to leave the realm, but added that 'substantial merchants intending to go to Bordeaux or other places for feat of merchandise' were not to be 'restrained by the force of the said proclamation.' Although this was intended only as a temporary restriction on travel in reaction to a possible threat from abroad, it was in accord with earlier statutory prohibitions which had long forbidden departure from the realm without license by anyone except 'great men of the realm and true and notable merchants, and the King's soldiers.'[57]

In light of Henry VII's well-known effort to control unlawful retaining, it is surprising that only one of his surviving proclamations dealt with that subject. Issued in 1502, it simply ordered enforcement of previous legislation 'upon the penalties in his said statutes limited and in avoiding his high displeasure and other dangers that may ensue.'[58] Once again comprehensive new legislation on the subject was introduced by statute. The next Parliament enacted

[55] *TRP* no. 17.
[56] *TRP* no. 46.
[57] *TRP* no. 47; 5 Richard II st. 1 c. 2.
[58] *TRP* no. 50.

19 Henry VII c. 17, which added penalties and a system of enforcement not in the earlier statutes or the proclamation. Justices of the peace were to examine persons suspected of offenses against the statute and to certify their names to the Court of King's Bench. Informers were also allowed to bring information against offenders to the Star Chamber, the King's Bench or the council. Court costs and a reward were promised to the informer upon conviction. In light of the assumption that proclamations were normally enforced in the Star Chamber, it is surprising that the King relied on a statute to introduce this method of enforcement.

Proclamations were sometimes used to change statutory penalties. On 3 June 1487 the penalties for tellers of false tales were modified by a royal proclamation. Whereas medieval legislation provided that they were to be put in prison until they revealed the author of the tale, the King now commanded that they should be placed in the pillory 'there to stand as long as it shall be thought convenient.'[59] Although this change was not afterwards incorporated in a statute, the alterations Henry VII made in the medieval vagabond legislation were quickly made statutory. At first Henry simply ordered that the existing legislation be enforced,[60] but on 18 February 1493 he used a royal proclamation to correct some of the problems resulting from the statutory procedures. One of Richard II's statutes had ordained that vagabonds who could not 'find surety of their good bearing' were to be imprisoned until justices of gaol delivery appeared.[61] This resulted in some inconvenience because of 'the great charges that should grow...for the bringing of the said vagabonds to the jail and the long abiding of them therein.' Therefore, the proclamation provided that vagabonds should be put in the stocks for three days and nights on bread and water and then released and 'sworn to avoid the town.' If they failed to do so they would then be placed in the stocks for six days and nights and imprisoned. Beggars who were able to work were to be returned to their last place of residence. Local officials were threatened with a fine of 20d if they did not enforce the proclamation.[62]

The Proclamation was issued at a time when no Parliament was in session, but when the next Parliament met, a statute repeated almost verbatim its provisions adding only a number of additional

[59] *TRP* no. 11. The earlier statutes were 3 Edward I c. 34; 2 Richard II st. 1, c. 5.
[60] *TRP* no. 16. The proclamation also forbade disturbance of the peace with weapons.
[61] 7 Richard II c. 5.
[62] *TRP* no. 30. The proclamation also ordered that 3 Henry VII c. 2, the statute for punishment of murderers made in the last Parliament, be put into execution.

clauses on unlawful games and allowing justices of the peace to remit the punishment when vagabonds were seriously ill or were pregnant women. A second statute on the same subject in 1503 lowered the period in the stocks to a day and a night for the first offense and three days and nights for the second. It also stated that the chancellor, treasurer and judges could inquire into neglect on the part of sheriffs or local officials in enforcing the statute.[63] Another proclamation on vagabonds, issued on 22 May 1490, ordered the expulsion of Scottish vagabonds from the northern counties. They were to return to Scotland immediately. If they did not, they would be imprisoned until 'such time they will make before the rulers and guiders of the said shires and marches solemn oath to depart.'[64] The next session of Parliament enacted a statute on the same subject. It repeated the proclamation and ordered stricter penalties. Those who did not leave would suffer 'forfeiture of all their goods and chattels and their bodies to prison.' In addition constables were commanded to search for vagabonds and convey them to Scotland. Those who neglected this order would be fined.[65]

These proclamations on vagabonds seem to have been emergency measures designed to meet an immediate problem which could not wait for the sitting of the next Parliament. When more permanent legislation was intended, statutes were used. This same procedure was followed in other matters. An unfound proclamation of 5 December 1496 is described as 'enlarging divers acts made in the last Parliament for divers artificers and laborers.'[66] The acts in question probably included 11 Henry VII c. 22, which set wages, hours of work, and holidays for laborers and artificers. It obviously did not succeed, because it was repealed by 12 Henry VII c. 3 in the next Parliament. The proclamation issued before Parliament met must have introduced a temporary change in a law that had proved unworkable.

The penalties in Henry VII's proclamations also do not reveal any effort to extend the powers of royal proclamations. It has already been shown that the King relied on statutes for severe penalties. Many proclamations did not include a penalty clause or stated the penalty in vague or general terms. When specific penalties were threatened, they were normally imprisonment, forfeiture or fine. One

[63] 11 Henry VII c. 2; 19 Henry VII c. 12.
[64] *TRP* no. 22. An unfound proclamation issued at the time of the war with Scotland in 1497 expelled all Scots from the realm: C 82/164; Appendix B item 5.
[65] 7 Henry VII c. 6.
[66] Charles L. Kingsford, *Chronicles of London* (Oxford, 1905), 217. Appendix B item 4.

PROCLAMATIONS OF THE TUDOR KINGS

of the distraints of knighthood proclamations included a severe fine of £200, but it seems to have been intended primarily as a threat and there is no evidence that it was actually exacted.[67] Often proclamations listed both a specific penalty and added further punishment 'at the King's pleasure.' When statutes were ordered enforced, the penalties decreed were commonly those in the statutes, but as has already been mentioned at times statutory penalties were altered. The death penalty was used only four times, and it always had a statutory or common law basis. Henry's first proclamation included the death penalty to curb unrest and rebellion in a situation that called for martial law. In 1487 violators of military regulations were threatened with death for offenses which were felonies at the common law. In 1502 the proclamation announcing the alliance with the Emperor ordered the death penalty for traitors and rebels who did not leave the realm. The only other proclamation containing the death penalty was the one mentioned above, dealing with individuals who impaired the coinage. As has been noted, this was the statutory penalty for that offense.[68]

Henry VII's proclamations were generally vague in referring to a method of enforcement. Many of them did not even list the officials who were charged with carrying out the provisions of the proclamation. Courts were almost never mentioned. None of the proclamations ordered enforcement in either the Court of Star Chamber or common law courts. The council was used only in the proclamation of 5 July 1504 directed against the clipping of coin. If local officials failed to enforce it, subjects were told to complain either to the King 'or to his council or to any justice of the peace' and if the accusations were proven the officials would be fined and imprisoned.[69] When enforcement clauses were included they normally simply ordered local officials to carry out the provisions of the proclamation. Orders were directed to sheriffs, mayors, bailiffs, constables, and especially justices of the peace. The proclamation of 23 December 1487 on vagabonds is a typical example. It ordered:

> all mayors, bailiffs, sheriffs, constables, and all other ministers and officers of every such city and town, that they and every of them make due search in every suspect house or place in the same city and town for all such vagabonds and other suspect persons; and them to arrest, take, and put

[67] Leonard, 'Knights and Knighthood,' 46, states that there is no evidence that the £200 fine was ever collected. Fines vary from £2 to £13 5s 8d.
[68] The proclamations ordering the death penalty are *TRP* nos. 1, 13, 52, 57.
[69] *TRP* no. 54.

in ward, in sure keeping, from time to time, as often as the case shall require.[70]

Proclamations on distraint of knighthood ordered sheriffs to seek out the names of the offenders and report them to the chancellor. Trade regulations were enforced by customers, comptrollers and officers of the creeks and ports, and they were sometimes threatened with loss of their office or a fine if they were negligent.[71] At times private citizens were encouraged to aid in enforcement. The proclamation of 5 April 1491 decreed that any person who brought Irish money into the realm would forfeit the money and suffer fine and imprisonment. One half of the forfeiture was to go to the King and 'the other half to the finder and seizer thereof.'[72] The proclamation which established the Staple of mines at Southampton stated that anyone who exported tin or lead in violation of the proclamation would forfeit the metal and half the forfeiture would go to the King and the 'other half to the finder of the same.'[73] Proclamations utilizing informers never specified, as was common in statutes, that informers could sue for half of the forfeiture by writ of debt in the common law courts. A final method of enforcement was by officers of the Staple or the Merchant Adventurers. The mayor and constable of the Staple were allowed to punish those who violated the regulations in the proclamation which set up a Staple of mines. The Merchant Adventurers were given the right to make and enforce their own ordinances without interference from the officials of Calais by the 1505 proclamation providing for a free mart at Calais. Informers who aided in enforcing these regulations were promised a reward of one third of the goods forfeited by the offender.[74]

Don Pedro de Ayala may have been right: Henry VII may have preferred 'to govern England in the French fashion'; but his royal proclamations provide no evidence that he attempted to do so. He knew the limits of his prerogative and he used proclamations freely in those areas where he had the right to act without Parliament. At times he may have pushed those limits a bit further than a strict constructionist or Stuart lawyers would have allowed. He did not hesitate to change or modify statutes when emergency situations demanded this, and his proclamation forbidding unlicensed grain export continued a policy that was technically in violation of at least the spirit of earlier statutes. But there is no evidence of an effort

[70] *TRP* no. 16. [71] *TRP* nos. 9, 31.
[72] *TRP* no. 25. [73] *TRP* no. 27.
[74] *TRP* no. 56.

or even a desire to rule without Parliament. He normally used statutes for major legislation even in prerogative matters. At times he incorporated changes made by proclamations in new statutes when Parliament was again in session. He does not seem to have had a philosophical devotion to statutory legislation alone, since he never sought statutory authority to issue proclamations, but then most of his proclamations were concerned with administrative matters and foreign affairs and very few of them could even be termed 'legislation.' The lack of enforcement clauses suggests that in many cases they were little more than propaganda devices or vague threats. He obviously considered royal proclamations a useful and necessary instrument of governing, but he never used them in a way that posed any threat to Parliament.

5

THE USE OF ROYAL PROCLAMATIONS: HENRY VIII–THE FIRST STAGE

The ten years which follow the fall of Wolsey are among the most momentous in our history. The monarchy at last realized its power, and the work for which Wolsey had paved the way was carried out with a terrible thoroughness... Parliament assembled only to sanction acts of unscrupulous tyranny or to build by its own statutes the fabric of absolute rule. All the constitutional safeguards of English freedom were swept away. Arbitrary taxation, arbitrary legislation, arbitrary imprisonment were powers claimed without dispute and unsparingly used by the Crown.

The old English liberties lay prostrate at the feet of the King. The lords were powerless, the House of Commons was filled with creatures of the court, and degraded into the mere engine of tyranny. Royal proclamations were taking the place of Parliamentary legislation.[1]

All three periods of Henry VIII's reign had a nefarious reputation among the nineteenth century proponents of the belief in Tudor despotism. Although Henry VII may have wanted 'to govern England in the French fashion,' and played a major role in the transition from the 'Lancastrian Experiment' in Parliamentary government to centralized royal government, it was not until the reign of Henry VIII that 'the monarchy at last realized its power.' Cromwell rather than Wolsey was the main villain. During his ministry Parliament enacted the 'English Lex Regia' and the remaining 'constitutional safeguards of English freedom were swept away,' so that in the last years of the reign Parliamentary legislation was replaced with legislation by royal proclamation. It is doubtful if any serious historian still holds this view. Even a casual acquaintance with the statute book and the proclamations issued during Henry VIII's reign reveals that proclamations were not used to replace statutes. Furthermore the safeguards in the Statute of Proclamations would have made it difficult for the government to govern by decree even if there had been a desire to do

[1] John R. Green, *A Short History of the English People* (New York, 1879), 340, 355.

so.[2] The debate no longer centers on the question of what was accomplished, but rather it has shifted to the more nebulous issue of what was intended. It is now argued that, although Henry VIII failed to achieve an unfettered right to legislate by decree, it was not for lack of trying.[3] Since it is extremely difficult to uncover surreptitious intent in history, the task of determining what the government sought is considerably more demanding than describing what was actually done. However, it can be logically assumed that the way in which proclamations were used during the reign should disclose a good deal more about the government's attitude towards them than assumptions about hidden motivations. In addition if one compares the royal proclamations issued while the Statute of Proclamations was in effect to those issued in the earlier part of the reign, it should reveal what was actually achieved by the act.

Three chapters are here devoted to Henry VIII's reign. A central concern of all of them is to explain the Statute of Proclamations. This chapter covers the years before 1539. It is divided into periods roughly corresponding to the age of Wolsey's dominance and Cromwell's ministry in order to contrast the differences between their attitudes towards and their use of royal proclamations. The next chapter takes up the problem of the Statute of Proclamations with the hope that a more convincing analysis can be offered after the use of proclamations in the years preceding 1539 has been studied. Finally, the third chapter attempts to determine the impact of the statute in the last years of Henry VIII's reign.

Wolsey (1509–29)

The statistical tables presented earlier do not reveal any significant differences between the proclamations issued between 1509 and 1529 and those of the previous reign. The incidence of use climbed only slightly from 0.24 per month to 0.30 per month. Subject matter remained fairly consistent except for a slight increase in the percentage of proclamations dealing with economics and social questions.

[2] Seemingly the clause of the Statute of Proclamations ordering proclamations to be obeyed 'as though they were made by act of Parliament' so shocked Whig sensitivities that less cautious historians ignored the restrictions on proclamations in other sections of the act. Merriman, who did comment on them, called them 'so guarded that they could easily be rendered nugatory.' Merriman, *Letters of Cromwell*, I, 124.

[3] An example is Stone, *Causes of the English Revolution*, 59 where he argues that Henry VIII and his advisors 'attempted to extend the legal authority of proclamations in a way we can only guess at.' Another is Joel Hurstfield, 'Was There a Tudor Despotism After All?,' *TRHS*, XVII (1958), 83–107.

HENRY VIII – THE FIRST STAGE

Almost half of the proclamations continued to have vaguely worded penalties. Although there was a six percent increase in the number of proclamations mentioning enforcement procedures, and although the Star Chamber was mentioned for the first time, the majority of them continued to be silent on the question of enforcement. The analytical table also does not disclose anything that would suggest a more arbitrary use of proclamations; in fact, the percentage of them devoted to enforcing existing law was considerably higher than in the previous reign. Thus the bare statistics do not reveal many changes. However, a close analysis suggests that although the overall pattern in the use of proclamations during this period posed no threat to statutory legislation, there were times, especially when Wolsey was at the height of his power, when they were used in a way that indicated that the person responsible for them had little patience with restrictions that stood in the way of achieving his goals.

The more arbitrary proclamations of the period were few in number and primarily concerned with enforcing existing legislation. Most proclamations continued to deal with matters clearly within the boundaries of the prerogative. One third of them were related to foreign policy questions, war and rebellion. The proclamations dealing with military matters and all but one of those on foreign policy questions were connected with the French wars.[4] In addition a prohibition on the unlicensed importation of Gascon wine in December 1512 can probably be explained by the first French war. This was done two months after the English army returned from its invasion of Gascony. No explanation was offered for the action except 'for certain great and urgent causes moving' the King and council.[5]

Proclamations which were related to the war effort did not always mention this. Five of them, issued between February 1522 and

[4] *TRP* no. 71 announced an alliance with Spain against France. No. 76 announced the treaty which ended the first French war and no. 79 announced the reconfirmation of the treaty after the death of Louis XII. No. 104 announced a truce with France in August 1525 and less than a month later no. 105 announced the peace treaty. No. 120 reported an eight months' truce with France and the Empire in June 1528, and no. 124 extended it for another eight months. No. 126 made public the end of the war with the Empire in August 1529. Musters against the threat from France or her ally Scotland were the subject of five proclamations: nos. 61, 69, 89, 90, 97. The 1513 expedition to France also resulted in five proclamations. Two were designed to provide victual for the army and the fleet (nos. 66, 67), a third dealt with transporting the army (no. 72) and the final two contained ordinances and regulations for the army (nos. 73, 74). The only one of the surviving proclamations of the period dealing with rebellion is no. 106, which was motivated by the riots in Coventry in the fall of 1525 and ordered that subjects 'desist, forbear, and cease their said confederations and combinations' and report or arrest conspirators or 'devisers of such seditious bills or writings.'

[5] *TRP* no. 68.

August 1523, resulted from the second French war, but only two stated this specifically. Wolsey agreed to the treaty of Bruges with the Emperor in August 1521. By the terms of the treaty England was to launch a naval campaign against France in 1522. While the terms were still secret and before the formal declaration of war, ships and men began to be gathered for a campaign against France or Scotland. In late February the requisitioning of empty wine casks was justified by the ambiguous phrase 'for certain causes and considerations his highness moving.' After the declaration of war in May 1522, Surrey led an army from Calais to pillage northern France. Two proclamations were issued to aid in victualling the army. The first in August 1522 specifically mentioned that the King had 'at Calais a puissant army lying, for the victualling whereof necessary it is that provision from time to time be made.' On 24 November a proclamation offering no explanation forbade the conveyance of grain out of Dorset except to Southampton and Portsmouth 'for such victualling as his highness shall appoint and assign there.' On the same date the arrest of French citizens and their goods was ordered, 'for certain causes we, and our council moving.' In August 1523 the provisions of the proclamation issued twelve months earlier to provide for the victualling of the army at Calais were repeated.[6]

The early part of Henry VIII's reign was also similar to Henry VII's in the percentage of proclamations which announced executive acts or dealt with administrative matters,[7] but the percentage which ordered the enforcement of existing law was almost double that of the previous reign. With the exception of two proclamations which ordered the keeping of watches,[8] all of them attempted to improve the enforcement of earlier statutory legislation. Sometimes they did little more than order the enforcement of statutes and make public their provisions. In other cases the changes were so major that one

[6] *TRP* nos. 87, 81, 94, 93, 96. On 24 November writs were also sent to the customers of London forbidding the export of victuals. An extremely severe penalty of a £200 fine was threatened for disobedience. C 82/524 (*LP* 3[2] no. 2685).

[7] Seven proclamations fall into this category. Two announced or confirmed pardons (*TRP* nos. 59, 60; no. 59 also included general orders for keeping the peace and providing justice). Two were concerned with the restitution of goods taken by French privateers (nos. 82.5, 83). Three dealt with miscellaneous subjects. No. 60.5 transferred cases pending before Commissions of Oyer and Terminer to the King's Bench, no. 64 granted English citizenship to children born in Calais and no. 109 ordered commissions in London or its suburbs to appear before Wolsey and the council in the Star Chamber the following Thursday.

[8] *TRP* no. 85.5 ordered watches and searches in the Cinque Ports. No. 92 ordered watches on highways to protect against robberies or felonies.

could almost consider them new legislation on the subject. The largest number fall into the first category, but the most interesting are in the second group. Those in the first group need little comment. One was designed simply to make public and translate a number of medieval statutes. The preamble complained of general lawlessness and a failure to execute the provisions of the Statute of Winchester as well as other statutes. Therefore, the proclamation was issued 'to the intent that none of his said subjects shall pretend ignorance or lack of understanding of the said Statute of Winchester, amongst the other good and necessary statutes for the commonwealth which hereafter ensueth.' The statutes were 'translated out of French into vulgar tongue of English' and their texts included in the proclamation.[9] A series of other proclamations on liveries, retainers, apparel, coinage and wool manufacture also did little more than order observation of existing statutes. Sometimes they included vague threats of the King's displeasure or more specific statements that offenders would suffer the penalties in the statutes 'without hope of pardon.'[10]

At times the government's effort to enforce statutes met with limited success. When this occurred, Wolsey's basic impatience with obstacles that stood in the way of enforcement led to major changes in the enforcement procedure. The most arbitrary proclamation of the period seems to have resulted from precisely this type of problem. Initial efforts to enforce earlier legislation failed, and rather than go to Parliament for new legislation, Wolsey used a proclamation to change the method of enforcement so radically that the limits of the prerogative were significantly expanded without actually introducing new regulations. The proclamation attempted to control the use of unlawful games, handguns and crossbows. Legislation on this subject was motivated by the belief that playing at games such as 'closh, quoiting, loggatting, tennis, dice, cards and tables,' and the use of handguns or crossbows resulted in the neglect of practice in developing skill at the longbow. Concerns about the neglect of archery were

---

[9] *TRP* no. 63, p. 86. The other statutes were 3 Henry VII c. 2, 12 Richard II c. 6, 12 Edward II c. 6, 23 Edward III c. 6 and 23 Edward III st. 3 c. 2. In some cases the provisions of the statute were simply summarized. A second proclamation of this nature was issued on 19 February 1517 and ordered London officials to make open proclamation of 'the Statute of Winchester, the acts of apparel, vagabonds and laborers.' In this case the text of the statutes was not given in the proclamation. *TRP* no. 80.

[10] *TRP* no. 77. No. 61.5 added to the penalties in the statutes such vague threats as 'to avoid our displeasure, and as you will answer unto us at your peril.' Other proclamations simply ordering enforcement of statutes are nos. 62 and 78.5 prohibiting retainers, no. 79.5 on apparel, nos. 83.5 and 83.6 on coinage and no. 117 on repairs in Calais.

already being expressed in the reign of Edward III at a time when England's archers were embarrassing the French with their skill.[11]

Medieval legislation was designed to insure that subjects maintained proper equipment, and that they used their leisure time to practice archery rather than play at unlawful games. Tudor statutes introduced prohibitions on handguns and crossbows while continuing the restrictions on unlawful games. Two acts in Henry VII's reign, which recited the advantages of the longbow and the mischief caused by the crossbow, forbade the use of crossbows by individuals who did not have significant income from freehold land.[12] All previous legislation on the topic was repealed by 6 Henry VIII c. 13 which added handguns to the prohibited list. No one was to shoot or keep in his house a crossbow or handgun unless he had an annual income of 300 marks. Disobedience would be punished by a £10 fine. Subjects who could legally use crossbows or handguns were allowed to seize them from those who possessed them unlawfully. The King was, however, allowed to license their use by others. This statute was revised by 14 and 15 Henry VIII c. 7, which made it unlawful to use or possess handguns or crossbows unless one had an income of at least £100 per annum. It also suspended all previous licenses and decreased the penalty for unlawful use or possession to 40s. Tudor legislation on unlawful games was initiated by 11 Henry VII c. 2, which forbade participation by servants and artificers (except at Christmas) under penalty of a day in the stocks. Householders allowing unlawful games in their houses were threatened with a fine of 6s 8d. Early in Henry VIII's reign more comprehensive legislation rehearsed the advantages of the longbow and lamented the decline in skilled archers caused by shooting with crossbows and playing at unlawful games. The new statute, 3 Henry VIII c. 3, recited the provisions of earlier acts and ordered them put in execution. Three years later the statute was made perpetual by 6 Henry VIII c. 2.

[11] Joseph Strutt, *The Sports and Pastimes of the People of England* (Detroit, 1968), 43. The concern that playing at unlawful games was leading to a neglect of archery was well expressed in an undated petition from the bowyers and fletchers of Shrewsbury who obviously had a vested interest in the question. Playing at unlawful games, they argued, might 'be tolerable to eminent inhabitants for their recreations,' but it was intolerable for others since the longbow had been 'the greatest defense against the enemy, so that our nation has not only been had in great terror by enemies but also in veneration by others as the country of valiant victories gotten thereby.' *HMCR* 15th Report Shrewsbury, 48-9. I was unable to locate this manuscript in the Shrewsbury archives, but the editor of the Historical Manuscripts Commission Report simply dates it 'Temp. Henry VIII.'

[12] 19 Henry VII c. 4 set the limit at 200 marks per annum. 3 Henry VIII c. 13 raised it to 300 marks. For medieval statutes see 13 Edward I c. 6, 2 Edward III c. 6, 12 Richard II c. 6, 11 Henry IV c. 4 and 17 Edward IV c. 3.

Although there is some evidence that local officials attempted to enforce the act,[13] a problem in enforcement had developed by 1526. The government reacted with a proclamation on 10 April which repeated the prohibitions on handguns and crossbows in 14 and 15 Henry VIII c. 7 and ordered the act observed. Local officials were commanded to enforce it and threatened with punishment 'in example of all other' if they failed to carry out their duties.[14] A proclamation on unlawful games a month later was more threatening. It complained that failure to enforce the 'laudable acts, statutes and provisions' for the maintenance of archery and the prohibition of unlawful games had caused 'the exercising of longbows and archery of this realm' to be 'almost utterly set aside and extremely decayed.' It ordered that 'no person within this his realm of what estate, degree or condition he or they be, do play or use the said unlawful games, nor any of them, nor any householder suffer them within their houses.' Violators were to suffer the penalties in the statutes, and all local officials were to see that the statutes were enforced in 'assizes, sessions, sheriffs' tourns, leets and other courts by inquiry, privy search and other knowledge.' Those who failed to carry out these orders would be 'further... extremely punished as is aforesaid, without favor or any manner redemption, and to be in our sovereign lord's indignation and high displeasure.' Since no exceptions were made for the upper classes, the far-reaching provisions of the proclamation would have denied the use of unlawful games to all classes. Wolsey seems initially to have been serious about enforcing this. Commissions were appointed in every county to enforce the proclamation and to see 'that in all places, tables, dice, cards, bowls were taken and burnt.' It must have been this effort to apply the legislation to all classes which resulted in significant resistance. Hall comments that 'the people murmured against the Cardinal saying he grudged at every man's pleasure saving his own, but the proclamation small time endured.'[15]

Even if the proclamation was not withdrawn licenses were already being issued by summer to 'keep' the forbidden games, 'any acts, statutes, ordinance or proclamation heretofore had made or passed

[13] Recognizances taken from innkeepers not to allow unlawful games are commonly found in the London records between 1515 and 1521. In addition the city government issued orders to enforce regulations on unlawful games and prosecuted offenders. CLRO Rep. 3/88d, 4/166, 5/172d; 3/89 and 5/103d reveal actual presentments of offenders.
[14] *TRP* no. 107.
[15] Edward Hall, *The Union of the Two and Illustrious Families of Lancaster and York* (London, 1550), II, 149. The proclamation is *TRP* no. 108.

to the contrary here or in any wise notwithstanding' as long as no 'apprentices nor light persons' were allowed to play.[16] Wolsey, however, did not give up the effort to see that the less limiting statutes were enforced. In November 1527 local officials were ordered to enforce the statutes 'with such circumspection and diligence as the King's highness shall not eftsoons have cause or need to send or give to them any further commandment in that behalf.' Those who failed to comply would suffer 'condign punishment for their negligent demeanor to the fearful example of other his subjects.' Shortly afterwards additional orders were issued to put pressure on local officials. Justices of the peace were held responsible for insuring that local officials executed the statutes. They were to punish negligent officials in accordance with previous legislation. Finally, they were to order them to appear 'upon pain of £100' before the King's council 'in the Star Chamber at Westminster... there to receive and abide such order and direction as by the King's highness and his said council shall be thought convenient.'[17] Orders were also sent to London giving specific instructions about enforcing the legislation on crossbows and handguns. The city government responded by agreeing to call the merchants of the steelyard and other foreigners and to command them 'on the King our sovereign lord's behalf' to provide the names of all members of their company who had crossbows and handguns 'according to the commandment lately given by the King's most honorable council in the Star Chamber.'[18]

The two-and-one-half year effort to enforce the existing statutory legislation culminated with a final proclamation in December 1528. It not only suggests that the effort had not been successful, but reveals Wolsey's total frustration with what were probably no more than half-hearted efforts by local officials to enforce the acts. The general public was called upon to aid in enforcement. A method of enforcement combined with penalties that far exceeded any in the earlier statutes in their severity and their disregard for established procedures was introduced. The proclamation began by rehearsing the entire problem in detail. It referred to the advantages of the longbow and the service it had provided in the defense of the realm and 'many notable exploits and acts of war' which had brought 'great and triumphant victories... to the great honor, fame, renown and

[16] CLRO LB 0/76. The license in question was issued to John Yans 'to keep from henceforth a game called nine pins with the casting of the half bowl playing at tables with dice not only in our said city but also in the said suburbs.'
[17] *TRP* nos. 118, 118.5. The second proclamation cannot be dated specifically, but it was probably issued shortly after the first.   [18] CLRO Rep. 8/7.

surety' of the realm. For this reason many statutes had been made to preserve that skill. They were, however, not being obeyed and 'shooting in longbows is sore and marvelously decayed and in manner utterly extinct.' In addition the use of crossbows and handguns was leading to felonies and the destruction of game in forests and chases. The restrictions on crossbows and handguns were then ordered observed. Anyone who saw another person using these weapons illegally was allowed to seize them and break them 'in pieces in the next market town or other town.' If individuals refused to yield the weapon, the person attempting seizure was to call upon other of the King's 'good and loving subjects' for their assistance. Furthermore, if anyone suspected that crossbows or handguns were being kept illegally in a house, 'then it shall be lawful to the said person or persons, knowing or probably supposing the same to be true, to enter into the said house or houses' and command the householder or anyone else present to deliver the weapon. If the occupants refused, 'the King's true and loving subjects near thereunto dwelling or being' were to be called upon 'in the King's name to go with him to the same house for his better aid and assistance in executing this the King's high commandment.' They were then 'to charge and command the said householder, or such as in his absence shall be then in the same to make delivery of the said crossbow or crossbows, handgun or handguns upon pain of death.' The remainder of the proclamation dealt with unlawful games and reintroduced the enforcement procedures which had caused so much 'murmuring' two years earlier. No one was to use unlawful games contrary to the laws. Individuals 'keeping any hostelry, inn or alehouse' were immediately after the proclamation to 'eschew all manner unlawful games to be used in their houses' and 'without contradiction' to allow individuals authorized by the King 'to take and burn the said tables, dice, cards, bowls, closhes, tennis balls and all other things pertaining to the said unlawful games.'[19]

The enforcement procedures in this proclamation certainly exceeded anything in the previous legislation. The violation of one's home to search for suspected weapons was in itself questionable. The penalty of death for refusing to turn over crossbows and handguns, although probably meant primarily as a threat to frighten individuals who were, after all, armed with rather dangerous weapons, must nevertheless be considered an arbitrary extension which violated individual rights even in an age when those rights were not so

[19] *TRP* no. 121.

precisely defined. We do not know how long the proclamation was in effect, but there is some evidence that at least some local officials responded to the orders. In London the city government ordered the aldermen to make a secret search for unlawful games 'according to the instructions late made for the same and put in print.' All such games were to be taken away and 'openly be burnt.' Crossbows and handguns were also to be seized and 'broken in two pieces.' On 28 December 1528, approximately three weeks after the proclamation, a special search of inns and alehouses was ordered in New Romney. Unlawful games were ordered seized and held until further orders were received.[20]

Wolsey's use of proclamations to introduce methods of enforcement which were considerably more stringent than those in statutes can also be illustrated in the enclosure legislation. Tudor regulations in this area began with two statutes in the reign of Henry VII which were directed against the engrossing of farms. In 1488 a statute penalized landholders on the Isle of Wight who accumulated farms. A more general act stated that landholders were to maintain houses and buildings necessary for the maintenance of farming on all holdings of twenty acres or more which had been let to farm at any time in the last three years. Violators were to be penalized by surrendering half the profits of the holding to the lord of the fee or the King until the buildings had been repaired.[21] Since these acts do not seem to have been effective, Wolsey introduced a new approach to the problem in 1514. The effort began with two rather radical proposals. The first was a draft bill which contained sweeping and certainly unenforceable controls on engrossing. It attacked engrossers of farms who were accused of holding as many as ten to sixteen farms and limited an individual to no more than one farm. The bill never

[20] KRO NR/CP/W7. References to enforcement in London are found in CLRO Rep. 8/10. Additional measures to enforce the proclamation in London are noted on 15 December when action was taken against three people who allowed unlawful games. On 17 December they were ordered to enter into a recognizance of £20 not to allow unlawful games; CLRO LB o/129d; Rep. 8/12d. The proclamation may still have been in effect in February 1529 when the aldermen of London were again ordered to 'put down all such houses' where unlawful games were being used and to put the 'occupiers' in prison: CLRO LB o/132.

[21] 4 Henry VII c. 16, 4 Henry VII c. 19. Engrossing was the amalgamation of two or more farms, which led to the pulling down or decay of houses and buildings on those farms. Enclosure, on the other hand, meant fencing or hedging a piece of property which had previously been open field or common land. The government was concerned about both practices because they often resulted in the conversion of land to pasture and a corresponding reduction in grain production which, it was feared, would aggravate the problem of scarcity. In addition it was believed that engrossing deprived small farmers of their livelihood and resulted in unemployment, an increase in the number of vagabonds and resulting social tensions. Joan Thirsk, *Tudor Enclosures* (London, 1958) has a good brief discussion of the problem.

became law, probably because it was an unworkable proposal. But a draft proclamation probably drawn up in the same year may have been issued.[22] Although considerably less radical, it also may have exceeded the controls acceptable to Parliament. It stated that 'by the lamentable complaint of his said subjects as by the credible report of his justices of the peace and commissioners' the King had become aware that the scarcity of grain and victuals was the result of the conversion of arable land to pasture and the engrossing of farms. In addition, the practice resulted in unemployment. As a result 'the King's subjects, for lack of occupation, hath fallen and daily do fall into idleness and consequently into thefts and robberies.' Converters of arable land to pasture and engrossers were called 'enemies of the commonwealth,' and all lands which had been in tillage since the first year of the reign of Henry VII were ordered restored to tillage by the following Michaelmas. 'Houses of husbandry yet standing' were 'to be inhabited and dwelt in by husbandmen or laborers according as it was before the engrossing of the said houses.' No provision was made for enforcement and the penalty was stated in general terms: 'upon such grievous pain as will ensue, and as they will avoid the King's highness' indignation and displeasure.'[23]

The Parliament which began to meet in February 1515 enacted the first enclosure legislation of Henry VIII's reign. The statute, 6 Henry VIII c. 5, may reveal the unwillingness of the members of Parliament to accept the more radical approach. It was considerably milder than either the bill or the draft proclamation. The act stated that lands which were 'the more part' occupied in tillage on the first day of the meeting of that Parliament were to continue in tillage. All land converted to pasture since that date was to be restored to tillage 'after the manner and usage of the county where the said land lieth.' All decayed buildings were to be rebuilt within a year. The penalties for violations were the same as those in Henry VII's legislation – half the profits from the land were to be forfeited until the violation was corrected. The statute was reenacted in the following year and made perpetual – probably only after some resistance from Parliament had been overcome.[24] The effectiveness of the

---

[22] The date on the draft proclamation is provided by a manuscript note SP 1/9/264 (*TRP* no. 75). The bill is undated (SP 1/9/262) but the editors of the *LP* attribute it to the year 1514 (*LP* 1[2] no. 3600 [1]). Thirsk, who calls it 'a sweeping and also an illogical proposal,' accepts that date. Joan Thirsk, 'Enclosing and Engrossing,' *Agrarian History*, IV, 215.   [23] *TRP* no. 75.

[24] 7 Henry VIII c. 1. Thirsk believes that 'the act which finally emerged in 1515 and was made perpetual in 1516 showed more understanding of regional diversity and seems to have been modified under pressure from members of Parliament.' Thirsk, *Agrarian*

legislation depended on the assumption that the lords of the fee would assume responsibility for enforcement. Obviously this was an unlikely possibility, for they were often directly involved in the enclosures.[25] As a result the act was ineffective. In 1517 Wolsey took further action. He appointed a commission of inquiry to investigate the combined problems of enclosure, destruction of houses and villages, and the conversion of land to pasture. The commissioners were to carry out their investigations in all but the four northern counties and to report back by Michaelmas 1518. Before the commission had even completed its inquiries Wolsey took another step. He issued a decree in chancery on 12 July 1518 'that all manner persons that hath pleaded the King's general pardon or submitted themselves to the king's mercy and grace for enclosures' pull down any enclosures which had been made since the first year of Henry VII's reign within forty days and restore the land to tillage. Those not complying would be fined £100 unless they 'shall bring sufficient proof before the King in his chancery' that the enclosures were 'more beneficial for the commonwealth of this realm than the pulling down thereof or that it may stand with the laws and statutes against the decay of houses and turning of tillage to pasture heretofore provided.'[26]

Although prosecutions based on the reports of the commissioners continued throughout Wolsey's ministry,[27] and the decree with its threatened fine of £100 surely indicates that Wolsey was very serious about enforcing the relatively weak statutory legislation on enclosures, his effort seems to have had limited success. In the last three years

History, IV, 215. Pollard also believed that the Parliament had passed the act only after 'considerable difficulty' and that 'it had refused or at least had omitted to authorize any means for carrying out the act.' His argument was based on evidence from the *Lords Journals*: 'The bill was read five times and twice committed to different committees in the lords before it was sent down to the commons. It reappeared and is said to have been read a third time on 5 April. Even so, it was to expire at Christmas; and a new bill was introduced to prolong it in the autumn session on 23 November.' A. F. Pollard, *Wolsey* (London, 1929), 86. It is not surprising that Wolsey had difficulty getting Parliament to accept limitations on enclosures since Cromwell, a much more effective Parliamentary leader, also had difficulty with Parliament on enclosure legislation. The original government bill for 25 Henry VIII c. 13 was significantly modified by Parliament. G. R. Elton, *Reform and Renewal* (Cambridge, 1973), 89–92, 102–6.

[25] I. S. Leadam, *The Domesday of Inclosures* (London, 1897), I, 9.

[26] SP 1/17/45 (*LP* App. 2[2] no. 53). The decree was signed by Wolsey and a manuscript note states that it was proclaimed in the Court of Chancery. The dating in the decree suggests that the draft proclamation was probably issued because it also prohibited enclosures since the first year of Henry VII's reign. Leadam believed the date was 'presumably fixed with reference to the three years retrospect limit in the act of 1488.' Leadam, *Doomsday of Inclosures*, I, 11. However, this is unlikely since the statute forbade only engrossing. The proclamation, on the other hand, ordered restoration of land to tillage which had been converted from tillage since the first year of Henry VII's reign.

[27] Thirsk, *Agrarian History*, IV, 216.

of his ministry Wolsey again turned to royal proclamations to enforce the enclosure prohibitions. The first one on 14 July 1526 stated clearly that the government was not satisfied with the results of the previous campaign against enclosure. It denounced the evils of enclosures in strong language and decried the fact that despite the 'industry and diligence' of Wolsey and the council 'to reform, remove and repress the aforesaid great enormities and inconveniences...very little reformation thereof as yet is had.' It ordered that 'all actors and offenders in the premises' who had allowed the decay of houses and villages or enclosed land and unlawfully converted tillage to pasture since the first year of Henry VII's reign 'whereof any inquisition of office is found and remaineth of record' to destroy their enclosures by 21 October unless they could prove in chancery that the enclosure was neither harmful nor in violation of the law. Land converted from tillage was to be restored by the same date. In a fashion similar to the first proclamation the penalty for failure to comply was stated in general terms: 'as they and every of them at their uttermost perils will avoid his high displeasure, and upon such pain and danger as may further ensue to them.'[28] The new proclamation again exceeded the statutory limitations on enclosures since it ordered that enclosures made since the first year of Henry VII's reign be torn down, while Henry VIII's statutes on the subject simply ordered that lands in tillage in 1515 be restored to tillage.

Shortly after the deadline in the proclamation had expired two more proclamations appeared. On 21 November all who had been summoned to chancery for enclosures were ordered to appear by the following Friday 'or else writs of attachment shall be awarded against them.' When that deadline expired a second proclamation made in chancery on 28 November stated that those called into the Court of Chancery for enclosures who had not yet entered into recognizances or 'devised for reformation' were to appear before 'commissioners appointed in that behalf and by the same commissioners to be ordered and not to depart, upon pain of 500 marks.' A year and a half later Wolsey turned to another method of acquiring information on offenders. A proclamation of 12 May 1528, again made in chancery, ordered all subjects to disclose to Wolsey secretly 'by writing and bills' the names of individuals who had more than one farm or who were guilty of illegal and harmful enclosures.[29]

[28] *TRP* no. 110.
[29] *TRP* nos. 113, 114, 119. These proclamations do not have the normal format of a royal proclamation, and as Professor Elton has argued, they may not belong in the canon of royal proclamations. Elton, *HJ*, VIII, 268.

Finally, on 15 February 1529 an even more radical procedure was introduced. Individuals were commanded to destroy enclosures 'contrary to the statutes and laws' which resulted in 'the decaying of husbandry and tillage' by 'the 15th of Easter next coming without any further delay or contradiction.' If they failed to do so they would not only suffer the pains in the 'laws and statutes' but the sheriffs' and King's commissioners would destroy the enclosures.[30]

The gradual increase in the severity of enforcement procedures is here quite evident. For over a decade and a half Wolsey had tried to enforce unpopular legislation. He must have become more and more frustrated by the continuing resistance. The proclamations therefore added new methods to force compliance and finally culminated in the order to sheriffs and commissioners to destroy enclosures. The proclamations and the decree in chancery also added to the statutory legislation on the subject not only by introducing methods of enforcement not prescribed in the statutes, but also in that they ordered enclosures made since the first year of Henry VII's reign destroyed, although the statutory date was 1515. Whether Wolsey had exceeded the limits of the prerogative by using proclamations in this fashion is difficult to determine, but it seems evident that he used them to introduce regulations which Parliament had been unwilling to incorporate in statutes. At least in one case, when the Sheriff of Northamptonshire destroyed some enclosures, the action was appealed as being illegal. After Wolsey's fall, the new chancellor, Sir Thomas More, upheld that appeal.[31] In dramatic contrast to Wolsey's practice proclamations were not again used in an attempt to control enclosures until the reign of Edward VI. Cromwell, who introduced a new approach to enclosures, relied on statutes both for the regulations and the enforcement procedures despite the fact that he encountered a good deal of difficulty in getting his bills accepted by Parliament.[32]

Wolsey also used proclamations liberally to introduce temporary economic measures. They normally responded to the problems brought on by a shortage of victuals caused by harvest fluctuations. That the supplying of London was a particularly serious problem is evidenced by three similarly worded proclamations issued between 1513 and 1527. They temporarily gave free license to all persons to bring victuals into the city notwithstanding 'any act, proclamation,

[30] *TRP* no. 123.
[31] Leadam, *Star Chamber*, II, lxxv–lxxvi.
[32] Elton, *Reform and Renewal*, 101 ff.

restraint, commandments or provisions heretofore had made, or granted to the contrary.' Each of them came after a bad harvest. The first on 11 March 1513 was probably also connected with preparations for the French war. A second in the winter of 1522 came after the bad harvest of 1521. The final proclamation in September 1527 was probably necessitated by the disastrous harvest of 1527.[33] The same bad harvest also resulted in considerably more stringent regulations. The harvest of 1527 was one of the most disastrous in the entire Tudor period. The result was a degree of scarcity exceeded only twice in the sixteenth century (the 1556 and 1596 harvests were even worse). The average price of grain was two-thirds higher than the norm. In Norwich there was serious unrest which the mayor felt bordered on revolution.[34] The situation became so critical that the central government had to take drastic action. On 26 September 1527 orders were sent to the justices of the peace in the county of Kent commissioning them to make searches for grain. The orders assumed that there was sufficient grain in Kent to supply the populace, but that individuals were withholding grain from the market for selfish gain. The justices were commanded 'to divide yourselves into sundry places and parts of the said county and not only to view search and try what grains and corns be in the houses, barns, garners or ricks' but also to seek out individuals who had more grain than was necessary for the supply of their household and for seed and to bind them by recognizance to bring the grain to market. Individuals who refused were to be imprisoned. The justices were to inform the council 'if you cannot conveniently so order the same... to the intent we may devise further remedy in that part.'[35]

Although we do not know the results of the search in Kent, the government must have been satisfied enough to institute it on a national scale two weeks later. On 12 November a general proclamation was directed both against middlemen who forestalled, regrated or engrossed grain and against producers who hoarded surplus grain. It sought to restrict the activities of middlemen who enhanced the price of grain by purchasing it on the way to market or before it had been harvested in order to resell it. Hostility toward middlemen was common in the Middle Ages. Both the central and

[33] *TRP* nos. 70, 86, 116; Hoskins, *AgHR*, XII, 44.
[34] *Ibid.* 34.
[35] C 193/3/108. Local authorities also took action in Shrewsbury. The common council agreed 'that proclamation be made at master bailiff's pleasure to make proclamation for bread to come into the town out of the country.' SCRO Assembly Book of the Bailiffs, Aldermen and Common Council 1526–32, no. 75.

local governments had legislated against their activities, which were considered in violation of the medieval concept of a just price.³⁶ The proclamation forbade regrating, forestalling and engrossing of grain and ordered people with surplus grain to bring it to market and to sell it at a reasonable price under pain of the King's displeasure and indignation as well as 'such other punishments as be provided by his laws and statutes in that behalf made.' So that no one was 'negligent in performing this the King's ordinance and high commandment,' people in every county were appointed as commissioners to search for grain and to compel the owners to bring it to market and to sell it at a reasonable price. Those who failed to obey were to be punished 'according to his said laws' and their names were to be certified 'to the King and his most honorable council in the Star Chamber at Westminster,' before 21 January. Because grain was particularly scarce in London, purveyors for that city were permitted to buy in counties where there was sufficient grain 'notwithstanding any words or restraint mentioned in this proclamation.'³⁷ A second proclamation seems to have been issued shortly afterwards. It survives only in a very mutilated printed version that is undated. But since it orders that offenders be reported to the council by 28 January rather than 21 January it was probably issued after the first proclamation which it resembles in most sections except that even more detailed instructions for the commissioners were included. They were not only to make searches, but they were to call local officials before them and inquire if they knew of any individuals who had hidden grain. The commissioners were to search out forestallers, regraters and engrossers and to inquire about offenders at sessions there to 'enjoin them upon pain to appear before the King and his said most honorable council at the day and place before mentioned; there to make answer to the premises.'³⁸

Although searches for grain became common later in the Tudor

---

[36] Holdsworth, *History of English Law*, IV, 357. Holdsworth offers the following definitions: 'A forestaller was defined as a person who purchased or contracted to purchase goods while on their way to market, or who attempted by any means to enhance the price of such goods or persuaded persons not to come to market or not to bring goods to market. A regrater was defined as a person who bought corn or other provision in a market within a radius of four miles. An engrosser was defined as a person who bought up growing corn or other victuals in order to sell them again.' Medieval statutes prohibiting these practices included 25 Edward III st. 3 c. 1 which forbade forestalling of wines and other victuals and merchandise; 27 Edward III st. 1 c. 5 which made it a felony to forestall Gascon wine; 28 Edward III c. 13 which forbade the forestalling of foreign merchandise; 31 Edward III st. 2 c 2 which forbade the forestalling of herring and 6 Richard II st. 1 c. 11, which forbade forestalling of fish.

[37] *TRP* no. 118.   [38] *TRP* no. 118.5.

period, this procedure seems to have been introduced by Wolsey. It also seems to have been relatively successful. Surviving documents indicate that it was carried out with great diligence. Six days after the first proclamation both writs and a general commission were directed to justices of the peace commanding them to carry out the proclamation. The writs, addressed to individual justices, ordered them to 'do all and every other thing to you appertaining according to the true tenor and purport of such instructions as we have annexed to this our commission.' The attached commission was a general order to all counties. It contained instructions for the justices to divide themselves in order to make searches in the various divisions of their shire. They were to make certification to the council of the type of grain found, the quantity, and the amount ordered to market 'according to the tenor of our proclamation.'[39] The critical situation must have had an impact on the justices, because there is a good deal of evidence to show that they did their jobs quite carefully. A series of detailed reports from a number of counties survive. They record the number of inhabitants in the various hundreds, the amount of grain, and the amount in surplus or the additional amount needed for an adequate supply. Some counties reported a surplus and also 'that since the beginning of the first view of corn the said markets have been sufficiently furnished with corn able to suffice all buyers coming and more.' Other counties clearly had a severe shortage and even the search did not provide sufficient grain.

One is struck by the thoroughness of the effort. The surviving reports record that hundreds of towns and thousands of people were surveyed. Although only a limited number of reports have survived, one can assume that other sections of the country were covered with equal care. The shortage was most severe in counties like Staffordshire, Essex and Yorkshire. In these areas the search did not resolve the problem although it may have alleviated the situation. In Northamptonshire the procedure must have been successful because there is no reason to doubt the consistent reports of the commissioners that the markets had been sufficiently furnished since the proclamation.[40] It also must have had positive results in Norfolk. The

[39] E 40/A14908 (*LP* 4[2] no. 3587[1]); SP 1/45/58–9 (*LP* 4[2] no. 3587(2).
[40] SP 1/45/60–1 (*LP* 4[2] no. 3587); SP 1/46/132–49 (*LP* 4[2] no. 3819). The North Riding of Yorkshire had a very critical shortage. The justices reported they had done precisely what the commission ordered, but they found no forestallers and they were 10,000 quarters of grain short of the needs of the Riding. E 163/10/13 (*LP* 4[2] no. 3822). Staffordshire also had a serious problem. The commissioners reported 'they cannot find

commissioners seem to have reported a surplus and asked for advice about selling grain. In February 1528 the Duke of Suffolk told them to allow the purchase of grain for other areas as long as there was enough left for the relief of London and Norwich. However, they were to inform him before 1 March of the surplus grain still left in their hundreds so that it could be disposed of for the relief of others.[41]

Possibly the unusual effectiveness of the search can be explained by the dire national emergency created by the extremely bad harvest. The danger of widespread unrest and even revolution may have stirred the justices to be especially diligent. In this case royal proclamations served the commonwealth well by helping to meet a critical problem that could not have waited for action by Parliament. However, the success achieved was temporary. In June 1528, shortly before the next harvest, Sir Edward Guildford, Warden of the Cinque Ports, wrote to Wolsey warning him that people were complaining that little corn was coming to market and that unreasonable prices were being charged. He suggested that people were hoarding grain and recommended an even more thorough effort to control hoarding than had been included in the two 1527 proclamations.[42]

We do not know if Wolsey followed his advice, because no proclamation has survived. But the 1528 and 1529 harvests were also bad and at least three proclamations were issued during those years in an effort to control hoarding and the middlemen. On 4 December 1528 subjects were charged to 'show and detect' to the justices of the peace 'as near as they can imagine or conjecture what should be the occasion or cause why grains should be so great and excessive prices,' and whether they thought it was as a result of forestalling, regrating and engrossing 'as it is thought to his highness and his honorable council that it should be.' Seemingly the government expected an affirmative answer, for the proclamation also ordered subjects to 'detect and show' the names of forestallers, regraters and engrossers. In addition, local officials were to 'diligently inquire and search for reformation of the premises' and to 'punish malefactors and offenders.'[43] On 19 August 1529 a proclamation stated that no

nor see that there is sufficient grain in the same shire to sustain the people there inhabiting except they may have their bargains made with other persons in other shires'. St Ch 2/27/159. See also St Ch 2/20/369 for the report from Nottinghamshire, which had a surplus.

[41] SP 1/6/220-1 (*LP* 4[2] no. 3883).

[42] SP 1/48/225-7 (*LP* 4[2] no. 4414). All corn was to be viewed and the number of acres of land were also to be listed. In addition producers were to be asked how much they had already sold and to whom and at what prices. Finally, regraters were to be forced to sell at the prices at which they had purchased the grain.

[43] *TRP* no. 121.

person was to regrate grain or to 'combine himself with others to make or set such unreasonable prices.' Individuals were ordered not to buy more corn than was needed for 'his household and seed corn for his land upon pain of the King's high displeasure and forfeiture of the same corn and grain.'[44] More detailed orders in October repeated the provisions of the earlier proclamation and added that individuals having sufficient corn should not buy more corn for seed unless they brought the same amount to the market to sell. Anyone with sufficient corn for his household and seed was again commanded to bring surplus grain to market. Any bargain made in violation of the proclamation was declared void and the money ordered exchanged. Offenders were threatened with imprisonment without bail at the King's pleasure as well as with the penalties of the earlier proclamation.[45]

Wolsey also used restraints on grain exports to attempt to alleviate the shortage. This may have been done by royal proclamations. Evidence of the action is found in a letter from Norfolk to Wolsey on 18 December 1528 which pointed out that the 'restraint as well of all manner grain as of all manner of victual' would hurt the King's revenues and that the inclusion of butter and cheese in the restraint was unnecessary because a surplus was being produced in East Anglia.[46] Although this total restraint on food exports was probably connected with the bad harvests in the two previous years, there is evidence that Wolsey also continued the policy of his predecessors in demanding a licence for grain export for less noble reasons. Although no proclamations on this subject have survived, one may very well have been issued in 1516, after three years of good or average harvests.[47]

Wolsey's use of proclamations ordering searches for grain and controlling the grain trade in a period of economic emergency seems justified in light of the seriousness of the problem, even though the searches for grain involved an intrusion on individual rights. Although it is likely that those with surplus grain were not particularly pleased about this use of the prerogative, we have no evidence that they complained publicly. However, there were objections to another proclamation designed to deal with an emergency situation. It was issued on 13 January 1518 in response to

[44] *TRP* no. 125. [45] *TRP* no. 127.
[46] SP 1/51/118 (*LP* 4[2] no. 5048).
[47] Gras, *Corn Market*, 225. Gras believes that a permanent policy of restricting unlicensed grain export was begun in 1516. He supports this by citing licenses issued for export beginning in January 1516. As has already been noted, it is likely that the policy began earlier.

a serious outbreak of the plague in London. It ordered that residents of houses infected by the disease set a ten-foot pole with straw at the end on the street side of the house so that passers-by would know there was plague in the house. People from the infected house were also ordered to carry a four-foot white rod. The pole was to be kept on the house for at least forty days after the last outbreak of the disease. Even this seemingly justifiable precaution was not well received. Three weeks after the proclamation people 'not only contempted' the proclamation 'but also have murmured and grudged and also have had seditious words whereby commotion or rebellion might arise within this city.'[48]

Only seven proclamations might be classified as having introduced new regulations. Although they were few in number, they provided another example of Wolsey's readiness to use royal proclamations in areas where earlier monarchs had used statutes. This is not true of all of them. One of them closely resembled Henry VII's 1505 proclamation in that it granted 'liberty and license' to merchants to use Calais as a market 'with as large and ample freedoms and liberties and immunities as they had or enjoyed at or in any mart' in the Low Countries, and set up regulations governing that mart.[49] A proclamation of 31 May 1517 was more questionable. It set regulations not only on the number of courses that could be eaten at meals, but also on the type of food that could be eaten. Anyone who disobeyed was to be 'taken as a man of evil order contemptuously disobeying the direction of the King's highness and his council,' and was 'to be sent for to be corrected and punished at the King's pleasure to the example of other.' Although sumptuary regulations of this type were common in the Middle Ages, they were normally instituted by statute. This is the only surviving proclamation regulating meals.[50]

[48] CLRO LB N/70; *TRP* no. 81.5.
[49] *TRP* no. 115. The proclamation differs from Henry VII's in that it does not seem to have been as directly connected with foreign policy. Sandman felt that it was made 'to facilitate the access of merchants to Calais, so that the town might compete with the fairs of Anvers and Bruges,' and he maintains it illustrates Henry VII's concern for the merchant class. G. A. C. Sandman, *Calais Under English Rule* (Oxford, 1908), 80.
[50] *TRP* no. 81. Baldwin maintains that sumptuary legislation was 'mainly, if not entirely' done by statutes in the Middle Ages and views this proclamation as an infringement on an area normally reserved to statutes. Frances E. Baldwin, *Sumptuary Legislation and Personal Regulation in England* (Baltimore, 1920), 165. Although Baldwin's treatment of the subject is based entirely on printed sources and is marred by an inadequate acquaintance with the proclamations, it is true that sumptuary legislation in the Middle Ages was commonly introduced by statutes. Examples of medieval statutes which regulated eating are 10 Edward III st. 3 which restricted the number of meat dishes to two courses except on feast days, and 37 Edward III c. 8 which restricted servants to one meat or fish meal per day.

The remaining 'new regulation' proclamations all dealt with financial questions and included the first Tudor debasement. Although later legal definition was to allow coinage matters to the King's prerogative, it has already been noted that Henry VII often used statutes especially when he sought to introduce comprehensive regulations. Furthermore, it was not at all clear that the King had a prerogative right to debase the coinage at the beginning of the Tudor period, because the crown had engaged in a long struggle with Parliament over that question during the Middle Ages. The only statute dealing with coinage matters in the period 1509–29 was 14 and 15 Henry VIII c. 12 which contained regulations for the coining of money. One proclamation was based on that statute. Issued in October 1524 it simply ordered that coins be accepted 'at such values and prices as they be expressed in the said act, upon pain of imprisonment and further to be punished' at the King's pleasure.[51]

The remaining five coinage proclamations were not based on statutory authority. The first three simply declared certain foreign coins legal tender and set their values in English money. On 25 May 1522 a proclamation announced that a number of unclipped gold and silver coins would be current in the realm at the following values: 'ducat, large of gold at 4s 6d...crown of the sun not clipped at 4s 4d...and every crown of gold, not soleil, nor clipped at 4s.'[52] The foreign coins were actually undervalued, but, nevertheless, there was some difficulty in getting people to accept them. On 7 June 1522 the Earl of Surrey wrote to Wolsey that soldiers were having difficulty finding people who would exchange crowns for 4s 4d despite the proclamation. He warned that 'more exclamation will arise' unless Wolsey provided 'a remedy for the same.' He recommended that letters be sent to the mayors of Winchester and Southampton and to the sheriffs of the county 'to see the King's proclamations put in execution and also such as have silver to change the said crowns for 4s 4d.'[53] Possibly as a result of the 'clamor' two more proclamations

[51] *TRP* no. 100. The statute 14 and 15 Henry VIII c. 12 stated that for every hundred weight of gold made into coin twenty pounds were to be made into half angles valued at 40d and for every hundred pound weight of bullion plate or silver made into coins fifty pounds were to be in groats and twenty pounds in half groats valued at 2d. These are the only two values set on coins in the statute.

[52] *TRP* no. 88. Feaveryear maintains it was connected with Charles V's trip to England to negotiate an alliance against the French and was done 'for the convenience of the visitors.' Feaveryear, *Pound Sterling*, 44.

[53] SP 1/24/17 (*LP* 3[2] no. 2357). Surrey also recommended that Wolsey send £400 or £500 in silver to use for exchange. He added: 'I doubt not this matter shall be displeasant to your grace, but not so much as it is to me for I am continually troubled with the clamor of the same.'

rated foreign coins at the same values during the next three years. In November 1522 the carolus and gold florins were added to the coins rated in the first proclamation. In July 1525 orders in the 1522 proclamation were repeated almost verbatim.[54] The 'clamor' that arose over a proclamation that simply set values on foreign coins is a bit surprising. It may indicate that coinage proclamations trespassed on a sensitive area even though they were well within the limits of the King's prerogative as defined by later legal writers.

In 1526 Wolsey issued two proclamations that touched an even more sensitive matter. He used them to announce the first Tudor debasement. Different from the later debasements, this one was quite minor and fully justified. Rather than being a scheme for the King to avail himself of a quick method of obtaining revenue, it was, as the proclamation stated, an effort to remedy the difference between the value of English gold coins and those on the continent. There was a danger that the kingdom might be depleted of its gold supply, because gold coins were rated higher in terms of silver in nearby Flanders than they were in England. Consequently gold coins were flowing out of the country despite the laws prohibiting export of coin.[55] On 22 August 1526 the values of English coins were raised by ten percent; however, even this was not sufficient, because the export of coins continued. Therefore in November 1526 the values of English gold coins were increased by twelve and a half percent. Two new gold coins, the george noble valued at 6s 8d and the crown of the double rose valued at 5s, were also introduced. Silver coins were reduced in weight from twelve grams for a penny to ten and two-thirds grams for a penny. The 'ancient standard' of twenty-three carats three and a half grams was reduced in the new crown to twenty-two carats. Foreign coins, because they varied in 'fineness and weights' were set at 'no certain valuation.' They were to 'be received and taken by any person at such value as the payer and receiver of them can agree.' All previous proclamations which 'may be prejudicial or contrary' to this proclamation were declared void and people were ordered not to raise prices because of the debasement. Local officials were ordered to see that people obeyed the proclamation and to arrest and imprison those who did not.[56]

[54] *TRP* nos. 95, 102.
[55] George C. Brooke, *English Coins* (London, 1955), 174ff; C. W. C. Oman, 'The Tudors and the Currency, 1526–60,' *TRHS*, new series IX (1895), 173.
[56] *TRP* nos. 111, 112.

The debasement was a moderate one, justified by economic necessity, but it did set precedents for later debasements. Eighteen years later, Henry VIII employed debasement for the purpose of raising revenue and introduced a policy that proved to be economically disastrous. In addition the use of royal proclamations for debasements helped to set precedents for later legal writers to include this as part of the King's prerogative. It has already been noted that both Morrice and Smith recognized that the King had a prerogative right to alter the coinage of the realm;[57] however, what later writers considered a part of the King's prerogative was not as readily accepted by medieval Parliaments.

Coinage debasements were rare in the Middle Ages, but when they occurred they often encountered strong opposition from Parliament. Furthermore legal treatises did not necessarily include this as part of the King's prerogative.[58] In 1311 the Lords Ordainers insisted that currency changes should have the consent of Parliament. Although the ordinances of 1311 were repealed in 1322, control of the coinage remained a controversial issue. The first reduction in the weight of silver coins by royal action in 1344 came only after Parliament had rejected this solution to the problem of coin export in the previous year. Two years later Parliament petitioned that further changes in money should not be made without the consent of Parliament. A second debasement in 1351 caused Parliament to petition the King to restore the old standard. In 1352 Edward III responded by promising to try to restore the coinage and agreeing that there would be no further debasements: 'It is accorded that the money of gold and silver which now runneth, shall not be impaired in weight nor in alloy; but as soon as a good way may be found, the same be put in the ancient state as in the sterling.'[59] For sixty years Parliament maintained control and refused to allow further debasement. In 1385 the chancellor's speech to Parliament called for an increase in the value of money, because coin was being exported, but no legislation followed. Finally in 1411, when the next reduction in weight was made, it was said to have been done 'at the request of the Commons, and it took the form of a statute though it was never enrolled as

[57] Morrice said he could 'enhance or abase the same at his good pleasure.' BM Add. 36081/255.
[58] C. M. Cipolla, 'Currency Depreciation in Medieval Europe,' *EcHR*, 2nd series xv no. 3 (April 1963), 420–1. Cipolla refers to the *Mirror of Justices* which states 'it was ordained that no king of this realm could change, impair or amend his money, nor make money of anything save silver without the assent of all his earls.' W. W. Whittaker ed. *Mirror of Justices* (London, 1895), 11.
[59] 25 Edward III st. 5 c. 13.

one.'⁶⁰ Although Parliament had controlled debasements for over half a century, in 1464 Edward IV reasserted royal control. He reduced the weights of coins largely as a financial expedient, and Parliament does not appear to have complained. Thus, as in the export legislation, the Tudors had Yorkist precedents for their actions. Nevertheless the royal prerogative to alter the coinage was still not uncontested. As late as the reign of Mary the judicial decision reported by Dalison stated that although the King could raise the coinage to a higher value for the benefit of his subjects, he could not diminish or debase the coin by royal proclamation, for that would be to the prejudice of his subjects. Although this section was deleted when the report was printed, and it is clearly in contradiction to later opinion,⁶¹ it does indicate that at least the right to debase the coinage was under challenge in the Tudor period.

Historians have long been aware that Wolsey 'was in no sense a constitutional minister, nor did he pay much heed to constitutional forms.'⁶² Consequently his use of royal proclamations does not reveal any particularly surprising feature of his method of government. It simply supports the long-held belief that he would have preferred to rule without interference from Parliament. When he could not accomplish his goals through existing statutory legislation or could not acquire new legislation he did not hesistate to introduce what must certainly be considered questionable methods of enforcement for the enclosure laws and the acts designed to assure the maintenance of archery. He also used proclamations to introduce what may have been the first Tudor search for grain when economic necessity demanded, and he continued to emphasize the prerogative right to regulate exports despite the limiting medieval statutes. Finally, the debasement of 1526, although again economically justified and in accord with Yorkist procedures, was another intrusion of the prerogative into a formerly contested area. Wolsey was impatient with any restraints that stood in the way of accomplishing his goals. Therefore he was prepared to stretch the proclaiming

⁶⁰ Feaveryear, *Pound Sterling*, 34. See pages 14ff for full discussion of medieval debasements, and John H. M. Craig, *The Mint: A History of the London Mint from A.D. 287 to 1948* (Cambridge, 1955), 61ff.

⁶¹ BM Harl. 5141/31. The King's right to alter the coinage by royal proclamation continued to be recognized long after Coke's decision. T. Cunningham, *Dictionary*, II, 117.

⁶² Mandell Creighton, *Cardinal Wolsey* (London, 1521), 128. Pollard stated: 'He denied the whole basis of government by consent...He had as little regard for the convocations of the church as for the Parliaments of the realm.' Pollard, *Wolsey*, 370. For a more recent evaluation see Stanford Lehmberg, *The Reformation Parliament* (Cambridge, 1970), 1; Wolsey 'preferred to rule without Parliamentary interference, no doubt partly because of his troubles with the Parliament of 1523.'

power to its outermost limits and possibly even beyond, if necessary, without seeking Parliamentary authority. Although no lasting damage was done to the legislative preeminence of Parliament and there is no reason to believe that he pursued a deliberate campaign to undermine the power of Parliament through the use of royal proclamations, he set precedents for expanding the power of proclamations which might have been exploited by later monarchs.

Cromwell (1529–39)

Henry VIII's next minister chose to follow neither Wolsey's nor Henry VII's approach in his use of royal proclamations. Rather he introduced a new concept by seeking statutory authority for royal proclamations. Although there were no major changes in subject matter in the 1530s,[63] Wolsey and Thomas Cromwell were dramatically different in the way they viewed the relationship between statutes and proclamations. As has already been pointed out, a series of statutes were enacted in the 1530s which delegated specific powers to royal proclamations. One fifth of proclamations in the period were specifically based on this type of statute. The vast majority of them set prices on meat or wine. A careful review of this legislation reveals a great deal about the new attitude towards royal proclamations which became evident in the 1530s. Because this legislation continued into the last decade of Henry VIII's reign, the chronological limits of this chapter will be exceeded in order not to break the tale at an awkward place.

The control of wine prices by royal proclamation was common during the Middle Ages.[64] Statutes were sometimes also used in the

[63] There were some changes as the first proclamations on religious matters appeared; and there was a significant drop in the number of proclamations on foreign policy and military matters. There were three military proclamations. *TRP* no. 137 ordered a muster for defense against the danger of Scottish invasion. No. 167 was issued for the purpose of victualling the army raised to suppress the northern rebellion, and no. 156 ordered members of Parliament to go immediately to their home counties to prepare 'for their defense and the annoyance of our enemies.' Foreign policy proclamations announced the peace treaty with Scotland in August 1534 (no. 147), declared neutrality in the struggle between France and the Empire in 1536 (no. 165) and ordered the government and citizens of London to treat the French ambassador with hospitality and courtesy in November 1534 (*TRP* no. 150). Another proclamation which was clearly motivated by foreign policy matters was no. 190, which made unlicensed shipping punishable by death.

[64] Schanz assumes that price controls on wine may have existed since the reign of William the Conqueror. The first evidence he cites is a royal proclamation issued in 1157. Schanz, *Englische Handelspolitik*, I, 643. Normally only the retail price was fixed, but this led to complaints because variations in the wholesale price made it difficult if not impossible to sell profitably at the fixed retail prices at times. So in 1354 a proclamation

attempt to regulate the price of wine, but normally the setting of specific prices was left to local officials or was done by royal proclamations. In 1381 5 Richard II st. 1 c. 4 set maximum wholesale and retail prices, but this was an exceptional measure and was repealed two years later by 7 Richard II c. 11 at the request of the Commons. For over a century afterward price controls were primarily in the hands of local officials or set by royal proclamations. With the single exception of a statute enacted in 1491 which set a maximum price on malmsey wine there were no more statutory regulations until the 1530s.[65]

The first wine price legislation in the 1530s revealed the pattern that was to be followed for the next two decades. The third session of the Reformation Parliament enacted 23 Henry VIII c. 7 which set specific retail prices on wine (8d a gallon for French wines and 12d a gallon for sweet wines). It also delegated power to a special conciliar committee to set wholesale prices by royal proclamation. The price was probably set at £4 a tun shortly thereafter.[66] The effort to enforce this price met with determined resistance, and the next session of Parliament added a new statute, 24 Henry VIII c. 6, to aid in enforcement. Merchants were ordered to sell at the set price or forfeit the value of the wine. Local officials were empowered to enter places where the wine was stored and to deliver it to persons desiring to buy it. After the passage of the statute a number of proclamations were issued which cited both statutes. In 1534 the price of the best Gascon and French wines was set at £4 a tun and local officials were ordered to utilize the procedures provided by 24 Henry VIII c. 6 to enforce that price. The effort to maintain the price again met with resistance. In 1536, when

ordered local officials to set the retail prices in consultation with the vintners and taverners. Margery James, 'The Fluctuations of the Anglo-Gascon Wine Trade During the Fourteenth Century,' *EcHR*, IV (1951), 144–5. Steele lists numerous proclamations pricing wine in his incomplete handlist of pre-Tudor proclamations. Steele, clvii–clxxvi. Many proclamations setting retail prices of wine are also found in the archives of the city of London at Guildhall.

[65] 7 Henry VII c. 7. This action was taken in retaliation for an additional duty which Venice had imposed on English shippers. Henry VII reacted by imposing his own increased duty on alien importers, and then a maximum wholesale price was fixed so that the increased duty would not fall on English consumers. The statute was not part of a consistent price fixing policy and was to 'endure no longer than they of Venice shall set aside the imposition of the payment of the iiij ducats.'

[66] Appendix B, item 15. The text of this proclamation has not been found, so we cannot be certain what price was set; however, it was under £5 a tun since 24 Henry VIII c. 6 accused merchants of selling wine 'some for five pounds the tun some for more and some for less, and so after the rate of excess prices...and above the prices thereof set by the right honorable Lord Chancellor, lord treasurer, lord president of the King's most honorable council...'

23 Henry VIII c. 7 (which was to expire at the end of that Parliament) was renewed, the preamble to the new statute complained that merchants were circumventing the price regulations by cheating on the quantity sold at the fixed price.[67] The statute was followed by a proclamation in January 1537 which raised the maximum wholesale price to £4 13s 4d a tun (7 marks sterling). A second proclamation in December of that year set the same price. The following year, however, probably in response to market pressures, the price was raised to £5. There must have been an abundant supply in 1539, because in November the price was again set at £4 a tun, but by December 1541 it was raised to £5 a tun.[68] The gradually rising wholesale price made it difficult for the vintners to sell at the statutory prices. In 1543 they petitioned Parliament for assistance. Parliament responded with 34 and 35 Henry VIII c. 7, which empowered the same group which had set wholesale prices to set retail prices also. Prices rose very quickly in the 1540s. New and often higher wholesale prices were set in a series of proclamations based on the authority delegated in 23 Henry VIII c. 7. The first surviving proclamation to take advantage of the new powers granted in 34 and 35 Henry VIII c. 7 was not issued until June 1546, but considering the increases in wholesale prices, it is likely that others that changed the statutory retail prices were issued earlier.[69]

The history of the wine price legislation provides an interesting study in the new respect for statute that was evident while Thomas Cromwell was the King's chief minister. The enactment of 23 Henry VIII c. 7 reflects Cromwell's unusual concern for statutory authority, because wine prices had been set by royal proclamations for centuries without any specific statutory authority.[70] But the new

[67] *TRP* no. 149; 28 Henry VIII c. 14.
[68] *TRP* nos. 170, 176.5, 187, 191.5, 206; Appendix A no. 191.5 (CLRO Journals 14/269). The growing pressure on his prices is evident in the account book of Henry Tooley, Ipswich merchant. In 1534 his prices ranged from £4 to £4 6s. 8d. For the next two years he sold at the price set in the 1537 proclamation, £4 13s. 4d, but in 1539 he was charging £5 6s. 8d and even £6, considerably above the price in the 1538 proclamation. In 1540 qnd 1542 he was able to maintain the prices in the 1539 and 1541 proclamations. IESRO Account Book of Henry Tooley, 1.
[69] In 1544 the price was set at £8 a tun for gascon wine and £6 for French (*TRP* no. 230). In 1545 the price dropped to £6 13s 4d a tun for Gascon and £5 6s 8d for French (no. 260). The first surviving proclamation setting retail prices was no. 267.
[70] 31 Edward III st. 2 c. 3, which granted the chancellor, treasurer, justices, and other of the King's council power to regulate the buying and selling of wines and fish at Bristuit was interpreted in a broad fashion by a proclamation in 1511 which summarized it to read 'the chancellor and treasurer and other of the King's council may make ordinance for prices of wines and fishes.' *TRP* no. 63. If Cromwell had been less careful he might simply have adopted the assumptions of this proclamation that statutory authority to set wine prices already existed.

approach also led to problems. The hope that wholesale prices could be manipulated by royal proclamations while retail prices were maintained at fixed levels set in the statute must have been based on the false assumption that wholesale prices could be kept within a range that allowed sufficient profit to the retailer at the statutory price.[71] When enforcement problems resulted, Cromwell did not use royal proclamations to introduce new procedures. Instead he turned to Parliament. Despite the additional legislation, the wholesale price could not be maintained at a low enough level. The fixed statutory retail price became a serious obstacle especially after the passage of the Statute of Proclamations in 1539, because those prices could not be changed except by a new statute. A solution was not provided until 1543 when 34 and 35 Henry VIII c. 7 authorized the King to use royal proclamations to set both retail and wholesale prices, thereby making the policy of price fixing more easily adaptable to economic pressures.

Reliance on statutory legislation also led to some problems in the meat price legislation.[72] Meat price controls were also primarily in the hands of local authorities during the Middle Ages. The intervention of the central government was unusual and sporadic. Statutes were seldom used and normally they did not actually set specific prices on meat.[73] Tudor legislation began with a series of efforts in the early part of Henry VIII's reign to control poultry prices by mayoral proclamations in London 'on the King our sovereign lord's behalf.' Wolsey did not hesitate to order the London government to take action on controlling prices, and without statutory authority the council actually set specific prices for London.[74] In April 1529 prices of beef, veal and mutton were set by direct order of the King's council and Wolsey. This order not only set specific prices per pound but ordered butchers to be bound in recognizances to sell

[71] If the wholesale price could have been maintained at £4 a tun the vintners would have done quite well, for at that price they paid less than 4d a gallon and they were allowed to sell at 8d by the statute. Schanz, *Englische Handelspolitik*, I, 649.

[72] The discussion that follows is with some additions a summary of my article in *HJ*, XII 4 (1969), 583–95.

[73] 37 Edward III c. 3, which attempted to control the price of poultry, is the only medieval statute of which I am aware that actually set specific prices.

[74] In June 1516 Wolsey presented to the Court of Aldermen 'a bill of certain articles.' Among the items was 'the inordinate price of victuals.' CLRO Rep. 3/86. Five days later, on 9 June, the assembly answered the articles and appointed a committee to join with members of the King's council to set prices of victuals. *Ibid.* 88. In February 1518 the council again intervened to set poultry prices. CLRO Journals 11/323. In May the mayor proclaimed on behalf of the King that no person was to sell poultry above the prices set by the King. SP 1/232/58 (*LP* App. 1[1] no. 206); CLRO Journals 11/335.

meat by weight and to have 'a beam with true balance and weight to the intent to weigh the said victual.'[75]

In contrast to Wolsey's method of controlling prices by direct orders of the council, Cromwell turned to statute. In 1533 Parliament passed legislation closely approximating to Wolsey's council order of 1529. Specific prices were set on beef, mutton and veal, and it was ordered that meat be sold by weight. In addition a committee of the King's council was empowered 'to diminish and abate the prices above rehearsed but in no wise to enhance the same.' Local officials who had previously had power to price meats were given the same authority.[76] This resulted in a great deal of resistance from the butchers of London. The mayor and aldermen of the city requested the aid of the King's council. On 3 July 1533, in response to that request, a proclamation was issued pointing out that the butchers were complaining that the prices charged by the graziers were so high that they could not sell at the statutory prices. Therefore the graziers were ordered to sell 'after such reasonable prices as the butchers may reasonably accomplish and perform the effects of the said act.' Graziers who did not obey were threatened with the King's 'indignation and displeasure and to suffer punishment for the same at his will.'[77] In addition a circular letter was sent to the justices of the peace in August instructing them how to enforce the proclamation. The wording of the circular reveals a great deal about the government's attitude towards statutes and the role of royal proclamations. The justices were told that the prices set by the statute 'must needs not only to us but also to all and singular persons of our realm be thought reasonable and indifferent as by all estates assembled agreed and consented unto, and by reason thereof like as every our subject must be content therewith.' However, the graziers were obstructing the operation of the statute by making it impossible for the butchers to sell at the prices ordered; therefore, 'the aid and help of our high power royal' was required. The justices were instructed to explain to the graziers that unless they sold at reasonable prices, 'the

---

[75] CLRO Rep. 7/50d, Journals 13/140.

[76] 24 Henry VIII c. 3. Professor Elton points out that the statute 'was cast in the form of a petition and given the private act assent.' Therefore he maintains the 'act cannot be safely assigned to Crown initiative.' Elton, *Reform and Renewal*, 111. However, as he also points out, the petition form and private act assent did not necessarily prove that the initiative did not come from the government. Furthermore, the statute so closely approximated the government policy imposed on London in 1529 that it seems likely that the statute was initiated by the government. In addition, as Elton points out, the two amending acts of 1534 and 1536 were clearly governmental acts.

[77] CLRO Journals 13/378; *TRP* no. 139.

constraints of the butcher were void and frustrate' and 'our people should want or our laws therein be frustrate.' After explaining this, they were also to warn the graziers that the King would 'lay unto their charge at their uttermost perils the inconveniences ensuing by their default and their contempt and disobedience to the mind of our laws.' In addition the justices were authorized to seize 'beefs, muttons, and veals' and to sell them 'according to the rate of the said statute.'[78] What the circular implies is that the statute must be obeyed and considered reasonable and just because it was a statute, because it was made 'by all estates assembled.' The proclamations and circular were, on the other hand, only an 'aid and help' to true legislation necessary in order to make it enforceable.

On 29 January 1534 another royal proclamation was issued. It denounced the butchers of London for not obeying the statute and maintained that the statutory penalty, a fine of 3s 4d for each offense, was not sufficiently severe to deter offenders. Butchers were again ordered to sell at the statutory prices and threatened with an additional fine set by the King's council. Local officials were commanded to see that offenders were put in prison 'there to remain without bail or mainprize until the King's pleasure be known in that behalf.' Both the proclamation and the circular had altered the enforcement procedures and the penalties in the statute, but they were used only as temporary expedients to meet an immediate problem. When Parliament reassembled, 25 Henry VIII c. 1 incorporated the provisions of both the proclamation and the circular.[79] In addition the statute provided that complaints against graziers for unreasonable prices would be heard by a jury appointed by the mayor or the justices of the peace, and that jury would fix the price. Graziers who disobeyed would be summoned before the Star Chamber. Finally, the King was empowered to suspend the statute by proclamation and to set more realistic prices when the economic situation demanded such a change.

The powers granted by the statute were used within a month. In February the butchers of London again complained that they could not maintain the statutory prices. On 12 March the Court of Aldermen petitioned the central government to allow a higher price

[78] SP 1/78/205–6 (*LP* 6 no. 1052).
[79] Parliament reassembled on 15 January. The proclamation (*TRP* no. 142) was issued two weeks later, because those 'resorting to this high court of Parliament' were complaining that the butchers were not observing the statutory prices. The proclamation seems to have been issued to deal with the situation during the period that Parliament was engaged in formulating the new legislation.

between Easter and Midsummer. The central government responded by using the powers granted in 25 Henry VIII c. 1 to suspend the statute until 24 June 1534 and to allow the butchers to sell beef at ⅝d a pound and mutton at ¾d a pound, the prices recommended by the Court of Aldermen.[80] The London butchers resented even the new prices. When the period of suspension was over, they again complained to the city that 'they can have no livings' at the statutory price. In October, the aldermen sent a committee to appeal to the chancellor. On 23 October 1534 another royal proclamation suspended the statute for London and its suburbs until 24 June 1535.[81] By Easter 1535, butchers outside of London were complaining about the special treatment received by the London butchers and about the prices charged by graziers. On 6 March 1535 William Sandys wrote to Cromwell stating that the butchers argued that they could not buy cattle at reasonable prices. He reported that he advised them to draw up a bill of complaints and present it to the King.[82] On 25 March 1535 the government responded with a royal proclamation which suspended the statute and permitted butchers throughout the realm to sell for higher prices until 24 June 1535. The act had no sooner gone back into effect than it was again suspended for the London butchers until 2 February 1536.[83] A month before that suspension expired the butchers again petitioned the Court of Aldermen asking that the statute be repealed or that another remedy be provided. On 8 February the government suspended the statute for all butchers until the following Pentecost and allowed them to sell as they had before its enactment. When Parliament met, a new statute extended the suspension to 24 April 1540. On 14 April 1536 the provisions of that statute were included in another proclamation.[84] After the statute came back into effect in 1540 the government twice more suspended it in response to new petitions from the London butchers.[85]

---

[80] CLRO Rep. 9/49; *TRP* no. 144.

[81] CLRO Rep. 9/69, 78d; *TRP* no. 148. The proclamation maintained that London butchers needed to be allowed a higher price since their costs were higher than those of butchers in other areas and that cattle were more expensive in the winter than in the summer.

[82] SP 1/91/22, 68 (*LP* 8 nos. 318, 350). The city officials in other cities also had difficulty in getting the butchers to comply with the prices. The assembly book of Shrewsbury records a series of complaints from the butchers in 1534 and 1535. SCRO Assembly Book of the Common Council 1532-41, no. 75.   [83] *TRP* nos. 154, 159.

[84] *TRP* no. 162; 27 Henry VIII c. 9; *TRP* no. 164.

[85] The butchers petitioned for the first suspension before the statute came back into effect (CLRO Rep. 10/159d) and the government responded with a proclamation that continued the suspension until November 1540 (*TRP* no. 193). On 20 April 1540 they again petitioned and the Court of Aldermen advised them to 'sue unto the lords of the higher house and they should have the favor of this court' (CLRO Rep.

Finally, in April 1542 the butchers with the support of the city government asked Parliament to repeal the statute. Parliament complied by repealing both 24 Henry VIII c. 3 and 25 Henry VIII c. 1.[86]

The repeal of these statutes ended the noble experiment in statutory regulation of meat prices. Reliance on statutory authority had proved a cumbersome technique to regulate something as variable as meat prices. Even the delegated authority to suspend the statute by royal proclamation had not resolved the problem because the prices in the statute simply could not be maintained in an inflationary period. However, the process again illustrates Cromwell's concern for statutory authority. He again sought this authority in an area where neither medieval monarchs nor Wolsey had felt it necessary. Proclamations were used either as emergency measures to correct oversights in the statute and to make enforcement procedures more effective, or they were based specifically on the authority delegated by Parliament to suspend the statute. In neither case were they used as long-term legislation. The changes introduced in 24 Henry VIII c. 3 by royal proclamation were immediately made statutory when Parliament was again in session. Even the power to suspend 25 Henry VIII c. 1, although specifically based on statutory authority, was only used to suspend the act for short periods of time. When a four-year suspension was desired, it was accomplished by a new statute. Furthermore, the whole procedure in the meat price legislation illustrates a realistic sensitivity on the part of the central government to the needs and requests of those most affected by the legislation. This very sensitivity, in fact, complicated the whole process and made it necessary to use the suspensory power so often that it finally became obvious that a new approach was needed. This approach was introduced after the enactment of the Statute of Proclamations and will be discussed in the chapter devoted to the last years of Henry VIII's reign.

Three other proclamations during the 1530s were also based on powers delegated in statutes. The powers granted in 27 Henry VIII c. 26, the statute on the governing of Wales, were used on 20 February 1537 when a portion of that statute was suspended until the following All Saints Day.[87] An act regulating apparel was twice suspended by

10/173). Parliament made no response during its session which lasted from 12 April 1540 to 24 July 1540, but on 27 October 1540 a royal proclamation suspended the statute for another year (*TRP* no. 196).   [86] CLRO Rep. 10/325; 33 Henry VIII c. 11.

[87] *TRP* no. 172. Dr Roberts believes that the statute may have been suspended because Cromwell and Audley received advice from Lee to delay the shiring. The government may have been concerned that the discontent expressed in the Pilgrimage of Grace would spread to Wales. Roberts, 'Tudor Settlement of Wales,' 191–3.

royal proclamations which cited a clause in the statute allowing the King to issue licenses to exempt members of the royal households from the regulations: 'the same license to be declared in writing by the King's highness or the lord steward of his most honorable household or the lord chamberlain knowing the King's most gracious pleasure in the same.' In February 1534 'officers and servants waiting or attending upon his guard, the Queen or the Princess Elizabeth' were allowed to 'wear all manner such apparel as they now have' until Palm Sunday. On 27 May 1534 the license was extended until All Saints Day.[88]

A large number of proclamations were used to provide temporary emergency solutions. Even in this area there was a marked tendency to rely on statutes whenever possible.[89] This has already been illustrated in the meat price proclamations, where emergency changes in earlier statutes were incorporated in new statutes as soon as Parliament was again in session. It is also documented in the regulations attempting to control vagabonds and regulate unlicensed grain export.

A significant change occurred in the approach to the problem of poor relief and the related problem of vagabonds and beggars in the 1530s. Earlier regulations on this subject were designed primarily to control the problem and to maintain law and order. Normally, statutes and proclamations simply ordered the punishment of vagabonds and commanded that they be returned to their birthplace or previously established residence. No distinction was made between able bodied poor, who were capable of working, and the impotent poor, who through no fault of their own were dependent on the charity of the community. It was assumed that there was sufficient work for all, and that beggars and vagabonds were capable of finding productive employment. Therefore the solution to the problem lay in punitive measures which would make vagabondage so unpleasant that vagabonds would be forced into productive employment.[90] At first the legislation of the central government tended to be less

[88] *TRP* nos. 143, 146; 24 Henry VIII c. 13.

[89] Nineteen percent of the proclamations issued in 1530–9 can be classified as temporary emergency regulations. Although this percentage is not significantly higher than other periods (fourteen percent of all the proclamations issued during the early Tudor period were used for this purpose), a significant number of the changes introduced by royal proclamation were later incorporated in statutes.

[90] The change in the attitude towards vagabonds in the legislation of the 1530s has been discussed in detail by Professor Elton. See especially G. R. Elton, 'An Early Tudor Poor Law,' *EcHR*, 2nd series VI (1953), 55–67. On vagabond legislation see also Peter Ramsey, *Tudor Economic Problems* (London, 1963), 158ff.

punitive than local regulations. While Henry VII's statutes simply provided that vagabonds be placed in the stocks and expelled from town, the city of London was already punishing vagabonds by whipping and branding early in the reign of Henry VIII.[91] In June 1530, however, more severe punishments were introduced by the central government in a royal proclamation. It was still assumed that the problem was due to 'that most damnable vice of idleness' and that the solution lay in stricter enforcement of earlier laws combined with an increase in penalties. Vagabonds or 'mighty beggars' were ordered to return to their previous dwelling place within two days or they would be 'stripped naked from the privy parts of their bodies upward (men and women of great age or sick and women with child only exempt) and being so naked to be bound and sharply beaten and scourged.' After the beating they were to be given a billet informing others that they had been whipped and sent on. If they remained in the same place or stayed in any town longer than one night on their way home, they would be whipped again. Local officials were ordered to carry out the punishments 'all vain pity and other excuses laid apart.'[92]

The proclamation was issued after the first session of the Reformation Parliament had ended; therefore it could be classified as emergency legislation introduced to deal with an increasingly severe problem. Since Parliament was not in session it might have been meant to endure only until these changes could be incorporated into a new statute when Parliament reconvened on 26 April 1530. However, the second session of the Reformation Parliament did not begin until 16 January 1531, so we cannot be certain. By that time the King had a new councilor and it is probably Cromwell's policy rather than that of those who devised the 1530 proclamation which was reflected in the poor law statute that emerged from the session.[93] The new legislation was the first which distinguished between vagabonds who were able to work and those who needed to be supported by public charity. It, therefore, revealed a new attitude

[91] CLRO LB N/49–49d. In September 1517 the city government ordered that any vagabond who returned to the city after being expelled be imprisoned and 'have a hole stricken in one of his ears with a stamp made for the same and then to be banished this city forever.' Whipping was commonly ordered before 1530; see CLRO Rep. 4/215, 7/21 for examples.

[92] *TRP* no. 128.

[93] Cromwell became a member of the council in 1531, and although he was not a member of the 'inner ring' until the end of that year, he was probably 'the council's expert on Parliamentary affairs' and his influence was significant in the second session of the Reformation Parliament. Elton, *Reform and Renewal*, 92. See also Lehmberg, *Reformation Parliament*, 132.

HENRY VIII – THE FIRST STAGE

and approach not in the proclamation. Justices of the peace were commanded to search for 'aged, poor and impotent persons which ...of necessity be compelled to live by alms' and these individuals were to be registered and given licenses to beg. The statute resembled the proclamation only in that it ordered that a sturdy beggar 'be tied to the end of a cart naked and beaten with whips...till his body be bloody.'[94] When major changes were introduced in the poor laws in 1536, this was also done by statute. Throughout Cromwell's ministry proclamations were used only to order enforcement of existing statutes and did not introduce even temporary changes in penalties or procedures.[95]

An equally strong reliance on statutory legislation is documentable in the effort to control grain export. For half a century proclamations forbidding unlicensed export had been issued even though 15 Henry VI c. 2 allowed free export as long as the price of wheat was not above 6s 8d a quarter and barley above 3s a quarter. Grain export was also limited in 1531. However, the statutory prices may have been in effect, for the price of grain had risen twenty-five percent between 1530 and 1531.[96] A restraint was issued on 9 April 1531, and sometime before 29 July 1531 a proclamation probably forbade unlicensed export. On 25 August 1531 a second restraint was issued.[97]

[94] 22 Henry VIII c. 12.
[95] A draft proposal prepared by Cromwell's staff (probably in 1534) contained an elaborate scheme for dealing with both impotent and sturdy beggars in an entirely new way. It included a proposal for an additional use of delegated legislation. Vagabonds were to be provided employment in a series of public works projects which would be supervised by a special council empowered to regulate the public works as well as the administration of relief to the impotent poor and to punish those who offended its order. 'What was exceptional were that this council's orders were to be proclaimed in like manner as proclamations made by the King and privy council.' Elton, *EcHR*, VI, 58. The draft never became law, but 27 Henry VIII c. 25 contained a similar philosophy. Although the provisions providing employment for sturdy beggars were not included, local officials were ordered to find work for them. Alms were to be collected and distributed by parishes for the impotent poor. The royal proclamations were *TRP* no. 131 which ordered vagabonds to leave London and to return to their homes in obedience to 22 Henry VIII c. 12, no. 138 which ordered enforcement of the statutes 'provided for idle beggars and vagabonds' and no. 141 which, after citing 22 Henry VIII c. 12, ordered vagabonds to leave the court. Hughes and Larkin base their text of this proclamation on a copy in the Public Record Office which does not include the preamble citing 22 Henry VIII c. 12, but a fuller copy in the British Museum includes a reference to that statute. BM Add. 9835/1.
[96] Alan Everitt, 'The Marketing of Agricultural Produce,' *Agrarian History*, IV, 487.
[97] This can be documented from a number of obligations entered into by exporters to convey grain to Calais. They mention restraints on 9 April 1531 and 24 August 1531. In addition there must have been a proclamation between the two restraints, for an obligation dated 29 July 1531 speaks of grain shipped 'after the foresaid restraint, but not after the King's letter of proclamation.' SP 1/66/193–4 (*LP* 5 no. 356); see also SP1/67/2–7 (*LP* 5 no. 381).

These efforts must not have been sufficient, because on 7 September 1531 a second proclamation complained of 'scarcity and excessive dearth of corn and other victuals' brought about by a bad harvest caused 'by unseasonable weather' and the continuing export of grain despite the King's commandments to the contrary. It spoke of the need for 'dreadful penalties' to deter violators and prohibited all export of victuals without making exceptions for Calais or for individuals who held licenses. It also sought to provide for effective enforcement by warning that if victuals above the value of 40s were found on any ship which had not been first reported to port officials they would be forfeited even if they were not being conveyed out of the realm. Port officials were ordered to seize all victuals being conveyed contrary to the proclamation 'and signify unto the Exchequer the names of such persons as they shall know to offend in the same.' Anyone who reported negligence on the part of port officials to the 'Lord Treasurer and other of the King's council' would receive half the value of the goods conveyed from the guilty port officials. Shippers were allowed to convey victuals to Wales and other English counties but they must first enter into an obligation of double value of the victuals and bring back a certificate proving they had delivered the victuals in England or Wales.[98]

The sweeping prohibitions caused some difficulties for Calais. Upon petition from the council certain exceptions were made for the victualling of Calais. Correspondence between Lord Lisle, who became deputy at Calais in March 1533, and Cromwell indicates that the problem of victualling the city remained an issue throughout 1533. Consequently, it is likely that the proclamation was in effect until Parliament met on 15 January 1534 or that new restraints were imposed.[99] That Parliament enacted 25 Henry VIII c. 2, which introduced a new approach to the export legislation by demanding

[98] *TRP* no. 134.
[99] Victuals were being exported to Calais and then being transported to France or other foreign countries. This was the reason there was no exception for Calais in the proclamation. The council at Calais petitioned for a change and the King, who seemingly blamed the Calais government for allowing export from the city, responded out of concern for the citizens of the town 'who being without default or blame of the abuse of the said liberties do suffer...for the offense of the heads and rulers.' SP 1/73/33 (*LP* 5 no. 1702). Even after the King's action Calais still did not have adequate grain. Lisle wrote to Cromwell in December 1533 complaining that very little of the grain supposedly shipped from England to Calais had actually arrived, and he suggested that the customers' books be searched. SP 1/82/3 (*LP* 7 no. 4). In January 1534, Lisle wrote again and warned that food was so short in Calais that if a war broke out, they would be in serious difficulty unless 'the council will set the restraint free and that this town may be victualed in general from all parts of the realm as we have been in time past.' SP 1/82/40 (*LP* 7 no. 5).

a license for the export of a long list of food items, including grain. This marked the end of the confusing practice of relying on price levels in the medieval statutes or the more questionable procedure of using royal proclamations to prohibit unlicensed export in violation of those statutes. Although the final statute was not the government's original bill,[100] the policy of using a statute in place of what was formerly done by royal proclamations in a piecemeal fashion is too much in conformity with Cromwell's other actions to have originated from any other source. In the next Parliament a new act, which was clearly the result of government initiative, completed the process of providing Parliamentary authority to give the crown freedom of action to regulate trade. The new statute, 26 Henry VIII c. 10, gave Henry VIII the right to repeal 'in part or in the whole' all acts made since the beginning of that Parliament 'for the restraint or let of any commodities of this realm.' As a result the Crown could both control food export by the issuing of licenses, and act in emergency situations to revise or repeal Parliamentary legislation.

There were, of course, times when it was necessary to use royal proclamations to deal with emergency situations without statutory authority. At least two proclamations containing regulations designed to supply the market with grain were issued in the 1530s. Cromwell had received advice in December 1532 and January 1533 that a search for grain was needed,[101] but there is no evidence that he responded. In 1532 he seems unsuccessfully to have sought a statute to deal with the problem. In November of 1534 he used a royal proclamation.[102] The preamble complained that the high prices of grain were caused by people who had 'plenty of their own growth,' but were still buying grain in order 'to make a dearth thereof.' Because 'there is no just ground or cause why such grain should be so high enhanced in price,' the proclamation ordered that no one was to buy wheat or rye for resale except for the supply of London and other cities, or for baking bread and the provision of the fleet. Those having sufficient grain for seed and for their household were not to buy more. Producers seeking to buy grain for seed had to prove before the commissioners that they needed it or to bring an equal

---

[100] The original bill probably introduced by the government was replaced in Parliament 'and it was this seemingly unofficial replacement which became law.' Elton, *Reform and Renewal*, 11.
[101] SP 1/72/165 (*LP* 5 no. 1650); SP 1/74/62 (*LP* 6 no. 51).
[102] *TRP* no. 151. Professor Elton calls it 'a temporary emergency measure for which statute would have been quite unsuitable,' but he maintains 'even so, Cromwell had in 1532 characteristically tried for a more lasting arrangement by means of a bill which had achieved two readings in the Commons.' Elton, *Reform and Renewal*, 164.

quantity of grain to market within eight days. Violators were threatened with fine and imprisonment at the King's pleasure. In addition the proclamation forbade the regrating or engrossing of grain 'upon pain of imprisonment and forfeiture of all their goods and chattels.' Subjects having a surplus were ordered to bring the grain to market 'by the order of the commissioners assigned for the same and there sell at reasonable prices' upon pain of imprisonment and fine. Local officials were ordered to insure that the proclamation was carried out and to report offenders to the commissioners or to the chancellor and the council.

The severity of the penalty for regrating and engrossing suggests that the situation was serious. The proclamation may even have been issued in response to local petitions for action. Although no petition survives, we know that shortly after the proclamation was issued Cromwell received a request from the Gloucester city government asking that the commissions directed to the county 'for the due search and view of corn' also be directed to the city.[103] A similar proclamation was probably issued in the autumn of 1535 on the advice of Audley who in September wrote from Essex that there had been a sudden increase in the price of grain even though it was commonly believed that there was a sufficient supply. He had therefore made proclamations in Essex and established commissions to search out corn. But he hesitated 'to make proclamations and commissions in other shires till the King's pleasure were therein known.' He advised Cromwell that quick action be taken. A proclamation must have been issued shortly thereafter, because on 30 September Audley sent Cromwell writs for the 'proclamation for corn.'[104]

Royal proclamations were also used to suspend statutes in emergency situations without specific statutory authority. A series of them suspended an act on wool cloth manufacture for periods that extended over five years. Although statutes were not normally suspended by proclamations during the 1530s unless there was Parliamentary authority for the action, the wool cloth legislation was probably suspended at least seven times during these five years. Because the use of proclamations in this matter seems at first glance somewhat in contradiction to the normal policy, it is necessary to tell the entire story if one is to understand why proclamations were used. The final act on this question was not enacted until 1542, for which

---

[103] The city officials were concerned that since the city was separate from the county, the writs addressed to the county would not apply to them. SP 1/87/26 (*LP* 7 no. 1417).

[104] BM Titus B ix/430 (*LP* 9 no. 358); SP 1/87/68 (*LP* 9 no. 487).

reason the chronological limits of this chapter will again be extended so that the story can be told in full.

Legislation attempting to set a standard size for various cloths and to prohibit the use of faulty materials and processes was common in the Middle Ages and the early Tudor period. Seemingly, these earlier statutes were not being enforced, because in November 1534 a royal proclamation ordered that the statutes were to be observed and added new threats against enforcement officials to stimulate them to be more diligent in enforcing the acts.[105] Although the government was concerned about enforcing standards, it does not seem to have intended to introduce new regulations. We do not know how well the effort to enforce fared, but seemingly the mercantile interests were not satisfied with the regulations. In the last session of the Reformation Parliament a bill was introduced which was probably the result of merchant concerns about the quality of cloth they were exporting. As was not unusual with statutes resulting from this type of vested interest, the formulators did not take into account the difficulty of applying the new standards included in the act.[106] The preamble complained of the 'great infamy and slander' that 'had arisen of late years in sundry outward parts beyond the sea of the untrue making of woolen cloths within this realm.' In order to assure a uniform and just standard the statute ordered that after Michaelmas clothiers were to weave 'his or their several token or mark' in their cloths and 'set his seal of lead unto every of the same' with the true length. Broad cloths were to be seven quarters in breadth instead of the previously acceptable width of two yards, while kerseys were to be one yard in breadth.[107] A change in the standard width of woolen cloth involved a major adjustment by the weavers which could not be accomplished in the few months allotted in the statute; therefore, it proved necessary to suspend the statute before it went into effect. On 5 October 1536 it was suspended for a year, because the cloth makers had not had sufficient time to acquire the 'looms, stays, and other instruments convenient for making of the same cloth.' However, they were ordered to equip themselves properly for complying with the statutory measurements during the period of the suspension.[108] The tone of the proclamation was conciliatory. It recognized

---

[105] *TRP* no. 152. See footnote to this proclamation for list of statutes.
[106] The statute was definitely not a government measure. In 1514, when the council was involved in determining whether or not the statute needed to be revised or repealed, it called upon 'Sir Richard Gresham knight and such others as were noted to be the setters forth of the said act' to defend the statute. Nicolas, VII, 154; see also Elton, *Reform and Renewal*, 110.   [107] 27 Henry VIII c. 12.   [108] *TRP* no. 166.

the impossibility of a quick conversion. Parliament was not in session at the time; and, therefore, a royal proclamation was the proper instrument for this type of emergency action.

However, the problem posed for the weavers must have been more severe than the government anticipated. A month before the statute was due to take effect, Robert Holdich, an ulnager from East Anglia, informed Cromwell in a letter that although he had warned the cloth manufacturers that the suspension would soon end, 'as far as I can hear and learn little or nothing as yet is done by the most part of them to the very due reformation thereof.' The letter concluded by asking Cromwell's advice on what action he should take if the clothiers did not comply.[109] A week before the suspension was to expire Cromwell received a letter from Audley informing him that 'divers' of the cloth makers had come to him 'declaring unto me that in case they shall be compelled to make cloths from Michaelmas forthwith according to the King's act' they would be forced out of business, for it was impossible 'to keep the breadth of the cloth limited by the act.' The weavers further argued that because they were poor it was difficult for them to acquire the looms necessary to weave cloth according to the measurements in the act. Audley reported that he had pointed out to them that the King had suspended the statute for a long time so that they could make the adjustment. He 'marveled much that they had been so negligent,' and stated that he did not think the King would delay the execution of the statute any longer. They responded that they could 'by no possible means make cloths according to the act' and they 'lamented very sorely saying they would leave their occupations.' Audley then warned them that if they left clothmaking and this resulted in the growth of sedition because of a lack of work 'then it would be laid to their charge to their perils and utter undoings.' They still answered 'they would do that which lay in their possible powers but more they could not' and pleaded with Audley to ask the King to suspend the act again. Although Audley reported to Cromwell that he told them he could not promise to do this, he nevertheless advised Cromwell to 'move the King's majesty hereof to the intent his grace's pleasure may be known whether his highness of his goodness will yet suspend the act for one year.' He ended by reminding Cromwell that swift action was necessary since 'Michaelmas is the last day of the old proclamation for this matter.'[110]

[109] SP 1/124/135-6 (*LP* 12[2] no. 605).
[110] BM Titus B v/187 (*LP* 12[2] no. 1737).

If we can believe Audley, he had made every effort to get the clothiers to comply with the act. But they still refused, either because they were very stubborn or (more likely) because they were telling the truth. They simply could not make the adjustment economically. Whatever the explanation, the government was faced with an impossible situation. Obviously the first suspension had been intended as a temporary one, but unless he was willing to risk mass unrest Cromwell had no choice but to take Audley's advice. One day before the suspension ended it was continued for another year. But whereas the first proclamation had recognized the necessity of the action and was very mild in tone, the second questioned seriously whether the clothmakers had really done all in their power to comply with the statute. It stated that the action was being taken because, despite the previous proclamation which the King had issued 'at the humble suit of the...clothmakers' in order to give them time to equip themselves to conform with the statute, clothmakers were still complaining that the weavers had not acquired the necessary looms. Consequently, they maintained they could not observe the statute. The King therefore was suspending it again so that the council could investigate the matter in order 'to determine and resolve his grace's pleasure for the due execution and observation of the same act, accordingly as for the advancement of the commonwealth of this realm shall be thought expedient.' The King had responded in a generous fashion, probably because he had no other choice, but a note of sarcasm and suspicion was included in the proclamation:

> The King's most royal majesty, not a little marveling at the negligence and defaults of the said subjects in this behalf, considering that they have had long time as well for provision for due execution of the said act as to prove the impossibility of observation of the same (if any such be) as they have alleged; and yet nevertheless, minding that the complaints and suggestions of his said subjects shall be duly and indifferently examined before the proceeding to the straight execution of the said act to their trouble and molestation...[111]

The major difficulty in complying with the statute seems to have been that it was all inclusive and demanded that even the makers of rough kerseys for foreign export conform to the set standard. These inexpensive kerseys were made from coarse wool on looms of varying size and could not be manufactured to conform to the standard without a major readjustment. The kersey makers, therefore, continued to try every available avenue to obtain a revision of the

[111] *TRP* no. 175.

regulations. The suspension expired on 29 September 1538, and the act may have gone into effect for a few months. Parliament met in April 1539 and the weavers of Suffolk and Essex prepared a bill repealing the 1536 act. In addition, they petitioned Cromwell for his aid. Their petition reads as though the act were in effect. The weavers complained that the clothiers had their own looms and their own weavers and that they were demanding that cloth from private weavers 'keep the full rate and size' although they were paying a set price for the cloth which did not take into consideration the added expense involved. The petition concluded by requesting Cromwell's aid in furthering their bill in Parliament. We do not know Cromwell's reaction, but the bill failed in the Commons, and unless there was another suspension the statute remained in effect.[112]

The kersey makers did not give up the struggle despite their defeat in Parliament. In March 1541 they petitioned the council that the statute 'might be dissolved or at the least the execution of the same deferred.' The council responded by agreeing that 'the execution of the said statute should be prorogued for a time.' Also, it ordered the clothiers to appear before the council in Easter term 'to say what they could why their suit should be further granted.' If their arguments were convincing, the statute would 'be annulled and they to occupy as they do at this point.' However, 'Sir Richard Gresham, knight, and such others as were noted to be the setters forth of the said act' were also to appear to defend the act. If the kersey makers' case was not as convincing as that of their opponents, they were to be given until 24 August 'to prepare all things necessary for them for the observation of the said statute.' Two days after the council recorded this decision, a royal proclamation mentioning the petition of the kersey makers suspended the statute until 24 June 1541.[113] On 20 May 1541 the kersey makers of Berkshire and 'certain merchant adventurers' appeared before the council. The council ordered that a test be carried out to measure the length and breadth of kerseys 'both dry and wet... to the intent they might know whether it were meet to mitigate the act concerning the length and breadth of kerseys or to suffer the same to continue in full force.' The clerk

[112] SP 1/151/128–31 (*LP* 14[1] no. 874); Elton, *Reform and Renewal*, 79, suggests the act may have been suspended again until 24 June 1539 by a now lost proclamation. This assumption is based on dating a petition from the kersey makers to the council in 1539 since that petition refers to a suspension until 24 June. I prefer a later dating for reasons discussed below (footnote no. 115). It does, however, seem likely that the statute was suspended again because the council's responses to the kersey makers' petition in 1541 reads as though the statute was not in effect. Nicholas, VII, 158.

[113] *TRP* no. 198; Nicolas, VII, 156 (*LP* 16 no. 625).

did not record the council's opinion, but it was reported that the matter was to be referred to the King. Since the previous suspension had almost expired, and probably also because the kersey makers had presented a good case, another proclamation was issued on 1 June 1541 which suspended the statute until Christmas. By the time the suspension ended, the Parliament of 1542 was about to assemble; so the statute was again suspended until 24 June 1542, probably to give Parliament enough time to act on the issue.[114] It is likely that shortly after Parliament began to meet on 16 January the kersey makers again petitioned the council requesting that Parliament debate the question and 'after relation thereof made to his highness what they shall think most convenient for the commonwealth of this realm in the premises that then it may please his majesty to take such order therein' as the King and council thought 'most expedient.'[115] Persistence finally had its reward when Parliament enacted 33 Henry VIII c. 18. The preamble to the new act mentioned the test, described in the council records, which had proved that kerseys made of coarse wool 'cannot be so certainly wrought as the same should and might keep any true or just certain length or breadth when it shall come to the water.' Therefore the act allowed coarse kerseys to be made of the same measurements used before the passage of 27 Henry VIII c. 12, although it confirmed the regulations in the act dealing with other cloths.

Thus the long struggle ended with what seems to be a justified victory for both the kersey makers and common sense, probably to the great relief of the government. A complex series of events was brought about by a carelessly drafted statute not of government origin. Because the matter was further complicated by a struggle between vested interests, it had necessitated the use of a series of proclamations. Throughout that five-year period the government had acted in an admirable way to deal with a situation not of its own making. Audley's and Holdich's letters reveal that efforts were initially made to obtain compliance with the statute, and that a second suspension was ordered only after information was received indicating this was not possible. The petitions of the kersey makers were given serious attention and the framers of the statute were allowed to present their arguments before the council. The council

[114] *TRP* nos. 202, 207; Nicholas, VII, 192 (*LP* 16 no. 842).
[115] St Ch 2/23/115. The petition is undated, but 1542 seems more likely than the 1539 date suggested by Professor Elton. The petition specifically mentioned that Parliament was in session, and that the act had been suspended until 24 June 'for divers and sundry considerations declared and proved before your honorable lordships.' This seems to be a reference to the test held in May 1541 and proclamation no. 207, which suspended the statute until 24 June 1542.

even ordered an experiment to test the truth of the kersey makers' arguments. Only after all the evidence had been considered was more permanent action taken in the form of a new statute. The whole tale reveals a remarkable responsiveness to the needs and complaints of various groups and an intelligent and necessary use of the proclaiming power. Once again the use of royal proclamations in this matter establishes that they were essential instruments for the orderly administration of the commonwealth. Despite the fact that they were used to suspend a statute temporarily over a relatively long period of time without statutory authority, that action was surely a justifiable and necessary use of the prerogative.

Royal proclamations not only suspended statutes, but they were also used to dispense from statutes and established customs. At least two proclamations were issued in the 1530s which gave subjects a general license to eat white meat in Lent. One of these, dated 11 March 1538, has survived. It is especially interesting because it gave a legal justification for the action and defended the use of proclamations to dispense with laws which might temporarily be detrimental to the realm. Abstinence from white meats during Lent was called 'a mere positive law of the church, and used by a custom within this realm, and of none other sort or necessity.' Therefore, 'the same may be upon good considerations and grounds altered and dispensed with from time to time by the public authority of kings and princes whensoever they shall perceive the same to tend to the hurt and damage of their people.'[116]

Another group of proclamations dispensed from or at least suspended the enforcement of statutes which had been ignored for some time. The tale is both complex and revealing and deserves telling in some detail. It involved four proclamations regulating exchanges issued in a thirteen-month period in 1537 and 1538.[117] The effort to control exchanges was closely connected with the serious concern about preventing the export of coin and bullion. There had been a good deal of statutory legislation on this subject, and this may explain why the statute book had to be searched when Cromwell in 1531 sought advice on how he might prevent the export of coin.[118]

[116] *TRP* no. 177. The other proclamation was issued in 1537 SP 1/117/158 (*LP* 12[1] no. 755); Appendix B item 22.
[117] Elton, *Reform and Renewal*, 117–20, discusses this legislation. What follows is based on this account; however, it has some additions and a slightly different emphasis.
[118] 5 Richard II st. 1 c. 2 forbade unlicensed export upon penalty of forfeiture of the sum carried. 17 Edward IV c. 1 made unlicensed export of gold and silver a felony for twenty years. This was revived by 4 Henry VII c. 23. That statute was revised in Henry VIII's first Parliament by 1 Henry VIII c. 13, which lowered the penalty to forfeiture of double

Although a series of medieval statutes had also forbidden unlicensed exchanges, neither the statutes forbidding export nor those forbidding unlicensed exchanges seem to have been seriously enforced. In July 1531 a proclamation based on 5 Richard II st. 1 c. 2 forbade all export of gold and silver. This also seems to have included the transfer of money by letters of exchange. But despite the wording of the proclamation, exchanges seem to have remained relatively free. Certainly, licensed exchange through the office of the keeper of exchanges continued.[119] New action must have been contemplated in 1535. In March of that year Stephen Vaughan wrote to Cromwell from Antwerp, informing him of foreign concerns about new restrictions on exchanges: 'The strangers speak much of an act made in England against exchanges, how and upon what considerations made I cannot tell but it so worketh with them that they say we will bring the world against us.' The following year legislation was introduced into Parliament, but it failed to pass the Lords after having been accepted by the Commons. The bill probably would have altered earlier legislation by ending all exchanges.[120] Having failed in the effort, the government in July 1537 turned to a royal proclamation which simply ordered compliance with the earlier statutes 'upon pain contained in the said several statutes, and also to incur into the displeasure and indignation of the King's said highness.'[121]

The effort to apply the medieval statutes was immediately greeted with a protest. John Hutton, Governor of the Merchant Adventurers in Antwerp, wrote letters on 6 August and 12 August warning of the dangers to trade which would result from restricting exchanges. He

the value of the gold or silver exported. The statute was to endure to the next Parliament. It was renewed by 3 Henry VIII c. 1 until the following Parliament. This statute was not renewed; consequently in 1531, when the statute books were searched, all the expired statutes had to be read carefully until a statute could be found that was still in effect upon which to base a proclamation.

[119] *TRP* no. 133. The proclamation was more limiting than the act of 5 Richard II c. 2 which only forbade unlicensed exports.

[120] SP 1/91/98–9 (*LP* 8 no. 392). Elton, *Reform and Renewal*, 118.

[121] *TRP* no. 173. Professor Elton argues that 'Cromwell's first turning to Parliament' in an area where 'all law and precedent authorized action by proclamation' was 'a strikingly unusual bit of constitutionalism.' But he maintains that this is an example of Cromwell resorting 'to a proclamation because he had failed to get an Act of Parliament.' Elton, *Reform and Renewal*, 164. Since the proclamation did little more than order compliance with earlier statutes, and the Parliamentary bill may have forbidden all exchanges, this is not really an example of using proclamations to introduce something that Parliament refused to grant. Rather it seems that since new regulations could not be obtained from Parliament, Cromwell was hesitant to introduce them on the authority of the prerogative alone; therefore he was content simply to order application of the previous statutes.

maintained that not only would the cloth trade be disrupted, but the legislation would have the opposite effect than was intended: 'great sums of coin shall by reason thereof be conveyed out of the realm for there is not laded the tenth part in merchandise for all such commodities as cometh out of France for the rest must be either made over by exchange or conveyed over in money.'[122] There must have been a series of other protests, because on 13 August 1537 a proclamation, issued 'at the humble petitions of divers and sundry merchants,' allowed them until 30 October 1537 to 'use their exchange and rechange as they did and used before his said proclamation' as long as they reported the sums exchanged before the council in Star Chamber. It further promised 'a final order and determination' after the council had investigated the question in more detail.[123] The government again found itself caught between two vested interests. By responding to the merchants' plea for free exchanges the profits of the office of the keeper of exchanges were affected. In December Audley, one of the keepers, wrote to Cromwell sending him a bill which he had presented to the King on the question of exchanges. He urged Cromwell 'to take some pain therein' because he felt 'the merchants will no way by their wills but to have their liberal exchanges without licenses.'[124]

The prohibitions on unlicensed exchange must have taken effect again in November 1537, because in July 1538 Cromwell received a new complaint. Richard Gresham wrote urging him 'shortly to make a proclamation that all outward merchants as well subjects as all other may continue their exchanges and rechanges frankly and freely as they have hitherto done.' He warned that unless this were done the clothmakers would be left with a great deal of cloth and merchants going to Bordeaux for wines would convey gold overseas. He stated that 'merchants can no more be without exchanges and rechanges than the ships in the sea to be without water.'[125] The argument had some impact because on 30 July free exchange was again allowed until November. 'Final order and determination concerning the said exchanges' was promised before that date.[126] But

[122] SP 1/124/24–9 (*LP* 12[2] no. 509); SP 1/123/240 (*LP* 12[2] no.464). Hutton argued that buyers of merchandise coming from France used letters of exchange to charge themselves to repay with money that they made from sales abroad. Thereby they did not have to export coin to pay for their purchases.
[123] CLRO Journals 14/41; Appendix A no. 174.5. Professor Elton was not aware of this proclamation; consequently he assumes that the prohibitions on exchanges remained in effect for a year.
[124] BM Cleo E IV/225d (*LP* 12[2] no. 1159).
[125] BM Otho E x/45 (*LP* 13[1] no. 1433).   [126] *TRP* no. 181.

Gresham was not satisfied. On 2 August he wrote again stating that Audley had sent him the proclamation, but, he argued, this was 'a very short time' because merchants traveling to Spain and France 'and to diverse other places so that it will be Christmas and after for the rechanges should return so that the said merchants shall be always in such fear as they were before.' He then requested that 'a proclamation may be made that it may endure unto such time' as Parliament could act on the question.[127] Gresham seems to have convinced Cromwell. On 6 August merchants were allowed free exchanges 'as they have done heretofore in times past without any exaction, loss, damage or penalty for the same, any act or statute to the contrary thereof notwithstanding, and that this present proclamation shall be sufficient warrant and discharge to them and every of them against his highness in this behalf.'[128]

This seems to have concluded the exchange manipulations until the reign of Edward VI when another effort was made to apply the earlier legislation. The four proclamations issued in the two-year period had first ordered enforcement of earlier legislation and then issued a temporary and finally an unlimited dispensation from those statutes. The dispensation was justified by the argument that the King was only giving up his own profit: 'Albeit the King's most royal majesty might justly and rightfully prove and take great advantage and profit by reason of exchanges and rechanges...by the express terms and words contained in divers and sundry statutes.' Furthermore it was pointed out that these statutes had 'not been commonly put in use for changes and rechanges on this side the mountains,' so that the action was only legalizing previous practice.[129] The whole process again documents an unwillingness to use the prerogative to introduce permanent new regulations and a responsiveness to the needs and requests of individuals affected by the legislation. The sweeping prohibitions of the 1531 proclamation must have been intended as a temporary measure. When more permanent legislation was sought, a bill was introduced in Parliament. The bill failed, and therefore a proclamation was issued the following year which went no further than to order observance of the statutes. When evidence was presented that the enforcement of this legislation would be harmful to merchant interests and to the commonwealth, royal proclamations were twice used to delay action until the council could carefully consider the issues. Only when Gresham presented

[127] SP 1/135/7–8 (*LP* 13[2] no. 13).
[128] *TRP* no. 182.   [129] *Ibid.*

compelling arguments that this type of temporary solution only created greater confusion was more permanent action taken and then probably only until Parliament could act as Gresham had suggested. But the 1539 and 1540 Parliaments had more pressing issues to consider. That may explain why no action was taken. The effort to regulate exchanges had failed,[130] but at least one important change had been brought about by the use of royal proclamations. What had once been allowed by simply ignoring the restrictions in the medieval statute, a method that could lead to disrespect for statutory prohibitions, was now made legal by a general dispensation. In this case royal proclamations again performed a necessary and useful function. Rather than compete with Parliamentary legislation, they in fact tended to reinforce respect for statute even when they were used to dispense from statutes.

Royal proclamations also served a useful function in the English Reformation. Although it is clear that the government did not rely on them for the major legislation of the English Reformation, they served to publicize and to order enforcement of statutes. At times new regulations were also introduced by this method. The first three proclamations dealing with religion in the 1530s do not belong to the period of Cromwell's ministry. The first was probably issued early in 1530 and may represent Sir Thomas More's policy. In an effort to stem the tide of Protestant influence in England, the medieval heresy laws were revived and applied. The lengthy document referred to the 'many devout laws, statutes and ordinances for the maintenance and defense' of the Christian faith 'against the malicious and wicked sects of heretics' and maintained that heresy was again entering England as the result of an influx of 'blasphemous books lately made and privately sent into this realm by the disciples, fautours and adherents of the said Martin Luther and other heretics.' It then summarized portions of the medieval heresy statutes. In conformity with those statutes it forbade preaching, teaching, writing books, or holding assemblies 'in any manner of wise contrary to the Catholic faith or diminution of the Holy Church.' It also forbade unlicensed preaching and ordered that heretical books be delivered to the bishop of the diocese within fifteen days. The enforcement clauses of the earlier statutes were repeated almost verbatim and the penalties threatened were those in the statutes. Only the concluding section of

[130] Elton, *Reform and Renewal*, 120, argues that the failure was beneficial to trade. 'It is arguable that by freeing the exchanges Cromwell did more for the export trade than by all the legislation designed to encourage it directly.'

the proclamation, which specifically listed fifteen prohibited books including works by Roy, Bullinger and Tyndale, was new in that it specifically applied the statutes to current problems.[131] Nevertheless, a 'policy of repression'[132] was introduced which was extended by a second proclamation on 22 June 1530.

The new proclamation, made with the advice of the clergy, added books by Tyndale, Fish and Firth to the earlier list and repeated orders to deliver the books within fifteen days. The last half of it concentrated on English translations of the Bible. Although it promised a new translation 'by great learned and Catholic persons' it ordered that all existing translations be turned in and that no one was to 'buy, receive, keep or have' an English, French or Dutch Bible except those appointed 'for the correction or amending of the said translation.' It included an order that no one was to print any English books 'concerning Holy Scripture' not previously printed in the realm until the book had been 'examined and approved by the ordinary of the diocese' and the printer had noted the examiner's name and his own on the book. Although the proclamation was largely based on medieval statutes, it did introduce new regulations on printing by 'establishing the first licensing system under secular authority.'[133]

The third proclamation attempted to protect Parliamentary legislation against papal interference. It referred to 'divers and sundry acts for the good order and reformation of divers abuses by the clergy' and warned that as a result 'ways and means' might 'be sought from the court of Rome' to hamper operation of those laws. The King, therefore, commanded that no one was to purchase, use or publish any bulls from Rome or elsewhere which were 'prejudicial to the high authority jurisdiction and prerogative royal of this his realm' or hindered the reformation of abuses in the English church.[134]

[131] *TRP* no. 122. The proclamation is misdated 'before 6 March 1529.' It should be dated before 6 May 1530. Elton, *Policy and Police*, 218 n. 5. The medieval statutes cited were 2 Henry IV c. 15 and 2 Henry V st. 1 c. 7. The proclamation repeated almost verbatim some of the clauses of these statutes which were of course directed against Lollardy. It even included sections which specifically mentioned the Lollards: 'to make utterly to cease, and destroy all manner of heresies and errors commonly called Lollardies.'

[132] Elton, *Policy and Police*, 219 comments 'This proclamation created the nearest thing, the Elizabethan and early-Stuart High Commission possibly apart, to an Inquisition that England was ever to know.'

[133] *TRP* no. 129. Frederick S. Siebert, *Freedom of the Press in England 1476–1776* (Urbana, 1965), 46. Siebert maintains that control of the press had previously been under ecclesiastical authority, but the crown gradually, 'almost imperceptibly assumed control over the press during the sixteenth century.' *Ibid.* 22.

[134] *TRP* no. 130.

The first proclamation that can be attributed to Cromwell's ministry was issued in July 1533. It announced that Henry's first marriage had been declared invalid and that Anne Boleyn had been crowned queen. Catherine should therefore no longer be styled Queen but rather Princess Dowager. Subjects who 'attempt or procure any manner process or do or move any act or acts to the let or derogation of any such proceeding, sentences and determinations, as is and have been done' concerning the annullment of the first marriage or the new marriage, or who continued to obey or address Catherine as Queen, were warned that they were in danger of the penalties of the Statute of Praemunire. The proclamation stated that it was 'made for a plain overture and publication of the premises, whereby as well all and every his loving subjects, as others, may (if they will) avoid and eschew the said great pains, dangers and penalties above specified.'[135]

The first proclamation to cite specifically the King's authority as supreme head of the church appeared in February 1535. It resulted from a dispute between the citizens and clergy of London over tithes. The question had long been a troublesome one. In May of 1533 the Court of Aldermen appointed a committee to bring the matter to the attention of the King's council for arbitration.[136] A committee of the King's council, including Cranmer, Audley and Cromwell, took up the matter. Before they rendered a decision they requested 'that the citizens should assemble in their several wards and there to treat whether they would be contented to abide their order and final determination.' The citizens agreed that 'whatsoever they shall do in the same the citizens shall be very well contented to perform the same.'[137] On 2 April 1534 a letters patent was issued to the officers of the city of London announcing a temporary solution. However, this was not intended as a final solution, because the officials were told to inform the citizens that paying the stated sums at Easter would not prejudice the 'definitive arbitration' which would be decided after Easter. The citizens of London agreed to pay this sum but they were clearly not satisfied and appealed the matter to Parliament.[138] The matter was still at variance the following February when the King issued a proclamation which stated that although the citizens of London had submitted the dispute to the conciliar committee and

[135] *TRP* no. 140. The statute was 16 Richard II c. 5.
[136] CLRO Rep. 8/275d. See Reginald Sharpe, *London and the Kingdom* (London, 1894), 383–4 for the previous history of the dispute.
[137] CLRO Journals 13/394, 400.
[138] CLRO Journals 13/404; the letters patent is included in *TRP* as no. 145.

HENRY VIII – THE FIRST STAGE

agreed to abide by its decision, they were refusing to do so. Subjects in other parts of the realm also 'grudged and murmured to pay their tithes.' Consequently, the King 'being the supreme head in earth under God of the Church of England' ordered them to pay at the rates decided, upon pain of imprisonment and fine at the King's pleasure. Subjects in other parts of the realm were to pay the amounts they had customarily paid. The proclamation was followed by a statute which ordered the citizens of London to pay tithes as set 'by the order of my lord chancellor and other of the King's most honorable council (and the King's proclamation)... until such time as any other order or law shall be made.' The Mayor of London was commanded to imprison those refusing to pay until they paid.[139]

The tithes matter involved an effort to enforce an administrative decision which had resulted from a request for arbitration, and the proclamation was followed by a statute ordering obedience to it. A second proclamation, also based on the King's authority as supreme head, was more questionable. It was issued in March 1535 and ordered that foreign Anabaptists 'as well such as have recanted and revoked their heresies as all other that have or do hold or teach those or any other erroneous opinions or heresies against God and his Holy Scripture' depart the realm within twelve days 'on pain to suffer death, if they, contrary to this proclamation, do abide and be apprehended or taken.' Local and ecclesiastical officials were to apprehend those who continued to believe or teach these heresies 'to the intent the offenders may receive due punishment and pains of death from time to time as the case shall require, according to their merits.' The proclamation actually added to the penalty for heresy. Even though it applied only to foreign Anabaptists, it decreed the death penalty even for heretics who had recanted. Although this was probably alleviated by the stipulation that local officials could apply the penalty 'from time to time as the case shall require,' it nevertheless was an unusually severe penalty.[140]

---

[139] *TRP* no. 153; 27 Henry VIII c. 21. This did not settle the dispute which continued until 1545 when 37 Henry VIII c. 12, after reciting the whole history of the matter, reported that the clergy and citizens had agreed to submit the final decision to a committee headed by Cranmer. The statute ordered that the decision of the committee was to be enrolled in chancery, and it was to be considered as valid as an act of Parliament. Anyone refusing to pay was to be imprisoned by the mayor of London or the chancellor until he paid. See SP 1/105/213–15 (*LP* 11 no. 204); SP 1/160/119–23 (*LP* 15 no. 722); 23 Henry VIII c. 7; CLRO Journals 15/18 for further information on the dispute.

[140] *TRP* no. 155. The death penalty for heretics who refused to abjure or relapsed after abjuration was stated in 2 Henry IV c. 15. This statute was repealed in 1534 and replaced

Another proclamation in January 1536 was directed primarily against a sermon by John Fisher. It ordered that anyone having a book containing the sermon or any book or writing which contained 'any error or slander to the King's majesty or to the derogation or diminution of his imperial crown,' deliver them to the chancellor or Cromwell within forty days upon penalty of the 'perils and dangers of his laws and statutes provided for the same' which the King intended to apply 'without pity or mercy to them to be given by his majesty in any behalf.' The second section of the proclamation attacked those who sold pardons and indulgences. The publication or selling of any papal pardon or indulgence was forbidden 'upon the pains comprised in his laws in that case provided.' The proclamation then applied the existing vagabond legislation to the punishment of 'pardoners.' If any persons went 'vagrant in any part of the realm, as pardoners, taking upon them anywhere to publish such indulgences and pardons' they were to be treated as vagabonds and be 'whipped, according to the act provided for valiant beggars and vagabonds.'[141] Another proclamation in October 1536, connected with the Lincolnshire rebellion, attempted to stop the spread of rumors and gathering of unlawful assemblies more by its threatening language than by any specific new penalties. Subjects were ordered to apprehend rumor spreaders and those who encouraged unlawful assemblies and to imprison them until the King's pleasure 'shall be further known therein.' Subjects were also ordered not 'to stir, move, or attempt any routs, riots or unlawful assemblies or enterprise any gatherings of our people together without our special license and commandment thereunto had.' If they had gathered in unlawful assemblies they were to return home to 'employ themselves about their lawful business without further enterprise or attempt.' If, after hearing the proclamation, they refused to disperse, the King warned them that he would withdraw his mercy and 'proceed against them with all our royal power, force, and minions of war which we now

by 25 Henry VIII c. 14, which confirmed two other medieval statutes (5 Richard II st. 2 c. 5 and 2 Henry V st. 1 c. 7) and provided that heretics who refused to recant would be burnt; however, heretics convicted for the first time were to have an opportunity to recant and do penance. Despite the wording of the proclamation, the death penalty does not seem to have been applied to heretics who recanted, for on 5 June 1535 Chapuys reported that Dutch Anabaptists who had been reconciled with the church were sent home rather than being burnt. *LP* 8 no. 826.

[141] *TRP* no. 161. The meaning of the first section of the proclamation was unclear to John Stokesley, Bishop of London, who wrote Cromwell asking him if the proclamation was meant to include all his 'books of the canon law and schoolmen which favor much the bishop of Rome.' SP 1/89/32 (*LP* 8 no. 55).

have in a readiness and destroy them, their wives and children with fire and sword to the most terrible example of such rebels and offenders.'[142]

Royal proclamations played no role in the major doctrinal formulations of the 1530s, nor were they used in the initial attack on ceremonies. The Ten Articles, which were accepted by convocation in July 1536, began the attack on ceremonies and moved cautiously in the direction of a Protestant position on the sacraments. They were followed by a series of royal injunctions which ordered the clergy to explain the Ten Articles to their parishioners and commanded them not to 'set forth or extol any images, relics, or miracles for any superstition or lucre, nor allure the people by any enticements to the pilgrimage of any saint.'[143] The movement towards reform was interrupted by the uprising in the North which brought about the proclamation on rumors and unlawful assemblies in October 1536. In the fall of 1538 a second series of injunctions was issued that to a great extent repeated those of 1536. They also added an order that a copy of Coverdale's translation of the Bible be placed in every church so that parishioners could read it, and that baptisms, marriages and burials be recorded in parish registers. The clergy were to 'provoke, stir and exhort' people to read the Bible but to avoid contention. Scriptural sermons were to be preached and superstitious practices discouraged.[144]

The 1538 injunctions continued the progress of moderate reforms, but two months after they were issued a lengthy proclamation dated 16 November 1538 partially reversed this trend. It had ten sections. The first eight attempted to retard the growing influence of Protestantism in England. The preamble complained that books were being imported and printed in England which contained 'annotations and additions in the margins, prologues, and calendars' which reflected the beliefs of 'Anabaptists and sacramentarians, which be lately come into this realm.' Furthermore, individuals were 'using some superstitious speeches and rash words of erroneous matters and fanatical opinions both in their preachings and familiar communication' which led to disputes on the sacraments 'in open places, taverns and alehouses' and influenced people 'to break, condemn,

---

[142] *TRP* no. 168. Elton, *Policy and Police*, 252, comments 'This excited document which sounds like Henry's own composition went out together with the King's *Answers to the Rebels* to restore the desired atmosphere of obedience.'

[143] Henry Gee and William J. Hardy, *Documents Illustrative of English Church History* (New York, 1910), 271. See Elton, *Policy and Police*, 247ff for a full discussion of the injunctions and their impact.   [144] *Ibid.* 271ff.

and despise of their own private wills and appetites other Holy Sacraments, laudable rites, and ceremonies heretofore used and accustomed in England.' The proclamation forbade the importation of English books without the King's license upon pain of forfeiture of 'all his or their goods and chattels' as well as imprisonment at the King's will. Nobody was to print any book in the English tongue unless it were first examined by the privy council or someone appointed by the King. Furthermore, printers were 'not to put these words *cum privilegio regali* without adding *ad imprimendum solum.*' English Bibles were not to be printed or imported with annotations 'or any prologue or additions in the calendar or table' unless viewed and approved by the King or his council. Translations were also to include the name of the translators. Anabaptists and sacramentarians were warned that the King intended 'to proceed against such of them as be already apprehended according to their merits and the laws of his realm.' Those not apprehended were ordered to leave the realm within eight or ten days after the proclamation 'upon pain of loss of their lives and forfeiture of all their goods, without any favor, remission or indulgence to be administered to any of the offenders against the tenor of this present article.' Another lengthy section, also directed against sacramentarians, stated that no one except 'learned men in Holy Scripture instructed and taught in the universities' were to 'reason dispute or argue upon the said Holy and Blessed Sacrament nor of the mysteries thereof, upon pain of loss of their lives and forfeiture of their goods, without any favor or pardon.' The proclamation also ordered that ceremonies not yet abolished were to be kept and that clergy who had married in violation of their oaths were to be deprived. Those who married after the proclamation would suffer the additional punishment of imprisonment and 'further punishment' at the King's will.

Although the first eight sections of the proclamation contained harsh punishments and severe regulations designed to halt the spread of Protestantism and to destroy the more radical forms of the new faith, the last two sections had a considerably different emphasis. Section nine ordered clergy to instruct their parishioners in 'the true meaning and understanding of Holy Scripture, sacramentals, rites and ceremonies' so that 'all superstitious abuses and idolatries' connected with those ceremonies would be avoided. Section ten attacked the adulation of Thomas Becket as a martyr and a saint. It first undermined the traditional version of the Becket story by presenting an account much less complimentary to Becket. It then ordered that Thomas Becket be no longer called a saint but rather be considered 'to have been a rebel and traitor to his prince.' His images and pictures were to be taken down and 'the days used to be festival in his name shall not be observed, nor the service, office, antiphons, collects, and prayers in his name read, but erased and put out of all books.'[145] The first eight sections of the proclamation clearly reveal the King's policy, because a draft of that part corrected in the King's hand survives. However, as Professor Elton has suggested, the remaining portion of the proclamation 'seems as clearly to come from Cromwell whose convictions and preoccupations it reflects.'[146]

The proclamation was modified three months later by a new proclamation which also reveals Cromwell's influence. It ordered the clergy to 'instruct the people the good and right use and effects' of the ceremonies mentioned in the first proclamation. It then proceeded to explain each ceremony in a way that emphasized their function as 'outward signs and tokens whereby we remember Christ and his doctrine' and condemned superstitious abuse of them. In addition the Anabaptists and sacramentarians were pardoned for 'such faults as they have committed by falling into such wrong and perverse opinions by words or writings, whereof they be not yet convicted nor condemned afore any judge or ordinary of this realm.'[147] Cromwell may even have sought a more liberal pardon. An undated draft proclamation with corrections in Cromwell's hand, probably drawn up late in 1538 or early in 1539, would have extended a pardon to all who offended against the first proclamation. The draft, furthermore, suggested that many ceremonies associated with superstitious practices would eventually be abolished, although it expressed a concern about both the extreme Protestant and Catholic parties 'whereof the one is too rash and the other too dull.'[148]

The growing religious divisions in the realm may have motivated another draft proclamation, probably drawn up in April 1539. The draft reflects the King's concern for unity of opinion, for it was corrected in his hand. The preamble attacked both those who sought

---

[145] *TRP* no. 186.

[146] Elton, *Policy and Police*, 257: 'How those disparate pieces ever came to be joined together is a mystery, though one may conjecture disputes in the council ending in a compromise; the main part of the proclamation represents a victory for the conservative faction, but the reformers managed to add a second part which, though harmless on the surface, would remind people that things had not changed right round again.' It is interesting that only the last item in the proclamation specified the advice of council.

[147] *TRP* no. 188. Elton, *Policy and Police*, 258, notes that the proclamation showed 'the revising hand of Cranmer and Cromwell had been at work.'

[148] SP 6/4/267-80 (*LP* 13[2] no. 1183). The editors of *LP* date the draft December 1538.

'to restore into this realm the old devotion to the usurped power of the Bishop of Rome, the hypocrite religion, superstitious pilgrimages, idolatry, and other evil and naughty ceremonies and dreams justly and lawfully abolished and taken away by authority of God's word' and those who used the Bible to 'wrest and interpret and so untruly allege the same to subvert and overturn as well the sacraments of Holy Church as the power and authority of princes and magistrates.' The draft lamented the disputes between the two factions 'in church, alehouses, taverns and other places and congregations' which resulted in 'slander and railing' at each other, and which was likely to result in 'sedition and tumult.' It announced that the King intended to deal with the problem in Parliament 'by advice of his prelates and clergy and other of his council.' But first 'in the beginning of his Parliament' it was necessary to take immediate action. No one was to call another papist or heretic unless he could prove it. No one was to teach, preach or expound Scripture except curates, licensed preachers and graduates of the Universities of Oxford and Cambridge. Those who read the Scriptures were to do so 'quietly and reverently' and 'for their own instruction and edification.' If they were in doubt about any section, they were not to trust to their own interpretations but to 'resort humbly to such as be learned in Holy Scripture for their instruction in that behalf.' Finally, all subjects were to use the Bible in English according to the King's 'godly purpose and gracious intent.' Offenders against any of these orders were threatened with the same penalty, but the draft left a blank space of at least four lines after the words 'upon pain of' where the penalty should have been written. Another curious aspect of the draft is that it claimed to be based on Parliamentary authority: 'according to an authority of Parliament already to his highness, successors and council granted.'[149] This seems to be a reference to the Statute of Proclamations, because the Act of Supremacy, the other likely source for this authority, did not mention the council.[150] If so, it indicates that the government was anticipating rapid passage of the statute, because the draft was drawn up at the beginning of that session of Parliament, possibly at the same time that the original bill for the Statute of Proclamations was introduced. The bill, however, lingered for six weeks before it passed both houses of Parliament. In the meantime the Act of Six Articles had been enacted. This may have been the planned, more

[149] BM Cleo E v/311; *TRP* no. 191.
[150] 26 Henry VIII c. 1; Professors Hughes and Larkin have surmised that the reference anticipated 'the authorities granted by Parliament in the Statute of Proclamations.' *TRP*, p. 285 n. 1.

permanent legislation referred to in the draft. Consequently the proclamation was no longer needed. There is no evidence that the draft was ever issued.[151]

The overall use of royal proclamations on ecclesiastical matters again indicates that the government did not rely on them for long-term legislation. They were used to revive old legislation, to remind subjects of the dangers of violating statutes, to order obedience to the laws and statutes, or, as in the case of the proclamation on London tithes, to announce a conciliar decision after the intervention of the central government had been specifically requested. However, they seldom made new regulations or even added significantly to penalties. The few that did can either be attributed to More's administration or to Henry VIII's influence, and it would be hard to argue that even these proclamations involved any really questionable use of the prerogative.

In contrast to the cautious use of royal proclamations on religious questions, two proclamations issued at the end of the period involved a more ambitious use of the prerogative. Both seem to have been connected with foreign policy problems. They were issued within two days of each other in February 1539 and were probably connected with a deteriorating foreign situation. In June 1538 Charles V and Francis concluded the Truce of Nice and in July the Pope met with the two monarchs. In December the Pope finally published the papal bull deposing Henry VIII. In January 1539 he sent Reginald Pole to convince the Emperor to join with the French and Scottish Kings to carry out the papal bull. The series of events was extremely threatening to England. Additional rumors indicated that a huge fleet was being collected in the Netherlands to invade England. In February the ambassadors of the Emperor and the French King were recalled from England and all English ships were stayed in the Netherlands. England responded with frantic preparations to meet the expected invasion. Old fortifications were strengthened and new coastal fortresses were built along the southern and northeastern coasts. In March troops were mustered in the southern counties to defend against the expected cross channel invasions, and Norfolk

[151] The bill for the Statute of Proclamation was introduced on 12 May, but it did not pass both houses until 26 June. The Act of Six Articles was introduced on 7 June after a long struggle in committee. The King may have anticipated more trouble with the Six Articles than with the Statute of Proclamations and therefore planned to issue the proclamation while the Parliament was debating the Six Articles. See Kenneth Pickthorn, *Early Tudor Government: Henry VIII* (Cambridge, 1934), 406, for a discussion of the passage of the Act of Six Articles.

raised troops in the North to guard the borders against the Scots.[152]

On 26 February 1539, when tensions were at a high point, a proclamation with an extensive and elaborate justification stated that beginning on 6 April alien merchants would pay the same duties as English merchants for the next seven years. The explanation for the action took up over half of the text. Rulers, it was argued, were duty bound to devise ways 'to advance, set forth, and increase their commonwealths...and to maintain and observe such ordinances and orders as by them should be devised for the same.' But if these ordinances did not work for the benefit of the commonwealth as originally intended, then they must 'revoke, repeal and reform their said ordinances and orders and establish new from time to time as the necessity of their commonwealth should require.' Although the King was 'justly and lawfully entitled in the right of his imperial crown' to collect more customs from aliens than he did from English merchants, and modification of this would work to the King's 'own detriment and loss,' the King felt that the ordinances establishing higher customs for aliens were not working for the benefit of the commonwealth because an increase in trade might result from an equalization of customs. Therefore, the King having 'more respect to the advancement of his grace's commonwealth than to his own singular profit,' and intending to test whether a change in customs demanded of alien merchants would really be beneficial, ordered the seven-year experiment. The long justification was probably included because it could be expected that the change would not be welcomed by English merchants. The proclamation, furthermore, included a rather severe penalty for customs officials who continued to charge alien merchants more than English merchants. They would lose their offices, pay a fine at the King's will and 'over that' pay 'to the parties grieved ten times so much as they shall exact and take contrary to this present proclamation.'[153]

The proclamation introduced a policy which Cromwell had been seeking to establish for some time, probably in the interest of encouraging trade. He seems to have sought Parliamentary action on this question in 1534 and again in 1535 without success; consequently, his use of a proclamation in 1539 seems to be an example of relying on the royal prerogative when Parliament would not yield. Further-

[152] R. B. Wernham, *Before the Armada* (New York, 1966), 141ff.
[153] *TRP* no. 189.

more, since legislation on alien and denizen customs had commonly been done by statute in the past, this also seems to be an intrusion of the prerogative into a new area.[154] However, it is likely that the proclamation was more concerned with foreign policy than with encouraging trade. Its introduction at this critical time has normally been interpreted as an effort to win the support of merchants in the Netherlands for a policy of neutrality and thereby also to wean Charles V from a war policy.[155] This interpretation is supported by the fact that when the crisis was over, 32 Henry VIII c. 14 virtually annulled the advantages to foreign merchants granted in the proclamation by limiting the concession to goods shipped in English vessels. Chapuys also thought the action was motivated by foreign policy. Complaining about the restrictions in 32 Henry VIII c. 14, he maintained that the privilege had been granted because the King was afraid of war, and once the danger was past this new 'ordinance' revoked the advantage Antwerp merchants had gained by the proclamation. The experiment cost the King over fifteen thousand pounds, but if it succeeded in helping to prevent war, it was certainly well worth the price.[156]

If the first proclamation is an illustration of using the 'carrot' to deal with the critical foreign situation, the second was surely applying the 'stick.' On 28 February 1539 the King reacted to the embargo on English shipping in the Netherlands with a restraint on all shipping. 'For divers respects and considerations moving his highness for the surety and defense of this realm,' the King commanded that no ships be allowed to leave the King's 'dominions, ports or jurisdictions' without a special license 'upon pain of death and forfeiture of all the lands, goods and chattels of the offenders in this behalf.' Orders were also sent to local officials commanding them to enforce the proclamation. They were told that the embargo was necessitated by the need to guard against piracy.[157] This

---

[154] Elton, *Reform and Renewal*, 115, comments 'this, however, was one reform which Cromwell wanted urgently enough to by-pass for once an obstreperous Parliament.' See T. C. Wyatt, 'Aliens in Social and Economic Life of England in the Reign of Henry VIII' (University of London MA Thesis, 1952), 86–8, for discussion of alien legislation.

[155] Wernham, *Before the Armada*, 144: 'It was...a strong encouragement to the Netherlanders to stand out again for trade and neutrality as they had done in 1538; a useful way of keeping the north German cities friendly and through them another line open to the German Lutherans in general.' James A. Williamson, *Maritime Enterprise 1485–1558* (Oxford, 1913), 126, called it an effort 'to buy off the hostility of Charles V, whose Flemish subjects were the chief gainers by it.'

[156] *CSPSs*, VI (1), no. 121 (*LP* 16 no. 13). E 122/195/17 (*LP* 16 no. 9) lists the total loss in customs 'by virtue of the King's proclamation' as £15,450 9s 3d.

[157] SP 1/143/210 (*LP* 14[1] no. 408).

justification was probably intended for the French King, for Cromwell wrote to Bonner on 1 March explaining that the proclamation had been issued because of the Emperor's embargo. However, Bonner was instructed to tell Francis I that the ships had been arrested 'for to provide by the same against such piracies and other practices' and to tell him that 'from time to time and little by little his ships shall be delivered and no detriment nor damage done unto them.'[158]

The proclamation seems to have been strictly enforced, and at first it even restrained the coastal trade between English ports.[159] The efforts of Wriothesley to convince the Queen Regent of the Netherlands to lift the embargo on English ships, which had been unsuccessful before the proclamation, finally bore fruit on 8 March when she at least agreed to allow loaded English ships to leave.[160]

The embargo, however, remained in force. Within three weeks there were serious complaints from East Anglia. Norfolk wrote Cromwell two letters in two days. The first on 17 March stated that daily applications for licenses to export corn were being made to him and that 'unless there be some enlargement granted to dispatch away part of the same' there would be no storage space left for corn. He added that 'force of suitors' compelled him to write, but he advised that if 'the Emperor will keep promise with the King's majesty, I think it were a good deed to suffer barley and malt only to go over as long as malt shall not be above 4s the quarter.'[161] The following day Norfolk wrote that he was under a great deal of pressure 'for the enlargement of the restraint of grain.' He again added that he felt licenses should be granted to export malt and barley. This, he maintained, would be 'a very meritorious deed' and would benefit the country.[162] Cromwell seems to have responded to that request. Probably in late March or early April the restraint was lifted with the stipulation 'that all ships laden with corn go to none other place than to Calais.'[163]

[158] Merriman, *Letters of Cromwell*, II, 183–5.
[159] KRO CPW/166, 168.
[160] *CSPSp*, VI (1), no. 43 (*LP* 14[1] no. 470).
[161] SP 1/144/126 (*LP* 14[1] no. 541).
[162] SP 1/144/139 (*LP* 14[1] no. 555). Cromwell received similar information from Audley who informed him that English shippers 'make much moaning in all creeks and ports here about' and suggested that the King should lift the restraint. BM Otho E xi/293(*LP*14[1] no. 682).
[163] E 36/143/129 (*LP* 14 [1] no. 655). The reference in Cromwell's remembrances is undated, but the editors of the *LP* place it at the end of March 1539. By 22 June the restrictions limiting shipments only to Calais were also lifted. John Husse wrote to Lisle on that date: 'The ships are set at liberty and merchants may land and go with their goods where they will.' SP 3/5/68 (*LP* 14[1] no. 1144).

This proclamation represents the most extreme use of the proclaiming power in the 1530s. The penalty, although probably justified by the national emergency, was exceptionally severe and was seemingly based on the authority of the prerogative alone.[164] It was clearly an unpopular measure as was the proclamation on alien customs. But both proclamations were temporary expedients clearly related to the critical foreign situation. Although the constitutionality of the embargo proclamation might be questioned, it was seemingly in accord with the opinion expressed by the Lord Chief Justice in 1531 that in times of great danger the King 'by the advice of his council might make proclamation and use all other policies at his pleasure and the said proclamations and policies so devised...should be of as good effect as any law made by Parliament or otherwise.'[165] Nevertheless, the extreme penalty is a bit surprising, especially since severe penalties were not common in the 1530s.

The use of harsh penalties may have been part of a trend towards more severe punishment in the year preceding the enactment of the Statute of Proclamations. Of the twelve proclamations surviving from the period March 1538 to March 1539, half included threats of penalties that were harsher than normal.[166] Three of them contained the death penalty. Two have already been discussed. The third, in April 1538, attempted to aid the King's officers in the performance of their duties by decreeing strict punishments for those who obstructed them. It maintained that the King's officers were often 'hurt, maimed, slain and murdered' and that offenders went unpunished because they claimed privilege of clergy or sanctuary. It ordered subjects to 'yield themselves to the arrests and attachments' of the King's officers 'without refusal, rescue or resistance,' and threatened those who hurt or maimed them with forfeiture of 'all their lands, goods, and chattels, and their bodies to be committed to perpetual prison.' If any person murdered these officers they would 'suffer death, without remission or pardon' and would be denied privilege of sanctuary or clergy. Anyone who 'from henceforth slay or murder any by occasion' in frays with swords would also 'suffer

[164] Elton, *HJ*, vii, 270, explains the use of the death penalty by listing the proclamations as one of those 'which in effect proclaim martial law.'

[165] BM Titus B 1/311d; Merriman, *Letters of Cromwell*, i, 410.

[166] The other six were *TRP* nos. 181 and 182, which contained no order and therefore did not include a penalty; no. 188, which offered a pardon and explained an earlier proclamation; no. 183, which simply summarized a number of statutes; no. 190.5, which was an exact duplicate of an earlier proclamation setting values on foreign coins (no 178); and no. 187, which followed the normal form of a wine price proclamation with the usual penalty.

death without remission or pardon, and shall lose his clergy and privilege of sanctuary.'[167] Although the punishments were common law penalties for the offenses, the proclamation added to the penalties by removing the possibility of avoiding punishment by a pardon, by privilege of sanctuary, or by benefit of clergy.

The remaining three proclamations included either heavier fines than normal or vaguely defined threats of extremely severe punishment. Officials who violated the February 1539 proclamation by collecting more in customs from alien merchants than permitted faced the loss of their offices, fine and payment to the offended party of ten times the amount collected. A proclamation of October 1538 which restrained export of leather, hides and tallow threatened forfeiture of double the value of the items illegally exported, imprisonment and fine at the King's pleasure. Although this was not an exceptionally severe penalty, it was harsher than the statutory penalty for illegal export of hides and untanned leather.[168] A third proclamation, issued in March 1538, which contained extremely threatening language may reveal the government's growing impatience with the half-hearted enforcement of earlier statutes. It was issued only after a series of efforts had been made to inspire local officials with greater diligence in enforcing statutes. Already in February 1536 a proclamation, which ordered compliance with statutes on archery, unlawful games, apparel and vagabonds, maintained that these statutes were not being observed largely because of the negligence of justices of the peace and other officers responsible for enforcement. Subjects were ordered to obey the acts upon the pains in the statutes which the King would 'not hereafter at any time remit, pardon, nor forgive to any of the offenders.' Enforcement officials were commanded 'without favor, affection or corruption' to 'put their effectual endeavor and diligences for the due observation and execution of the said statutes and every of them.'[169] In the following year subjects were ordered to obey the recently enacted statute on crossbows and handguns. Local officials were again instructed 'to put their effectual endeavors for the due execution of the said statute and this proclamation and for the punishment of offenders thereof as they will answer to his grace for

---

[167] *TRP* no. 179.

[168] *TRP* no. 184. 27 Henry VII c. 14 ordered forfeiture of the leather or hides exported.

[169] *TRP* no. 163. Householders and lords were also to see that the statutes were observed by their servants and families upon pains in the statutes and the King's 'most dreadful indignation and displeasure.'

the same at their uttermost perils and will avoid the King's most high displeasure and indignation.'[170]

These threats were mild in comparison to those in the proclamation of March 1538. It ordered enforcement of a series of statutes that included those on rumors, vagabonds, unlawful games, archery, apparel and sewers. It lamented that 'for lack of due execution of which good statutes, the offenders for whom they were made daily increase and be encouraged.' It argued that the fault lay with local officials 'which for the most part so negligently, dulcetly, favorably, and willingly use their offices that justice is decayed, no punishment is done for common and open offenses.' Law enforcement officials were ordered to carry out their duties 'without dread, corruption, affection or partiality.' If they did this, the King promised he would 'assist them and, for the same, love them, favor them, and in all their reasonable suits most graciously hear them.' But if 'after this his most gracious admonition no amendment be had, nor respect to their duties,' they would not only receive the King's 'high indignation and displeasure,' but he would 'pursue them as very enemies of his commonwealth, and punish them in their bodies, lands, and goods, and after their demerits that it shall be to their confusion and undoings, to the most terrible example of such offenders.'[171]

These proclamations may document a need to compensate by angry threats or by more severe penalties for an inadequate system of enforcement. A growing concern about the enforcement of proclamations existed in the 1530s, but there is no indication that any set system of enforcement was established or that the methods used were successful. Over half of the proclamations at least stated a method of enforcement, but specific courts were still seldom mentioned. The vast majority of proclamations simply ordered local officials to see that the proclamations were obeyed. Proclamations based on statutes usually simply repeated the enforcement procedures in the statutes, but sometimes there were changes. The proclamation of 18 July 1531 which forbade the export of gold and silver provided that informers could give information in either the council or the exchequer and receive half of the forfeiture on conviction.[172] It was based on

---

[170] *TRP* no. 171. The proclamation added to the statute (25 Henry VIII c. 17) by including a provision that even those subjects permitted by the statute to use handguns could not use any with a stock under 2½ inches in length.

[171] *TRP* no. 138. The editors date the proclamation 'After 1532'. Elton, *Reform and Renewal*, 165 n. 16, has noted that the proclamation should be dated March 1538. There is abundant additional evidence to establish that this dating is correct. A reference in the London records dates the proclaiming of the proclamation on 11 March 1538. CLRO Journals 14/69.   [172] *TRP* no. 133.

5 Richard II st. 1 c. 2, which did not include this procedure. The proclamation of 7 September 1531 which prohibited unlicensed export of victuals was the only one not based on a statute which allowed enforcement in the exchequer. It ordered port officials to seize the grain illegally exported and to 'signify unto the Exchequer the names of such persons as they know to offend in the same.'[173] The number of proclamations which mentioned the council increased slightly, but if we are to judge from the statements in the texts of the proclamations, the council still played a minor role in enforcement. Six proclamations provided for enforcement by the council. One, already mentioned, dealt with the export of gold and silver; two others were concerned with ecclesiastical matters; a fourth used the council to deal with negligent officials; and the proclamation of 11 November 1534 which ordered punishment of grain hoarders, provided that local officials were to report offenders to the chancellor or the council. A final proclamation mentioning the council was that of 29 January 1534, which ordered enforcement of the statute on the sale of meat. It gave the King and council the right to set fines and penalties for violations.[174]

With the exception of these examples there was still a good deal of vagueness on the matter of judicial enforcement. Just as the authority of proclamations was not clearly defined, it was probably also not clearly established where they could be enforced. Since most of them were based on statutes, one would assume that the methods provided for in the statutes would be used. But proclamations ordering enforcement of statutes normally were issued because those methods had not proved sufficient. Furthermore, those not based on statutes needed to have an acceptable method of securing speedy and efficient punishment of offenders.

There is a good deal of evidence to establish that the problem of enforcement caused Cromwell deep concern, especially as the decade came to an end. This was so largely because existing methods were not working very effectively. Although enforcement is dealt with in detail in a later chapter, it is necessary at this point to provide some examples which will illustrate the concerns of the government in 1539.

The difficulty of enforcing proclamations is possibly best shown by the effort to enforce the export legislation, because it began at the outset of Cromwell's ministry and continued throughout the 1530s.

[173] *TRP* no. 134.
[174] *TRP* nos. 133, 129, 186, 134, 151, 142.

HENRY VIII—THE FIRST STAGE

One of the greatest problems facing port officials seeking to prevent illegal export was to distinguish between ships that were legally transporting victuals to ports in England or to Calais and those which were bound for foreign ports. To prevent shippers from listing a destination in England or Calais and then shipping to foreign ports, merchants were required to state their destination and to sign an obligation often amounting to double the value of the goods shipped. They were then required to bring a certificate within a specified length of time from the port officials in the indicated port to prove that the shipment had actually been delivered. Although the system seemed to promise effective regulation, it depended upon careful supervision to make sure that the certificates were returned to the originating port, and that the obligations were collected if the shipper failed to return with a certificate. Obviously this was not being done in a systematic fashion. In late 1531 the King instructed Cromwell to pay special attention to this matter. He ordered that obligations for exporting grain 'be called out of the hands of the customers' and that a search be made 'who hath carried corn and grain as well uncustomed as against the King's commandment and restraint, and sharp process to be made against them for the same without any delay.'[175] Cromwell carried out the task with his usual efficiency. Shortly afterward he must have compiled a book listing obligations for export from ports throughout England. The book listed 332 bonds. The government then began process on 258 cases in a serious effort to enforce the laws. It was found that only 73 individuals were able to present certificates to prove that the grain had been delivered to its stated destination.[176] The effort at strict enforcement continued for four years, but seems to have enjoyed limited success. In October 1535 Cromwell wrote to John Gostwick, outgoing auditor in the Exchequer, indicating that he had given up hope of collecting on

[175] BM Titus B 1/486 (*LP* 5 no. 394).
[176] E 36/257/2–73 (*LP* 5 no. 1706). The books were obviously intended to carry out what Cromwell noted in his remembrances in October 1533: 'to cause a docket to be made by the King's attorney or such as doth sue the King's process to know how many be in suit at the King's suits and how furth the suit is entered as well against them that be sued for conveyance of corn as for other debts.' BM Titus B 1/446 (*LP* 5 no. 1381). The first forty-three pages simply list the bonds entered into between 1530 and September 1531. The last section is headed by a note in Cromwell's hand, 'the book of the King's process sued against divers for corn.' It is divided into three sections. Seventy-three names are listed under the first section, headed 'of them that showed their certificate and did put in pleas which were entered in Trinity time last past.' The second heading listed thirteen cases as having pleaded 'the sealing of the obligations not to be their deeds.' Finally, the last heading lists 172 individuals as having 'made no answer and therefore contempts be entered against them.'

many of the obligations. But he ordered Gostwick to attempt to arrive at a settlement with those parties whose obligations were still outstanding and to take new obligations from those who were unable to pay at that time. It is difficult to know if this was successful, but ten years later a case involving one of the obligations taken in 1530 was still pending in the Exchequer.[177]

Throughout the 1530s complaints that grain was too expensive and that officials were allowing illegal export or that exporters were finding clever ways to evade the regulations continued to come to Cromwell's desk.[178] In 1535 he received advice that stricter penalties might deter those who were driving up the price of grain by regrating. Stephan Vaughan wrote in September that 'the people need your help against regraters everywhere.' He stated that it would be beneficial for all 'if his grace executed some terrible punishment against anyone that were found a regrater.'[179] In the spring of 1538 Cromwell seems to have lost his patience with a notorious offender, the mayor of Rochester. Lord Cobham wrote in May that the mayor was allowing malt and corn to be exported. He asked Cromwell to write him a letter because 'we can have no reformation of it because of their liberties, for the mayor is searcher himself by the King's charter.'[180] Cromwell responded in an angry letter which ordered the mayor to allow 'no more corn to be conveyed out of these parts where you have jurisdictions' and to appear before him 'immediately upon the receipt hereof to answer for that ye have hitherto done and permitted. For the which if you cannot the better declare yourself I shall look upon you as it shall be too heavy for you to brave.'[181]

---

[177] BM Titus B IV/115 (*LP* 9 no. 647). On 17 June 1545 the customer and treasurer of Calais reported that they had located evidence that a certain Philip Crayer who had entered into an obligation 'bearing the date of xvith of April in the xxth year of the King's majesty's reign,' had in fact delivered the victual to Calais. Philip Crayer had since died but the Exchequer was now bringing action against his widow. SP 1/202/87 (*LP* 20[1] no. 961).

[178] Early in 1534 Cromwell received information complaining that the mayor of Lynn was allowing illegal export. Customers were taking obligations but the informant was afraid that they would 'never be put in suit but dropped as many others heretofore hath been.' SP 1/82/145 (*LP* 7 no. 141). John Mawdysley wrote to Cromwell in the same year that people were hiding wheat, cloth, tallow and other merchandise under wool in barges and carrying the wool from Norwich to Yarmouth and then loading it on ships bound for Spain and Portugal in violation of the restraint. SP 1/239/116 (*LP* App. 1[1] no. 967). In September 1534 Cromwell wrote to Lord Lisle complaining that 'divers and many things are daily conveyed out of this realm into parts of beyond the seas contrary to the statutes and provisions.' He complained that the searchers at Calais were remiss in carrying out their office and he sent two men to Calais to make a special search. SP 1/85/206 (*LP* 7[2] no. 1179).   [179] SP 1/96/83 (*LP* 9 no. 375).

[180] BM Vesp. F XIII/204 (*LP* 13[1] no. 362).

[181] SP 1/132/94–5 (*LP* 13[1] no. 980).

Cromwell's missive seems to betray his frustration at not being able to control what must have been widespread evasion of the laws. The matter was serious enough to cause the King to appoint a commission to investigate the problem. In May 1538 it reported that the laws were not being obeyed and advised that unless swift and certain justice were guaranteed the laws would continue to be ignored:

> If all such forfeiture of victuals as corn, beefs, muttons, veals, porks, butter, cheese, tallow and other victuals or any of them by virtue of this commission now forfeitured be not briefly and consequently executed or called upon after presentment had into the King's exchequer and the fines whereof quickly levied such offenders and trespassers will not regard dread nor fear but rather have more comfort in their wrongful usages to the evil example of others.[182]

Cromwell did not have to be convinced of the desirability of speedy and sure justice. Throughout his administration he attempted to improve the efficiency of law courts both by setting up new courts and seeking to reform the old.[183] However, the report of the commissioners combined with the continuing problem of enforcing proclamations must have made the question of finding a more effective way of securing obedience to proclamations a major concern of Cromwell in 1538 and 1539. The severe penalties in some of the proclamations may reveal a desperate effort to deter offenders in accordance with the kind of advice offered by Stephan Vaughan in 1535. But severe penalties were not Cromwell's normal way of dealing with a problem, and it is unlikely that they were really effective. As the commissioners stated, unless certainty of punishment could be assured, evasions of the law would continue. Cromwell may also have been concerned about the authority of proclamations in 1539, for he was forced to use them in a particularly questionable way to deal with the critical foreign situation. Throughout his ministry he had shown a preference for statutory authority even in areas where the use of proclamations without that authority would not have involved any departure from past precedent. Consequently, it would not be surprising if he felt a bit uncomfortable about issuing those two proclamations designed to deal with an emergency situation on the authority of the prerogative alone, despite the Lord Chief

---

[182] SP 1/132/136 (*LP* 13[1] no. 1026).
[183] Elton, *Reform and Renewal*, 141ff.

Justice's opinion in 1531. In addition there may have been some practical problems in the courts when the government tried to impose the felony penalties decreed in the proclamation that imposed the embargo on shipping. How these matters may have influenced the drafting of the bill for the Statute of Proclamations in the spring of 1539 is discussed in the next chapter.

6

THE STATUTE OF PROCLAMATIONS

Tudor and Stuart ideas on proclamations are a subject on which it is hard to be precise. It was generally felt both that a King had a right to make them and that they should not become an acceptable substitute for Acts of Parliament, but this comfortable ambiguity could only be preserved by moderation and a lack of definition. The 1539 Act is an attempt at definition: it recounts that some people have not been obeying proclamations to the dishonour of the King, 'who may ill bear it,' and gives the government statutory authority to punish breaches of proclamations. We know that the act was substantially amended during its passage, but we do not know how. Whether this act is simply designed to clear up ambiguities, or whether it embodies the same principle of delegated legislation, giving statutory authority to council regulations, which Cromwell had been using for some time, whether it is concerned with enforcement, or whether it is a serious attempt to give the King a legislative power without Parliament, we cannot say. The act only remained in force till 1547 and its effects are obscure.[1]

This comment in a recent survey textbook sums up the mystery still surrounding the meaning and intent of the Statute of Proclamations over four centuries after its enactment. Since so much of the controversy over the role of royal proclamations in the early Tudor period has focused on this enigmatic act, it is fitting that a full chapter be devoted to it. The available evidence has been sifted and interpreted by so many writers that one must begin with a review of previous interpretations. Complete coverage is obviously neither practical nor necessary, but at least some acquaintance with the opinions and contributions of other historians is needed in order properly to understand the act in the context of the historical debate.

Previous interpretations

The consideration given the Statute of Proclamations by later historians contrasts dramatically with the lack of attention paid to it

[1] Conrad Russell, *The Crisis of Parliaments: English History 1509–1660* (Oxford, 1971), 119–20.

when it was enacted. What was later analyzed as a major constitutional crisis was hardly noticed by contemporaries. Chroniclers seemingly considered the statute of such minor importance that they failed even to mention it.[2] Foreigners were more interested in it than Englishmen. The French ambassador, Marillac, noted its passage, but his understanding was so distorted that it is hard to recognize it as applying to any statute passed in the 1539 Parliament much less the Statute of Proclamations. A year later in another comment, he became the first to interpret the act as having set up a royal despotism in England. On 6 August 1540 he wrote to Montmorency stating that an act had been passed 'que les estatz ont entièrement transféré leur auctorité et puissance à leur roy, duquel doresnavant la seulle opinion sera d'aussi grand efficace que les actes qu'ilz soulloient faire en parlement.'[3]

That a good deal of debate had taken place in Parliament over the statute was mentioned by John Husse in a letter to Lord Lisle on 25 June 1539: 'Parliament is not broken up. They remain out upon one act nor hath not done this fifteen days, which is concerning proclamations, but now they are at a point and tarry but the making out of the bill.'[4] Another reference to the debate in Parliament over the bill was made eight years later in Gardiner's letter to Somerset. He stated that 'many liberal words were spoken and a plain promise that, by authority of the Act for Proclamations, nothing should be made contrary to an act of Parliament or Common Law.'[5] The first clear statement accusing Henry VIII of seeking more than he obtained in the statute came from John Aylmer in 1559. He commended 'those that in King Henry VIII days would not grant him that his proclamations should have the force of a statute' and called them 'good fathers of the country, and worthy commendation in defending their liberty.'[6] James I, addressing a Commons' delegation in 1609, specifically accused Henry VIII of seeking tyrannical powers. He again commented on what had happened in Parliament:

[2] I have not been able to find a single reference to the statute in any contemporary chronicle. Wriothesley who even describes a number of the acts of the 1539 Parliament including the Act of Six Articles, remains silent on the Statute of Proclamations. Wriothesley, *Chronicle*, 101.

[3] J. Kaulek ed., *Correspondance Politique de MM De Castillion et de Marillac* (Paris, 1885), 211 (*LP* 15 no. 954). His comment in a letter to Francis I on 5 July 1539 described the act as allowing the King to tax without the consent of Parliament and threatening those who refused to pay with penalties of treason. He maintained it had been passed 'avec grandes difficultez qui ont esté' débatues longtemps en leurs assemblées et avec peu de contentement. *Ibid.* 107 (*LP* 14[1] no. 1207). [4] SP 1/152/103 (*LP* 14[1] no. 1158).

[5] Muller, *Letters of Gardiner*, 391.

[6] John Aylmer, *An Harborre for Faithful and Treuue Subiects* (Strasbourg, 1559), H3.

I commend Bacon who when Henry VIIIth sought by Parliament to make his proclamations law, and this with such violence thrust on your house, or none durst stir his finger. Then did Bacon as would, stand up and speak with boldness against it, for the King's seeking in that point was tyrannical.[7]

Although by the Stuart period it was believed that Henry VIII had sought more than he obtained in the Statute of Proclamations, the limitations on the proclaiming power in the act were generally remembered so that Henry was not accused of having succeeded in setting up a royal despotism. Even Coke, although he maintained that the statute gave 'more power to the King than he had before,' still noted that 'there is declared that proclamations shall not alter the laws, statutes, or customs of the realm or impeach any in his inheritance, goods, body, life, etc.'[8]

The first major comment on the statute in a general history also clearly recognized these limitations. The earliest detailed discussion of the act which I was able to find is in a work by Nathaniel Bacon first published in 1651. Bacon, the grandson of Nicholas and a nephew of Francis, was a puritan and a fierce parliamentarian, hostile to the power of the monarchy; nevertheless, he did not feel that the Statute of Proclamations had increased the King's powers. He attributed it to the machinations of Stephen Gardiner, who allegedly on his return from an embassy to the Emperor stressed the dangers from both France and the Empire. He maintained that it would be 'a dangerous thing' if the King 'should be at disadvantage either with the Emperor or French King, for want of power in these cases of sudden exigencies.' In addition, 'at home the point concerning religion was coming to the test.' High passions made it necessary that 'the King should steer with a shorter rudder, that this care might meet with every turn of Providence, which otherwise might suddenly blow up the peace and good government of this nation.' According to Bacon this was the justification which 'made way for

[7] Henry Yelverton, 'Narrative of Sir Henry Yelverton,' *Archaeologia*, xv (1806), 43.

[8] Coke, *Reports*, IV, 297. In the Commons debate over proclamations in 1607 Alford referred to the Statute of Proclamations but argued that it limited the power of proclamations: 'In Henry VIII time, no man to be touched in his life, goods, liberty or member by any proclamation.' *CJ*, I, 1035. The only comment I have found in the reign of James which did not note the limitations was by an anonymous writer who was urging James to enforce the proclamations against building in London. He cited Henry VIII's reign as a period of strict enforcement and stated that 'Henry the Eighth raised his voice until he made his will a law and the law made answerable to his will, which he left in force to his successor. Look the xxxith year of his reign and your majesty shall find that things commanded by proclamation by him or his successor should be obeyed and kept as if they were confirmed by Parliament.' The writer, however, was so ill informed that he does not seem to have been aware of the repeal of the Statute of Proclamations. BM Harl. 305/338–9.

the King without shame to ask what no King before him suffered ever to enter into conceit: I mean a legislative power.' But this is not what he received. Since the bill was altered by the Commons, the final statute imposed significant restrictions on the use of proclamations which were satisfactory to neither party. It was 'neither much to the desire of Commons, that so much was given; nor to the good liking of the King, that there was no more.' In Bacon's estimate the King actually lost more than he gained. For, he stated, it 'can be no precedent to the future, unless to inform Kings that the Parliament hath a power to give more authority and prerogative to Kings than they or the Crown have by common right; and to give it with such limitations and qualifications as seemeth good to them.'[9]

Bishop Burnet also recognized the limitations imposed upon proclamations. He pointed out that the act laid the burden of interpretation on the judges 'since there were such restrictions in some branches of it, which seemed to lessen the great extent of other parts of it, so the expositors of the law had much referred to them.' Though he had no supporting evidence, he attributed the statute to the fact that the King's 'injunctions' in religious matters had been challenged as being contrary to law 'since by these the King had without consent of Parliament altered some law, and laid taxes upon his spiritual subjects.' He seems to have been unaware that the statute was repealed in 1547, for he mistakenly maintained that the religious changes of Edward's reign were based on the Statute of Proclamations.[10]

The tradition of interpreting the statute as having actually set up a royal despotism seems to have begun in the eighteenth century with Blackstone and Hume. Blackstone stated in a brief comment:

By the statute 31 Henry VIII c. 8 it was enacted that the King's proclamations should have the force of acts of Parliament; a statute which was calculated to introduce the most despotic tyranny, and which must have proven fatal to the liberties of this kingdom, had it not been luckily repealed in the minority of his successor.[11]

[9] Nathaniel Bacon, *An Historical and Political Discourse on the Laws and Government of England* (4th ed. London, 1739), 125–6. The first part of the work appeared in 1647, but the second part which included the section of the Statute of Proclamations was not published until 1651. An edition published in 1665 was suppressed by the government. It was reissued after the revolution of 1688 with a new title page maintaining that the work was based on the manuscript notes of John Selden. *DNB*, 1, 836–7.
[10] Gilbert Burnet, *History of the Reformation of the Church of England*, J. Pocock ed. (Oxford, 1865), 1, 193.
[11] William Blackstone, *Commentaries on the Laws of England* (London, 1836), 1, 270.

Hume was far more eloquent, considerably more detailed, and even more radical in his interpretation. He felt that the Parliament of 1539 might very well have been the last one to sit in England, if Henry had so willed, since Parliament 'made by one act a total subversion of the English constitution' by giving 'the King's proclamations the same force as to a statute enacted by Parliament.' He dismissed the restrictions on proclamations as 'stupid or willful blindness in the Parliament' because they pretended that there were still some limitations on the King's proclaiming power.[12]

Nineteenth century historians usually concurred with Hume's view, although they tended to be more moderate in their interpretation and offered considerably more documentation. Lingard introduced Marillac's account to show that opposition was encountered in the Commons. He attributed the statute to Cromwell contending that Cromwell's favorite doctrine, 'what pleaseth the King has the force of law,' was 'nearly accomplished.' He was however more careful about the actual results, maintaining that, although Hume felt 'it laid prostrate at the foot of the throne, the liberties of the whole English nation,' the act passed Parliament with great difficulty and only after certain restraints had been imposed on the proclaiming power.[13] Albert Dicey, in his Arnold Prize Essay of 1860 on the privy council, was less cautious. He argued that the Tudor monarchs had consistently sought 'to give proclamations the force of laws, and thus to render the King's Council a legislative body.' This effort 'was for a moment crowned with success' when 'Henry VIII obtained from the most servile of Parliaments' the Statute of Proclamations.[14] Interestingly, the only really thorough study of the act in the nineteenth century did not result in such a radical appraisal. Richard Dixon, who included comments on the course of the bill's passage through the Parliament and mentioned Husse's and Gardiner's letters, felt that 'the act bears rather the appearance of a timid attempt to draw the prerogative within the limits of regular legislation than a surrender of the constitution to the prerogative.'[15] The most influential of nineteenth century constitutional historians, William Stubbs, returned to the most extreme interpretation, calling Parliament's actions in passing the act a 'virtual resignation of the

---

[12] David Hume, *The History of England* (New York, 1879), III, 177–9.
[13] John Lingard, *The History of England* (Edinburgh, 1902), V, 133.
[14] Albert V. Dicey, *The Privy Council* (London, 1887), 92–3.
[15] Richard W. Dixon, *History of the Church of England from the Abolition of the Roman Jurisdiction* (London, 1887), II, 126.

essential character of Parliament as a legislative body' and describing the statute as a 'lex regia.'[16]

Stubbs' appellation provided a label for the statute which was often repeated and which immediately identified it as a tyrannical act. Even the dean of English legal historians, Frederick Maitland, in his Rede Lecture of 1901, called the statute 'the English *lex regia* which gives the force of statute to the King's proclamations.'[17] However, Maitland never applied his talents to a careful exposition of the circumstances surrounding the passage of the statute, and his passing remarks in the Rede Lecture, which have been used to place him in the same school of interpretation as Hume and Stubbs, do not reveal his actual opinion. Even though he tended to believe that the constitutional position of proclamations had been changed, he also recognized that although 'statute may give to the King a subordinate legislative power...what one statute has given another may take away.'[18] In his introduction to his edition of the letters of Cromwell, Roger Merriman attempted to prove that Cromwell was responsible for the act. He viewed it as a tyrannical measure which Cromwell had been planning for some time. Quoting from Cromwell's letter to Norfolk, he even suggested that the statement made by the chief justices (that proclamations were of as 'good effect as any law made by Parliament') came 'at a hint from Cromwell.' Merriman also falsely maintained without documentation that Cromwell's remembrances included 'frequent mentions of an act to be passed in Parliament' to give proclamations the force of law.[19]

Until Robert Steele published his calendar of proclamations, writers concentrated only on the statute and the facts surrounding its passage. They completely ignored the contents of the proclamations issued either before or after 1539. Although Steele published only brief summaries of the actual texts, his volume supplied the material that later interpreters of the statute used to support their conclusions.[20] Using the evidence provided by Steele, Pollard was

---

[16] William Stubbs, *Constitutional History of England* (Oxford, 1906), II, 619.

[17] Frederick W. Maitland, *English Law and the Renaissance* (Cambridge, 1901), 69.

[18] Frederick W. Maitland, *The Constitutional History of England* (Cambridge, 1931), 253.

[19] Merriman, *Letters of Cromwell*, I, 124; Adair, *EHR*, XXXII, 39, first noted Merriman's error. I have checked all of Cromwell's remembrances in manuscript and have been unable to locate any statements which would support Merriman's conclusion.

[20] Steele felt that the Statute actually limited the powers of proclamations: 'It gave to the Council when constituted in a particular way, parliamentary sanction for the infliction of fines and imprisonment in matters affecting religion and public order, precisely similar to those it was already in the habit of imposing in case of riot, etc. Moreover, the parliamentary sanction...was obtained in exchange for a distinct limitation of the powers of the Council.' Steele, lxxix.

one of the early writers who noted that the statute did not significantly affect the use of proclamations. Since he could not find any proclamations which seemed to depend on the act for their validity, he maintained that 'either Henry VIII did not interpret the statute as conferring new powers of legislation on the crown or else he refrained from using them.'[21] Holdsworth, who attempted the first real description of the use and content of royal proclamations, also based his comments entirely on Steele's bibliography. He believed that the Statute of Proclamations was an effort to define 'the large vague powers of legislation possessed by the medieval Kings' which 'had never been expressly defined or curtailed.' The act could not be viewed as a 'lex regia,' both because it limited the power of proclamations and because Steele's list clearly showed that Henry did not use it in this fashion.[22]

In the January 1917 issue of *The English Historical Review*, E. R. Adair finally gave the controversy the detailed scholarly treatment it demanded. Adair's views were to some extent new and dramatic because he rejected all interpretations which implied that a change had been made 'in the legality of proclamations.' He pointed out that the preamble clearly recognized that the King had the right to issue proclamations. As long as they did not alter common law or make provisions inconsistent with it, the King's right to legislate by proclamations could be extended over a very wide field. Thus the statute limited rather than increased the King's power because it established a clearly defined restriction.[23] He also cited Steele's bibliography which showed that 'no proclamation seems to have been issued during the period 1539–47 which might not have been enforced either before the Statute of Proclamations became law, or after it had been repealed.' If the statute had given increased powers, a King of Henry's character would have used them. He maintained that proclamations were, in fact, used in a more arbitrary fashion after the repeal.[24] Thus the statute was not passed to increase the King's powers, rather, it was meant to improve enforcement of proclamations:

The outstanding characteristic of a law lay in its sanction, in the method whereby its observance might be enforced and its infringement punished.

---

[21] A. F. Pollard, *The Evolution of Parliament* (New York, 1934), 266. Pollard believed the Act was passed both 'to revive the waning respect for royal proclamations,' which resulted from the increase in statutory legislation and 'to put into practice the theory of the act of supremacy.' *Ibid.* 268.

[22] Holdsworth, *History of English Law*, IV, 101–3.

[23] Adair, *EHR*, XXXII, 39–41.   [24] *Ibid.* 44.

Any person who disobeyed an act of Parliament could be tried by a common law court; breakers of royal proclamations, however, unless a proclamation were merely declaratory of an act of Parliament, or issued by virtue of some such act, were punished in a prerogative court, such as the council or the star chamber. Under the early Tudors it seems very probable that the great increase in administrative business with which the council had to deal was causing considerable delay in the transaction of minor details of a judicial nature. The act of 1487, 'Pro Camera Stellata,' represents an attempt to ensure that the more pressing judicial business was disposed of promptly and efficiently, and at the root of the act of 1539 there seems visible a similar desire to find a method of enforcing royal proclamations which might prove more convenient than trial before the privy council.[25]

Adair was misled by his lack of information about the enforcement of royal proclamations in the period before 1539, but his solution to the problem of the Statute of Proclamations was perceptive and original. He was one of the first historians to note that its major concern was enforcement. He also tried to explain the opposition in Parliament by suggesting that the government's original intention may have been that 'breaches of proclamations should be punished in the ordinary courts, for it is clearly stated in the statute that proclamations shall be obeyed, observed, and kept as though they were made by act of Parliament.' The setting up of a special conciliar court was the result of a compromise with the Commons, who objected to the original government bill. However, the compromise failed to work, and Adair noted that in the failure of this special court to justify its existence 'lies the secret of the repeal of the Statute of Proclamations.'[26]

Despite its inaccuracies, Adair's work was the most scholarly and convincing study available for almost half a century. But it failed to win universal acceptance. Although serious historians no longer repeated the extreme interpretations of the eighteenth and nineteenth centuries, some felt, as Tanner did, that Adair had depreciated 'rather too much the importance of the act.'[27] Others felt that Adair had failed to explain adequately the opposition to the government's original bill. Lawrence Stone commented briefly on the Statute of Proclamations in May 1951. After noting Adair's explanation, he suggested that although the original bill was no longer extant and therefore the point could not be proven, the government probably

---

[25] *Ibid.* 41–2.   [26] *Ibid.* 43.
[27] J. R. Tanner, *Tudor Constitutional Documents A.D. 1485–1603* (Cambridge, 1922), 530. Plucknett, *Concise History of the Common Law*, 45, also found Adair's explanation inadequate, commenting that his 'extreme scepticism is rather difficult to justify.'

sought a good deal more from the statute than Adair surmised. He felt that the statute was 'an attempt – which failed – to give proclamations the full force of law.' Cromwell's comments in his letter to Norfolk, Marillac's remarks in April 1539 and James I's opinion that the first draft of the bill had been 'tyrannical' were cited in support of the belief.[28] The view that the statute gave the King new powers was also again expressed in 1958. Sir Charles Ogilvie argued that the portion of the statute which decreed the penalties of treason for those who left the realm to escape punishment for breaches of proclamations allowed the conciliar tribunal to 'inflict the penalties of treason' which 'could not be assumed by the council without statutory sanction.'[29]

The continuing debate finally induced G. R. Elton to write a lengthy article on the act. The article, which appeared in the April 1960 issue of *The English Historical Review*, was the most complete and scholarly analysis of the statute ever attempted. It sought to answer three questions which Professor Elton felt needed further comment: what were the meaning and effect of the Statute of Proclamations as it was finally passed; what was the nature of the original bill proposed by the government; and what changes did Parliament make in that bill? He began by reviewing more carefully and thoroughly than any of the previous writers each section of the statute, noting the strong emphasis on enforcement. However, he maintained that 'it will not do to regard this as its sole purpose. The preamble ranges wider and so, in part, does the enactment.'[30] The preamble clearly revealed that there was no need or intention to create a right to issue proclamations, for it assumed that right and gave both the causes and reason why the statute was necessary: 'The trouble about proclamations was in part that they were being evaded but in part too that their basic validity seems to have been called in doubt.'[31] The statute did not add to the powers of proclamations, because it took 'an unquestioned royal prerogative' which was asserted in the preamble and rested it 'on the authority of a parliamentary

---

[28] Lawrence Stone, 'The Political Programme of Thomas Cromwell,' *BIHR*, xxiv (May, 1951), 2.

[29] Charles Ogilvie, *The King's Government and the Common Law 1471–1641* (Oxford, 1958), 62.

[30] Elton, *EHR*, LXXV, 210. Elton stated that he preferred to abandon Adair's suggestion which he had accepted earlier. G. R. Elton, *The Tudor Revolution in Government* (Cambridge, 1953), 343. He rejected Adair's explanation because he felt that 'the setting up of such a statutory body is too clearly in line with other early-Tudor practice to come from anyone but the government. Since Adair could offer no evidence, however slender, and since I now feel that the probability is against his notion, I prefer to abandon it.' *Ibid.* 212 n. 3.   [31] *Ibid.* 210.

statute.' Rather than creating an independent royal legislative power, it 'subjected the prerogative to the sovereignty of the King in Parliament.'[32] Thus the statute as it was finally enacted was surely not 'a weapon of despotism or even of the prerogative.' It was 'an attempt to reorganize the machinery for the enforcement of proclamations' which 'also provided a general statutory justification for proclamations' and 'in the process limited the independent powers of the Crown by resting them on parliamentary authority.'[33]

Elton then turned to the more difficult problems of attempting to determine what was contained in the original government bill and to explain the opposition of the Parliament. He reviewed in detail the passage of the bill through Parliament and established that it faced strong opposition in both the Lords and the Commons. The Lords' amendments are noted in the original act in the Parliament office. They all tended to 'limit the independent vigour of royal proclamations' by adding the words 'by authority of this act' at key places in the text. The Commons, on the other hand, were more concerned about property rights. They were probably responsible for adding section II, which barred proclamations from imposing the death penalty and exempted freehold of all kinds from the operation of proclamations.[34] Thus the original bill was not 'quite as innocuous' as Adair thought. 'The chances are that it did not expressly bar proclamations from invading life and property, and it may have said more simply than the final act that proclamations were to have the same force as statute.' However, the history of Henry VIII's reign made it difficult to conjecture that Henry intended to rule without Parliament. The statute as it finally emerged must have been a compromise between Crown and Parliament which the Crown accepted because the changes introduced did not undermine the major purpose of the government in seeking it.

The story of this act is incomprehensible unless, on the one hand, there were serious differences between the Crown's views and those of both Lords and Commons, and unless, on the other, those differences were not so fundamental as to make a compromise between them impossible. After all, the bill was redrafted, not thrown out; after all, it received the King's assent... Furthermore, while enforcement of proclamations was the most obvious purpose of the act, their validity and scope entered fully into its drafting and there is every reason to suppose that it was this constitutional and legal question rather than the machinery for trying offenders which caused the trouble in Parliament.[35]

[32] *Ibid.* 211.
[34] *Ibid.* 218.
[33] *Ibid.* 214.
[35] *Ibid.* 221–2.

There was no serious challenge to Elton's interpretation for six years. In the intervening period the texts of the early Tudor royal proclamations were published, making new evidence readily available. However, the first major comment on the Statute of Proclamations after 1965 did not even cite a single proclamation. In his address to the Royal Historical Society on 8 October 1966, Professor Hurstfield readily admitted that he had 'not mentioned a single new document but only material which is perfectly well known to historians,'[36] and that his major concern was to resurrect the concept of 'Tudor Despotism' from the historical 'dustbin.' The original bill submitted by the government rather than the Statute of Proclamations was a central concern in his argument, because he maintained that although 'the statute gave very little to the Crown that it did not already possess,' the Crown had sought a great deal more. It was the Crown's intent, rather than what was achieved, which Hurstfield felt supported his belief that the Tudors attempted to set up a despotism.[37]

Hurstfield began by examining the preamble to the statute. He asked why 'the large claims of the preamble' were 'at variance with the minimal powers claimed by subsequent clauses.' He answered this question by stating that the preamble was 'the declaration of government claims and intentions' while 'the enacting clauses' were all that they were successful in achieving after Parliament changed the original bill.[38] To establish that the intent of the government was 'tyrannical,' he cited all the old evidence, including Aylmer's, James I's and Gardiner's statements. The oft-repeated arguments that a statute which rested on the consent of Parliament could not pose a threat to Parliament and that proclamations were thought of as emergency legislation did not impress him. He reminded his listeners that the German Reichstag had also granted Hitler the right to govern by edict 'in time of emergency.' He also used Cromwell's letter to Norfolk which he stated gave 'a clue to his [Cromwell's] processes of thought.'[39] He agreed that Cromwell may have preferred a statutory basis but questioned whether the use of statute precluded a despotism: 'Of course Cromwell preferred to support every extension of the royal power by statute; that made it all the more powerful and all the more secure, and it gave the illusion of popular consent.' The Crown needed the authority of Parliament to give proclamations the force of law,

---

[36] Hurstfield, *TRHS*, XVII, 107.
[37] *Ibid.* 93.
[38] *Ibid.* 95.
[39] *Ibid.* 97.

because 'there were no other means open to it if it wanted to gain those powers lawfully. But is a thing less tyrannical because it is lawful?'[40] The government failed in its effort, but 'in asking ourselves whether there was a Tudor despotism we are also asking whether the government was trying to establish a Tudor despotism.' Professor Hurstfield was convinced that the original bill for the Statute of Proclamations was intended to do precisely this.[41]

It is not surprising that Professor Elton responded to Hurstfield's attempt to reintroduce the concept of Tudor despotism. That response included an additional comment on the Statute of Proclamations. In his effort to refute the argument that royal proclamations might have posed a threat to parliamentary legislation, Elton maintained that 'the royal prerogative to issue proclamations did not enfranchise any personal legislative authority in the Crown, before, under, or after the act of proclamations.'[42] He also insisted that the government never had intended to establish an independent legislative power: 'So far was this much maligned act from wishing to augment the King's power that rather surprisingly it expressly asserted the opposite intention.' The preamble stated that the 'one reason for legislative action' was 'the fear that in his eagerness to make the people behave themselves the King might extend the liberty and supremacy of his royal power. This expansion beyond the limits set by the law the statute treats as undesirable, and it therefore must be regarded as limiting.'[43] Elton further questioned Hurstfield's documentation since he relied 'on the memories of opposition and the terms of the preamble.' Elton noted that the fact that the original bill was replaced by Parliament with a new bill proved 'nothing about the intensity of opposition or the character of the original bill' since this was a common practice in Tudor parliaments.[44] He argued further that Hurstfield had misread Cromwell's letter to Norfolk. It did not show that Cromwell was 'pleased at being able to use proclamations instead of statutes. It shows only that he was unfamiliar with the power of proclamations at common law, with the massive precedents for the use of proclamations touching coin and with a relevant statute of Richard II's.'[45] He also cited Cromwell's use of

---

[40] *Ibid.* 98.   [41] *Ibid.* 99.
[42] Elton, *Tudor Men and Institutions*, 278.
[43] *Ibid.* 279.   [44] *Ibid.* 280.
[45] *Ibid.* 281–2. Elton also offered evidence that 1531 was a more convincing date for the letter than 1535 and noted that 'Cromwell's apparent ignorance of the power of proclamations is explained now that we know he expressed it early in his official career while the eight years between the letter and the act of proclamations make quite sure that he

proclamations to set meat prices. This documented Cromwell's preference for statute even where there was an undoubted right to act by royal proclamation. Finally, he noted that Somerset, who was responsible for the repeal of the Statute of Proclamations, had 'issued far more ominous proclamations than Henry VIII had done with or without the act.'[46]

These are, to my knowledge, the major interpretations of the Statute of Proclamations to the present date. They reveal that a good deal of intensive research on the events surrounding the passage of the statute and a thorough analysis of the wording of the act have not provided adequate evidence to resolve the controversy satisfactorily. What has been lacking is a concerted effort to apply a study of the actual use of royal proclamations to an understanding of the statute. Only Professor Elton, in his most recent comment, has bothered to cite this type of evidence in support of his arguments. At least on the basis of the citations in their footnotes it does not seem that any of the other commentators have even looked at the text of a single proclamation. Thus it would seem that a 'new look' based on the evidence in the proclamations' texts and on the actual use of royal proclamations in the early Tudor period is in order.

A new look

Three questions are basically at issue in considering the meaning and impact of the Statute of Proclamations: (1) What was actually achieved by the statute? (2) What did the government seek in the original bill? (3) Why was the statute repealed? The first question is the easiest to answer on the basis of the evidence already presented. The statute provided first a general definition of the prerogative power to issue royal proclamations. In doing so it established some very clear boundaries which curtailed the King's power. Although proclamations had seldom been used in a manner which exceeded these limits, there were times especially when Wolsey was the King's chief minister that they were used in a fashion which would not have been legal under the provisions of the statute. Because legal writers and judges had said very little about the powers of proclamations before 1539, it would be difficult to argue that Wolsey's use of them was unconstitutional. If we are to believe Cromwell's account in his

did not, in consequence of what he had learned, lay up a thought of substituting proclamations for statutes throughout the time of his ministry. The date of 1531 makes the letter entirely useless for Dr Hurstfield's purposes.' *Ibid.* 282 n. 34.
[46] *Ibid.* 283.

letter to Norfolk, which even those who view the statute as a tyrannical measure seem ready to believe for their own purposes, some judges allowed very broad powers to proclamations in times of emergency. The Lord Chief Justice, after all, had stated that when there was 'so great a danger' the King with the advice of council could 'make proclamations and use all other policies at his pleasure ...for the avoiding of any such dangers and that the said proclamations and policies...should be of as good effect as any law made by Parliament or otherwise.'[47] The limitations in the Statute of Proclamations which prevented proclamations from infringing the common law and statutes, or inflicting penalties of death and loss of freehold except in cases of heresy, were certainly the generally accepted boundaries in normal times, but there may have been some question if they applied in times of 'so great a danger.' The restrictions on penalties had been exceeded when Wolsey was the King's chief minister even when no great danger could be argued. In 1539, during what was certainly a time of 'great danger,' a proclamation also threatened penalties which would not have been legal after the passage of the Statute of Proclamations. Thus the statute first defined and limited the powers of proclamations.

Secondly, the statute ordered that proclamations be obeyed like parliamentary statutes, but it did not state that even in their limited sphere were they to be considered permanent legislation in the same way as parliamentary statutes were. The statute spoke of them as temporary legislation. The preamble refers to 'sudden causes and occasions...which do require speedy remedies and that by abiding for a Parliament in the meantime might happen great prejudice to ensue to the realm.' What has not normally been noticed is that even the infamous enacting clause implies that they are temporary legislation, for they are to be obeyed 'as though they were made by act of Parliament *for the time in them limited* [my italics].' One would have to view the statute with a very jaundiced eye indeed to argue that it considered proclamations permanent legislation in the same manner as statutes. The whole emphasis of the act and the justification for its enactment are that they are necessary to provide emergency solutions when Parliament cannot act swiftly enough. Of course, this is precisely the way they were generally used in the eight years preceding the statute. Therefore, this understanding of the terms of the statute is in accord with the evidence gleaned from the study of the actual use of proclamations.

If what has been said so far is true, it would seem that the govern-

[47] BM Titus B 1/311d.

THE STATUTE OF PROCLAMATIONS

ment lost more than it gained. One is therefore naturally inclined to ask why the Crown was willing to accept the statute in its final form, because it is hard to conceive of any government deliberately seeking to limit its powers. Certainly the Crown must have gained something which made the concessions they may have granted in the revised version of the original bill worthwhile. The obvious answer is that the statute granted first a general parliamentary authority for all proclamations. This, as has been shown in detail, was a major concern of Thomas Cromwell. He sought parliamentary authority for proclamations even in areas where it was generally accepted that such authority was unnecessary. Thus in this respect the statute involved little more than a continuation, although in a considerably more sweeping way, of the policy that had been followed throughout the 1530s. However, unless we are prepared to assume a greater philosophical devotion to statutory authority on the part of Thomas Cromwell than would be plausible for a practical statesman, it is hard to accept that this was a sufficient reason for the act. The Crown must have gained something in addition to statutory confirmation of its prerogative right to issue royal proclamations, and it clearly did.

Any objective reading of the statute cannot miss the strong emphasis on enforcement throughout the act. The title of the act, 'that proclamations made by the King shall be obeyed' emphasizes enforcement. The preamble complained that proclamations were not being obeyed and stressed the need that 'an ordinary law should be provided...for due punishment, correction and reformation of such offences and disobediences.' The first enacting clause deals only with enforcement. Proclamations are to 'be obeyed, observed, and kept as though they were made by act of Parliament.' With the exception of section VIII, which stated that proclamations issued during the minority of a King must be signed by the majority of the privy council, the other clauses all had some relationship to enforcement. Section II limited the penalties which could be imposed. Section III attempted to make sure that lack of knowledge of a proclamation would not provide excuses for disobedience. The next two sections set up the special conciliar court and allowed the issue of process under the great or privy seal. Sections VI and VII tried to provide a safeguard against the accused leaving the realm or hiding to avoid prosecution within the eighteen months' limitation. Section IX attempted to make sure that justices of the peace paid strict attention to enforcement. Finally, the last section allowed the court to diminish the penalties in proclamations.

The statute was obviously intended to improve the efficiency of enforcement by providing for a special court with speedy process to deal with offenders, and by making sure that proclamations were given sufficient publicity and that justices of the peace carried out their duties. Even though it said nothing about the jurisdiction of other courts, it probably also cleared up doubts about whether proclamations could be enforced in ordinary courts, using methods normally decreed in penal statutes. What the government achieved is quite clear. It obtained a general statutory basis for all proclamations, and most important, it acquired what was hoped would be an improved method of enforcement. In return it agreed to certain limitations on the power of proclamations which had been generally observed anyway. Thus any government willing to observe the traditional limits of the royal prerogative had sacrificed very little. Only one which intended to use royal proclamations as a weapon of despotism would have been severely inhibited by the statute. There is no indication from the use of royal proclamations in the 1530s that there was any effort in that direction while Thomas Cromwell was the King's chief minister.

Nevertheless, one cannot ignore the clear evidence that the original bill was altered by Parliament and that the government failed to achieve its full objectives. Therefore, one must seek to determine what the government sought in the original bill in order to answer Professor Hurstfield's contention that the Statute of Proclamations involved an effort to establish legislation by decree and that it failed. Since it is always more difficult to deal with questions involving hidden motivation than to document what actually happened, it is not easy to provide an answer that cannot be challenged, even using the evidence presented in this study. How proclamations were used after the statute was passed has no relevance because the government did not achieve its full objectives and the man normally accused of being responsible for the statute was executed in 1540. One must therefore rely on whatever additional evidence can be marshalled to reveal what led to the original bill and what changes Parliament made in it.

It seems fairly clear that Professor Elton was right in his contention that section II was added by the Commons. As he pointed out, it is a proviso and it seems to be imprecise in its drafting.[48] In addition,

[48] 'The drafting of this clause leaves something to be desired. As it stands it does not protect subsequent legislation from infringement by proclamations which could have been a very serious matter if the act had lasted. Nor is it at all plain what the exception about heresy meant.' Elton, *EHR*, LXXV, 211.

THE STATUTE OF PROCLAMATIONS

by the Elizabethan period it was believed that this is precisely what had happened. Alymer's remarks are not specific enough for us to know what he meant when he commended those who defended 'their liberty' and 'would not grant' the King 'that his proclamation should have the force of a statute.' But another probably more authoritative comment in the Elizabethan period was quite specific. In the 1576 Parliament a bill was sent from the Lords to the Commons already engrossed with the Queen's signature. The Commons, nevertheless, added a proviso to the bill. The Lords argued that since the bill had already been signed by the Queen the Commons could not add to it or alter it. In the ensuing debate a number of precedents were cited for the action. The account in Thomas Cromwell's diary reads as follows:

Diverse precedents also were recited in like cases namely that to a bill preferred and subscribed by King Henry VIIIth that it might be lawful for him by proclamation to make a law that there was a proviso added by the house which took away the whole body of the act.[49]

Since this remark was made over thirty years after the event its reliability might be doubted, but in at least one respect it agrees with the other evidence. The only proviso that could have been added which could be interpreted as having taken 'away the whole body of the act' would have been section II. This is what Professor Elton suggested, and combined with the evidence he offered, it seems likely that the original government bill did not contain the limiting clause.

If this is true, one is left with what could be used to infer some ominous intent on the part of the government. Without the safeguards in section II proclamations might have posed a threat to parliamentary legislation if the government had been intent on governing by royal decree. But was this the intent of the government which drafted the bill? All the evidence submitted earlier on how proclamations were used surely established that, unless there was some radical change in policy in the months preceding the Parliament of 1539, Cromwell's government preferred statutory authority; proclamations were used primarily as temporary emergency legislation or they were based on statutes. Only if we totally ignore the way in which they were used in the 1530s can we assume that there was a desire to govern without Parliament in 1539. Furthermore, there is at least some scattered evidence which suggests what may have led to the

---

[49] Trinity College MS 1045(4)/131. The debate is described in J. E. Neale, *Elizabeth I and Her Parliaments 1559–81* (New York, 1958), 358. Thomas Cromwell was the grandson of Henry VIII's minister.

drafting of the original bill. All of it reveals a concern about enforcement. This should not be surprising because the preamble, which was probably in the original bill, complains that proclamations were being 'willfully condemned and broken' and the statute was primarily concerned with enforcement.

It has also been shown that in the late 1530s Cromwell made repeated efforts to improve enforcement. There must have been a special problem with proclamations on religious matters because the records contain numerous references to resistance to those proclamations, especially in the late months of 1538 and the early part of 1539.[50] People were particularly reluctant to obey that portion of the proclamation of 16 November 1538 which abrogated the festival and service associated with Thomas Becket. Sir William Walgrave, J.P. in Suffolk, wrote to Cromwell in December 1538 that his grandmother had a chaplain who was a papist and 'hath in his mass book daily this Thomas Becket's name with all his pestiferous collects,' and that 'for all proclamations or injunctions' there was 'no punishment.' He went on to comment that as a result of his effort to enforce the proclamation he was 'suspect and except I have commandment from your lordship I dare not meddle.'[51] In January 1539 the parson of Gislingham, Thomas Tyrrel, was accused before the sessions at Ipswich of violating the November 1538 proclamation. Witnesses testified that the parson had been shown the proclamation but he 'said unless he had a commandment from his ordinary he would not obey it.'[52] In March 1539 Miles Coverdale reported to Cromwell that in Henley on Thames 'the image of Thomas Becket with the whole feigned story of his death is suffered to stand still.' He blamed the Bishop of Lincoln for 'great and notable negligence.'[53] The government must have been concerned about the resistance to ecclesiastical proclamations in the spring of 1539, because the draft proclamation probably drawn up in April 1539 refers to this problem. It is also interesting that this proclamation would have been the first proclamation based on the Statute of Proclamations if it had been issued.[54]

[50] Elton, *Policy and Police*, 258 comments that the vacillations in the religious policy in the late 1530s 'did not assist a coherent policy of either reform or stand-still nor did they help at all in the task of enforcement.'
[51] SP 1/140/225 (*LP* 13[2] no. 1179); *TRP* no. 186.
[52] SP 1/142/62 (*LP* 14[1] no. 76).
[53] SP 1/144/35 (*LP* 14[1] no. 444). Other reports of violations of the same proclamation are found in SP 1/150/170-1 (*LP* 14[1] no. 821); SP 1/152/1-2 (*LP* 14[1] no. 1053).
[54] *TRP* no. 191; BM Cleo. E v/311. Curiously the penalty section was left blank in the draft possibly because it was drawn up while the question was being debated in Parlia-

THE STATUTE OF PROCLAMATIONS

The problems over religion coincided with the serious foreign threat that developed in the early months of 1539. The proclamation of 28 February forbidding unlicensed shipping on pain of death an forfeiture of lands, goods, and chattels was issued in reaction to that threat. This must have been what Gardiner had in mind when he wrote to Somerset to protest against the 1547 injunctions. He was endeavoring to convince Somerset that the King could not command against an act of Parliament. In what seems to have been the first draft of the letter he stated:

Since that time, being of the council, when many proclamations were devised against the carriers out of corn, when it came to punish the offenders, the judges would answer, it might not be by the laws, because the act of Parliament gave liberty, wheat being under a price. Whereupon at the last followed the Act of Proclamations in the passing whereof were many large words spoken.[55]

This statement supported Gardiner's argument, but it was obviously untrue, because 25 Henry VIII c. 2 had already forbidden unlicensed exports. Therefore the medieval legislation on the subject which would have given 'liberty' when wheat was under a certain price did not apply. Proclamations forbidding export of corn could not have been declared illegal by the judges on the grounds of violating an act of Parliament. Gardiner seemingly recognized this. In a second and expanded draft of the letter he introduced an interesting revision which offered less support for his argument, but which was probably closer to the truth:

Since that time, being of the council, when many proclamations were devised against the carriers out of corn, at such time as the transgressors should be punished, the judges would answer, it might not be by the laws. Whereupon ensued the Act of Proclamations in the passing of which act many liberal words were spoken, and a plain promise that, by authority of the Act for Proclamation, nothing should be made contrary to an act of Parliament or common law.[56]

ment. At approximately the same time Calais was experiencing troubles over religion, and the council was divided over the punishment of those accused of 'erroneous opinions on the sacrament' and 'evil opinion concerning scripture.' SP 1/151/253–4 (*LP* 14[1] no. 1042). It may have been this controversy which caused Husse to remark in a letter to Lord Lisle on 2 May 1539 'after my singular opinion if any man accept contrary in doings or sayings to the King's highness' proclamations and injunctions it should stand with reason that he were punished according to the extent of the same or else otherwise as it should be thought requisite and expedient by your lordship and the council there.' SP 3/4/59 (*LP* 14[1] no. 913).

[55] Muller, *Letters of Gardiner*, 391. The injunctions are included in *TRP* as no. 287. Gardiner maintained that the injunction violated 34 and 35 Henry VIII c. 1. See below pp. 205–6.

[56] *Ibid.* Muller believed that this second draft was the final version.

The difference between the two versions is important. The second draft deleted the section referring to an act of Parliament giving liberty and stressed that the judges answered 'it might not be by the laws' when the time came 'as the transgressors should be punished ...whereupon ensued the Act of Proclamations.' Gardiner does not say, as he did in the first draft, that the judges said that a proclamation could not violate a statute. Rather, they said that the punishment 'might not be by the laws.' The only extant proclamation which might have resulted in this type of decision was that of 28 February forbidding unlicensed shipping.

If this is true, then Gardiner's statement provides what may be the missing link in reconstructing the events surrounding the drafting of the bill for proclamations. Throughout the 1530s, there had been a growing concern about the enforcement of proclamations. This concern reached a crisis point in the last years of the decade. Enforcement must have been hampered by the lack of definition, for it was not clear what courts had jurisdiction over proclamations or even what penalties might be imposed.[57] In addition local officials must have at times been notoriously negligent in carrying out their duties, or the severe threats to them in some proclamations of the late 1530s would not have been necessary. Furthermore, the effort to enforce the export legislation seems to have had limited success, possibly as a result of the lack of effective judicial enforcement and the negligence of port officials. In February 1539, when severe measures were needed to deal with a deteriorating foreign situation, these problems became especially serious. Both the embargo imposed upon shipping and the granting of equal customs to foreign merchants were probably issued in response to the serious threat of an invasion from the Continent. The first proclamation of 26 February 1539 allowing foreign merchants the same customs rates as English merchants was probably very unpopular, for similar measures had failed in Parliament, but it provided an important foreign policy weapon. In order to make sure that customs officials complied with this unpopular legislation, severe penalties including loss of their office and a fine of ten times as much as they took in additional

[57] This is suggested by one of the earliest comments on the Statute of Proclamations. *The Discourse Upon the Statutes*, probably written early in the reign of Elizabeth, stated 'but therein hath been doubted of what effect such proclamations have been, and what pain he that breaketh them should have. And some said that the pain is the loss of his allegiance. As for the authority of them an act of Parliament was made in 31 Henry VIII which is now repealed...' Thorne, *Discourse*, 105. This seems to imply that before the enactment of the Statute of Proclamations there was a debate over the penalties that could be imposed.

THE STATUTE OF PROCLAMATIONS

customs from foreign merchants were threatened. The second proclamation, which imposed felony penalties for violating the embargo, also included severe penalties to deter offenders. But in light of the Lord Chief Justice's statement in 1531, even these penalties did not seem to be illegal when the commonwealth was facing 'so great a danger.' However, when this was tested in court other judges may have thought otherwise and stated 'it might not be by the laws'; so a bill was drafted which would have provided parliamentary authority for the use of even the most severe penalties when 'sudden causes and occasions...do require speedy remedies.' It may even have been Gardiner rather than Cromwell who suggested the need for these sweeping powers, as Nathaniel Bacon maintained,[58] but the rest of the bill surely reflects Cromwell's concerns about enforcement and statutory authority.

Thus the original bill was probably influenced by the events in the spring of 1539, but it ranged further than this. It was meant to clear up any doubts about judicial jurisdiction and to provide for a systematic, orderly and efficient system of enforcing proclamations. Furthermore, it would have allowed the government to impose even the most severe penalties in an effort to deter offenders. But it was in no way intended to equate proclamations with statutes as permanent legislation. The statute as it was enacted referred to them as temporary emergency measures. Cromwell's use of proclamations before 1539 suggests that the original bill did not differ on this point. The King, who had a special concern with proclamations on religious matters, may have been responsible for the specific references to religion and the exception granted to proclamations 'for and con-

[58] Bacon's account of the events leading to the Statute of Proclamations is curiously unique and may have been based on information no longer available. This could even have been an oral tradition in the Bacon family, since Nathaniel was the grandson of Nicholas Bacon and the nephew of Francis Bacon, who may have given James I his information that a certain 'Bacon' led the fight in Parliament against the government bill. There is no evidence that this was Nicholas because we do not even know if he sat on the Parliament of 1539, but it is interesting that Bacon's name should be mentioned. Nathaniel Bacon probably altered his account to fit his preconceptions, but his explanation of the events leading to the Statute of Proclamations is in conflict with his effort to prove that Henry VIII sought 'what no King before him suffered ever to enter into conceit; I mean a legislative power' and that a vigilant Commons blocked the effort. He first stated that what was sought was power to act in sudden emergencies so that the King would not 'be at disadvantage either with the Emperor or French King' and to deal with a tense religious situation. He is able to make the transition to his conclusion that the King sought 'a legislative power' only by maintaining that the events he described provided the rationalization for what followed: 'These and the like represented a fair face to that which followed...' Bacon, *Discourse*, 125.

cerning any kinds of heresies against the Christian religion.'[59] This may also have resulted from the difficulty encountered in enforcing those proclamations in 1538 and 1539.

Of course, much of this is conjecture, but every explanation of the Statute of Proclamations has been forced to rely on conjecture to some extent because the evidence for a definitive statement is not available. Furthermore, the explanation fits the known facts surrounding the enactment of the Statute of Proclamations, and, more important, it is in accord with the solid evidence gained from the study of the use of royal proclamations. Finally, it explains why the government accepted a statute that had been so extensively revised by Parliament. The Elizabethan commentator was wrong. The changes introduced by the Commons did not take 'away the whole body of the act.' They simply imposed certain limitations which the government was willing to accept, because except in the crisis brought on by the events in the spring of 1539, they had not normally been violated. The more important concerns of Cromwell were not removed, for both the enforcement procedures and the general statutory authority for proclamations remained in the final statute. Although the full objectives were not achieved, the final statute must have reflected what was the major purpose of the government in seeking the act.[60]

If the statute and the intentions of the government were really as innocent as stated above, why was the act repealed in the first Parliament following the death of Henry VIII? Earlier explanations which attributed the repeal to Somerset's concern that the act was tyrannical will obviously not suffice if the act was not tyrannical. In addition, as will be shown, Somerset used proclamations more extensively and in a more questionable fashion than anyone else in the early Tudor period.[61] Professor Elton believed that the repeal can

[59] He even corrected with his own hand the draft proclamation on April 1539 which would have been the first proclamation specifically based on the Statute of Proclamations (BM Cleo. E v/311; *TRP* no. 191).

[60] If it is true that the references to religion reflect the King's concerns, it may have been his influence that prevented the Commons from applying the limitations in section II to religious proclamations. If so, his objectives were also achieved in the final statute.

[61] Professor Jordan argued that the Statute of Proclamations was repealed 'to mitigate the heavy penalties with which Henrician proclamations were buttressed and to posit the effective power of proclamations on more nearly acceptable constitutional grounds.' Jordan, *The Young King*, 174. Since Jordan admits that 'There is no evidence whatsoever of any timidity in the employment and expansion of royal power by the use of proclamations under the tenure of the Duke of Somerset' (*ibid.* 350), his explanation of the repeal of the Statute of Proclamations is surprising even if one assumes that he did not know that Somerset used severe penalties more often than others had.

be explained by the clause which specified that at least half of the council must sign proclamations during the King's minority, because it militated against the ascendancy of one man. This explanation is more reasonable, but it also does not stand the test of recently discovered evidence. Chancery warrants reveal that proclamations were signed by the council both while the statute was in effect and after its repeal. Furthermore, Somerset did not obey the clause requiring twelve signatures even while the statute was in effect.[62] Except for a passing remark which Somerset made to the Spanish Ambassador, Van der Delft, in November 1547, which would have to be interpreted very liberally to make it apply to the repeal of the Statute of Proclamations,[63] the records are silent on the motives for the repeal; therefore, one must search elsewhere for evidence. Fortunately at least some evidence can be gleaned from Parliamentary records.

In 1543, 34 and 35 Henry VIII c. 23 revised the Statute of Proclamations by lowering the quorum in the statutory court set up by that statute. According to the preamble of the amending act the action was necessitated because 'diverse and sundry informations' had been presented to the court 'and the same information after issue joined and witnesses published have taken no effect, end, or perfect determination' within the statutory time limit 'for and in default that there hath not been present so many of the King's most honorable council' as were required by the Statute of Proclamations. Surprisingly, this procedural change encountered parliamentary opposition which resulted in the amendment of the original bill. On 3 March 1543 a 'bill of certain of the King's majesty's council to give judgment and take order against offenders and breakers of proclamations' was introduced in the House of Lords.[64] No mention is made of that bill in the Lords' Journal until 19 April, six weeks later. However, on 18 April the reading of an 'act for the authorizement of the King's majesty to make proclamations and the same so made to stand in no less strength than if the same had been enacted by authority of Parliament' is recorded. This act must have been the

[62] Elton, *EHR*, LXXV, 214; Hoak, 'Edward VI's Council,' 210.
[63] Van der Delft wrote to the Queen dowager on 9 November 1547: 'Being desirous of discovering something about the reasons for the convocation of this Parliament I mentioned the matter to the Protector, and after much conversation he told me that they had decided to abolish and to modify several of their laws which at present were too severe, and to give to the subjects a little more reasonable liberty without in any way releasing them from the restraints of proper order and obedience.' *CSPSp*, I, 197. This is clearly a reference to Henry VIII's treason legislation, which was repealed in the same Parliament, rather than to the Statute of Proclamations.   [64] *LJ*, I, 212.

Statute of Proclamations, for the title leaves no other possibility. The following day the original bill was given a second reading. At the next meeting of Parliament on 21 April it was given its third reading and sent to the Commons, but the Lords' Journal records a dissenting voice: 'Billa against breakers of proclamations cui omnes proceres assenserunt preter Dominum Mountjoye.'[65] The Lords obviously had some doubts about the bill, because they had the Statute of Proclamations read before proceeding to the second reading, possibly to assure that there were adequate safeguards on the question of penalties. But even then at least one of the members opposed the bill. The bill now disappeared in the Commons until 8 May when it was returned to the Lords, 'with new words thereunto annexed.'[66] The Commons had enough objections to amend the bill. Fortunately their addition can easily be determined by looking at the original bill in the House of Lords Record Office. The act is written in a very precise clerk's hand with no additions or corrections until the last sentence, which is in an entirely different hand. This must have been the amendment added by the Commons. The sentence reads: 'This act to endure during the King's majesty's life which our Lord long preserve.'[67]

Thus the Commons were responsible for restricting the duration of the statute to Henry VIII's reign, and that limitation may have proved quite significant. With the death of Henry VIII the statute was no longer in effect. Therefore Edward's councilors were faced with the same unwieldy court that had originally necessitated the passage of 34 and 35 Henry VIII c. 23. Somerset might have tried to extend the act, but he must have been aware both of the opposition in 1543 and that the Commons had been responsible for limiting the statute to the lifetime of Henry VIII. Without 34 and 35 Henry VIII c. 23, the conciliar court was certainly less effective and the Statute of Proclamations may now have seemed more of a hindrance than a benefit, for Somerset had recently been reminded by Gardiner of the limitations imposed by the act in the letter which accused him of issuing injunctions in violation of a statute. Thus by repealing what seems to have been an unpopular statute, Somerset lost nothing, because he preferred using the council to enforce proclamations in a quasi-judicial manner, and he does not seem to have been concerned about statutory authority for proclamations. Furthermore, he was able to gain both a greater freedom in the use of proclamations

[65] *Ibid.* 224.   [66] *Ibid.* 230.
[67] House of Lords Record Office, M, 34 and 35 Henry VIII c. 23.

and possibly win the gratitude of Parliament. Although one would prefer more evidence, this explanation of the repeal fits Somerset's use of royal proclamations more than other interpretations and is consistent with the only interpretation of the Statute of Proclamations that seems reasonable.[68]

[68] This explanation is not entirely new. Adair, relying entirely on the preamble of 34 and 35 Henry VIII c. 23, surmised a connection between the failure of the statutory court and the repeal of the Statute of Proclamations. 'In the failure of this special court to justify its existence lies the secret of the repeal of the Statute of Proclamations.' Adair, *EHR*, xxxii, 43. The repealing act, 1 Edward VI c. 12, also repealed 34 and 35 Henry VIII c. 23, but this must have only been a formality since the act was clearly limited to the lifetime of Henry VIII.

7

THE USE OF ROYAL PROCLAMATIONS: HENRY VIII – THE SECOND STAGE

The point that most forcibly strikes the student of history, as distinct from the student of law, is the extent to which this act [Statute of Proclamations] remained a dead letter. It may be that it was Cromwell's rather than Henry VIII's proposal...Cromwell fell in 1540, the year after the Statute of Proclamations was passed...and the act was almost ignored. A hundred and twenty proclamations are known to have been issued between the passing of that statute and Henry's death, and not one of these seems to depend for its validity on the statute...Either Henry VIII did not interpret the statute as conferring new powers of legislation on the crown, or else he refrained from using them.[1]

Historians have long been aware that the Statute of Proclamations did not result in any radical change in the use of royal proclamations. Pollard had already noticed this in 1920. However, since his analysis was based entirely on the titles and summaries in Steele's list, he did not know that the act had an impact on some of the proclamations issued while it was in effect. Although it did not grant the King 'new powers of legislation,' it did not remain 'a dead letter.' Approximately twelve percent of the surviving proclamations issued during the remainder of Henry VIII's reign referred to it. Since they provide an important test of how the act was used, a careful comparison of these proclamations with those which did not cite the statute should make it possible to determine how government regarded the act. Unfortunately, if the statute 'was Cromwell's rather than Henry VIII's proposal,' we may never know how Cromwell planned to use it. He fell from power in June 1540. Only two of the proclamations issued during the last year of his ministry have survived. Neither of them cited the Statute of Proclamations. The first set wine prices on the authority of 23 Henry VIII c. 7. The second continued the suspension of the meat price statute until November 1541.[2] Fittingly the final two proclamations which might still be ascribed to Cromwell were both based on specific statutory authority.

[1] Pollard, *Evolution of Parliament*, 260.
[2] *TRP* nos. 191.5, 193.

HENRY VIII – THE SECOND STAGE

On 16 February 1541 new and severe penalties for unlicensed export and a new method of enforcement were introduced by the first surviving royal proclamation that mentioned the 1539 act. It forbade unlicensed export of corn, grain, meal, billet, timber, tanned leather or hides upon pain of forfeiture of the items shipped and 'all other their goods and chattels and also to have imprisonment at the King's majesty's will and pleasure.' Mariners who transported the goods were threatened with the loss of their ships and also of their goods and chattels in the ships. Port officials who allowed the export would forfeit their offices as well as their goods and chattels. Informers were allowed to sue for one-quarter of the forfeiture before the conciliar court set up by the Statute of Proclamations.[3] Although the regulations on leather and timber export may have been new,[4] the prohibitions on grain export were in conformity with the restrictions on unlicensed export in 25 Henry VIII c. 2. However, the statutory penalty was only forfeiture of the item shipped. The statute also did not include penalties for shippers or negligent officials.

The severity of the penalties and the use of the conciliar court suggest that the government was making a determined effort to secure effective enforcement of the troublesome export legislation. Cromwell had difficulty enforcing these laws throughout the 1530s. These problems continued after 1540. A series of depositions from the Exchequer, dated January 1540, reveals that in the last six months of 1539 exporters were still using a variety of clever methods to evade the restrictions.[5] Late in 1540 a number of accusations were

---

[3] No surviving copy of this proclamation has been found. It must, therefore, be reconstructed from bills brought before the conciliar court which cited offenses against it. Hughes and Larkin have included a copy based on one of those bills as *TRP* no. 197.6; however, it is not a complete copy. Since that bill did not accuse port officials of allowing illegal export, that portion of the proclamation was not included in the bill. A more complete copy is found in St Ch 2/2/170. Another copy is found in St Ch 2/23/183. None of the bills included the enforcement clause, but it can be reconstructed from 34 and 35 Henry VIII c. 9, which referred to the proclamation. Offenders against one section of that statute were threatened with forfeiture both of the grain shipped and of their ships if they failed to enter into security with the customer at Bristol not to transport the goods abroad, 'whereof the King our sovereign lord to have three parts thereof and the party that will sue for the same the fourth part before the King's most honorable council according to the King's proclamation in that behalf made and provided.'

[4] This was the first of a series of proclamations which introduced wide prohibitions on unlicensed export including leather and wood. There does not seem to have been any statutory basis for those on leather and wood. 27 Henry VIII c. 14 forbade the export of salt hides and prohibited export of leather by tanners, but did not include any sweeping prohibitions on unlicensed leather export. The Emperor felt that the restraints imposed were new, but he maintained the council argued that 'such other necessary commodities of the realm have always by old laws and statutes been prohibited which they could never transport without license.' SP 1/166/202–6 (*LP* 16 no. 1085).

[5] E 36/120/123–35 (*LP* 15 no. 61).

brought to the council by the notorious informer, George Whelplay, alleging both extensive illegal export and serious malfeasance of duty by port officials.[6] Even if these charges were not proved they must have had an influence on the penalties for negligent officials included in the proclamation. Chapuys reported to Charles V that illegal export had been common because 'there was no other penalty for the transgressors except the confiscation and loss of such prohibited goods.' He felt that with the more severe penalties 'they will now take good care not to' continue these violations.[7]

The proclamation failed to make an exception for the victualling of Calais. In April the Deputy and Council of Calais complained to the council that the provision of victual for their city was being seriously hampered. In May a letter addressed directly to the King spoke of a serious shortage in Calais since 'no man dare bring it [victual] over for fear of the proclamation.' The letter requested that Calais might be victualled in the 'old fashion before the proclamation.'[8] Two weeks later a new proclamation, again made by the authority of the statute, commented on the need for a 'more speedy remedy for the victualling of his said town of Calais and castles.' It allowed export to Calais without license as long as the exporters bound themselves by an obligation amounting to double the value of the goods shipped and brought back a certificate from officials in Calais that delivery had been made. However, if shippers 'falsely and untruly convey such victuals and things to other places out of his [the King's] dominions' or if the supplies after being delivered to Calais were then exported to foreign ports, the violators would suffer the full penalties of the earlier proclamation.[9] This was the first modification of the February 1541 proclamation. It was changed a number of times during the remainder of the reign, but without

---

[6] For Whelplay's activities see G. R. Elton, *Star Chamber Stories* (London, 1958), 58ff. Whelplay maintained that of some 3,750 quarters of grain shipped from Yarmouth in a two-month period between November 1539 and January 1540, 1,800 quarters had been illegally exported and he provided the names of twelve offenders. SP 1/243/169-70 (*LP* App. 1 no. 1490[3]). He furthermore accused port officials in a series of ports of 'untrue dealing in their offices.' Despite Whelplay's reputation, the council took the accusations seriously and asked the Duke of Norfolk, who as lord treasurer was responsible for the customs service, to investigate, reminding Norfolk that the King 'taketh' the matter 'very earnestly'. Nicolas, VII, 57, 60-1. In November Whelplay and his assistant, Ellis Brooke, were examined by the council on 'information put in by them against the customers, comptrollers and searchers.' They were unable to prove all the articles and they were given more time, but at least one port official 'being specifically accused by the foresaid parties seemed culpable of certain matter laid to his charge and upon the which it was agreed that the Duke of Norfolk should take order with him in that behalf.' *Ibid.* 78.

[7] *CSPSp*, no. 153 (*LP* 16 no. 554).

[8] SP 1/165/69-70, 180-5 (*LP* 16 nos. 703, 808).   [9] *TRP* no. 201.

HENRY VIII – THE SECOND STAGE

citing the Statute of Proclamations. Most of these changes involved temporary adjustments to provide for victualling of the armies during the French war; however, the basic regulations and penalties imposed by the 1541 proclamation may have remained in effect until the death of Henry VIII. There was no further statutory legislation on the subject and there is no evidence that it was ever revoked.[10]

A second group of proclamations based on the Statute of Proclamations was concerned with matters involving hunting and hawking. On 3 November 1541 Hatfield Chase in Yorkshire was enlarged by the addition of two manors recently acquired from the confiscation of monastic property.[11] The action was probably unpopular with tenants on those manors, for it brought them under the strict control of the forest laws. But at least in the opinion of Coke it was legal. He maintained that although the King could not afforest his subjects' lands, he could 'in his own grounds...make a forest.'[12] The King scrupulously avoided breaching this limitation. When two years earlier he had added lands not held by him to his chase at Hampton Court, he had proceeded by a statute. Nevertheless, the action was so unpopular that it was rescinded in the next reign as the result of a complaint to the council.[13] The limits of the royal prerogative were not exceeded in the proclamation on Hatfield Chase. But, possibly because it could be expected to be an unpopular action, it was based on the authority of the Statute of Proclamations.[14]

Two additional proclamations dealing with the King's 'disport

[10] It was certainly in effect late in 1544 since a case alleging violations of that proclamation in September 1544 was heard by the statutory court set up by the Statute of Proclamations (St Ch 2/17/195). The other export proclamations were *TRP* nos. 225, 239, 241, 255, 258, 259, 262, 263, 266, 269.

[11] *TRP* no. 205. Hatfield Chase was on the Lincolnshire boundary north and east of Doncaster. It had come into Crown hands in 1346 and remained Crown property until the reign of Charles I. The manors added were Armthorpe, which was part of the possessions of the Abbey of Roche, and Crowle which had been in the possession of the Monastery of Selby. After the dissolution of the monasteries these properties had become royal lands. Joseph Hunter, *The History and Topography of the Deanery of Doncaster* (London, 1928), I, 87–8.

[12] Edward Coke, *The Fourth Part of the Institutes of the Laws of England* (London, 1671), 301. For a discussion of the forest laws see Holdsworth, *History of English Law*, I, 94ff; G. J. Turner, *Select Pleas of Forest* (London, 1901).

[13] 31 Henry VIII c. 5; Dasent, II, 190–2.

[14] Hunter, *History and Topography of Doncaster*, I, 88, speculates that the proclamation may have been intended to extend the forest laws to the areas bordering the chase rather than actually to enlarge the chase. 'The proclamation seems to have been intended not so much to make an actual extension of the chase, properly so called, as to bring the inhabitants of this place, bordering on that which was actually stored with the King's deer, more completely under the authority of the officers of the chase, for Armthorpe was not kept in the King's hands with the rest of the chase, but was granted out to that great subject John Dudley, Duke of Northumberland.'

and pastime' were concerned with hawking. They followed two statutes on the same subject. The first statute had made the stealing of hawk's eggs from nests on the King's manors a felony. The following Parliament extended the prohibition to nests in woods or grounds anywhere in the realm. In April 1542 the King 'by his royal power dilated and confirmed by act of Parliament' issued a proclamation. It ordered that no one was to steal or without the King's license 'take, keep or otherwise by conceit or covin, directly or indirectly convey any egg or eggs, bird or birds of any goshawks, tercels or lannerets within this realm...or cause to be kept or brought up any sore hawk or any kinds of hawks above remembered' for a year. Violators were threatened with a fine of £100 and imprisonment at the King's and council's discretion. Informers were promised £40 for successful prosecution. Shortly before the expiration date the regulations were continued for another year.[15]

The severity of the penalty and the size of the reward promised to informers indicates that the government was serious about enforcement. Nevertheless, the penalty for disobedience, despite the size of the fine, was not as severe as the statutory penalty. This must have been because the conciliar court set up by the Statute of Proclamations could not deal with felony cases. The King was obviously interested in efficient and swift enforcement to deter offenders, but in this case certainty rather than severity of punishment was considered the best way to accomplish this purpose. The proclamation, while remaining within the limitations imposed by the Statute of Proclamations, included a penalty that was severe enough to cause potential offenders to give serious thought to the consequences of disobedience and a reward that was large enough to encourage private prosecutions. The conciliar court must have been intended as a method of insuring speedy and sure application of the penalty. It is interesting that the government was quite selective in deciding when to use this court. A series of other proclamations, which simply forbade hunting or hawking in specific areas, did not cite the Statute of Proclamations.[16] The whole procedure suggests that the statute was invoked when prompt and effective enforcement was deemed especially imperative.

[15] TRP nos. 211, 217. The editors transcribe the informer's reward in no. 211 as 'one tenth' of the fine, but both surviving manuscript copies read £40. CLRO Journals 14/319; BM Harl. 422/141. The statutes are 31 Henry VIII c. 12, 32 Henry VIII c. 11.

[16] TRP nos. 222, 247, 254. The proclamations simply applied the existing laws to specific areas. The penalties decreed ('high and grievous displeasure' for no. 222, and 'imprisonment and additional punishment at the King's pleasure' for the other two) do not suggest the same kind of urgency that the severe penalties in the two hawking proclamations imply.

Other proclamations may have omitted reference to it in order not to overload the conciliar court with less important matters.

The need for more effective enforcement probably also explains why the Statute of Proclamations was cited in three other proclamations. In May 1543 a royal proclamation set the price of sugar after a number of other methods of imposing controls had been tried. Sugar prices in London were set by the King's council in February 1538 in order to curb a steep rise in price. However, the action was rescinded in May by the mayor on the King's behalf 'for diverse considerations.' The price was then set at 7d a pound in a mayoral proclamation made 'on the King our sovereign lord's behalf and by his most gracious special and dread command.' Three years later, after consultation with sugar merchants, a similar proclamation raised the price to 8d a pound.[17] These efforts do not seem to have succeeded in maintaining a reasonable price level, for the 1543 royal proclamation maintained that sugar which had 'been at 2d, 3d and 4d the pound' was now '9d and 10d the pound against all reason and equity.' It also accused individuals of buying sugar for resale and mixing in impurities which made it 'unwholesome for man's body.' The proclamation, which quoted directly that part of the Statute of Proclamations which stated that proclamations should be obeyed 'as though they had been made by act of Parliament for the time in them limited,' set the price of the best sugar at 7d a pound and imposed a fine of 3s 4d for every pound sold above that rate together with one month's imprisonment. Anyone guilty of adding impurities to sugar would furthermore 'lose and forfeit all his goods and chattels and also suffer imprisonment at the King's will.' Informers were allowed to 'sue' for a share of the forfeitures 'by original writ, bill, plaint, or information in any of the King's courts, in which action or suit no wager of law shall be admitted nor any essoin or protection allowed.'[18]

This was the first early Tudor proclamation to use the formula normally found in the enforcement clauses of penal statutes. It allowed enforcement in common law courts even though it was not based on any statute except the Statute of Proclamations. The severity of the punishment for adulterating sugar and the statements in the preamble that sugar had risen sharply in price as well as the previous history of the efforts to control the price of sugar indicate that the situation in May 1543 was considered serious. This probably explains

[17] CLRO Rep. 10/81d; Journals 14/133, 237d.
[18] *TRP* no. 218. Informers would receive half of the 3s 4d a pound fine but only a third of the severe forfeiture for adulterating sugar.

why the government again resorted to the authority granted in the Statute of Proclamations. It may be that informers were also allowed to use other courts, because by 1543 the conciliar court was experiencing trouble in dealing with the heavy load of cases being brought to its attention.[19] What is most interesting is that the government did not hesitate to use the procedure of enforcement normally reserved for penal statutes in a proclamation based on the authority of the Statute of Proclamations alone.

In the following May, another proclamation which set prices on meat used a similar method of enforcement. The difficulty in enforcing meat price regulations has already been documented. With the repeal of the meat price statutes price controls seem to have been left to the local governments until 1544. A new procedure was necessitated by a below-average harvest in 1543 and 'a great dearth among cattle' and a sharp rise in meat prices in the spring of 1544.[20] London immediately felt the impact. On 4 April 1544 the city government set the price of beef at $\frac{3}{4}$d a pound and mutton at 1d a pound until the following summer. In May they requested the help of the central government. The mayor and aldermen set prices of beef, mutton, pork, veal, lamb and poultry, 'and agreed that a bill shall be made of them and all others the premises concerning victuals ready to be delivered upon Monday next in the afternoon unto the King's most honorable council.'[21] The proclamation issued shortly afterwards set the prices reommended by the mayor and aldermen. It was probably based on the Statute of Proclamations because of the problem encountered in enforcing the earlier meat price legislation. The penalties threatened were obviously meant to frighten potential offenders, for the fine of £10 for every violation was considerably higher than the fine of 3s 4d in the earlier legislation. Informers were also promised a handsome reward – half of the relatively large fine. They were allowed to:

sue for the same by information, bill, plaint, action of debt, or otherwise in any of the King's Courts of his Exchequer, King's Bench, or Common Pleas or else before such of the King's most honorable council, as be appointed to hear and determine the same by authority of the said act [Statute of Proclamations]; in which suits none essoin or protection shall be allowed nor wager of law received or admitted for the defendant.[22]

---

[19] 34 and 35 Henry VIII c. 23, the act which amended the Statute of Proclamations by lowering the quorum on the statutory court, had just passed Parliament. The preamble to the act clearly states that the court was not working effectively and that it was overloaded with cases.   [20] Hoskins, *AgHR*, XII, 42.

[21] CLRO Rep. 11/58d, 66d.   [22] *TRP* no. 231.

This time common law courts were specifically named together with the conciliar court. Again one can assume that this was done to assure both swift and efficient enforcement in a particularly troublesome matter and to avoid overcrowding the statutory court.[23]

The rise in meat prices was accompanied by a steep increase in the cost of grain. In November 1544, the government used a proclamation again based on the Statute of Proclamations to order a search for grain.[24] As was common in these proclamations, it was argued that prices were being increased by individuals who were accumulating more grain than they needed for seed and their household. Prices had already risen excessively and 'worse are like to be hereafter unless speedy remedy be provided.' Therefore the King ordered justices of the peace to gather and search for surplus grain within twenty days after the proclamation. Individuals with surplus were to be given a bill signed by the justices of the peace 'declaring the days, places, number and certainty of the bringing of the said corns and grain to the said market.' Those refusing to carry out these orders would be fined 3s 4d for every bushel they failed to deliver. Half of the fine was again promised to those who sued 'by information, bill, plaint, action of debt or otherwise' in the Exchequer, King's Bench, Common Pleas or the conciliar court. These restrictions were to remain in effect till the following All Saints Day.[25]

The remaining two proclamations based on the Statute of Proclamations do not seem to have cited the act for purposes of better enforcement. They were used first to suspend and then to reinstate a statute on handguns. Shooting with handguns and crossbows was limited by 25 Henry VIII c. 17 to subjects having a yearly income of at least £100 a year. These regulations were changed by 33 Henry VIII c. 6, which, although it allowed individuals living in rural areas to use handguns in the defense of their houses, continued

---

[23] The procedure does not seem to have coerced the butchers, who again maintained they could not comply. On 17 June 1544 the wardens of both the butchers and the poulterers were called by the city government to appear and 'to declare why they do not obey the King's proclamation.' CLRO Rep. 11/78. Foreign butchers stopped selling in London and on 19 June the London butchers were ordered to sell more meat and at the prices in the proclamation. The same day the poulterers appeared and said they could not sell at the prices 'to have a living thereby' but they agreed to do the best they could to serve the city 'until such time as they can get some dispensation for the said proclamation.' Ibid. 79.

[24] Bowden, *Agricultural History*, IV, 848. The price of grain in 1544 was higher than any year since 1535. It was about twenty percent higher than it had been in 1543. The Chronicler, Wriothesley, noted that 'wheat and other grain was very scant.' Wriothesley, *Chronicle*, 147.   [25] *TRP* no. 242.

to limit the general use of handguns to the upper classes.[26] The government seemingly still held a low opinion of the military usefulness of these weapons. It was not until two years later that a new attitude became evident. A royal proclamation made 'by the authority of the act made for proclamations' argued that it was 'expedient' to have individuals skilled in the use of handguns 'as well for the defense of the realm against enemies as annoying of the same in time of war and hostility.' Consequently, all subjects over sixteen were given liberty to fire handguns as long as they did not use them for hunting or shooting in inhabited areas 'except it be at butt, hill, or bank.' The action involved a major shift in policy which might be resented by the privileged classes whose monopoly in the use of handguns was being eliminated. This may be why the additional authority of the Statute of Proclamations was cited.[27] The proclamation, however, seems only to have been intended as a temporary measure and was probably related to the French war. A month after the peace with France was proclaimed in June 1546, a new proclamation again based on the authority of the Statute of Proclamations rescinded the earlier action and ordered the enforcement of 33 Henry VIII c. 6.[28]

These are the only surviving proclamations which mentioned the 1539 act. It seems clear that in each case the statute was cited because of a particularly compelling reason. Seven of the ten proclamations seem to have involved the statute for purposes of more effective enforcement. Those on Hatfield Chase and handguns may have sought additional authority because the action taken was unpopular. The last proclamation on handguns probably cited the statute because it was rescinding a proclamation based on the act.

[26] The statute also incorporated changes made in the earlier legislation by *TRP* no. 194 which maintained that individuals who had obtained licenses to use handguns and crossbows were shooting them in populated areas and endangering peoples' lives. The proclamation issued on 27 July 1540 therefore limited shooting in populated areas to 'places of the marks, pricks and butts appointed for the shooting and exercising of the said handguns or hacks.'

[27] *TRP* no. 225.5. Cruickshank, *Army Royal*, 80, calls it 'a daring experiment by throwing open the use of handguns to a wide section of the population.' The government may have taken the action by proclamation only after a bill in Parliament failed. The London records mention a 'bill put into the Parliament for the taking away the restraint of shooting' handguns on 16 May 1543. CLRO Rep. 10/251d.

[28] *TRP* no. 271. Cruickshank feels the proclamation may have been issued because the government realized that 'if too many people had guns it would encourage lawlessness in a variety of forms and in the long run it would put dissident groups into a position to challenge the authority of the crown.' Cruickshank, *Army Royal*, 81. Local governments were obviously delighted that the dangerous practice was over and they issued city orders that the statute be observed (GCA Byelaw Roll Oct. 1546).

HENRY VIII – THE SECOND STAGE

One is surprised that the vast majority of the proclamations issued between 1539 and 1547 never mentioned the statute. In some cases this can be explained by the fact that there was obviously no reason for additional authority or for using the enforcement procedures in the statute. This would apply to those which were little more than public announcements and contained no specific orders or penalties.[29] The same is surely true of those which limited access to the court because of the plague, adjourned and continued law terms, regulated legal pleading, or established an authorized Latin grammar and an English primer.[30] Another large group was concerned with military matters or directly related to the French war. Again one would not expect that they would need to cite additional authority.[31] A final series of proclamations was based on authority granted in other statutes. Five priced wines and a sixth changed the sanctuary from Chester to Stafford on the basis of the authority provided by 33 Henry VIII c. 15.[32]

If one consideres the lamentations in the preamble of the Statute of Proclamations about failure to obey religious proclamations, it is interesting that none of those on ecclesiastical matters issued while the Statute of Proclamations was in effect mentioned it. There were, in fact, surprisingly few religious proclamations. Even if the three

---

[29] *TRP* no. 220, which announced the commencement of the war with France, and no. 268, which announced the peace treaty as well as no. 208, which changed the royal style by adding the title 'King of Ireland' and no. 273, which encouraged Englishmen to colonize French territory, would fall into this category. The proclamation changing the royal style followed action taken by the Irish Parliament. The council was concerned that it was 'couched as though they gave this thing unto his highness by a common consent of themselves.' SP 1/166/144 (*LP* 16 no. 1019). It was followed by 35 Henry VIII c. 3, which made it treason to deny the title. The proclamation simply announced the title 'to the intent that our said subjects should not be ignorant of the alteration of our said style.'

[30] *TRP* nos. 216, 219, 223, 237, 248, 249, 256, 257, 270.

[31] Five of these proclamations dealt with the navy. Two exempted mariners from the press (*TRP* nos. 212.5, 221). Two encouraged privateering (nos. 243, 246), and one raised the wages of mariners (no. 245). Two proclamations ordered the gentry to go to their homes for military service (nos. 252, 261); two ordered punishment of deserters (nos. 236, 244); one ordered suppression of military rumors (no. 229). A number of proclamations gave as their justification the French war, although they may have been partially motivated by other concerns. In December 1543 a proclamation prohibited unlicensed imports from France since 'there is open war proclaimed' (*TRP* no. 224). Chapuys, however, felt the proclamation was motivated more by the desire for financial gain from licenses (*CSPSp*, VI, no. 271 (*LP* 18[2] no. 527)). Three proclamations ordered alien French to become denizens or leave the realm since as a result of the war 'all Frenchmen not being denizens may and ought to be reputed and taken for his grace's enemies' (*TRP* nos. 227, 233, 234). However, after four months the order was rescinded 'unto such time as his grace by his proclamation shall determine his further pleasure in that behalf' (*TRP* no. 238). The order may have been motivated by the financial gain which would accrue from the costs of denization since Henry had not dealt similarly with French citizens in previous wars. Wyatt, 'Aliens in England,' 78–81.

[32] *TRP* nos. 191.5, 206, 230, 260, 267 price wines. No. 212 changed the sanctuary.

which allowed the eating of white meats during Lent are counted,[33] there are only six surviving proclamations on religious matters. The first of these was not issued until May 1541. It simply repeated the order in the 1538 injunctions that a copy of the Bible be placed in every parish church 'there to be used as is aforesaid according to the said former injunctions.' It, however, specified 'Bibles of the largest and greatest volume,' a reference to the Great Bible first printed in April 1539. It was probably a response to a request from Anthony Marler, a book merchant who had been granted the right to sell the Great Bible by the council on 25 April 1541.[34] A second proclamation two months later changed the 1536 injunctions which had abolished certain feast days falling in harvest time and during law terms.[35] It restored observation of the Feasts of St Luke, St Mark, and St Mary Magdalen 'considering that the same saints been often and many times mentioned in plain and manifest Scripture.' It also condemned 'superstitious and childish observations' used on other feast days and commanded that they be 'clearly extinguished throughout all this his realm' because 'the same do resemble rather the unlawful superstition of Gentility than the pure and sincere religion of Christ.'[36]

A third proclamation in July 1546 was designed to control the influx of Protestant ideas. It was related to an earlier draft proclamation and a statute on the same subject. The relationship between the three documents is somewhat difficult to unravel. A statute, enacted by Parliament in the spring of 1543, banned Tyndale's translation of the Bible and all English books which taught contrary to the doctrines set forth since 1540. It allowed translations other

[33] Proclamations repeating verbatim the text of the 1538 proclamation on this subject were issued in 1541, 1542, and 1543 (*TRP* nos. 197.7, 209, 214). Since they maintained that the proclamation was necessary because fish was in scarce supply and the price had risen 'so that if the King's loving subjects should be enforced only to buy and provide herring and other salt store of fish...all this holy time of Lent...the same might and should undoubtedly redound to their importable charge and detriment,' I have included them under the listing 'economic' in the subject-matter classification even though they also involved a religious question.

[34] *TRP* no. 200; Nicolas, VII, 185. Marler petitioned the council for a proclamation ordering every church to have a copy of the Great Bible on 1 May. He maintained that unless this action were taken 'being charged as I am with an importune sum of the said books now lying on my hand, I am undone forever.'

[35] The 1536 injunctions actually ordered observation of earlier 'articles likewise devised put forth and authorized of late for and concerning the abrogation of certain superfluous holy days.' Gee and Hardy, *Documents*, 270. The earlier articles are found in Foxe, *Acts and Monuments*, v, 164.

[36] *TRP* no. 203. The practices referred to were 'children be strangely decked and appareled to counterfeit priests, bishops and women, and so be led with songs and dances from house to house, blessing the people and gathering of money and boys to sing mass and preach in the pulpit.'

than Tyndale's, but ordered that all annotations and preambles be blotted out, and limited the reading of Scripture to the upper classes. It also contained a proviso allowing the King during his lifetime 'to change and alter this act and provisions of the same.'[37] A draft proclamation containing regulations on printing not in the statute was probably drawn up at approximately the same time. Printers were to put their name and the name of the author and the date of printing on all English books, ballads and plays, and a copy was to be presented to the Mayor of the town where the printer lived. Probably in order to give the mayor time to decide if the work should be published, no other copies were to be circulated until two days later. It was also considerably more limiting than the statute on Bible translations since it would have forbidden all translations 'except only the Bible of Great Volume.' In addition, although the statute had forbidden books containing doctrines contrary to those set forth since 1540 without mentioning specific books, the draft cited books by 'Firth, Tyndale, Wycliffe, Joy, Roy, Basille, Bale, Barnes, Coverdale, Turner, Tracy' as well as books that 'contained matter contrary to the doctrine set forth and established by the King's most excellent majesty in his high court of Parliament holden at Westminster the — year of his grace's most noble and victorious reign.' Curiously, the year of the Parliament was left blank. Furthermore, the 1546 proclamation, which resembled the draft, did not include this sentence, but rather spoke of books teaching contrary to the *King's Book – A Necessary Doctrine and Erudition for any Christian Man*. This suggests that the draft was certainly composed before 29 May 1543, when the *King's Book* was published. It is likely that it was drawn up before the enactment of 34 and 35 Henry VIII c. 1, for although it is specifically cited in the 1546 proclamation, the draft fails to mention it. The only references to a statute in the draft are the statement cited above and another equally general reference (added by Wriothesley, who corrected the draft) to 'the Act of Parliament made.'[38] It may be that the King originally intended to

[37] 34 and 35 Henry VIII c. 1. The statute also confirmed the act of Six Articles. It forbade reading of Scriptures by artificers, servants, laborers upon penalty of one month's imprisonment. Gentlemen were allowed to read the Bible to their household and merchants and gentlewomen could read the Bible privately. Clergy preaching contrary to the King's doctrines were allowed to recant on the first offense, but on the third they would be burnt at the stake and forfeit their goods. Laymen, on the other hand, would merely forfeit their goods and suffer perpetual imprisonment for their offense.
[38] SP 1/169/116–26. The editors of *LP* list the document twice. First they date it approximately March 1542 (*LP* 17 no. 117) and then they correct their original dating by calling it an 'undated draft' of *TRP* no. 272 (*LP* 21[1] no. 1233).

proceed by proclamation and to introduce more restrictions than those in 34 and 35 Henry VIII c. 1. However, for some reason he changed his mind and turned to Parliament. But by including the clause allowing the statute to be altered during the King's lifetime, he retained his freedom of action to use proclamations to introduce changes at a later date.

In late 1545 the King may have sought new legislation on books, but despite the proviso in 34 and 35 Henry VIII c. 1, he seems to have gone to Parliament. In December 1545 Paget, who was on the Continent involved in the negotiations for peace with France through German intermediaries, wrote to Petre asking for news of the Parliament. Petre responded that 'the bill of books, albeit it was at the beginning set earnestly forward is finally dashed in the Commons House as are divers others whereat I hear not that his majesty is much miscontented.'[39] We do not know if the 'bill of books' was originally a government bill, but it seems likely, for Henry VIII was seriously concerned about the importation of heretical books even after the meeting of Parliament.[40] In July 1546 he issued the proclamation which introduced new regulations on books. It may be, as Professor Smith has suggested, that the bill in Parliament was allowed to die because Henry VIII did not want to upset the sensitive negotiations involving German Protestants as intermediaries. One of the German intermediaries had expressed his concern in December that the statute, which he felt would have condemned Protestant doctrine and books, was close to enactment. This is what had motivated Paget's letter to Petre and may have caused Henry VIII to have second thoughts about the bill.[41] The proclamation was issued after the negotiations had been completed. It contained regulations which may have been similar to those in the bill. Whatever the explanation, it resembled the earlier draft closely with the important exceptions that it specifically mentioned the *King's Book*, and referred to an 'act of Parliament...in the 34th and 35th year of the King's majesty's most victorious reign.'[42] Although other explanations of the relationship between the draft, the statute and the proclamation are certainly possible, the one offered above fits both the general policy of the government in religious matters and

---

[39] SP 1/212/36, 111 (*LP* 20[2] nos. 985, 1030).

[40] In June 1546 the King expressed concern to Mary of Hungary about heretical books being imported into England and in May the council had directed the mayor of London to examine two men 'touching certain heretic books of Bales' making, lately brought in a hoy of Flanders.' Dasent, I, 407, 409 (*LP* 21[1] nos. 755, 1098).

[41] Lacey B. Smith, 'Henry VIII and the Protestant Triumph,' *AHR*, LXXI (July 1966), 1257.   [42] *TRP* no. 272.

the fragmentary evidence discussed above. The government continued to rely on Parliament rather than the prerogative for ecclesiastical legislation throughout the period 1539–47. The only proclamation which introduced anything approaching major changes seems to have been issued only after efforts had been made to secure Parliamentary legislation.

The only other proclamation which was at all related to religious concerns was issued in October 1544. It forbade all plays and interludes in London unless they were in the houses of nobles, city officials, substantial citizens or in the guildhalls or open streets of the city. The government was concerned about plays set forth in 'many suspicious, dark and inconvenient places,' and those performed on Sunday and holy days conflicting with church services. It was argued that those plays attracted the youth 'and many other light, idle, and evil-disposed persons.' An earlier statute, 34 and 35 Henry VIII c. 1, had prohibited plays which contained Protestant doctrines, but had allowed those which were 'for the rebuking and reproaching of vices and the steering forth of virtue' as long as they did not 'meddle... with interpretations of Scripture.' The proclamation seems to have been more concerned about the 'sundry kinds of vice and sin' which young people might be encouraged to commit as the result of improper plays rather than about false doctrine. It may have been the result of an appeal by the city government which had prohibited plays and interludes the previous year.[43]

During the last years of Henry VIII's reign only a few proclamations either introduced major changes or impinged on areas formerly regulated by statutes. One of them was used to announce the 'Great Debasement' of 1544. The debasement had been preceded by the issuance in 1540 of coins for Ireland that had a debased silver content. However, the importation of these coins into England or the use of them for payments in England, Wales, Berwick or Calais was forbidden in November 1540.[44] The proclamation announcing the debasement of English coins was issued on 16 May 1544. It gave as its justification the same argument used for the valid debasement in

---

[43] TRP no. 240; CLRO Rep. 10/322d; Journals 14/319. Another proclamation dealing specifically with London may also have been motivated by a petition of the city government although the petition has not survived. The proclamation closed London brothels and forbade bear-baiting near London Bridge in April 1546 (TRP no. 265).

[44] TRP no. 197. The King had ordained that these coins were to be current in Ireland for the support of the army there, but people were bringing them to England 'to the great detriment and hurt of his grace's land of Ireland and of his said army and subjects of the same but also to the great deceit of his highness' loving subjects in this his realm of England.'

1526. It was maintained that coin was being exported from England because it was worth more in France and Flanders; therefore, the King, because he was concerned 'above all things' with 'the wealth and enriching of this his realm and people' and since 'for the remedying whereof there can be none other means and ways studied and devised' was forced to change the value of gold and silver in England. The plan for the debasement had, in fact, been in operation for two years and it was carried out purely for the King's financial gain. Therefore the justification for it was pure hypocrisy. The proclamation cited no special authority even though it was introducing major changes which would have serious long-term consequences for the commonwealth. However, since the royal prerogative to alter the coinage had been established by earlier precedents, it must have been felt that despite the medieval struggles over this question the King's prerogative was sufficient authority for the action.[45]

Two proclamations which set prices on weapons and armor impinged on areas previously regulated by statutory legislation, but they seem to have been short-term measures designed to deal with an emergency situation. Prices of bows and arrows had been set by statute in the late Middle Ages and in the reign of Henry VII. In February 1541 the first proclamation to speak on the subject simply ordered that bowyers and fletchers observe the statute designed to assure 'that his majesty's subjects may have bows and shafts...at reasonable prices.'[46] Nevertheless, the price seems to have risen enough that in May 1542 William Boys, justice of the peace in Kent, maintained that 'the commons complain because they cannot get bows nor arrows but at excessive prices.' He argued that if a remedy could be found 'there would be as great a number of archers in our parts as hath been in many years before.'[47] In August 1542 prices were set on 'bows, arrows, bills, harness, and other habiliments for the war' because, it was maintained, subjects were not able to acquire these items except 'at such unreasonable and excessive prices.' The prices were ordered observed on pain of imprisonment and a £10 fine for every offense. Local officials were told that, upon 'every complaint or information given to them' by any person seeking to buy these items, they were to commit the offender, to search his shop, and to sell the items found at the specified prices 'saving and keeping the

---

[45] *TRP* no. 228. On the debasement, see R. B. Outhwaite, *Inflation in Tudor and Early Stuart England* (London, 1969); P. H. Ramsey, *The Price Revolution in 16th Century England* (London, 1971).

[46] *TRP* no. 197.5; the statutes were 22 Edward IV c. 4; 3 Henry VII c. 13.

[47] SP 1/170/100 (*LP* 17 no. 303).

HENRY VIII – THE SECOND STAGE

money to the use and behoof of the owners thereof.'[48] In August 1544 another prolamation motivated by the French war maintained that armor was being sold at 'unreasonable and excessive prices.' Because large quantities of armor would soon be needed as a result of the recent muster, it was necessary to set maximum prices. The penalty for disobedience was imprisonment and a £5 fine. Local officials were ordered to insure that the proclamation was 'put in due execution,' but the clause in the earlier proclamation allowing them to search shops and to sell at the stated prices was not included.[49] Neither of these proclamations cited any special authority, but they did include the rather unusual phrase 'advice and consent' of the council.

The remaining proclamations issued during the period were all related to statutes. Some continued to be used to suspend statutes. The wool cloth manufacture statute was suspended three times during the period.[50] Two other statutes were suspended for brief periods of time. On 11 February 1544 34 and 35 Henry VIII c. 3, which had introduced new regulations for fuel being brought to London, was temporarily suspended. The action was justified by the contention that a large quantity of fuel which might not meet the regulations in the new act had been sent to London before the statute was passed, but severe weather had delayed delivery. Therefore it was suspended until 1 March, because if the fuel were not allowed to be sold, the citizens of London 'should lack wood for their necessary relief.'[51] A statute which announced the intention to enforce earlier statutes dealing with aliens and introduced more stringent regulations was also suspended for brief periods. Among the provisions of the act was an order that leases held by aliens who had not become denizens by Michaelmas be declared void and that no alien who was not a denizen be allowed to take any new lease after that date. Parliament adjourned at the end of July 1540, so that aliens had only three months to become denizens if they hoped to meet the deadline in the statute. As might be expected, chancery was overwhelmed with applications for denization, for which reason on 1 September 1540 the government extended the deadline until the following Easter. Even this extension was not sufficient, and in April 1541 the suspension was extended until midsummer.[52]

[48] *TRP* no. 213.
[49] *TRP* no. 235.
[50] *TRP* nos. 198, 202, 207.
[51] *TRP* no. 226.
[52] *TRP* nos. 195, 199. The Statute was 32 Henry VIII c. 16. See Wyatt, 'Aliens in Social and Economic Life,' 75ff for a full discussion. He estimates that over 16,000 aliens were living in England and the number of aliens applying for denization was triple that of even the next mass movement for denization which resulted from the proclamations connected with the French war.

Two proclamations were related to statutes dealing with the export of wool. The first of these (in June 1545) attempted to deal with abuses in the winding and packing of wool. Wool winding was a skillful operation done by specialist wool winders who had the opportunity to practice a good deal of deceit in carrying out their profession. They could easily wind impurities, such as sticks, dirt, dung, rocks and other small objects into the wool, thereby adding to the weight. Consequently the occupation had long been regulated by a statute which ordered that packers and winders of wool take an oath before the mayor of the Staple that they would carry out their tasks without deceit and obey the rules of the Staple. The statute, 27 Edward III st. 2 c. 23, however, carried no penalty for disobedience. Since honest packing and winding was of special concern to areas like Flanders, which bought large quantities of English wool, regulations governing packers were also written into trade treaties. Some of these carried the stipulation that winders be sworn to carry out their office honestly. If they did not they would lose that office and be punished by the King.[53]

Additional regulations on wool winding were introduced in the reign of Henry VIII by a new statute which threatened a fine to any person who added impurities to wool in order to increase the weight.[54] The problem seems to have continued and become increasingly serious in the last years of Henry VIII's reign, so that a royal proclamation was issued. It referred to Edward III's statute and maintained that despite the act the industry was being plagued by individuals who were winding impurities into the wool to the 'great slander of this realm' and to the 'great hindrance and deceit' of the Staplers and the 'great loss and prejudice' of the cloth makers. The statutory regulations demanding an oath of wool winders and forbidding the addition of impurities were repeated. The oath was to be taken before two justices of the peace or the mayor of the Staple, and a sealed certificate indicating the oath had been taken would be given to the wool winder. Anybody working without such a certificate would be punished together with his employer by ten days' imprisonment and 'be set upon the pillory in the next market town with a fleece of wool hanging about his neck.'[55] Whereas this proclamation tried to insure compliance by adding penalties to the earlier statutory legislation, the second only added the names of a number of counties

[53] *TRP* no. 45 refers to a treaty including such a clause.
[54] 23 Henry VIII c. 17. The statute was made to endure to the next Parliament when it was renewed by 28 Henry VIII c. 8.   [55] *TRP* no. 253.

which seem to have been inadvertently left out of a statute. The act, 37 Henry VIII c. 15, forbade the purchase of wool for resale by anyone except merchants of the Staple and manufacturers of yarn, hats, girdles and cloth in a number of counties specifically named in the statute. The proclamation simply stated that 'forasmuch as the shires of Middlesex, Stafford, Oxford, and Berks be omitted and left out in the said act,' they were now also to be included.[56]

Three proclamations attempted to deal with the vagabond problem. The first (in 1541) applied existing poor law legislation to vagabonds following the court. They were ordered to leave within twenty-four hours or suffer the pains in the statutes. In addition no one was to keep more servants than allowed to them or to allow vagabonds to come 'unto their chambers or offices contrary unto the King's ordinances in that behalf heretofore made.'[57]

A second proclamation has been given a title that sounds quite menacing. However, the title 'Ordering Vagabonds to the Galleys' is somewhat misleading. Issued during the French war in May 1545, it actually only forbade the keeping of more servants than allowed 'by the laws and statutes of this realm, or be retained by the King's majesty's license.' The preamble, which lamented the increase in the number of idle people, vagabonds and 'ruffians' in London despite the laws and statutes, stated that 'for reformation whereof' the King 'hath thought convenient and doth determine to use and employ all such ruffians, vagabonds, masterless men, common players and evil-disposed persons to serve his majesty and his realm in these his wars in certain galleys, and other like vessels which his majesty's highness intendeth to arm forth against his enemies.'[58] It did not condemn vagabonds to slavery in the galleys, as the title supplied would lead one to believe. Rather, it seems the King was simply announcing that he intended to impress idle men to serve in his fleet during the war. The proclamation was designed to prevent these men from being unlawfully included as servants in someone's household, thereby shielding them from the King's press gangs.

Another proclamation probably issued in 1546 again sounded the laments about enforcement so common before 1539. It complained about failure to enforce statutes for sewers and those dealing with vagabonds 'much to the King's displeasure and discontentation, the

---

[56] *TRP* no. 264. See G. D. Ramsay, *The Wiltshire Woollen Industry in the Sixteenth and Seventeenth Centuries* (London, 1965), 8ff, for a discussion of the statute.

[57] *TRP* no. 204. The statute was 22 Henry VIII c. 12, which had been renewed by 33 Henry VIII c. 17. The proclamation also included regulations on keeping of hounds, greyhounds and ferrets at court. [58] *TRP* no. 250.

whole default whereof his majesty imputeth to his justices of peace and other ministers being authorized and having charge of the same.' It ordered those ministers 'with all diligence and dexterity of the uttermost of their powers' to see to the enforcement of these laws 'at their uttermost perils' and the King's 'high displeasure and indignation.' It added a final ominous warning that if they failed to do so 'his majesty intendeth to proceed against the offenders as enemies of his commonwealth to the terrible example of all other.'[59]

A final proclamation supported London in a dispute involving the jurisdiction over the Thames. It provides a good illustration of the type of resistance that could develop when the King encroached on a sensitive area. The problem involved the regulation of fishing on the Thames and the price of fish sold in London, but it was complicated by a jurisdictional struggle between the lord admiral and the city of London. A series of statutes beginning in Edward I's reign had granted the citizens of London rights of jurisdiction over the waters of the Thames and the Medway.[60] A dispute began in February 1542 when an extremely diligent water bailey sought to correct illegal practices by fishermen on the Thames. The fishermen resented the intrusion and appealed to the lord admiral for his support. In 1542 a draft bill was prepared which accused the water bailey of abuses and would have given the admiral and his deputies authority 'to make ordinances and statutes' for the regulation of fishing on the Thames.[61] The bill, however, failed to become law, and the dispute continued. In December 1542 the city appealed to the chancellor for his support since 'a great number of the said fishermen are not contented to use themselves according to certain of the said articles and ordinances concerning the laying down and taking away of their trink nets and nets called pridenets,' and would not cease fishing near London Bridge.[62] A committee was sent to see the chancellor and lord privy seal for their 'advice and aid.' Two days later they reported that they had spoken to the chancellor on 'the matters in

[59] *TRP* no. 274.

[60] 13 Edward I c. 47 and 17 Richard II c. 9 had granted the city rights to punish offenders in the waters of the Thames and Medway. 4 Henry VII c. 15 stated that the mayor of London had jurisdiction over the Thames and added to that jurisdiction over breaches and creeks made in the river by floods. See John P. McManus, 'The Trade and Market in Fish in the London Area During the Early Sixteenth Century 1485–1563' (University of London MA Thesis, 1952), 188ff for a discussion of the dispute over the Thames.   [61] SP 1/169/5–22 (*LP* 17 no. 29).

[62] CLRO Rep. 10/297d. In order to preserve fish, only certain kinds of nets were allowed at certain times of the year. Fishing near London Bridge was controlled because this was where fish gathered for breeding. McManus, 'Trade in Fish in London,' 199ff.

variance between this city and the fishermen of the Thames and the officers of my lord admiral concerning the governance and punishment of the said fishermen,' but they were asked to wait until Christmas for a decision. In January another committee was sent to the chancellor. On 1 March a delegation was sent to the lord privy seal 'for the matter of the Thames and the prices of fresh fish lately assessed.'[63] This time they were successful because on 6 March 1543 a proclamation was issued which the city immediately ordered printed 'at the charge of the city' and proclaimed in towns along the river and posted on the church doors of those towns.[64]

The appeal of the city was never mentioned in the proclamation. Rather the high price of fish was stressed and individuals were ordered to observe the prices set by the mayor and aldermen 'with the consent and advice of our council.' Furthermore, fishermen were commanded to keep the market well supplied with fish. Finally, the proclamation stated that the mayor of London by royal grant and 'divers and sundry acts of Parliament...have of long time had and enjoyed the conservancy of our river of Thames and of the fish, broad and fry of the same river...and also the punishment and just correction of all the fishermen within and upon the same river.' Fishermen had 'obstinately, stubbornly, and contemptuously' refused to obey the mayor, wherefore they were ordered not to use unlawful nets or 'impugn, deny, resist or disobey the said mayor or his successors or his or their deputies or ministers' in exercising their jurisdiction. Offenders were threatened with imprisonment and the King's indignation and displeasure.

The proclamation had simply supported the traditional and statutory jurisdiction of the mayor of London, but the fishermen seemingly were not coerced into obeying. At times they even openly denied the King's authority. A fisherman from Barking who spoke 'very lewd, seditious and unseeming words at the time of the King's proclamation there made,' was punished by the council by being placed in the stocks.[65] Another fisherman refused to pay a fine which had been ordered by the court. One even questioned the authority of the King's proclamation. The water bailey had thrown some undersized fish overboard which had been caught by one William Smith. Smith asked upon what authority the water bailey had acted. He answered, 'here is the King's proclamation for mine authority;

[63] CLRO Rep. 10/299d, 302, 314d.
[64] *TRP* no. 215; CLRO Rep. 10/314d.
[65] CLRO Rep. 10/323. The council records also note the punishment. The fisherman's name was John Glover. Dasent, I, 105.

is not this sufficient?' Smith answered, 'No, bring a proclamation under my lord admiral's seal, and I will obey it or else not.' The water bailey then commanded him to appear before the mayor's court at Guildhall, but Smith said, 'Let him come to me' because he had 'other business' and 'he would neither come on Sunday nor none other days.'[66]

The water bailey continued to have trouble with other fishermen who questioned his authority, and he finally informed the Court of Aldermen that he was told that the lord admiral had given orders to arrest him. The court ordered the water bailey to continue to exercise his office and said they would aid him if arrested.[67] Meanwhile they turned to Parliament. A document that may have served as a preamble to a bill in Parliament is included in the London records. It defends the jurisdiction of the mayor over the Thames and maintains it was not only based on statutes but it 'is ratified and confirmed by a proclamation.' The city 'supposing by virtue of the said proclamation that they should have no more trouble nor business ensue concerning the premises,' nevertheless the lord admiral and others 'unlawfully procured divers fishermen to disobey the said statutes orders and punishments thereof.'[68] The bill must have been presented to the 1544 Parliament, for the city requested the aid of the council 'for their favor for the preferment of the bill in Parliament house concerning the river of Thames.' The council 'agreed to further it as much as they lawfully might do,' but the bill nevertheless failed to pass the Lords.[69] The dispute was temporarily resolved in December 1545 when the lord admiral wrote to the city concerning the 'matters as are now in question between the city and his lordship concerning the right and jurisdiction of this city upon the river of Thames.' In response the mayor and aldermen 'for certain reasonable considerations' agreed to return the nets taken from the fishermen 'that the said matter may be more fully examined.'[70]

The struggle about the jurisdiction of the city of London over the Thames seems a proper place to conclude the discussion of royal proclamations issued while the Statute of Proclamations was in effect because it graphically documents what has been an obvious theme of this chapter. The act did not significantly change the role of royal

---

[66] CLRO Rep. 10/328d, 346. [67] CLRO Rep. 10/346, 348d.
[68] CLRO Journals 15/40.
[69] CLRO Rep. 11/42. The bill was introduced in the Lords on 29 January and is described simply as 'concerning the preservation of the Fry of Fish.' It received a secon reading and seems then to have been dropped. *LJ*, I, 241, 244.
[70] CLRO Rep. 11/232.

proclamations in Tudor government, nor does it seem to have greatly increased the respect given to them. If Thames fishermen backed by the lord admiral could so blatantly ignore and even question the authority of a proclamation which did little more than confirm earlier statutes, surely this is an indication of the problems the King and council faced in getting subjects to obey proclamations. This was the very issue which the statute had attempted to settle by improving enforcement procedures, and this is how the government used it. The proclamations which seemed to pose the greatest problems in enforcement or the ones which the government was most interested in having enforced were the ones which specifically cited the authority of the act. But it is curious that the government did not rely on that authority very often. In the last two years of the reign only one surviving proclamation cited it, probably because it rescinded a proclamation based on that act. The statute was clearly considered more important by later historians than it was by Henry VIII and his council. Although it did not have a major impact on the role, authority or respect for proclamations, it did change the method of enforcement both by setting up a special court and by making available the system of enforcement used in penal statutes. Proclamations were to be 'obeyed, observed, and kept as though they were made by act of Parliament.' The Statute of Proclamations set up the machinery to make this possible, and the government used the act when it was particularly concerned about enforcement. Whether or not the system worked is the concern of another chapter in this study.

8

THE USE OF ROYAL PROCLAMATIONS: EDWARD VI

The great and mature development of proclamations as instruments of policy occurred under Edward VI when a total of 113 proclamations were issued, or just short of an average of 19 proclamations in each year of this reign. Further, the great bulk (77) of these proclamations date from the period of Somerset's tenure of power, Northumberland being inexplicably cautious in the use of this means of imposing his policy.[1]

Although Professor Jordan's figures are slightly inaccurate because he based his count on only the items contained in volume I of *Tudor Royal Proclamations*, his overall conclusion is indisputable. There was a massive increase in the use of royal proclamations in the reign of Edward VI. The incidence of use under Somerset was more than double that of any previous period. Even Northumberland used proclamations more extensively than either Henry VII or Henry VIII. In addition specific penalties were more commonly listed, and enforcement procedures were stated in over half of the surviving proclamations. There was also a substantial increase in the number which named a court or courts for dealing with offenders. These statistics suggest that if there was an effort to equate royal proclamations with Parliamentary legislation and to rely on the prerogative rather than Parliament for new legislation, it occurred in Edward VI's reign rather than in Henry VIII's. In fact, proclamations seem to have posed a greater threat to statute after the repeal of the Statute of Proclamations than they did while the act was in effect. This significant expansion in the use of the prerogative occurred largely during Somerset's protectorate. Although the number of proclamations issued during the last years of the reign makes it difficult to describe Northumberland as 'being inexplicably cautious,' there was a noticeable change in the way they were used. Broad generalizations are always dangerous, but there are at least some comparisons between Northumberland's and Cromwell's policy which contrast rather dramatically with Wolsey's and Somerset's approach.

[1] Jordan, *The Young King*, 349.

EDWARD VI

Somerset (1547-9)

At least twenty proclamations were issued before Edward VI's first Parliament repealed the Statute of Proclamations. However nothing in their texts would reveal that the act was still in effect. They failed either to cite its authority or to use the statutory court for enforcement. The religious injunctions issued in July 1547 even violated the limitations set by the act.[2] Of course, most of these proclamations did not need special enforcement procedures or additional authority. Three were concerned with the accession and coronation of Edward VI, three provided for the payment of Henry VIII's debts or the collection of the subsidy granted in his last Parliament, and one ordered religious pensioners to present their patents and grants for their pensions before the deputy of the Treasurer of the Court of Augmentations. Two more made regulations for the court. Another simply ordered that French prizes be released and the treaty of peace with France be observed.[3] Five were closely related to some of Henry VIII's proclamations. One was a verbatim repetition of the proclamation of 18 April 1538, which was designed to protect the King's officers in the execution of their duties.[4] Two complained that the King's deer were being 'hunted and disquieted' in violation of 'former orders and proclamations' made by Henry VIII and ordered that these regulations be observed. A fourth contained regulations on legal pleading which modified slightly those that Henry VIII had introduced on 27 June 1546.[5] The fifth repeated, with only slight adjustments that adapted the wording to the new reign, the provisions of the proclamation of 4 March 1546 which had altered 37 Henry VIII c. 15 by adding certain counties to those specifically mentioned in the statute. However, it also included a clause not in the statute or the earlier proclamation. The statute was designed to control the middleman's or brogger's activities in

[2] *TRP* no. 287.
[3] *TRP* nos. 275, 276, 277, 279, 282, 283, 289, 290, 291, 293.
[4] *TRP* no. 288. This may have been a reproclaiming of no. 179 at the order of the London city government. In October 1549 the Court of Aldermen ordered that the sheriffs were to have the same proclamation 'to be duly proclaimed in the city omitting the Duke of Somerset's name there in.' CLRO Rep. 12(1) 159d. It may be that a similar order resulted in no. 179 being proclaimed at the beginning of Edward's reign.
[5] *TRP* no. 294 was similar to Henry VIII's proclamation (no. 270) which had declared that no one was to be allowed to be a pleader at the courts at Westminster unless he had 'read in court.' The new proclamation allowed 'utter barristers' and students at the inns of court to plead in all courts except the Court of Common Pleas. The proclamations on hunting also authorized the King's officers to seize 'hounds, greyhounds, crossbows, handguns or other his or their engines' from offenders. *TRP* nos. 284, 286.

the sale of wool. It forbade the purchase of wool by anyone except merchants of the Staple and those who manufactured cloth, yarn, hats and girdles. This may have led to the practice of clipping or plucking wool from Staple fells for the purpose of resale; consequently the proclamation added that 'no manner of person or persons, what, estate or degree soever he or they be, shall pull, pluck, or clip the wool of any fell that is merchantable to the Staple of Calais' on pain of a fine equal to double the value of the fell and additional punishment 'at his majesty's will and pleasure.' Although the addition to the statute was minor, violations of this regulation were to be brought to the attention of the Exchequer on the basis of the authority of the proclamation alone.[6]

Another proclamation issued while the Statute of Proclamations was still in effect is interesting, primarily because it reintroduced the medieval method of controlling grain export and seems to indicate that proclamations sometimes continued in force after the death of the monarch who had issued them. Issued on 16 March 1547, it rescinded Henry VIII's proclamation of the previous June which had prohibited unlicensed export. It was maintained that grain was now in plentiful supply; therefore it could be exported without a license so long as the price of a quarter of wheat was not above 6s 8d and barley, malt and rye were not above 5s or 'unto such time as his highness by his other proclamation under his great seal of England shall determine the contrary.'[7] That it was felt necessary to revoke Henry's proclamation suggests that at least Somerset and the council believed the restrictions in a proclamation continued after the death of the monarch who issued them. Although it did not state so specifically, the proclamation was actually granting a sweeping dispensation from the restraints on unlicensed export imposed by 25 Henry VIII c. 2. The use of price levels to regulate export was probably a concession to the grain farmers and exporters after the abundant harvest of the previous year,[8] but it was a shortsighted policy. It quickly became necessary to withdraw the concession six months later, when the price of grain rose above the specified levels.[9] Nevertheless, Somerset did not abandon the policy. Although he did not acquire new statutory legislation in Edward VI's first Parliament, grain export was again allowed in March 1548 as long as the price of

---

[6] *TRP* no. 278. The editors have mistranscribed the word 'clip' as 'slip.' BM Titus B II/4. See below p. 278 for Exchequer cases.
[7] *TRP* no. 280. Henry VIII's proclamation was no. 269.
[8] Hoskins, *AgHR*, XII, 45, lists the 1546, 1547, and 1548 harvests as 'abundant.'
[9] *TRP* no. 295.

grain was below the stated level, 'until such time as his highness by his other proclamation under his great seal of England shall determine the contrary; any act, statute, law, proclamation or restraint to the contrary hereof in anywise notwithstanding.'[10]

Somerset seemingly did not feel it was necessary to acquire new authority even though he was in effect changing the statutory policy. Although this type of price-support policy may have been initiated because it might serve to encourage landholders to retain land in tillage rather than converting to pasture, it was extremely confusing for merchants. The rapid changes in the price of grain made it difficult for them to carry on their business efficiently and still remain within the limits of the law. The Johnson brothers, for example, found that their business was made considerably more complex by the vacillating policy. In early spring 1548 Otwell Johnson was seeking a license to export grain when the proclamation in March made it unnecessary. He wrote to his brother, John, that he could ship the grain he had purchased without a license for the time being, but in order to guard against future restraints he was arranging for a friend to acquire a license.[11] This was a wise decision because, possibly as the result of the increased exports, the price of grain rose, and the London authorities petitioned the council for a new restraint. On 26 September 1548 another proclamation forbade unlicensed export. Two weeks later even more severe restrictions were imposed. All previous licenses were revoked, and export was forbidden unless a new license was obtained 'after the date of this proclamation.'[12] The Johnson brothers were at the time shipping grain to the Low Countries. Rather than wait to obtain a new license Otwell decided to take a risk with the corn that had already been loaded. He told his brother that he would 'pretend to enter my corn that I will now load upon Calais trusting within the time limited for a certificate to be brought (which is four months) to get the license that I have written for.'[13] That the Johnson brothers had to risk breaking the law, and that London authorities had to petition for a new proclamation when the

---

[10] *TRP* no. 301.   [11] SP 46/5/254.
[12] *TRP* no. 315. The earlier proclamation is found in CLRO Journals 15/282d (Appendix A no. 313.5). The London authorities blamed the rise in prices on the great quantities of grain that had been exported (CLRO Rep. 11/468d). They had requested a restraint on butter, cheese and tallow in April 1548 because extensive exports were causing a rise in prices and the council also responded with a proclamation (*ibid.* 11/426; *TRP* no. 304).
[13] SP 46/5/298. After a successful sale of the malt at a reasonable profit the Johnson brothers decided not to export more grain because the price had risen sufficiently to make it more profitable to sell in England (*ibid.* 305, 310, 315).

price of grain rose, suggests that the policy was not realistic. Licenses and occasional restraints were a more effective way to control grain exports. The end of the experiment of using price levels to control exports, which was necessitated by a series of bad harvests beginning in 1549,[14] was probably greeted with relief by city residents and by merchants. The effort may have been economically justified, but it was a more confusing policy for merchants than the one it replaced. More significantly for the purposes of this study, it involved the use of royal proclamations to issue sweeping dispensations from 25 Henry VIII c. 2. Although this was certainly legal, it would have been constitutionally more proper to have repealed 25 Henry VIII c. 2 in the 1547 Parliament if Somerset had really intended to introduce a permanent new policy.

The remaining proclamations issued while the Statute of Proclamations was in effect were related to ecclesiastical matters. Here Somerset's use of the royal prerogative was certainly somewhat questionable. His religious policy in the first year of the reign was one of cautious and slow progress toward a moderate Protestant settlement. Although he had the support of the majority of the council, a small group of bishops led by Gardiner vigorously opposed the changes. In addition a vocal minority of the population, who desired more rapid change in the direction of a considerably more radical form of Protestantism, did not hesitate to use direct action to obtain their goals.[15] The proclamations reflect both the desire to inhibit the more radical elements within society, and a willingness to use the royal prerogative to introduce the type of moderate change Somerset favored. In May 1547 a proclamation was directed against those who spread rumors 'of innovations and changes in religion and ceremonies of the Church feigned to be done and appointed by the King's highness, the Lord Protector and other of his highness' Privy Council.' It maintained that the King and the council had 'never begun nor attempted' changes of this type and ordered that the statutes on rumors be put in 'full execution.' All subjects were urged to aid in enforcement by reporting persons spreading these tales to the privy council or to a justice of the peace who would imprison the accused

---

[14] The policy had probably already ended before the 1549 harvest. In January 1549 a proclamation imposed a three-months restraint on grain, tallow and a variety of other food items (*TRP* no. 319) and it may be that another restraint was imposed when the time limit expired because in August a proclamation allowed free victualling of Calais 'whatsoever restraint heretofore made notwithstanding' (*TRP* no. 349). This suggests that a restraint was in effect at the time.

[15] Jordan, *The Young King*, 125ff.

until he revealed the author of the tale. Subjects and justices of the peace were encouraged to perform their civic duty both by the threat of imprisonment for failure to carry out the commands in the proclamation and by a promise of 'convenient and good reward for faithfully doing his most bounden duty therein.'[16]

At the same time that Somerset was assuring citizens that no changes were being contemplated in religion, the first major changes to be introduced by prerogative action were already under consideration. At the end of July 1547 a series of royal injunctions introduced modifications in the worship of the English Church that led to strong protests from the spokesman of the conservative clergy, Stephen Gardiner. Although technically not a royal proclamation, the injunctions had the effect of introducing a series of new regulations on the authority of the royal prerogative alone.[17] At first glance they do not seem radical, for they basically ordered observation of Henry VIII's injunctions of 1536 and 1538. However, they went beyond these orders in forbidding all pilgrimages and ordering that all images which had been 'abused with pilgrimage or offerings' be taken down and that 'henceforth no torches nor candles, tapers, nor images of wax' were to be placed before any image or picture. Clergy were to instruct their parishioners in the true use of images and to take down and destroy images and ornaments in their churches and homes. Every church was to have 'a comely and honest pulpit,' the whole Bible in English and a copy of Erasmus' *Paraphrases*. The most controversial section of the lengthy injunctions read:

> Because through lack of preachers in many places of the King's realms and dominions the people continue in ignorance and blindness, all parsons, vicars, and curates shall read in their churches, every Sunday, one of the *Homilies* which are and shall be set forth for the same purpose by the King's authority, in such sort as they shall be appointed to do in the preface of the same.[18]

The homilies were twelve sermons written by Cranmer in the reign of Henry VIII. They were submitted to Convocation in 1542 but never authorized. They contained Protestant doctrines and three of them definitely taught the doctrine of justification by faith alone. Gardiner recognized the danger these homilies posed to the teachings of the medieval church. Already in June 1547, he had protested

---

[16] *TRP* no. 281.
[17] Injunctions were issued in quarto rather than in broadside. More important, they were meant to be published in churches rather than publicly proclaimed.
[18] *TRP* no. 287.

against their use both to Somerset and to Cranmer. In a letter to Somerset he argued that Convocation had never authorized the homilies and that they could not be imposed 'without a new authority from the King's majesty that now is.'[19] He further told Cranmer that they involved a repudiation of the *King's Book* of 1543. After the injunctions had been issued he wrote two letters to the council. In the first he again argued that the doctrine of justification by faith taught in the homilies was in contradiction to the teachings of the *King's Book*. In the second he reminded Somerset and the Council that 34 and 35 Henry VIII c. 1 forbade teaching contrary to the *King's Book*; therefore the injunctions were a command to violate a statute. In a letter written to Somerset shortly afterward, he developed that argument further. He maintained that the King could not command against an act of Parliament and he specifically cited the limitations imposed on proclamations in the Statute of Proclamations in support of his argument.[20]

Gardiner had a strong case. Although it is not clear whether royal injunctions were technically included under the limitations imposed by the Statute of Proclamations, Gardiner certainly thought they were. Furthermore, the principle that an action based on the royal prerogative should not violate a statute surely applied despite the technical difference between royal proclamations and injunctions. Whatever the merits of Gardiner's arguments, they were undermined by Edward's first Parliament which repealed both 34 and 35 Henry VIII c. 1 and the Statute of Proclamations.[21]

Before the repeal of the Statute of Proclamations, a final proclamation, issued on 12 November 1547, attempted to deal with those who were using direct action to bring religious change. It denounced attacks on priests and scholars by serving-men and apprentices, and individuals were commanded hereafter not to use 'such insolence and evil demeanor towards priests as reviling, tossing of them, taking violently their caps and tippets from them without just title or cause.'

---

[19] Muller, *Letters of Gardiner*, 362. The first two letters are found on 296–8. See Jordan, *The Young King*, 159–60, for further discussion of the contents of the homilies.

[20] Muller, *Letters of Gardiner*, 391. This is the same letter in which Gardiner reported the judicial decision discussed earlier. See above p. 43. Gardiner's second letter to the council is found *ibid*. 369–73.

[21] 1 Edward VI c. 12. James A. Muller, *Stephen Gardiner and the Tudor Reaction* (New York, 1926), 164 feels that Gardiner's case was 'constitutionally impeccable' and that the 'only constitutional answer Somerset and the Council vouchsafed to give him was the repeal in the next Parliament of the law on which he took his stand.' Jordan, *The Young King*, 210, agrees that 'there was for the moment an impressive merit in Gardiner's position, though it was to be entirely swept away just a few weeks later by the great repealer statute of Edward's first Parliament.'

Those who did so would, upon trial before the council, mayor, sheriffs 'or other sufficient judges to whom complaint shall be made' suffer imprisonment 'or other corporal pain' as determined by Somerset, the council or the judges. The proclamation implied that the penalty would be severe, for it added that it 'shall be such that by the punishment of a few, all other may be afraid to use such insolence, violence, and ill demeanor.'[22]

Parliament concluded its meeting on 24 December 1547. Between that date and Somerset's arrest in October 1549, a period of less than two years, at least fifty-seven additional proclamations were issued. Somerset had used the prerogative powers freely while the Statute of Proclamations was still in effect, but he used them even more extensively after the repeal. The average number of proclamations per month climbed from slightly under two during the first eleven months of the reign to over three during the remainder of Somerset's tenure. He continued to use them freely on ecclesiastical matters. Furthermore, he may even have planned initially to rely on the prerogative rather than Parliament to continue the reform of the church along Protestant lines.[23]

More religious proclamations were issued during the brief period of Somerset's protectorship than in any other subdivision of the early Tudor period. However, despite indications that Somerset was prepared to rely on the royal prerogative to introduce religious changes, most of the remaining religious proclamations were designed to restrict innovations rather than to introduce them. The first session of Parliament had continued the cautious policy of change by repealing many of Henry VIII's statutes on religion, dissolving the chantries and providing for the administration of communion in both kinds to the laity while imposing fines and imprisonment on those who spoke irreverently of the sacrament.[24] The proclamations which followed the session of Parliament continued this slow and cautious

[22] *TRP* no. 292.
[23] Hoak, 'Edward VI's Council,' 238–9: 'By 2 February 1548, for instance, Paget knew that Somerset had resolved to continue the reformation of the doctrine and institution of the Church by royal proclamation and not by statute.' Paget cautioned against this and Somerset listened to this advice; however, Hoak maintains, 'if we are to believe Paget, Somerset had not in fact intended to convene the session of Parliament which sat from 24 November 1548 to 14 March 1549 for the purpose of submitting the government's religious policies to the '"body of the realm"' (*ibid.* 239).
[24] 1 Edward VI c. 12 repealed 25 Henry VIII c. 14, 31 Henry VIII c. 14, 34 and 35 Henry VIII c. 1 and 35 Henry VIII c. 5 in addition to the two medieval heresy statutes: 5 Richard II st. 2 c. 5 and 2 Henry V st. 1 c. 7. 1 Edward VI c. 14 dissolved the chantries; 1 Edward VI c. 1 dealt with the sacrament and another statute on religion; 1 Edward VI c. 2 allowed the appointment of bishops by letters patent.

policy. Shortly after Parliament was prorogued people who engaged in vain and irreverent controversy over the Eucharist were condemned in a proclamation that forbade preaching, teaching or debates about the Eucharist in terms other than those expressly stated in Scripture. Individuals were ordered to accept the real presence of Christ's body and blood and to teach in accord with the recently enacted statute on the Eucharist 'until such time as the King's majesty, by the advice of his highness' council and the clergy of this realm shall define, declare and set forth an open doctrine thereof.' Offenders were threatened with prison and further punishment at the King's pleasure. Justices of the peace were ordered to imprison offenders and submit their names to the council. The proclamation dealt with the same issues as the recently enacted statute, but it introduced the council into the enforcement procedure and hinted that additional doctrinal statements on the Eucharist would be forthcoming from the King with the advice of the council and clergy[25].

Additional efforts designed to restrict those who would break too quickly with old forms were made in the first three months of 1548. In January observation of the Lenten fast was ordered both for the possible spiritual benefits which might ensue and more significantly 'to spare flesh and use fish for the benefit of the commonwealth and profit of this his majesty's realm, whereof many be fishers and men using that trade of living.' Offenders were threatened with the King's indignation and imprisonment. Local officials were ordered to imprison those accused by two witnesses of a violation. The next session of Parliament passed a statute dealing with the same matter and offered a similar justification. It differed from the proclamation primarily in that the penalties, a 10s fine and ten days' imprisonment for the first offense and 20s and twenty days' imprisonment for the second offense, were more specific and informers were allowed to sue for half of the forfeiture in any court of record.[26]

In February those who not only tried 'to persuade the people from the old and accustomed rites and ceremonies, but also themself bringeth in new and strange orders' were denounced in a proclamation that forbade these practices upon pain of the King's indignation, imprisonment 'and other grievous punishments at his majesty's will and pleasure.' It also stated that no one was to preach unless licensed by the King, the Archbishop of Canterbury, the bishop of the diocese or the King's visitor. Once again the council

---

[25] *TRP* no. 296. The statute was 1 Edward IV c. 1.
[26] *TRP* no. 297; 2 and 3 Edward VI c. 19.

was involved in enforcement. Local officials and church wardens were told to imprison offenders and report them to the council. Finally, further reform by royal action was suggested, for it was maintained that the King, the protector and the council were 'studying all the ways and means which can be to direct this church and the cure committed to his highness in one and most true doctrine, rite and usage.'[27] The following month a new proclamation in an even more specific way informed the public that further reform would be forthcoming by royal action. Referring to 1 Edward VI c. 1, which had allowed communion in both kinds, it warned of 'unseemly and ungodly diversity' that might arise. Subjects were ordered to take the sacrament reverently and not to put forth new ideas 'by their own private authority.' They were finally told that the King intended 'by the advice of our most dear uncle and other of our privy council with all diligence and convenient speed so to set forth the same as it may most stand with God's glory and edifying and quietness of our people.'[28]

Despite additional prerogative action in February commanding the removal of all images in all churches in the realm, the government continued to be plagued by the impatience of that radical and vocal element of the population (centered especially in London) who were not satisfied with the slow progress of reform. In April new and stricter regulations on preaching were introduced. No one was allowed to preach unless licensed. The license was to be shown to the 'parson and curate, and two honest men of the parish beside, before his said preaching.' Rumors that bigamy was not prohibited 'by God's law, but by the Bishop of Rome's law' were declared false. The clergy were ordered to punish those who committed bigamy 'according to the ecclesiastical laws, with grave and severe punishment.'[29] In September 1548 preaching was further limited. Maintaining that even licensed preachers 'behaved themselves irreverently and without good order in the said preachings,' the proclamation, after again promising that the King intended 'to see very shortly one uniform order throughout this his realm and to put an end of all controversies in religion,' forbade all sermons. Services were to be conducted with prayers and the reading of Cranmer's homilies. Local officials were ordered to imprison 'infringers or breakers thereof' and to report them to the council.[30]

The long-promised reform finally came in the form of the first

[27] *TRP* no. 299.
[28] *TRP* no. 300.
[29] *TRP* no. 303.
[30] *TRP* no. 313.

Edwardian prayer book. The Parliament which began meeting in November passed the first Act of Uniformity, enjoining the use of the prayer book and providing penalties for not using it.[31] Thus despite the statements in the proclamations suggesting that Somerset intended to use the prerogative to introduce additional reform, after the innovations introduced by initial injunctions, proclamations were used largely to restrict overzealous reformers rather than to change the religious settlement. In the process some new restrictions were introduced by royal proclamations. But the overall pattern was to use them to enforce and explain existing religious practices and to inform the general population that additional changes would be forthcoming.

Many of the proclamations issued during Somerset's ascendancy need only a brief comment. They dealt with the same subjects and were used for the same purposes for which they had been used throughout the early Tudor period. Since this was a period of extensive military operations, an impressive number were concerned with military matters. Others pardoned rebels, dealt with administrative matters and imposed court regulations, or restrictions on hunting.[32] Another simply added threats and penalties for officials who failed to enforce 21 Henry VIII c. 10, prohibiting the export of bell metal. In June 1548 controls were again placed on the export of leather and hides because, it was argued, extensive exports were causing scarcity and a resulting rise in prices. Finally, a rather unique type of price control proclamation in August 1549 fixed a maximum price of $2\frac{1}{2}$d per meal upon those who were lodging noblemen and gentlemen in the King's service in London.[33]

Other proclamations, especially those concerned with economic matters, deserve more attention because they reveal that Somerset was not at all restrained in his use of the prerogative. Those dealing with the wool trade and wool cloth manufacture are a good example of this. The first proclamation on this subject has already been discussed. It simply revised 37 Henry VIII c. 15 by including the

---

[31] 2 and 3 Edward VI c. 1. After the Parliament adjourned, Somerset used a proclamation in June 1549 to set prices on the new prayer book: *TRP* no. 335.

[32] *TRP* nos. 298, 314, 318, 325, 329, 330, 343, 348, 350 dealt with military matters; no. 308 pardoned rebels; no. 305 summoned judges and justices in London and suburbs to appear before the council; no. 312 adjourned Michaelmas term; no. 324 announced payments of the King's debts; nos. 307 and 316 provided for payments to religious pensioners; 311.5 (Appendix A CLRO Journals 15/273) limited access to the court because of the threat of the plague; no. 320 prohibited arms near court; and no. 347 prohibited hunting without special authority within the precincts of Whitehall or adjoining parks and chases.

[33] *TRP* nos. 306, 310, 346. The last proclamation was issued at a time when London was particularly crowded due to the unrest and rebellion in the land. This necessitated keeping large numbers of troops in the city. Jordan, *The Young King*, 446.

names of several counties inadvertently left out of the statute and adding a provision forbidding pulling, plucking and clipping of wool fells. The statute, however, was too restrictive. The poor spinners of Norwich, who were dependent upon middlemen for buying small quantities of wool, were adversely affected by the prohibitions on the buying of wool for resale, because it eliminated their suppliers. Consequently, Edward VI's first Parliament enacted 1 Edward VI c. 6, which exempted people in Norwich from the prohibitions in 37 Henry VIII c. 15. Parliament, however, did not renew the earlier statute which had been made to expire at the end of the next Parliament. Rather, after Parliament adjourned, a proclamation reiterated the restraint on the buying of wool anywhere in the realm by anyone except merchants of the Staple. It seems to have been carelessly drafted because it did not include the exemption for Norwich that had been granted in 1 Edward VI c. 6. Within three weeks the government seemingly recognized this. On 18 May 1549 a second proclamation repeated the provisions of the first with certain changes. It did not include the sweeping application to all counties; rather the East Anglian counties were significantly omitted from the list of those included in the proclamation. In addition the provision on plucking and clipping wool fells in the earlier proclamation was repeated, and merchants of the Staple were ordered not to sell any wool within the realm except 'refuse, coarse wools shot and shorted by the shooter such as be not meet for the said Staple.'[34]

The same rise in wool prices resulted in a temporary restraint on the export of wool in August 1549. The restraint was necessary because 'divers men of late use to engross and gather into their hands divers great quantities of wools to the intent to enhance and raise prices and so to convey the same into the parts beyond the seas.' Therefore wool export by all except merchants of the Staple was forbidden 'until such time as by like proclamation his majesty shall release this restraint.' Offenders would suffer forfeiture of double the value of the wools shipped and imprisonment at the King's pleasure. Port officials who allowed the wools to be loaded would lose their offices and be imprisoned. It is not clear how long the temporary restraint lasted, but it was seemingly an unpopular measure. Even if the restraint was not lifted, licenses were soon issued that allowed the export of wool despite the prohibitions in the proclamations.[35]

[34] Grafton, *Proclamations*, 42d–44d (Appendix A no. 330.5); *TRP* no. 331.
[35] *TRP* no. 345. The licenses were issued in response to complaints from both foreign and English merchants. SP 46/2/25.

In April 1549 a proclamation introduced new regulations on the manufacture of cloth. It complained of 'untrue and false cloths within this realm now within few years practiced and used' which caused 'great infamy and slander' to the realm. In order to end these slanders 'and to set forth such an order in his commonwealth that truth may rule and falsehood be utterly banished,' the proclamation established 'a perfect order of the making of cloths in all places of this his highness' realm.' Precise standards were set for the length and breadth of cloth, the amount of shrinkage allowed and procedures for the dyeing of cloth. Local officials were ordered to visit cloth manufacturers quarterly to 'view the cloths' in order 'to know whether they be truly made and dyed according to this proclamation.' They were told to 'present the names of all such offenders, with their misdemeanors' to Somerset and the council. The proclamation gave no indication that it was a temporary measure. The precision and detail of the orders suggest that permanent new regulations were intended. However, the method of enforcement was surely impractical, for if even a small minority of the clothiers offended against the act, and if local officials carried out their responsibilities, Somerset and the council would have been so overwhelmed with work that they would have had little time to attend to their other responsibilities.[36] Of course, we cannot be sure that these arrangements were intended as long-term legislation. Possibly, Somerset would have turned to Parliament for new legislation if he had remained in power, but in light of his general disregard for statutory authority in other matters involving the cloth and wool trade it seems unlikely. After Somerset's fall a statute was enacted which repeated many of the provisions of the proclamation, but it arranged for the appointment of overseers of cloth who would carry out inspections. Informers were allowed to sue for half of the fines and forfeitures in the normal manner provided for in penal statutes.[37]

Other new regulations were introduced by proclamations on coinage. Henry VIII's debasement had significantly lowered the bullion content of coins, but it had only slightly reduced their weight. Because the coins were valued at a rate considerably exceeding the actual value of the bullion in the coins, counterfeiting became

[36] *TRP* no. 328. Jordan, *The Young King*, 390-1, calls it 'an ambitious effort...to reform the standard of English cloth manufacture by incredibly precise regulations governing shrinking, dyeing, and quality, with instructions for inspection and the amazing requirement that violators be reported directly to the privy council.'

[37] 3 and 4 Edward VI c. 2. Another statute in the 1552 Parliament repealed all previous acts on dyeing, dressing, pressing, searching and sealing cloth, and introduced new regulations: 5 and 6 Edward VI c. 6.

profitable and widespread. At first Somerset continued to use the debased coins with the dies of the previous reign, but in April 1548 a proclamation indicated that a movement towards reform of the coinage was beginning. It stated that the teston, a silver coin valued at 12d, was particularly easy to counterfeit because of its size and value.[38] Therefore the King, 'minding the due reformation hereof' and to prevent counterfeiting, ordered that testons be withdrawn from circulation. After 31 December they would no longer be current and no one was to 'buy or amass into his or their hands any of the said testons for a peculiar gain to be had thereof to him or their wards, upon pain of forfeiture.' Those who held testons could bring them to the mint where they would receive their value in other coins.[39] On 31 January 1549 the time limit in the earlier proclamation was extended by allowing testons to continue as legal tender until 1 May 1549. It was argued that so many testons were in circulation that the deadline could not be met without serious inconvenience. The proclamation also tried to deal with those who were making unreasonable profits on the exchange of testons by forbidding any gain above 2d for every 20s exchanged upon pain of forfeiture of the money exchanged.[40]

However the movement towards reform had already ended. Against the advice of at least some of his council, Somerset had by this time decided on another debasement. This debasement was carried out cleverly. Probably because it was believed that a smaller but finer coin would be more difficult to counterfeit, new coins were issued that contained less alloy. But they were considerably lighter in weight. On 24 January 1549 a proclamation announced values for 'certain new coins of gold and silver to be made.' Subjects were ordered to accept the coins at those values on pain of imprisonment and further punishment at the King's pleasure.[41] On 11 April 1549 a detailed proclamation dealt with a number of matters involving the coinage. It forbade export of coin on pain of the King's displeasure and imprisonment 'over and besides such pains and forfeitures' as were in the statute. New and in some cases higher values were set on gold coins. Individuals who bought or sold coins above those values were to suffer forfeiture and an additional fine of ten times the value of the coins. Individuals who were buying coins to 'cull and try out the finest and heaviest and melt them down,' were accused of acting

---

[38] The teston was the largest silver coin. This helps explain why it was so commonly counterfeited.   [39] *TRP* no. 302.
[40] *TRP* no. 322.
[41] *TRP* no. 321; Jordan, *The Young King*, 394–5.

'contrary to the laws and statutes of this realm.' If they continued to ignore these laws they would suffer forfeiture and imprisonment. Finally, local officials were commanded to 'make the most diligent search and inquiry' to locate counterfeiters and to punish them by death and forfeiture of lands, goods and chattels 'as by the laws of the realm counterfeiters of the King's majesty's coin and their adherents, fautors, abettors or concealers hath been wont and accustomed.'[42]

In May the time limit for turning in testons was extended to 31 July 1549. Individuals were accused of 'abusing his highness' clemency' in the previous proclamation by not turning in testons. People were allowed to buy testons for the purpose of bringing them to the mint but at 'no less price than after $11\frac{1}{2}$d the piece and not under.' If the buyer bought at less than that 'to the damage of the poor men who would sell the same,' he would not only forfeit the testons but would be fined ten times their value.[43] Both of the last two proclamations used common law methods of enforcement to deal with those who sold above the stated values even though this section of the proclamation was not based on statutory authority. However, this may have been the normal method of enforcement. The proclamation of 11 April allowed informers to bring accusations 'in any of the King's majesty's courts, by bill, action of debt, or information, *as in such cases heretofore hath been accustomed* [my italics].' It was not until 1552 that a statute provided new authority for proclamations setting values on coins by decreeing that no one was to take or receive more in value for coins 'than the same is or shall be declared by the King's majesty; his proclamation to be current for within this his highness' realm.'[44]

The foolish and irresponsible debasement combined with the domestic disorders brought on by Somerset's enclosure policy and the first bad harvest in three years, all contributed to a steep rise in the price of food in 1549.[45] In early July the government intervened by setting prices on meat, butter and cheese. This was the only one of Somerset's proclamations to cite a statute granting authority to the King's proclamations. The statute was 25 Henry VIII c. 2, which simply provided that the council could set prices of victuals. But Somerset considerably exceeded the powers granted in that

[42] *TRP* no. 326.   [43] *TRP* no. 332.
[44] 5 and 6 Edward VI c. 19. The penalty was forfeiture, fine and imprisonment and informers were allowed to sue for a share 'in any Court of Record.'
[45] Bowden, *Agrarian History*, IV, 848. The price index on agricultural products rose from 182 in 1548 to 221 in 1549.

statute. The proclamation introduced a new approach to the setting of meat prices. Rather than setting a maximum price per dressed pound, it priced live whole animals. Furthermore, because cattle and sheep were more plentiful in the spring and summer, higher prices were allowed in the winter. Penalties were set at a £5 fine for cattle sold above the set price and 10s for sheep. Another clause based on the King's 'authority and power royal' provided for the supply of markets. It ordered local officials or individuals specifically appointed by justices of the peace to see that the markets were well supplied by compelling farmers and graziers to bring their animals to the market and to sell at the set prices. The proclamation concluded with a stern warning to those who would use self-help to deal with individuals who violated it:

If any subject, of what degree or estate soever he be, shall contrariwise and unlawfully, that is to say, otherwise than by complaint or order of law, seek, begin, or enterprise to redress his own cause, or the cause of any other, be the same never so just; then his majesty ascertaineth and letteth the same to know, that without any manner favor or grace to be hoped upon, he and every of them, so offending, shall surely feel, by extreme punishment, the King's highness' utter indignation; and in such case no extremity to be spared, but to be taken and accepted, not only as unkind, unnatural, unloving, and disobedient subjects, but also as high traitors and rebels against the King's majesty's own royal person, his crown, state and dignity.[46]

The proclamation, which had begun by simply applying powers granted by statute, thus went considerably beyond that authority. The order compelling farmers to supply the market was of course not based on the statute, but it did not exceed similar orders in earlier proclamations. However, the last section which on the authority of the King's prerogative alone made it treason to use methods other than those set by law in dealing with offenders against the proclamation would certainly have been illegal under the provisions of the Statute of Proclamations. It could only be justified by the national emergency in the summer of 1549. The country was plagued by riot and rebellion. Under those circumstances any actions that might lead to further violence must be discouraged in the strongest possible terms.[47]

The internal unrest in the summer of 1549 was to a great extent

[46] *TRP* no. 336.
[47] Professor Elton also viewed this proclamation as one 'which might be read as introducing a new capital offense'; however he explained it by arguing that 'even this in fact only extended the concept of rebellion to cover major rioting.' Elton, *HJ*, vii,

brought about by Somerset's campaign against enclosures. In a manner similar to Wolsey's approach, Somerset used proclamations to enforce existing statutory legislation. The procedure had disastrous consequences, both because it aroused the fierce opposition of landholders, who, as Wolsey had learned, would accept anti-enclosure laws only as long as they were ineffective and not enforced, and because it encouraged the general populace to hope for more rapid and far-reaching reform than was feasible. The attack was initiated in June 1548 with a royal proclamation. A good deal of it was devoted to justifying the action. The oft-recited evils of enclosures were reviewed in detail. It was argued that enclosures were detrimental to the defense of the realm, because 'force of men and the multitude of true subjects' rather than 'flocks of sheep and droves of beasts' were needed to meet external threats. Furthermore the recent 'great rots and murrains both of sheep and bullocks' might even be 'the due punishment of God for such uncharitableness.' After having made an extensive effort to convince subjects that enclosure statutes ought to be enforced, the proclamation simply announced that commissioners were being appointed so that 'a view and inquiry' could be made of all illegal enclosures 'contrary to the wealth and profit of this realm of England and the said godly laws and acts of Parliament.[48]

A commission headed by the radical reformer, John Hales, was appointed for the Midlands. Hales, who was one of the most vocal and bitter opponents of enclosures, carried out his work with a zealous thoroughness. The work of the commission was interrupted by the meeting of Parliament which began in November 1548. Although Hales was a member of that Parliament and drafted two bills on enclosures, the only new legislation affecting enclosures was 2 and 3 Edward VI c. 36, which simply imposed a special tax on sheep. The program of enforcing enclosure legislation was already resulting in the resentment of the landholding classes, and discontent was growing among the poor because the hopes for changes were not being carried out swiftly enough.[49] Nevertheless, Somerset issued

---

271. The proclamation does not, however, even refer specifically to creating a major riot. One would be considered a traitor if he in any way 'otherwise than by complaint or order of law' sought 'to redress his own cause or the cause of any other.'

[48] *TRP* no. 309.

[49] The commissioners had broad powers and there must have been widespread hope for a major reform. Jordan, *The Young King*, 429, describes these procedures as follows: 'In each place visited a jury of twelve was empanelled to which a commissioner, usually Hales, set out the instructions under which they served and recited in detail the information that was required. Witnesses were placed under oath and could be sent to ward if they

a new proclamation in April 1549. It began by referring to the Tudor enclosure statutes and the earlier proclamation. It then announced that the King and council as a result of the commissioners' reports were now aware that the statutes were not being observed. It recited specifically the types of offenses that had taken place and announced that the King intended to enforce the laws and 'to see them executed against all such as shall be found culpable, without pardon or remission.' The King's 'officers and ministers' were ordered to proceed 'with all speed and earnest endeavor' to the punishment of offenders.[50]

By the end of May serious disturbances were breaking out. In an effort to curb them, a new proclamation condemned those who 'under pretense of the said proclamation' had 'taken upon them his majesty's authority' and were destroying enclosures 'at their will and pleasure.' Subjects were assured the King intended to see that enclosures were 'reformed according to his majesty's laws and statutes,' but they were commanded to stop rioting and gathering in unlawful assemblies. Individuals having knowledge of unlawful assemblies gathered for the purpose of destroying enclosures or for any other purpose were commanded to report them to the justice of the peace. Those who did not cease their unlawful activities were warned that the King intended 'to prosecute by the sword, and with all force and extremity, all such offenders; and also when they shall be departed from their houses to any assembly for any such unlawful purpose to spoil and rifle their houses and goods to their utter ruin and destruction.'[51] Disorder continued to spread. In June another proclamation promised a pardon to enclosure rioters and speedy reform of illegal enclosures through proper channels. It warned that future rioters would be punished by loss of the pardon and 'death, loss of lands, goods and chattels as by the laws of the realm in such case is provided.'[52]

By July the Western rebellion and Ket's rebellion were raging out of control. Five proclamations were issued in rapid succession, applying a variety of remedies ranging from merciful pardons to irresponsible threats. On 8 July rewards were offered to those who reported rumormongers in a proclamation which accused criminals,

were contumacious. After information taken, the commission called offenders before it and of its own authority could forgive past illegalities, order enclosures to be removed, and command land illegally under sheep to be returned to tillage.' See *ibid.* 410ff for full discussion of Somerset's efforts to enforce the enclosure legislation.

[50] *TRP* no. 327. [51] *TRP* no. 333.
[52] *TRP* no. 334.

deserters and 'loiterers' of spreading rumors which mislead the 'King's true subjects' to gather in unlawful assemblies.[53] Three days later an effort was made to aid Lord Russell, who was attempting to suppress the Western rebellion. The rebels were besieging the city of Exeter, but Russell maintained he still was not adequately reinforced to come to the relief of Exeter. The proclamation attempted first to frighten the rebels into submission by ordering them to submit to Russell or be treated as traitors and forfeit their 'goods, chattels, offices, pensions, manors, lands, tenements, farms, copyholds, and other hereditaments.' It then attempted to encourage the uncommitted to join Russell by promising that the lands, goods and chattels of those who persisted in the rebellion

> shall grow, come and be unto all and every such person and persons as shall first have, take, possess, and attain to the same goods and chattels, or shall first enter into the said manors, lands, tenements and hereditaments; and the same shall have, hold, possess, and enjoy, to his and their own proper use, commodity, and behalf, in as large and ample sort as his highness, by means and right of the said forfeiture and confiscation, ought and may dispose of the same; and shall have thereof such assurance from his majesty by his letters patent, or otherwise, as they or any of them can or shall best imagine or devise.[54]

Somerset informed Warwick in a letter on 22 July that he had specifically mentioned copyholds since 'the matter of copyholds being so general a living to a number of those shires shall be as much a terror as any other thing that can be possibly devised.'[55] The penalties were certainly legal, but the promise to those engaged in subduing the rebellion was an irresponsible one which Somerset would later regret. After Russell's victory in August, Somerset was distressed by the large scale redistribution of property which was carried out by Russell in summary fashion. He wrote to tell him that he did not have the authority to distribute lands arbitrarily 'and that the proclamation under whose authority Russell claimed to proceed was not meant to deny due process of law.'[56] Although Somerset had probably not meant to encourage the type of actions which followed, the wording of the proclamation seemingly allowed the procedures which Russell adopted. Both this proclamation and the one setting meat prices, issued slightly over a week earlier, illustrate the type of

[53] *TRP* no. 337. Somerset had still not given up the effort to reform enclosures. Printed instructions were issued to the enclosure commissioners on the same day: *TRP* no. 338.
[54] *TRP* no. 339.
[55] Nicholas Pocock, *Troubles Connected with Prayer Book of 1549* (London, 1885), 32.
[56] Jordan, *The Young King*, 475.

irresponsible language which Somerset resorted to when he was threatened.

In contrast to the vindictive threats made on 11 July, the following day those who had submitted and repented of their offenses 'committed in sundry unlawful and riotous assemblies' were pardoned. Furthermore, those who had suffered 'any manner of grief, damage, or loss' from these riots and unlawful assemblies were ordered not to 'force, punish, avenge or correct any manner of offense, trespass or unlawful act committed by the same offenders.'[57] On 16 July a fourth proclamation again threatened extreme punishment to those who called or gathered in unlawful assemblies in order to tear down enclosures 'or to redress anything which shall and may be by the force of the King's majesty's commission reformed, redressed, and amended.' It spoke of the instructions issued to the enclosure commission and stated that the commissioners were prepared to introduce the desired reforms. This was being 'delayed only by the folly of the people seeking their own redress unlawfully.' It threatened offenders with death to be 'executed by authority and order of law martial, wherein no delay or differing of time shall be permitted or suffered.' It ordered officials to apprehend offenders, imprison them and to certify their names to Somerset and the council 'to the intent most speedy order may be given for the execution of the offender.'[58]

Somerset's methods of dealing with the rebellion were criticized by Thomas Smith in a letter to William Cecil on 19 July. Smith stated that the proclamations, directed in a general fashion to local officials, would not result in effective enforcement 'because when the proclamations be directed so generally every man looketh upon another.' He added that he did 'not mean that the proclamations should be otherwise directed; but I would wish letters directed to one or more special men of trust in every shire to be attendant upon the execution thereof' who could summon gentlemen, yeomen and households 'as need or occasion shall be so' to deal with the rioters.[59] Possibly in response to this advice, a letter was sent to special men in each county. The letter complained that 'our said clemency proclamations and other commandments and admonitions notwithstanding many idle vagabonds and other lewd and seditious persons' were not being punished and they were continuing to raise unlawful assemblies. The letter ordered the men to whom it was addressed 'to have a special

[57] *TRP* no. 340. [58] *TRP* no. 341.
[59] SP 10/8/33. Smith concluded by praising Lord Grey's work in Oxfordshire where his violent actions to suppress the rioters were described as 'better than ten thousand proclamations and pardons for the quieting of the people.'

and earnest regard to the observation of our said proclamations and the severe punishment of such as shall offend.' They were to cause justices of the peace and other officers to inquire about those who had stirred people into unlawful assemblies so that they could be apprehended and 'without delay hanged and executed openly to the terror of others.'[60] The fifth proclamation, issued on 22 July, criticized 'bailiffs, constables and headboroughs' for not suppressing unlawful assemblies as their offices obligated them to do. It accused them of sometimes being the 'very ringleaders and procurers.' They were ordered to 'forbear and abstain from the raising or assembling of any of his highness' subjects for any act or purpose other than such as by the laws and statutes of this realm is limited for them to execute and do' upon pain of death and forfeiture of 'lands and goods forever, with like penalties as to cases of treason is reserved.'[61]

By September both major rebellions had been crushed. The armies which had defeated the rebels were now used against Somerset. In October he was removed from power in a bloodless *coup d'état*. The events that led to his fall have been well chronicled elsewhere[62] and need not be reviewed here except to reiterate that his foolish policy on enclosures carried out through the use of royal proclamations was an important factor. He persisted in that policy even when it led to riot and rebellion. When he tried to deal with the turmoil, he displayed the same recklessness and high-handed use of the prerogative power characteristic of his brief rule. Although the harsh penalties used to deal with rebellion were certainly within the law, Somerset used severe penalties more often than they were used in any other period. The statistics are somewhat mitigated by the fact that the penalties in eight of these proclamations were common law or statutory penalties,[63] but there were cases when the death penalty was applied in an extremely questionable fashion. As has already been pointed out, the threat of treason penalties to those who

[60] SP 10/8/66.
[61] *TRP* no. 342. In August another proclamation (*TRP* no. 344), probably also motivated by the internal turmoil, introduced a temporary prohibition on all plays and interludes throughout the realm. It may have been stimulated by a request from the London government on 4 July for 'aid and advice for the staying of all common interludes and plays within the city and suburbs thereof' (CLRO Rep. 13(1)/100). However, it was issued approximately a month later and applied to the whole realm. The preamble commented on interludes and plays which 'contain matter tending to sedition and contemning of sundry good orders and laws; whereupon are grown and are daily like to grow and ensue much disquiet, division, tumults and uproars in this realm.'
[62] See especially Jordan, *The Young King*, 494ff.
[63] *TRP* nos. 288, 325, 326, 330, 334, 339, 341, 342.

EDWARD VI

used self-help to deal with offenders against the July 1549 meat price proclamation involved a rather broad interpretation of the treason laws. A proclamation of 19 February 1549 declared that anyone who aided pirates would 'be taken for a pirate or fautor of them and suffer such pains of death, loss of goods, and forfeitures, as the pirates themselves or their fautors by the laws of this realm should or ought to do.' Although this might be considered a justifiable extension of the statutory penalties for piracy, it came extremely close to introducing the death penalty on the authority of the prerogative alone, because there were no laws which specifically applied the death penalty to those who aided pirates.[64]

In addition to those proclamations which ordered the death penalty, there were a number that decreed more severe penalties than normally were used for the offense in question. The two which specified a forfeiture of ten times the value of the money exchanged at rates other than those set by the proclamations exceeded by far the normal penalty for an offense of this nature. It was also greater than the penalty included in a statute enacted three years later.[65] On 29 April 1549 the most severe penalties ever used in the early Tudor period in proclamations dealing with rumors were imposed by a proclamation which complained that rumors were being spread of military defeats and maintained 'that all other punishment heretofore appointed will not suffice for the redress and amendment hereof.' It ordered local officials to apprehend the sowers of false tales and imprison them until they revealed the author of the rumor. If they did not they would be considered the author, and 'every such author or maker of such false tale or news shall be committed into the galley, there to rot in chains as a slave or forcery during the King's majesty's pleasure.'[66] The use of exceptional penalties in times of stress might be justified by the needs of the commonwealth, but Somerset used unusual penalties even for less important matters. In June 1548 a proclamation maintained that it was being reported that the King intended to deforest the forest of Waltham in Essex and as a result

[64] *TRP* no. 323. This was the second of two proclamations dealing with pirates. The first (in January 1549) announced a pardon for 'honest mariners' who had been taken prisoner by pirates, and who had 'served under the said pirates' if they sought it by 31 March (*TRP* no. 317). Elton, *HJ*, VII, 270, states that the penalty in the second proclamation does not create a new capital offense although 'it comes close to it by including aiders of pirates among the pirates liable to death by statute.'

[65] *TRP* nos. 326, 332. The full penalty in the first proclamation was a fine of ten times the value of the coins and imprisonment. The second proclamation did not include imprisonment. The statute 5 and 6 Edward VI c. 19 ordered forfeiture of the coins, a year's imprisonment and fine at the King's pleasure.

[66] *TRP* no. 329.

individuals were killing and destroying the King's deer in that forest. It stated that the King intended to keep the forest of Waltham in its present state and it ordered that no one was to kill, hunt, or disturb the King's deer in that forest unless they were licensed to do so. Anyone continuing to hunt, chase or kill the King's deer would be imprisoned for three years and pay a fine 'at our will and pleasure if they have wherewith so to do, and shall find good surety to do no more hurt, and if they have not whereof so to do that they shall abjure this our realm.'[67] Although it is doubtful if the more arbitrary penalties were carried out in practice except possibly to make an example of a few unfortunate individuals, the penalties were heavy enough to discredit the assumption that Somerset was more liberal in his use of proclamations than his predecessors.[68]

Somerset may have relied on severe penalties more often than normal because there was no adequate and efficient method of enforcing proclamations after the repeal of the Statute of Proclamations had eliminated the special statutory court. One of the biggest contrasts between Somerset's proclamations and those issued earlier was the extensive use of the council. Only two proclamations specifically mentioned or implied that informers could use 'any of the King's courts of record' to sue for their share of the forfeiture.[69] Although those based on a statute might use the method of enforcement in the statute during Somerset's tenure, it was rare for proclamations simply to order enforcement of a statute or to be based on a statute. Most of his proclamations either relied on local officials or

[67] *TRP* no. 311.

[68] Jordan, *The Young King*, 174, explains the repeal of the Statute of Proclamations in the following way: 'The evident intention here was at once to mitigate the heavy penalties with which Henrician proclamations were buttressed and to posit the effective power of proclamations on more nearly acceptable constitutional grounds.' In light of the heavy penalties in Somerset's proclamations, this explanation is unacceptable; in fact, at the very time the repeal of the Statute was under consideration, the proclamation which ordered punishment of those who behaved in an insolent way towards priests threatened in general terms what must have been intended to sound like a very severe punishment to potential offenders (*TRP* no. 292).

[69] *TRP* nos. 326, 332. No. 336, which was specifically based on a statute, also stated that the King could 'have his recovery and remedy by information, bill, plaint, or action of debt in any of his highness' courts of record,' but a reward for informers was not included. Two other proclamations which used informers remained fairly nebulous on where they could sue for their share of the forfeiture. One simply used the phrase 'according to the laws of this realm' (*TRP* no. 319). The second implied that complaints would be made to local officials (*TRP* no. 322). This proclamation, which forbade a higher rate of gain in the exchange of testons than 2d for every 20s, might have been based on 25 Edward III st. 5 c. 12, which forbade the taking of profit on exchanges and allowed informers to sue in any court of record, but the statute was not cited and this method of enforcement was not specified.

the council for enforcement. Fifteen specifically mentioned the council.[70] The burden imposed on the council in the enforcement of fifteen separate proclamations in a period of less than two years would have made it impossible to find time for other business if it had seriously tried to deal with all infractions. Clearly this was not what was intended. The council could do little more than make an example of a few notorious offenders. The task of enforcing the laws more thoroughly was dependent on local officials. The repeal of the Statute of Proclamations, therefore, had its most significant impact in enforcement, in that it removed the special court which had been used to enforce proclamations which the government considered especially important. It also left unclear whether proclamations not specifically based on statutes could be enforced in common law courts. Therefore, Somerset had to rely on the council or local officials. The severe penalties suggest that this was not a satisfactory method. Because this problem must have become increasingly evident in the last years of the early Tudor period, a new effort was made to deal with it before the end of Edward VI's reign.

Northumberland (1549–53)

The first proclamation issued after Somerset's arrest revealed the general insecurity of a government that had just deposed a popular leader. On 30 October 1549 'certain lewd and seditious persons (more favouring the said Duke [Somerset] than remembering their duties to his highness and natural country)' were accused of causing 'sedition and division' by spreading rumors that 'the good laws made for religion should be now altered and abolished and the old Romish service, mass, and ceremonies eftsoons renewed and revived.' These rumors were pronounced false and local officials were ordered to apprehend those who were spreading the rumors and to imprison them until the King with the advice of his council 'signify unto them what they shall think convenient to be done for their punishment as their offense and doings shall require.'[71] Parliament began meeting on 4 November. In reaction to the turmoil the country had just experienced, a new statute was enacted which made it high treason for twelve or more persons to assemble for the purpose of tearing down enclosures or threatening any member of the privy council.

---

[70] *TRP* nos. 281, 292, 296, 299, 303, 313, 313.5, 314, 315, 328, 329, 330.5, 331, 337, 341. In two cases, proclamations which utilized the council for enforcement were later made statutory and the statutes used common law courts. *TRP* nos. 328, 331; 3 and 4 Edward VI c. 2; 5 and 6 Edward VI c. 7.   [71] *TRP* no. 352.

The statute included the specific words of a proclamation to be made in the King's name ordering such unlawful assemblies to disband.[72]

After Parliament ended its session on 1 February, Warwick ruled without Parliament for almost two years. Somerset was pardoned shortly afterwards and restored to the council in April, but his influence was never again paramount. Most of the proclamations issued during the remainder of the reign probably reflect primarily Warwick's influence. Many dealt with relatively uncontroversial questions, some of them reflecting the uneasiness of the government about internal unrest. In February a proclamation 'stayed the killing of flesh in Lent.'[73] The peace treaty concluded with France and Scotland was announced in March, and Trinity term was adjourned in May 'for divers urgent and great considerations.'[74] The same day individuals who had not lived in London for at least three years or who were unemployed were ordered to leave the city and return to their home counties or 'where they last dwelt by the space of three years together according to the tenor, form and effect of the statute in that behalf' and 'upon the pains in the same statute limited and expressed.'[75] This proclamation seems to have been motivated by the concern about internal unrest. The same concern may have led to a restraint on victuals, fuel, tallow and hides. The high price of victuals and the scarcity brought on by the bad harvest of 1549 were cited as the reason for the action. By the spring of 1550 this had become a major problem which might have led to serious discontent, especially among the poor.[76] On 17 May another proclamation graphically illustrated the nervousness of the government. It spoke of 'divers evil-disposed persons' who 'in conventicles and secret places' were plotting 'enterprises and disorders, tending to rebellion, murder, and unlawful assemblies.' It offered a very generous reward of £20 to any subject knowing of any 'conspiracy or other privy intent of insurrection or rising to be made, moved or attempted' who would report it to the King, the privy council, or the lord lieutenant of the county where the conspiracy was being planned.[77] The uneasiness reached a high point in June and July

[72] 3 and 4 Edward VI c. 5; *TRP* no. 353.5.
[73] CLRO Rep. 12(1)/201b (Appendix B item 34).
[74] *TRP* nos. 354, 355. Trinity term was again adjourned by proclamation the following year. *TRP* no. 369.
[75] *TRP* no. 356. The statute referred to must have been 3 and 4 Edward VI c. 16, which revived 22 Henry VIII c. 14.
[76] *TRP* no. 357. In April the city council in Norwich noted that grain would be so scarce during the year that 'the poor people shall not be able to provide for themselves.' NNRO Mayors Court Book 1549-55, 62.   [77] *TRP* no. 358.

when efforts were made to forestall possible trouble from unemployed military personnel. In June a proclamation complained of captains who 'neglect their duties but also break the good order that were convenient they should keep,' and commanded all captains 'as are retained in our wages for serving in any part of our dominions being absent from their charges' to return immediately. At the end of July captains and soldiers 'not presently entertained in his highness' wages' were told to leave London within three days upon pain of imprisonment and further punishment.[78]

In May 1550 Henry VIII's proclamation on wool winding was repeated almost verbatim with two additions. In order to increase the weight of their wool, it was maintained 'divers covetous persons' who were not 'satisfied with such increase of wools of their sheep as God hath given them' were allowing their sheep to 'remain unshorn and unclipped by the space of three weeks or a month after their said washing and drying' so that 'their said wools might be the weightier, partly by means of their sweating and partly also through other filth which doth increase by reason of their long deferring the shearing and clipping of the same.' In order to prevent this it was commanded that sheep after having been 'washed and dried' should be shorn within five or six days, upon pain of a 40s fine for every 100 sheep allowed to remain unclipped for a longer period. It was certainly a laudable effort to control a questionable practice, but it is doubtful whether it could be strictly enforced. The last section of the proclamation threatened local officials with a rather large fine of £20 for failing to enforce any section of the proclamation. This clause, which was not in Henry VIII's proclamation, is particularly interesting because it hinted that local officials might have at time deliberately refused to punish offenders. The clause read:

> that whatsoever justice of peace, mayor, sheriff, bailiff, or other officer do refuse to punish any person or persons so to him or them presented according to this present ordinance, and his or their faults duly known and proved shall forfeit to the King's majesty our sovereign lord £20 to be paid in his Exchequer and further to incur his grace's high displeasure.[79]

The same enforcement problems which hampered the effort to control wool winding also plagued the government's program designed to deal with high food prices and to regulate the coinage. These were the two most common subjects for proclamations in the last period of Edward VI's reign. Six proclamations on food prices

---

[78] *TRP* nos. 360, 363. W. K. Jordan, *Edward VI: The Threshold of Power* (London, 1970) 61.   [79] *TRP* no. 359. Henry VIII's proclamation was no. 253.

and thirteen on money matters were issued in a year and a half. The two subjects were related because the government was stimulating inflation with its coinage manipulations and trying to control it with the price regulations. It was an impossible situation and it is not surprising that enforcement problems developed. The food shortage reached critical proportions in the summer and fall of 1550 after another bad harvest aggravated an already serious situation. In July the restraint imposed the previous spring was reinforced by a proclamation which added more stringent penalties and attempted to improve enforcement. It began with a lengthy justification that stated the King's concern because 'things here needful for the commodious living of his highness' natural subjects' were being exported, causing scarcity and high prices. It therefore forbade export except to Calais and revoked all previous licenses 'until hereafter upon further respects it shall please his majesty to enlarge the same.' Offenders would suffer the penalties in the statute and would forfeit the item shipped 'the one half to be immediately confiscated to his highness' coffers, and the other half to the presenter of the same into his grace's Court of Exchequer.' In addition the ship used to export the goods would be forfeited. Both the 'offenders' and those 'aiding and consenting to the shipping' would be imprisoned and fined at the King's pleasure. Presentments were allowed for three years after the offense and those involved in illegal exports were encouraged to turn against their associates. Anyone bringing accusations 'in case he were before aiding or consenting to the said principal offenders act' was promised 'pardon of his imprisonment, fine or other penalty.'[80]

Even this effort was obviously not sufficient. In September new regulations with more severe penalties to assure an adequate supply of victual at reasonable prices were introduced. This proclamation had a very interesting background. It was devised while Warwick was away from the council taking baths for his health, but there must have been a discussion about its provisions and some agreement before he left. The council then changed it while Warwick was absent and sent him a copy 'which the lords have penned according to their opinions and so sent it unto him praying his lordship to peruse it and to amend it as he shall see cause, and thereupon to return it to the Lord Chancellor to set forth.'[81] Warwick seems to have been more than a little irritated. In his response to Cecil he

[80] *TRP* no. 361. Some exceptions to the restraint were made by the following month when the council issued new licenses. Dasent, III, 106.   [81] *Ibid.* 125.

wondered why the 'proclamation could not have been dispatched according to such devices as were thereupon talked of and fully concluded.' Warwick also did not believe that the councilors had earnestly sought his advice before making the changes, as they claimed. He expressed surprise 'that my said Lord Chancellor hath sought me and traveled the streets afore only to speak with me who can show him no more than others that were first privy before me.' He was also surprised that the chancellor did not know where he was since 'the master of the horse knoweth of my being here for I made him privy to it.' Nevertheless, he stated that since he could not 'attend to visit nor commune with you about it without I should omit that which is so necessary for my health,' he would agree to 'what my Lord of Somerset, the master of the horse and you with others do resolve in it.'[82]

The proclamation, issued on 24 September 1550, seems to reveal Somerset's influence. Not only had Warwick mentioned Somerset as one of the three men who were the devisers of the proclamation, but, typical of the proclamations issued when Somerset was dominant, it relied on severe penalties and showed little concern about statutory authority. It contained a three-pronged attack on the problem of scarcity and high prices. First the export of victuals, leather, tallow, wood and wool was forbidden, 'any license, grant or dispensation to the contrary heretofore granted in any wise notwithstanding.' Although it mentioned the 'many good laws, statutes, and other orders' forbidding export 'in time of need' no specific statute was cited, and the penalties exceeded those in any earlier statute. Offenders would 'forfeit as well all the goods and chattels that he or they have to their own use, their aiders or consenters, at the time they shall be found to offend this proclamation.' The ships and the things transported would also be forfeited. Half of the forfeiture was to go to those 'that shall find and present and approve the same' and the other half to the King 'or to the lord or lords of the franchises who hath authority to have the same by his highness' grant or other lawful means.' More courts were mentioned than in any previous proclamation, including the Star Chamber: 'The first presenter and party grieved shall have their remedy by bill or information, before the King's highness' Privy Council or any two of them, the Star Chamber, his grace's Courts of Exchequer, King's Bench or

---

[82] SP 10/10/30. Jordan, *Threshold of Power*, 36, was, I think, misreading the document when he stated that Warwick was 'chiding' Cecil 'gently' in his response. It seems fairly evident that Warwick was quite irritated by the proceedings.

Common Pleas or before four justices of peace of the shire where the offense shall happen.' In a fashion similar to Somerset's early proclamation on export, it allowed grain to be exported as long as the price was below a stated level (wheat 6s 8d a quarter, malt or rye 5s, beans or peas 4s and oats 3s 4d).

The second section of the proclamation attempted to eliminate the middleman in all grain sales except in absolutely essential circumstances. It again used exceptionally severe penalties to frighten potential offenders. The buying of grain in the market for resale was forbidden to all except those who sold to bakers, brewers and innkeepers, upon pain of forfeiture of the grain 'and the moiety of his or their goods, chattels, leases, and farms, for term of life, lives or years, or at will which he or they have to their own use.' Informers were again allowed to sue in any of the courts mentioned in the first part of the proclamation for a share of this potentially very lucrative forfeiture. Finally, another search for grain by justices of the peace was ordered. They were to compel farmers to bring surplus to market. Those who refused to do so would be fined £10 and suffer three months' imprisonment.[83]

Throughout the month of October major efforts were made to get local officials to enforce the proclamation. On 2 October letters were sent to justices of the peace to have special care to see to the 'inviolable observation' of the proclamation and the punishment of offenders.[84] The next day letters were sent 'to special persons in every county' directing them to see to the enforcement of the proclamation. The letter mentioned the 'special letters' written to the justices of the peace and commented that although the council hoped they would carry out their duties, 'some slackness hath in times past been found in many of the said justices.' These letters were, therefore, being addressed so that they might not only 'use such good ways and means as you may think best for the execution of the said proclamations' but also to see that the justices did 'their duties therein without all respects of any person.'[85] The same day letters were sent to the lords lieutenant of the counties informing them of the two previous letters and adding, 'we have thought good to send unto you the copies of both our letters mentioned to the intent you may give

---

[83] *TRP* no. 365. The proclamation contained considerably more severe penalties than an order issued to justices of the peace in November 1549 commanding a search for grain. The order simply threatened those who failed to bring their surplus to market as well as regraters and forestallers with imprisonment until the council decided what punishment they deserved. SP 10/9/55.

[84] Dasent, III, 125.   [85] SP 10/10/40.

the like order in all shires within the limits of your commission.'[86] On 8 October, a second letter was sent to the justices of the peace 'to put in execution the proclamation of victuals.' A week later 'letters of second charge to the justices of the peace for the execution of the proclamation for victuals at the special commandment of the King's majesty' were sent.[87]

The series of letters establishes that there was a determined effort to get local officials to enforce the proclamation, but they probably also indicate that the effort was not very successful. Even the severe penalties and the rich rewards promised to informers, who were allowed to use both prerogative and common law courts, could not deter merchants from seeking more profitable sales abroad or prevent the middleman from exploiting the situation. Therefore a second proclamation was issued on 20 October. It maintained that despite the earlier proclamation, unscrupulous profiteers were still creating 'great dearth and scarcity, more than necessity requireth...not only by unlawful engrossing, forestalling, and regrating of the same, but also by unlawful transporting and conveying the same victuals and other premises into sundry parts beyond the sea.' The proclamation may reflect what Warwick had originally intended to do before Somerset and others of the council revised it. Although it resembled the earlier proclamation, there were some important differences. The changes were not of the type one would expect if it had simply been intended as a way of forcing compliance with the earlier proclamation. The first section cited 25 Henry VIII c. 2, which gave the council power to set prices on victuals and forbade unlicensed export. 'According to the tenor of the said act' it set maximum prices on grain, butter and cheese. In addition, the order that a search be made for surplus grain was repeated. The prohibition on export was also reiterated, but the provision that export would be allowed as long as grain was under a certain price was not included. Finally, subjects were ordered 'upon his or their duty of allegiance' not to 'meddle or enterprise to put any article or clause of this proclamation in execution by color or pretense of the same, but only the justice of the peace or such other as have special authority by this present proclamation.' The prohibition against self-help resembled that in Somerset's proclamation in July 1549, but with the important difference that the penalties were not nearly as severe. This was characteristic of the entire proclamation. Illegal export would be punished by forfeiture of the items exported 'and

[86] SP 10/10/43.   [87] Dasent, III, 137, 140.

further to incur the danger, pains and forfeitures of the King's laws and statutes in that behalf.' Failure to bring grain to market was punished simply by 'imprisonment during the King's pleasure.' The controversial penalty on regraters was not repeated, and the penalties for selling above the prices in the proclamation were fines of 13s 4d for every bushel of grain and 2s for every pound of butter and cheese.[88] The whole procedure is difficult to understand. If it was simply intended as a follow up to the first proclamation, it seems incongruous that the penalties were lighter and that price controls were introduced, for the lighter penalties and the limitation on prices in the English markets would only encourage more illegal export. It may be that the first proclamation reflects Somerset's influence and the second was the one originally 'talked of and fully concluded' before Warwick left the council to take baths for his health. If so, it again documents Somerset's pronounced reliance on severe penalties even when compared to Warwick.[89]

Whatever the explanation of the second proclamation, it was a bad solution. Prices were set at such an unreasonably low level that they could not be enforced even with the best of intentions. On 4 November complaints were already being heard. The sellers of cheese and butter in London complained to the city government, and a committee was appointed 'to resort to the council and there to make their humble suit.'[90] Within the month it became obvious that real problems were developing in the effort to get people to bring grain, butter, and cheese to market to sell at these prices. A letter was again sent to special persons in the county appointing them as commissioners to guarantee that the market was supplied and dismissing the former commissioners. The letter complained that 'the great number of such as have greatest quantity of grains, butter, and cheese in their hands...do refuse to bring their corn, butter, and cheese to the market in such sort as hath been commanded,' and that the King would no longer 'suffer these lewd behaviors unreformed.' The new commissioners were again ordered to assemble the justices of the peace for a search. If anyone refused to bring his surplus to

---

[88] *TRP* no. 366.
[89] The belief that severe penalties would deter offenders is of course not an unusual assumption. The lower classes, whom Somerset sought to protect from exploitation, held similar opinions. William Mordewe, a baker from Norwich, had a simple solution for those 'men of the county' who he maintained were responsible for the 'great costs of grain and victual' because 'they would not obey the King's proclamations.' He stated 'if it please the King to make him head man he would hang a fourth of them that would not obey.' NNRO Session Interrogations and Depositions 1549–54, 37d.
[90] CLRO Rep. 12(2)/278.

market, it should be taken from him and brought to market and he should be sent to the council 'to be here further punished.' Furthermore, since the 'wilfulness of many is very great,' the sheriff, who was included in the commission, was authorized 'to assemble the force of the shire if necessary.' The letter finally hinted that the council now realized that the prices set may have been unrealistic. The commissioners were told that 'if anything for the prices in respect proclaimed of that shire may seem to need redress upon humble suit and knowledge from you, therein his majesty will graciously get such order for reformation as may seem requisite.'[91]

The council continued to try all available means to encourage enforcement. Letters were sent to the Presidents of the Councils of the West and North instructing them to make sure that the proclamation was carried out in their areas.[92] Local officials in some areas made a diligent effort to enforce it but others responded with excuses that may or may not have been legitimate. Lord de la Ware and Edward Sheeley reported from Sussex that they had tried to assemble the justices of the peace 'according to the King's proclamation' but only a few appeared because some were in London and others were sick, 'so for lack of help we could do nothing.' However, they had personally made a search 'as far as our limits do stretch' and had at least found some surplus grain which would be shipped to market. They also promised 'with all diligence' to 'send the copies of these last letters to the rest of the justices of peace of this shire for the further expedition hereof.'[93] Even when a careful search was made, the markets could not always be supplied. On 19 November the mayor of Boston wrote to Cecil that 'the poor town of Boston' was 'now in great distress by reason of want of wheat and other grain.' Despite the fact that the justices had 'made a diligent view and search from town to town in all their allotments according to the King's majesty's proclamation,' they could not find enough grain to 'furnish the market.' Therefore the mayor requested a license to buy in other counties. Four justices also signed the letter vouching 'that the premises are true.'[94] Sandwich was also in desperate condition by December. The mayor commented on the 'great enormity that is like to ensue to the inhabitants of this town for lack of corn.' A committee was appointed 'to solicit by way of a letter to be addressed from the town unto the lords of the King's majesty's most honorable

[91] SP 10/11/5.   [92] SP 10/11/6.
[93] SP 10/11/10. [94] SP 10/11/11.

council declaring the lack of the premises requiring their lordship's aid and furtherance therein.'[95]

Seemingly at least in some areas local officials had tried to carry out the proclamation, but probably because the regulations were not economically feasible the government was finally forced to rescind them. Possibly the decisive factor bringing about the revocation was a comment from Sir John Mason, ambassador at the French court, who wrote to Cecil on 4 December stating that he had heard 'a great bruit of discontention of our people upon a late proclamation touching cheese and butter.' Mason, who was normally a cautious diplomat, then frankly questioned the wisdom of its provisions:

I have seen so many experiences of such ordinances; and ever the end is dearth and lack of the thing that we seek to make a good cheap. Nature will have her course *etiam si furca expellatur*, and never shall you drive her to consent that a penny-worth of new shall be sold for a farthing. If good cheap follow this device, then hereafter will I think it were good the like were still used. But this I am sure, the thing shall not be so plentiful as it was, and then I report me to you whether it will be better cheap. For who will keep a cow that may not sell milk for so much as the merchant and he can agree on?[96]

Mason's argument was good economic sense. The unreasonable price controls could only bring scarcity. This is precisely what happened, and on 6 December the government admitted its mistake by revoking the proclamation. A letter was sent to the justices of the peace which reviewed the whole effort, including the two proclamations and the letters ordering enforcement. It reported that even though the prices seemed at the time reasonable, complaints had been heard from Hereford and 'from sundry other parts of our realm' that the prices could not be kept since the scarcity 'is found greater than at the beginning was thought.' Therefore 'upon humble suit made unto us from sundry parts of the realm...we have been and be pleased to revoke and make void our said later proclamation for the price of grain, butter and cheese.' The price was now 'to be at liberty and none other than the buyers and sellers can reasonably agree upon.' Justices were ordered to publish the revocation 'in such sort as among you may be thought best' and to 'see our former proclamation for

[95] KRO AsAc 3/242d.
[96] Patrick E. Tytler ed., *England Under the Reigns of Edward VI and Mary* (London, 1839), I, 341. Mason quickly covered up his criticism with a statement typical of a diplomat, 'See what babbling I make being clean ignorant of the case. I doubt not my lord saw what they did and therefore I may hold my peace like a fool.' *Ibid.* 341–2.

bringing of grain and victual to markets well and uprightly kept and observed.'[97]

If the second proclamation really reflected Warwick's approach, it must have been extremely embarrassing for him to have to withdraw it. But it was the result of a very shortsighted policy. The prices set were first unreasonably low,[98] and as Mason had pointed out, in times of scarcity it is impossible to maintain both low prices and an adequate supply. The result was that the proclamation served to aggravate the scarcity rather than to increase the supply, and it had to be withdrawn to prevent further dislocation.

Another insufficient harvest in the summer of 1551 added to the inflationary spiral, so that once again the government was forced to intervene. However, before this occurred further coinage manipulations added to the problem. In April 1551 the government decided that the coinage must be reformed. But before the reform was carried out, one last debasement was decided upon, in order to pay the government's debt and to finance the reform. The plan was to mint £160,000 of even more debased coin containing three ounces of silver to nine ounces of alloy (compared to four ounces of silver to eight ounces of alloy in the worst of Henry VIII's coins). When these coins had been disbursed, the value of silver coins would be lowered in steps first to two-thirds and then to half of their original value. The government hoped thereby to make a profit of 11s 8d for every £1 of money. However, the plan involved further deception of the public.[99]

The success of the enterprise depended on secrecy, for information

[97] SP 10/11/15. This was a rererence to *TRP* no. 365, but it is interesting that only the section dealing with the supply of the market was to be enforced.

[98] In January, a month and a half after the revocation of the proclamation, prices were set in the market at Norwich by the local government. The prices were invariably higher than those in the proclamation. Butter was twice the price in the proclamation and a bushel of wheat was 4s higher, while rye was 6s higher (NNRO Mayors Court Book 1549–55, 173).

[99] Feaveryear, *Pound Sterling*, 61–82. Two earlier proclamations on the coinage may have also involved some effort at deception. On 14 August 1550 a proclamation raised the value of French coins to 7s without offering any explanation (*TRP* no. 364). The council records, however, reveal that the change in value was proclaimed because gold coins were being exported and it was hoped that this would 'give cause to strangers to bring in' French crowns. However, an additional reason was 'for the King's majesty's more advantage now in the setting forth of them' (Dasent, III, 94). This must have been a reference to the first installment of the payment of 400,000 crowns from France, agreed to in the French treaty on 24 March. The installment was due on 27 July 1550 so it coincided closely with the date of the proclamation. The money went largely to pay soldiers in Calais, Ireland and along the Scottish border. The additional value in English money was obviously to the King's advantage and it probably more accurately reflected their real value. Jordan, *Threshold of Power*, 125. However, after the last installment from France was paid in October 1550, a new proclamation on 1 December lowered the value to 6s 4d stating that crowns would still be accepted at the mint at the old rates until the end

about the plan could lead first to a further loss of confidence in the coinage and secondly to economic confusion. The first hint of the reform occurred in a proclamation issued on 28 April 1551, which dealt in part with rumors. It began with an overlengthy justification stating that the King was deeply concerned about 'false lies, tales, rumors and seditious devices against his majesty, his councilors, magistrates and justices.' It maintained that 'no prince in the world is more loath to use the extremity of correction upon his subjects than is his majesty, nor no councilors more unwilling to advise his majesty thereunto than his highness' councilors be.' But if this 'contempt' of the King, his laws and his ministers continued, 'his majesty will severely and sharply look upon, correct and punish the offenders.' The explanation continued by stating that the King intended 'to study, devise, and put in use by the good advice of his council, all good ways, and means that may reduce again this realm unto that prosperity, estimation and wealth which by sundry occasions in process of time hath and is decayed.' The body of the proclamation dealt with four subjects. First, law enforcement officials were ordered 'earnestly, truly, and uprightly to execute and see executed all his majesty's laws, statutes and proclamations.' Second, vagabonds in London were ordered to depart within four days upon the pains in the statutes and additional penalties which the King might inflict 'by his prerogative royal.' Third, subjects were ordered not to invent rumors 'touching his majesty, his council, magistrates, justices, officers, or ministers' and to report rumors and their authors to the council that they might be punished. Finally, strict controls were imposed on the press and on plays and interludes. Nobody was to print, sell or distribute anything abroad in English unless it was first approved by the King or the council. In addition, plays in English were prohibited unless they were approved and licensed in the same way. Local officials were ordered 'diligently to inquire for and search out all manner offenders... and to punish the same without remission.'[100]

The proclamation again suggests that the government was extremely uneasy about the internal situation and possibly also

of December (*TRP* no. 367). Since French crowns were at the time unofficially being bought for 7s 3d and 7s 4d and being exported (Feaveryear, *Pound Sterling*, 63) the lowering of the value made little sense unless it was to encourage the sale of crowns to the government at the old rates, before the rate dropped. Since the real value was above the 7s, the government could again reap a profit by these transactions.

[100] *TRP* no. 371. The restrictions on printing may have been motivated by 'books and slanderous bills against the council to move men to rebellion' which were being circulated in London (Dasent, III, 262).

worried about rumors which might undermine the coinage manipulations that were about to begin. The first step in the coinage reform was taken two days later. The proclamation rehearsed Henry VIII's debasement which, it stated, was done to finance 'his last wars.' Even though the first debasement was 'greatly beneficial unto his said majesty's father,' the King felt that an 'amendment of the coin shall be both great honor to this realm, and also a marvelous benefit unto the whole commonwealth, for the bringing down of the high prices of all things.' Therefore he 'like a most gracious prince determined to reform the same.' Since this could not be done unless shillings and groats were valued 'at a value more near unto the goodness and fineness of the same,' after 31 August the value of shillings would be lowered from 12d to 9d and groats from 4d to 3d. All subjects were to 'pay and receive' these coins at those values after that day, upon pain of fine, forfeiture and imprisonment.[101] The proclamation was followed by the issuance of an even more debased coinage. This resulted in a growing distrust of the government's intention and a general panic. People refused to believe that a reform was actually going to be carried out, and prices increased dramatically. In addition there was a widespread protest and outcry against the policy.[102]

In response to the deteriorating situation, a proclamation was issued on 11 May which seemingly hoped to persuade people more by the elegance of its language than by any specific penalties. It reviewed the earlier debasement and the need for reform 'for the which all good subjects hath of late, as it were with groanings longed.' It stated that the King had attempted to begin the needed reform, but prices were 'purposely enhanced beyond all expectation and the gracious meaning' of the King and council was 'utterly perverted and sinisterly abused.' People who acted in this fashion were accused of living 'only for themselves, and as it seemeth by their doings neither respect God, King, the surety of his majesty's crown, nor any other Christian creature.' Rather they were 'going about to eat and devour, as well the estate of the nobility as the lower sort...and further maliciously overthwarting and hindering all the good purposes of the King's majesty and his council.' Nevertheless, the King did not intend 'in ire or passion to execute his indignation, but justly with good ground hath first by advice of his council thought meet to admonish all kinds of people in their degrees and to let them clearly understand his pleasure and determination in this behalf.' The

[101] *TRP* no. 372. [102] Feaveryear, *Pound Sterling*, 62.

proclamation then announced again that the King's purpose was 'to amend his coin and to reduce it to fineness of silver.' It blamed the price rise on 'fraudulent engrossing of farms, grain, victual, as well butter and cheese as other grosser things.' These practices were to cease or offenders 'shall suffer with his extreme indignation the justice of his laws to the uttermost.' But first the King 'partly of clemency of nature' was admonishing, and 'by this admonition the punishment shall be more just and necessary.' Finally, the proclamation condemned 'the lower sort of people lacking indeed that part all manner of reason, and being like to those sick madmen that either will have no physic or else will be their own physicians' who were 'attempting redress of things after their own fantasies, with force.' These people, who used self-help to deal with abuses, were also warned that the King would 'not fail but minister unto them sharp terror of his sword and laws.'[103]

The proclamation was remarkable in that for all its threatening language, it contained no specific punishment. Even the threats to those who used self-help were less severe than in previous proclamations. Therefore it must have been intended primarily as a propaganda device. Two other efforts to deal with the situation in May relied less on words and more on practical measures. On 10 May, city officials in London were called before the council and informed that merchants 'in contempt of the proclamation made for the reforming of coin' had 'suddenly raised the prices of all things.' They were ordered to call before them the 'wardens of every company and the aldermen of every ward to see this matter amended.'[104] On 20 May, a new proclamation complained of seditious bills being posted in London which contained slanders against the King and council 'as other noble personages within this realm.' Anyone seeing those bills was to destroy them; if they did not they would be considered the author, and after having been lawfully convicted before a justice of the peace they would be fined and imprisoned. Even though this expanded somewhat on the earlier legislation by stating that even one who did not tear down or destroy a seditious bill would be considered the author, the penalty remained rather mild.[105]

By summer the council was becoming uneasy about the whole scheme. On 10 June the old statutes forbidding unlicensed exchanges were revived upon the penalty in those laws and the King's 'great indignation and displeasure,' because gold and silver were being

[103] *TRP* no. 373.   [104] Dasent, III, 272.   [105] *TRP* no. 374.

exported 'to the great impoverishment of this his said realm.'[106] By the middle of June the coining of base money was temporarily stopped, but it was resumed again in a few days to pay for the fortifications at Berwick and Calais. However, it was finally permanently ended by the middle of July.[107] On 8 July a proclamation declared that shillings and groats were to be devalued immediately rather than waiting until 31 August, as the earlier proclamation had stated. The action was necessitated, because even though the King's 'meaning was much favorable to his people in setting so long a day,' it was being abused by those who were raising prices excessively. This made it 'very needful to shorten the former day.' Every effort was made to keep the proclamation secret until the day it was proclaimed. Special letters were sent to local officials ordering them not to divulge the contents 'until the very time of publication.'[108]

The new proclamations caused even more unrest and confusion. The merchant classes were especially affected. The Johnson brothers wrote a series of letters in June and July which both illustrate the disruption of trade and reveal that rumors about an additional devaluation were widespread. Otwell wrote to John in Calais early in June sending him the proclamation on exchanges. He commented that 'most merchants are brought into a wonderful perplexity of their trade and very few or none can understand the grounds of the council's meaning therein.'[109] On 20 June he reported that there were rumors that a proclamation would soon be issued 'for stay of buying and selling of gold of the King's coin or other.'[110] Almost three weeks before the date for the devaluation of shillings and groats was advanced, Otwell wrote 'but above all things in case you conclude any bargain the money must here be delivered me very speedily because most men doubt the sudden proclaiming of our money down to take effect before the end of this next month.' The same day that the proclamation was issued advancing the date for the devaluation, Otwell wrote that things were so confused that there were few who could 'assuredly comprehend or rather compass the well doing of their things.'[111] By 18 July rumors of another devaluation were already being spread. Ambrose Saunders wrote to John Johnson:

the people do so much fear another change of our money that they make as much danger to sell now for ready money as they did before the proclamation took effect saying that by the end of August our shilling shall be

[106] *TRP* no. 375.
[107] Feaveryear, *Pound Sterling*, 62.
[108] *TRP* no. 376; NNRO Mayors Court Book 1549-55, 125. See above p. 25.
[109] SP 46/6/159.
[110] SP 46/6/160.
[111] SP 46/6/163.

but 6d...fearing much the same thing I am in great doubt to buy until I hear from you.[112]

It was precisely this type of rumor that the council tried to deal with in a proclamation, issued on 24 July 1551. It maintained that rumors were being spread that 'because his highness hath already somewhat abated the value of his said coin therefore his majesty should yet more abase it.' These rumors kept people from bringing victual to market 'fearing their loss in the fall of the money.' Therefore, there was scarcity 'where no scarcity ought to be, and a marvelous dearth where plenty is of all manner of victuals.' In order to control this, new punishments were added to the rumor legislation. Those spreading rumors would be imprisoned for six months and fined at the discretion of the justices of the peace. If anyone was unable to pay the fine, he would be placed on the pillory, 'and one of his ears cut off, or both, if the grievousness of his offense shall seem to the justices, mayor or other officer so to require.' Anyone hearing a rumor and not reporting it would be punished as though he had spread the rumor and the same punishment would be inflicted on local officials 'to whom the accusation shall be given in case that upon the trial thereof they do not put the effect hereof in execution upon the offenders.' Those who accused the officials would 'be rewarded at the King's majesty's hands for the uttering and declaration of the officer's fault in not executing his charge.' Although the proclamation ordered the unusual punishment of mutilation, its effect was mitigated because it was to be applied at the discretion of local officials. Evidence from local records reveals that at least in those cases where we can establish that penalties were inflicted for violations of this proclamation, mutilation was not used.[113]

On the same day additional efforts were made to deal with the problem of high prices by means of a proclamation which announced that the King intended to enforce the laws against engrossing, forestalling and regrating. The contents of three statutes were summarized and local officials were ordered to enforce them. No new penalties were ordered, but individuals were warned that if the laws were not obeyed the King was 'resolved to provide in such wise for redress and repression of such greedy disordinate enhancers of prices as shall be more sharp and penal than any former law or procla-

[112] SP 46/7/7.
[113] *TRP* no. 378; NNRO Mayors Court Book 1549-55, 143, 145 lists a number of cases.

mation heretofore made or ordained hath been.'[114] None of the statutes cited really dealt with the offenses in an adequate way; so the next Parliament enacted a new statute which finally provided the much-needed comprehensive legislation. It may have been the 'more sharp and penal' law threatened in the proclamation, for the penalties for the third offense were pillory, forfeiture of the offender's 'personal estate' and imprisonment during the King's pleasure.[115]

One of the major problems inhibiting the effort to control engrossing, forestalling and regrating was lax enforcement by local officials. A letter sent to the sheriffs with the proclamation ordering enforcement of these laws illustrates the government's concern about 'the negligent administrations of the ministers that suffer our laws to be violated.' It maintained that this was the 'greatest occasion' for the 'number of enormities grown in our commonwealth,' and that in many cases justices of the peace 'which should have most regard unto the good order of the rest have been the greatest doers in unlawful matters.' Those who were guilty of 'offending in the points of our proclamations' were ordered to reform themselves 'as the rest may take example at you.' They were warned that if they failed to do better than they had done in the past, 'either must we wax sharper than we would be or suffer our people to perish.' Possibly because Warwick hoped that local officials would be more inclined to enforce legislation enacted by Parliament, they were reminded that the proclamation was 'none otherwise set forth than the statutes require it.' The letter ended with a plea: 'we pray you therefore so to look unto it upon this warning as we may have cause to think you good ministers.'[116]

On 16 August 1551, in blatant violation of the assurances given in the proclamation condemning rumors, the government again devalued the coinage. Once again the justification given was the need to control excessive prices: 'for the remedy thereof nothing is thought more valuable than the speedy reducing of the said coin more near its just fineness.' The shilling was now valued at 6d and the groat at 2d. Those who did not pay and receive these coins at the stated values would forfeit the coins and suffer fine and imprisonment at the King's pleasure. The proclamation was once again sent out with letters ordering local officials not to reveal its contents until it was made public.[117] Since the new devaluation should have helped

[114] *TRP* no. 377. The laws referred to were 51 Henry III c. 25, 25 Henry VIII c. 4, 3 and 4 Edward VI c. 19.
[115] 5 and 6 Edward VI c. 14.   [116] SP 6/13/31.
[117] *TRP* no. 379; NNRO Mayors Court Book 1549–55, 140.

reduce prices, London officials attempted to get fishmongers to sell 'according to the abasing of the coin at more reasonable prices than they now do.' Prices were also set by the city on meat, fish, butter, cheese, wood and candles, but a committee was sent to the council 'to declare unto them that they cannot perceive how the victuallers and fuelers of the city for all the abasing of coin can be able to abate or ease the prices...without their lordship's aid.'[118]

It is not clear what type of aid was being requested, but less than a month later the central government issued the most comprehensive meat price proclamation of the entire early Tudor period. It was based on the authority of 25 Henry VIII c. 2, and set retail prices on meat and cheese. Prices were also set on whole animals so that graziers could not charge so much for their animals that the butchers would be unable to sell at the stated prices. The proclamation again referred to the effort to reform the coinage carried out to the King's 'own great loss' under the assumption that 'the excessive prices of all things of good congruence should consequently fall and abate as by natural reason and equity necessarily it ought and should.' It again condemned the 'greedy people' who were increasing prices 'for their own wealth and filthy lucre' and stated that this was why the setting of prices had become necessary. Rather large fines which ranged as high as £20 for those who sold the best oxen above the set prices were threatened. Careful attention was given to enforcement. Informers were allowed to sue 'by bill, plaint, information or action of debt' both at justice of the peace sessions or in any court of record. Justices of the peace were told 'to assemble themselves and to take order by division or otherwise for the good and perfect execution of this proclamation.' If they were negligent they would be 'severely and sharply' punished. In addition special commissioners were appointed 'for the hearing and examination of the defaults and negligent doings of the said justices in the premises if any hap to be so.' Finally, the proclamation forbade any 'attempt to take from any owner any cattle or victual aforementioned against the will of such owner, otherwise than is aforesaid, or by delivery of the justices of the peace.' Offenders were threatened with 'loss of all their goods and chattels and to suffer imprisonment during the King's pleasure.'[119]

The proclamation again reveals the concern with negligent enforcement in that it not only threatened justices of the peace with severe punishment in general terms, but it also appointed commissioners to verify that they carried out their duties. It included

[118] CLRO Rep. 12(2)/365.   [119] *TRP* no. 380.

penalties for those who sold above the stated prices that were more severe than those in Somerset's proclamation.[120] However, the punishment for those who used self-help was still moderate compared to Somerset's use of treason penalties in the 1549 proclamation. Seemingly Warwick was not reluctant to use large fines, but he continued to be more moderate than Somerset in applying unusually severe penalties.

At first there seems to have been a considerable effort to enforce the proclamation. At least six cases were brought to the Exchequer which alleged offenses against it, and at least in Cornwall, if we can believe their report, the justices of the peace were quite diligent in carrying out their duties.[121] The London government also took immediate action. On 24 September it ordered the butchers who had been buying cattle to report in writing 'what answers they have received of the graziers and other having fat cattle to sell.' On 15 October the wardens of the butchers were commanded to provide the names of those 'that have denied to sell their cattle according to the proclamation.'[122]

The council also became involved in enforcement. On 22 October John Baker, a grazier, was punished for selling oxen at £5, almost twice the price allowed by the proclamation. However, by that time problems were also developing. On 27 September the council sent letters to all justices of the peace and sheriffs, ordering them 'to use more circumspection and better diligence in seeing the King's majesty's late proclamation concerning the prices of cattle observed and the transgressors thereof duly punished.' On 2 October further letters were sent to the Earl of Sussex and the justices of the peace of Norfolk, ordering them 'if they can by any good mean or authority redress the fault they find with the enhancement of prices of beefs and lack of butter and cheese out of Suffolk.'[123] On 17 October the mayor of London allowed cheese to be sold at higher prices than in the proclamation, 'the proclamation made of late limiting less price of the same notwithstanding.'[124]

On 20 November, a little over two months after the proclamation had been issued, the government confessed defeat. A new procla-

---

[120] *TRP* no. 336 had a fine of £5 for selling oxen above the price in the proclamation. The fine in no. 380 was four times as large.

[121] See below p. 278 for the Exchequer cases. The Cornwall justices of the peace reported a series of steps they took, including making sure that the graziers delivered cattle to market to sell at the prices in the proclamation and arbitrated disputes arising between the butcher and the grazier in the prices of the animal as a result of differences in the size of animals (BM Titus B II/65).   [122] CLRO Rep. 12(2)/379, 293d.

[123] Dasent, III, 394, 366, 376.   [124] CLRO Rep. 12(2)/395.

mation first reviewed the terms of the earlier one and then added that the King and council had intended 'that the said proclamation should no longer have continued nor been in force than until the next session of Parliament which was to be holden the 13th day of October next after the said proclamation.' The King 'intended that further order should have been provided by authority of Parliament as occasion should then have required.' However, Parliament had been prorogued first till November and then till January, and in the winter the cost of raising animals was considerably higher, 'which is not provided for and fully set forth by express words within the said proclamation nor otherwise provided for by his majesty and his council in Parliament.' Therefore, the proclamation was revoked, but subjects were assured that 'his highness meaneth and intendeth hereafter to provide at the next session of the Parliament, for his said subjects in the premises to the common utility and profit of his grace's realm and of all his subjects of the same as occasion and the case shall then further require.' Meanwhile, sales of victuals were to be made 'in such charitable manner as his majesty's subjects may have no cause to be grieved' and local officials were to 'see all the markets well and sufficiently furnished.'[125]

The proclamation is especially interesting in that it clearly stated that the original meat price proclamation was intended as a temporary measure until Parliament could act on the subject. However, the 1552 Parliament did not pass new legislation on meat prices. In May 1552 the council again sent letters to London authorities concerning 'the reformation of the victuallers of this city and the excessive prices that they do take for the victuals.' The city government which had already set prices in December 1551 now set retail prices again and threatened fines that were substantially higher than those in the proclamation.[126] Once again the policy followed by Warwick reveals a surprisingly cautious use of the prerogative and a much greater reliance on statutory legislation than Somerset's. It may be that he had learned from Somerset's mistakes or possibly the insecurity of his position made him reluctant to introduce penalties or procedures in proclamations that might offend a great many

[125] *TRP* no. 382.3. The council was serious about this last order. Three days after the proclamation orders were sent to appoint commissions for the marches of Wales 'to see the proclamation for the furniture of markets observed and offenders punished.' Commissioners were also appointed for York on 26 November 'for the proclamation of victuals' (Dasent, III, 427–8, 431).

[126] CLRO Rep. 12(2)/430, 484. The fine for selling meat above the set retail price was £5 for every offense in the regulations set by the city government. The fine in *TRP* no. 380 was 6s 8d.

people. It is interesting that in the 1552 Parliament Northumberland returned to Cromwell's policy of having Parliament grant authority to proclamations. A new statute on the buying and selling of wool allowed the King to repeal it by proclamation. Another statute sought to buttress the proclamations setting values on coins by forbidding 'giving, receiving or paying more in value' for a coin than was stated in the King's proclamation.[127]

The second statute may have resulted from the difficulties encountered in the effort to reform the coinage. On 30 October 1551 a new coinage of considerably purer standard was announced. People were instructed to bring their old coins to the mint where they would receive new coins in exchange at the values set in the earlier proclamation.[128] However, the government was extremely naïve if it thought people would bring testons to the mint to receive 6d in exchange, because all but the extremely debased coins issued in 1551 had a silver content worth more than 6d.[129] Consequently, people melted down coins to sell them for their silver value. This was contrary to a number of statutes. On 11 September a proclamation had stated this and had reiterated the statutory prohibitions adding to the pains in those statutes imprisonment and further punishment at the King's pleasure.[130] However, it seems to have had little effect. In December a proclamation attempted to correct false rumors about the new coinage.[131] On 21 December another proclamation again told of the King's desire to reform the coinage and rehearsed the steps already taken. It complained about 'sundry covetous merchants, some greedy goldsmiths and other like' who were raising 'the prices both of gold and silver far above the order appointed by his highness' and buying and selling coins 'far above the values rated' in the earlier proclamation. The King had already had some of the offenders 'openly punished according to their demerits and intendeth henceforth to pardon none that shall be found faulty in that behalf.' In addition anyone who sold gold or silver at prices

[127] 5 and 6 Edward VI c. 7; 5 and 6 Edward VI c. 19.
[128] *TRP* no. 382. On 11 October a proclamation had been issued calling in testons and groats to the mint 'and have fine silver of twelve pence for two testons.' Strype, II(1), 488 (Appendix B item 38).
[129] Feaveryear, *Pound Sterling*, 66. 'The testons of Henry VIII of 9 oz. fineness were worth as bullion at this price, 1s 10½d; those of 8 oz. 1s 8d; those of 6 oz. 1s 3d; and those of 4 oz., together with Edward's lighter 6 oz. coins of 1549, 10d. Who then was likely to sell any of them to the mint at 6d each?'
[130] *TRP* no. 381. The statutes cited were 9 Edward III st. 2 c. 3, 17 Richard II c. 1, and 4 Henry IV c. 10. The penalty in the statutes repeated in the proclamation was forfeiture of four times the value of the coin melted.
[131] BM Royal 18/cxxiv; Strype, II(2), 213 (App. B item 39).

higher than those stated in the proclamation would suffer forfeiture and 'open punishment and abide such fine as shall please his highness.' Furthermore, nobody was to melt or export coins. The proclamation tried to encourage enforcement by promising those who reported offenders a reward of a quarter of the money sold, melted or exported. It even encouraged the buyer to accuse the seller, or 'the conveyor of any money, gold, or silver into any foreign parts' to accuse the 'sender or owner' for the promised reward.[132] Parliament began meeting in January 1552 and it may have been the difficulty encountered in getting subjects to observe the rates set in the coinage proclamations that caused the government to seek statutory authority for them.

Throughout the remaining year and a half of Edward's reign proclamations continued to be used in a cautious fashion and for relatively uncontroversial purposes. In February 1552 prices were set on wine according to the authority granted in 23 Henry VIII c. 7.[133] Later in the month a curious proclamation complained of people who were irreverently quarreling, fighting, and shedding blood in churchyards and churches as well as those who were shooting doves with handguns and bringing 'horses and mules into and through the said churches.' Since these activities were increasing, the King commanded that they cease under pain of imprisonment and the King's indignation. The proclamation, issued while Parliament was in session, was followed by a statute on the same subject, containing considerably more severe penalties.[134] In March another proclamation ended the restraint on exchanges. It was issued as a result of 'the lamentable complaints and humble suits of divers and several merchants.' It pointed out that although the restraint 'was made according to our laws and grounded upon many good and just considerations mentioned in our proclamation set forth and published in June last past,' the King was 'pleased that exchanges and rechanges of money shall be at liberty' and used as they were before the proclamation 'during his majesty's pleasure;' however,

[132] *TRP* no. 382.5. Professor Jordan does not believe this proclamation was issued, but he offers no documentation in support of his opinion. Because a printed copy has survived, I tend to doubt his belief (Jordan, *Threshold of Power*, 460 n. 4).

[133] *TRP* no. 383. The statute was renewed in 1552 by 5 and 6 Edward VI c. 17. In Edward's last Parliament a new statute, 7 Edward VI c. 5, set retail prices although the King had the power to do so by proclamation.

[134] *TRP* no. 384. 5 and 6 Edward VI c. 4 included suspension of clerics for quarreling or brawling in the churchyard, excommunication for striking a person and a loss of an ear, or branding as well as excommunication for drawing a weapon with intent to strike.

gold and silver were not to be exported except as was permitted by the laws.[135]

The only proclamation that was at all controversial was issued in response to Knox's complaint about the stipulation in the 1552 prayer book on kneeling at communion. The council ordered that a rubric explaining the meaning of kneeling at communion be added to the prayer book which had already been sanctioned by Parliament. The proclamation dated 27 October 1552 did little more than explain in a similar fashion to the so-called 'black rubric' that kneeling did not imply adoration of the elements in the Eucharist or that 'Christ's natural flesh and blood' were physically present in the sacrament.[136] On 14 February 1553, shortly before Edward's second Parliament began to meet, a proclamation ordered observation of 2 and 3 Edward VI c. 19, which commanded that the Lenten fast be kept for economic reasons. This was one of at least three proclamations on this subject during the last years of Edward's reign. It suggested that the earlier legislation was not being observed, and it added that 'notable and incorrigible persons' were to be cited to the council so that 'some grievous open punishment' might be applied as an 'example to all others.'[137]

The last surviving early Tudor proclamation was also related to a statute. Issued less than two weeks before the King died, it attempted to correct an oversight in a statute passed by the Parliament which had just ended. The statute had reintroduced the penalties for felonies for export of gold and silver. If the legislation had been interpreted strictly it could have placed honest merchants engaged in legitimate business in jeopardy of their lives and lands. Consequently, the proclamation made an exception for merchants and others 'lawfully passing out of this our realm.' They were allowed to carry £4 'for their reasonable costs and expenses,' and were not to be subject to the penalties in the statute for carrying 'any rings or signets of gold or silver upon their fingers.'[138]

---

[135] *TRP* no. 384.5. Three other proclamations issued during the year seem to have done little more than order enforcement of statutes. Two proclamations in October 1552 ordered people with 'great horses' to have them ready for service. This seems to have been based on 33 Henry VIII c. 5, which specified the number of stallions to be kept by members of the nobility. The third in November ordered that 5 and 6 Edward VI c. 5. which stated that as much land was to be kept in cultivation as had been in 1 Henry VIII, be observed. Strype, II(1), 592 (App. B item 42); Strype, II(1), 588 (App. B item 43); Strype, II(1), 15 (App. B item 44).

[136] *TRP* no. 385.

[137] *TRP* no. 386. The first proclamation on this subject is dated 9 March 1551 (*TRP* no. 368). A second proclamation was issued in 1552 (Strype, II(2), 214; App. B item 40).

[138] *TRP* no. 387. The statute was 7 Edward VI c. 6.

Within a month Northumberland had been toppled from power after his attempt to change the succession failed. He had ruled badly in some respects, and had been guilty of opportunism at times, but he cannot be accused of misusing the King's power to issue royal proclamations. Although this might be attributed to the basic insecurity of his rule rather than any sincere commitment to Parliamentary government,[139] the fact is that proclamations were used in a more cautious way and with a greater concern for statutory authority than in any other period since Cromwell's rule in the 1530s. The only new regulations which were introduced by proclamations were the restrictions on printing and the coinage regulations, which were both certainly within the purview of the royal prerogative. Even though the judges in Mary's reign would argue that Northumberland's coinage manipulations were illegal, this probably reflected the malice of the judges towards a man they considered a traitor rather than an accurate statement of the law, because later legal writers certainly accepted the King's right to raise or lower the value of coins by royal proclamation.[140] As has been illustrated, penalties were also less severe under Northumberland than they were under Somerset. Only three proclamations could be cited as having decreed severe penalties without the authority of Parliament. One may reflect the influence of Somerset rather than Northumberland. Another threatened those who used self-help with loss of all goods and chattels, but this too was a considerably less severe penalty than that used by Somerset for a similar offense. The only other proclamation with a severe penalty threatened those who spread rumors of another debasement with loss of one of their ears. But even this penalty was mitigated because it was to be applied at the discretion of local officials who seemingly did not choose to punish with mutilation.

Although enforcement was a constant problem for Northumberland, in comparison to Somerset he did not use the council very often. Six proclamations implied or mentioned that the council would act as a court to deal with offenders. One probably cannot be

---

[139] See Jordan, *Threshold of Power*, 531, where he offers the following appraisal: 'His reign had from the outset been weak and fearful because he ruled under the shadow of Somerset's undoubted popularity and under the hatred of many Englishmen of all classes, who regarded him as the judicial murderer of the Protector.'

[140] The decision reported by Dalison spoke of Northumberland as 'le graund traytor' (BM Harl. 5141/31). The printed version of the report deleted the section stating that the King could not diminish or abase the coinage to a lower value without statutory authority. Morrice stated clearly that the King could 'enhance or abase' the coinage of the realm 'at his good pleasure' (BM Add. 36081/255).

attributed to Northumberland. Two used the council to determine the punishment for those who spread rumors – an offense which was commonly punished by the council. One stated that the privy council would punish captains not returning to their posts, and two used the council to punish individuals breaking the Lenten fast.[141] The last proclamation limited the council's role to punishment of 'notable and incorrigible persons.' This was similar to the role the council was designed to play in a new plan suggested for the enforcement of proclamations at the end of the reign. Northumberland relied on informers more often than in previous periods. This procedure had been used only occasionally before the Statute of Proclamations was enacted, but seven proclamations used this method while it was in effect. Somerset rarely used informers probably because he relied so heavily on the council acting in a quasi-judicial manner. In contrast almost eighteen percent of the proclamations issued while Northumberland was dominant encouraged informers to initiate prosecution and two more promised rewards to individuals reporting offenders.[142]

Despite his less extensive and more moderate use of royal proclamations, Northumberland was obviously very concerned about effective enforcement. The collection of proclamations printed by Richard Grafton, probably in December 1550 or January 1551, seems to have been related to enforcement. The preamble stated that the collection was being made because subjects 'often violated proclamations which happeneth either by ignorance or else for that when the print is passed, they cannot come by them.' The collection was printed in the form of a small handbook similar to those published to aid justices of the peace in their work. Grafton's intent was 'every second year (or oftener if it shall be requisite) to add hereunto such other proclamations as shall happen to be published by like authority.'[143] Even if there was no government involvement in the printing of Grafton's collection, there was clearly a well-planned effort to improve enforcement at the end of the reign. In March 1552 a proposal to create a committee of ten men 'for execution of penal laws and proclamations' was submitted to the council. The committee was to 'consider what penal laws be most necessary to be executed for the commonwealth' and to investigate the 'best ways they shall judge expedient and likewise due execution

---

[141] *TRP* nos. 365, 352, 371, 360, 368, 386.
[142] *TRP* nos. 357, 361, 365, 366, 367, 380, 382.5; 358 and 378 promised rewards to those reporting offenses.   [143] Grafton, *Proclamations*, preface.

furthered beginning with the greatest offenders.' They were to see that the 'execution of the same laws and proclamations be made in the proper courts of justice so as the authority of the law may bear the burden.' Their work was to begin after the 1552 Parliament ended. They were to assemble before every law term to see that 'the same causes may be effectively followed in every court where they ought to be.'[144]

A more detailed set of instructions for the committee ordered 'laws and proclamations as have good appearance of truth to be furthered in such ordinary courts or places as by the same laws and proclamations is appointed that they may both speedily and justly come to execution.' The committee was also to 'have regard and respect to the justices of peace how they execute their offices in such things as by the laws and proclamations they have authority and charge' in order that those who were 'continually negligent or otherwise unfaithful' might be 'amended' or replaced. Informers were to play a major role in the new enforcement procedures. The committee was to 'devise the best they may that such as be informers of such penal crimes may both be reputed as honest men and so by their good policies encourage men of known honesty to complain where cause is and in just complaints to see them maintained and regarded.' Finally, the committee was to act as a clearing house for complaints addressed to the council 'touching the information of breakers of laws and proclamations,' and to make regular reports to the council. Possibly as a result of the experience with the statutory court set up in the Statute of Proclamations, the presence of only six of the ten members of the committee was required for a quorum.[145]

Although the plan does not seem to have been put into effect, it was the most elaborate attempt to improve the enforcement of royal proclamations since the enactment of the Statute of Proclamations. The plan was designed to make enforcement in the ordinary courts of the land more efficient and to encourage the only police force the nation possessed, private informers, to aid in enforcement through the use of a conciliar committee. Whether or not this would have worked cannot be known for it was not implemented, but the fact that it was even devised surely indicates that the government was having serious problems enforcing royal proclamations at the end of the early Tudor period. This was the problem which had consistently plagued Tudor governments. The Statute of Proclamations had for a brief time introduced a new approach. Its repeal meant that another

[144] SP 6/14/16.   [145] SP 6/14/17.

solution had to be devised. Somerset turned to the council to resolve the problem. Northumberland used threatening language, propaganda, and the ordinary courts of the realm. The evidence already presented suggests that none of these solutions was adequate. However, since enforcement was clearly a major concern of a series of Tudor governments, the problem deserves a more thorough study based on the records of both central and local courts.

9

THE ENFORCEMENT OF ROYAL PROCLAMATIONS

The said commissioners shall consider from time to time what penal laws and proclamations be most necessary to be executed for the commonwealth and shall cause due inquisition to be made of the observation of them in the counties where and in such manner as they shall see most needful and expedient. Whereupon they shall cause such information of the breach of the said laws and proclamations as have good appearance of truth to be furthered in such ordinary courts or places as by the same laws and proclamations is appointed that they may both speedily and instantly come to the execution, and the examples of the executions of the laws may profit, and in this they shall begin with the greatest offenders first. Item, they shall also have regard and respect to the justices of peace how they execute their offices in such things as by the laws and proclamations they have their authorities and charge.[1]

The instructions given to the 'commissioners for consideration and execution of penal laws' at the end of the early Tudor period conveniently sum up what were the primary concerns in the enforcement of royal proclamations throughout the period. There were two major requirements for effective enforcement. First, the administrative personnel, to whom the instructions for carrying out the proclamations were addressed, must effectively publicize them and assure that the instructions were obeyed. These instructions, as has been noted throughout this work, involved a great variety of tasks. Unless the local officials (to whom these orders were normally directed) performed their duties with dedication and efficiency, the effectiveness of the proclamation was threatened at the outset. Since probably no official was more important in this task than the justice of the peace, it is not surprising that the instructions to the commissioners specifically mentioned the need to oversee their work and 'how they execute their offices.' Second, if proclamations were to be more than vague threats or propaganda devices that were used to impress on the public that the laws should be obeyed for the good of the commonwealth, violators had to be punished. Efficient

[1] SP 10/14/17.

law enforcement depended upon quick and sure punishment. Therefore, the instructions provided that commissioners were to 'see such informations of the breach of the said laws and proclamations as have good appearance of truth to be furthered in such ordinary courts or places as by the same laws and proclamations is appointed' and to make sure that the cases 'both speedily and instantly come to execution.'

The instructions were probably issued because the government was not satisfied with the existing procedures. It can be assumed that provisions were included for dealing with administrative personnel, because they were at times lax in carrying out their duties. It is also likely that the emphasis on furthering cases in the 'ordinary courts' and speedy 'execution' reveal problems in judicial enforcement. The evidence submitted in earlier chapters establishes that there was a concern with enforcement throughout the period and in many cases an inadequate response. However, the importance of the question justifies the more thorough and systematic study which this chapter seeks to provide. It deals with three basic questions: (1) How and where were royal proclamations enforced? (2) How effective were these procedures? (3) Were there any significant changes in enforcement in the course of the early Tudor period? Unfortunately the questions are easier to formulate than to answer. Previous studies provide very little assistance. The early Tudor period is still lacking a work on law enforcement similar in scope and quality to the pioneer study of Margaret Davies for the reign of Elizabeth.[2] Furthermore, the nature and volume of records are formidable obstacles. In addition to the voluminous records of the central courts, local court records are scattered in county and city archives throughout England. Records are also often disappointing in the information they provide. Especially on the local level survivals are not uniform and often the final result of a case is not available. What follows is of necessity based only on a sample of existing records, but since it is a rather large sample, one would hope that the conclusions based on that evidence are reliable.[3]

[2] Margaret G. Davies, *The Enforcement of English Apprenticeship* (Cambridge, 1956). The most useful works on enforcement for the purposes of this study are DeLloyd J. Guth, 'Exchequer Penal Law Enforcement 1485–1509,' (unpublished PhD thesis, University of Pittsburgh, 1967); Elton, *Star Chamber Stories*; and my own work, 'The Enforcement of Royal Proclamations Under the Provisions of the Statute of Proclamations 1539–47,' in *Tudor Men and Institutions*, A. J. Slavin ed., 203–31.

[3] Local court records include the Corporation of London records, records of nineteen boroughs (Norwich, Chester, Lincoln, Grimsby, Nottingham, York, Sandwich, Faversham, New Romney, Colchester, Hereford, Ipswich, Canterbury, Harwich, Shrewsbury,

Administrative enforcement

The problems discussed above make it extremely difficult to arrive at a defensible generalization on how well or how poorly local officials carried out the orders and instructions directed to them in royal proclamations. Records are often spotty and incomplete. Although there is abundant evidence to suggest that local officials at least made sincere efforts to enforce some proclamations, there are long periods in which the records are totally devoid of any references to royal proclamations. Since it is always dangerous to argue from silence, one cannot be sure whether this means that the proclamations and orders from the council were ignored or that the response of local government was simply not noted in the surviving records. As might be expected, evidence of poor enforcement cannot normally be obtained from local records, so that one must often rely on other sources which may at times be highly suspect. As a result, it is not possible to determine conclusively whether administrative enforcement was better in some periods than in others, but one can illustrate how the council attempted to get local officials to act and at least in some cases trace their response.

The council used a variety of means to influence the work of local officials. In addition to the orders and threats in the proclamations, numerous examples of letters to specific local officials have been cited throughout this work. This type of letter seems to have been especially common in the reign of Edward VI; however, this may only seem so because council records are more abundant for that period. The letters which followed the proclamations ordering a search for grain and those pricing meats are examples. Letters were also sent to individual local officials in connection with the proclamations in the summer of 1549 dealing with enclosure riots, and with the proclamation of 24 July 1551 prohibiting rumors of an additional coin debasement. After the shilling was again devalued, a letter was sent to the Earl of Shrewsbury instructing him that those who spread rumors about 'the further fall of the shilling' were to be 'so punished as they may be a terror to others.' The mayor of Exeter was also instructed 'from time to time to punish the offenders

Leicester, Coventry, Southampton and Rye), and county quarter sessions records for Norfolk and Middlesex. Ecclesiastical records from Norwich, Lincoln, York and Canterbury were also used. Research in central court records included a thorough study of all the Exchequer King's Remembrancer Memoranda Rolls between 1485 and 1553, all surviving records of the Court of Star Chamber, and all the materials for the early Tudor period classified KB9 Ancient Indictments of the King's Bench. In addition a few plea rolls of the Court of King's Bench and Common Pleas were quickly surveyed.

that spread any rumor of the coin according to the proclamation in that behalf.'[4] More general circular letters to all the justices of the peace and sheriffs were also employed. Cromwell seems to have sent annual circular letters to the justices instructing them to see to the execution of laws, and these often included orders dealing with matters covered by earlier proclamations.[5] Letters sometimes ordered local officials to make searches for offenses against the proclamation or to examine individuals suspected of violations.[6] At times the council even ordered that specific persons named in the letters be punished. On 2 March 1552 the mayor of Bedford was ordered 'to carry John Wyar and certain others to the next justice of peace for raising of a bruit touching a new fall of demi shillings that he may be put on the pillory according to the proclamation.'[7] The council sometimes called in the London authorities to give specific instructions. On 10 May 1551 the mayor of London 'with certain of the chiefs of the city' were called before the council because merchants were raising prices 'in contempt of the proclamation made for the reforming of the coin.' They were told to call the wardens of the city companies and the aldermen 'to see this matter amended by their good wisdom and diligence.'[8]

The examples of conciliar instructions and letters could be multiplied considerably, establishing that the council attempted to insure that proclamations were enforced, but it is not so easy to determine how local officials responded. A sincere effort to see that a proclamation was enforced can at times be shown from the issuance of orders to others. Thus, probably as a result of the conference with the council on the raising of prices, the London officials ordered the wardens of the city companies to assemble their companies and to

---

[4] Dasent, III, 354 (*TRP* 378) for letters dealing with the enforcement of the proclamation on enclosure riots (*TRP* nos. 333, 334); see SP 10/7/31.

[5] Elton, *Policy and Police*, 253–4. For examples of circular letters see BM Cleo E IV/8 (*LP* 13[1] no .1304); SP 140/211–17 (*LP* 13[2] no. 171). In the reign of Edward VI a circular letter was sent out ordering 'more circumspection and better diligence' in the enforcement of the last meat price proclamation (*TRP* no. 380). Dasent, III, 366.

[6] Wolsey followed up his proclamations on unlawful games (*TRP* no. 121) with an order for a search to be made of inns and alehouses (KRO NR/CP W7). On 22 October 1551 the council ordered that John Baker, a grazier who was reported to have refused to sell cattle at the prices in the proclamation, should be examined and 'finding the matter to be as it is, reported to cause the said grazier to be apprehended and so punished as his fault deserved.' Dasent, III, 394. On 23 March 1541 the council sent a letter to port officials in Chichester to hold a Flemish ship loaded with wheat and to sell the wheat and keep the money until 'it were tried out whether the said were forfeit or not to the intent the said money made of the said wheat might be restored either to the King's majesty or to the party as the case should require.' Nicolas, VII, 162.

[7] Dasent, III, 494–5; *TRP* no. 378.   [8] Dasent, III, 272.

warn them not to raise prices 'as they will answer at their perils to the contrary.'⁹ So too, when the city received a proclamation forbidding the killing of meat during Lent in February 1550, they called in the wardens of the butchers and ordered them to 'refrain themselves from killing of any flesh' and to report the names of offenders to the Court of Aldermen.¹⁰ Sometimes the city government simply stated that a proclamation would be enforced, or they commanded other forms of positive action such as the search for handguns, crossbows and unlawful games ordered in London on 3 December 1528.¹¹ Other actions included the appointment of special officials to aid in enforcement, or the calling in of offenders and ordering them to cease violating a proclamation. Norwich, for example, appointed a water bailey on 24 October 1543 for better enforcement of export legislation since 'leather, tallow and divers kinds of victual' were being exported 'contrary to the laws of this realm.'¹² On 12 January 1545 'certain players of interludes' were called before the mayor and aldermen of London and 'enjoined no more to play within the city except in houses of lord mayor, sheriffs, aldermen and other substantial citizens.'¹³

Local officials sometimes sought the council's advice on how to proceed on a matter involving the violation of a proclamation. On 20 April 1538 the Bishop of Lincoln wrote to Cromwell about his concern that people in Oxfordshire were eating meat in Lent 'contrary to the King's proclamations' as well as the customs of the Church. He asked Cromwell 'to know your pleasure what order shall be taken with them; if this example be not punished, I feel that more will follow.'¹⁴ The same kind of advice was sought by justices of the peace when enforcing the proclamation on rumors in March 1538. After the justices apprehended a rumormonger in Oxford, they sought Cromwell's opinion on 'what shall be done with the lewd fellow.' In April the justices in Leicestershire met to carry out the 'King's highness' proclamation lately directed.' Information was presented about 'certain words that should be spoken' by a clergyman. Having

---

⁹ CLRO LB R/115.   ¹⁰ CLRO Rep. 12(1)/201d.
¹¹ CLRO Rep. 8/10 in response to *TRP* no. 121. In June 1549 the Lincoln city council ordered that tithes would be paid 'as they be now bounden by the King's highness' late proclamation.' LCRO L/1/1/1/2/60. On 9 February 1548, after they had received *TRP* no. 299, the London aldermen agreed to 'earnestly endeavor themselves and use good diligence for the due execution thereof' (CLRO Rep. 11/349).
¹² NNRO Folio Books of the Proceedings of the Municipal Assembly 1491–1553, 205.
¹³ CLRO Rep. 11/135. No proclamation was mentioned, but the order was probably based on *TRP* no. 240 issued three months earlier.
¹⁴ SP 1/131/176 (*LP* 13[1] no. 811).

'proved the words by witness,' the justice placed the man 'in custody' and sent the bill to Cromwell, requesting his 'further pleasure how we shall order him.'[15]

As might be expected, local officials responded well to those proclamations that involved their self-interest. This has already been documented for the meat price proclamations and the proclamation concerning the Thames. It seems to be equally true of the vagabond legislation. Lincoln reacted to the proclamation of 19 February 1517 which ordered enforcement of the statutes on vagabonds by instructing the constables of the city to make a search and to report to the mayor and council the names of 'idle persons and they which will not work for their living.'[16] References to concerns about vagabond legislation occur in the Lincoln records throughout the period. In February 1547 orders were given that all vagabonds were to be called up and put to work 'or be otherwise found hereafter and ordered according to the King's highness' proclamation in that behalf provided.'[17] Similar references to the enforcement of proclamations on vagabonds are found in the Sandwich and London records. However, often boroughs concentrated on enforcing their own legislation against vagabonds, possibly because penalties were considerably more severe in local regulations than in the proclamations or statutes.[18]

Ecclesiastical officials could also be zealous about the enforcement of proclamations which reflected their theological position. Bishop Longland in August 1539 repeated his concern that people were eating in Lent and acting contrary not only to the customs of the Church but 'to the King's gracious injunctions and proclamations which commanded all honest ceremonies to be observed.' He was afraid that if offenders were not punished the practice would spread. Therefore, he asked Cromwell, 'I beseech you some punishment may be done therein.'[19] John Bird, Bishop of Chester, expressed a similar concern to Henry VIII in November 1541 about practices that offended the sensitivities of those who had rejected the old faith. He maintained that in his diocese people who claimed to be exempt from the bishops' jurisdiction were not observing the proclamation order-

---

[15] SP 1/139/95 (*LP* 13[1] no. 555); SP 1/131/168 (*LP* 13 [1] no. 801). The proclamation was probably *TRP* no. 138.
[16] LCRO E/1/1/1/1/70d. The proclamation was *TRP* no. 80.
[17] LCRO L/1/1/1/2/49.
[18] KRO SaAc 3/74. The references in the London records are too numerous to cite. As noted earlier, London was whipping vagabonds long before this was ordered by proclamation or statute. See above p. 118.
[19] SP 1/153/46 (*LP* 14[2] no. 71). The proclamation was *TRP* no. 186.

ing that 'idols and images accustomed to be worshipped' be taken down. They were allowing people 'to make oblations and offerings in that place after the accustomed manner.' He requested power to visit all areas in the diocese and to 'repress things out of order and to execute your grace's precepts, commandments and laws.'[20] Bishop Bonner of London was diligent in the enforcement of the proclamation of 8 July 1546 forbidding heretical books. He reported a list of eighty-nine books which he had burnt in obedience to the proclamation. At least in some areas the enforcement of that proclamation became so zealous that even Bibles 'not condemned by the proclamation' as well as 'the King's majesty's books concerning our religion lately set forth and his primers' were being taken out of churches and houses and burnt.[21]

Although scattered examples of good enforcement are relatively easy to find, there is no way of telling in general how consistent and how good local enforcement was. We know from other studies that local officials were not especially eager to enforce legislation which was not beneficial to them, or vital for the peace of the community, and which might involve conflict with their neighbors. Furthermore, if they were diligent in trying to enforce all the legislation that came under their purview, the amount of work involved in doing so, especially for justices of the peace and constables, would have been overwhelming. Although they often put forth a good deal of effort enforcing the regulations of their own community or legislation of the central government which was important to that community, they had neither the time nor the desire to attend to all the legislation of the central government.[22]

When local officials did a bad job of enforcing proclamations, this was, of course, not usually mentioned in local records; therefore one must document this largely from the admonitions and complaints of the central government or private individuals. This type of evidence is scattered. A good many examples have already been given. Many of the complaints of the central government about poor enforcement were included in the proclamations texts, but at

---

[20] SP 1/168/7-8 (*LP* 16 no. 1377). The proclamation could have been either *TRP* no. 186 or no. 188.

[21] Foxe, App. XVIII, 566 (*LP* 21[2] no. 173) records Bonner's activities. Richard Cox wrote to Paget on 29 October that although the proclamation 'meant well' some were deliberately misinterpreting it, 'some that knew what was to be done, yet, for fear of danger made away all. Other that...cast away all, good and bad. The third which had none to cast away, rejoiced much that they might remain still in their old ignorance and superstitious folly.' SP 1/226/16 (*LP* 21[2] no. 321).

[22] Davies, *English Apprenticeship*, 161ff, 248ff.

times the council wrote letters to officials personally chastising them for failure to enforce proclamations.[23] Government officials even criticized justices of the peace in general meetings for the slackness of their efforts. Wriothesley appeared in person at the sessions in Hampshire in April 1539 and criticized those justices of the peace who 'did so use their power and justice but only for the purpose that men should follow the bent of their bows.'[24] A much more severe criticism was delivered by Chancellor Richard Rich in a speech made to justices who had been specifically called into the Star Chamber in 1549. The speech was filled with animadversions about the justices' neglect of their duties. Rich specifically mentioned that the council had learned that 'the King's majesty's proclamations' were not being 'executed.' He maintained 'we are informed that many of you are so negligent, and so slack, in that it doth appear that you do rather look as it were through your fingers than diligently see to the execution of the said laws and proclamations.' He accused them of being so slack 'that in some shires which be further off, it may appear that the people have never heard of divers of his majesty's proclamations, of if they have heard, that you are content to wink at it.'[25]

The speech was, of course, delivered after the Statute of Proclamations was repealed. Two sections of that act were devoted to resolving the problems mentioned by Rich. One threatened officials who failed adequately to publicize proclamations with the penalties in the proclamation. Another provided that justices of the peace should, within fourteen days of a proclamation, divide themselves in such a way that they could see to 'the due and speedy execution of the contents of the same proclamation,' upon the pains in the proclamation. These sections may have been included because proclamations were not being adequately publicized or enforced by the justices before 1539, but unfortunately one searches in vain for evidence that justices were more diligent while the statute was in effect. If we are to believe Rich's complaints, the problem certainly continued after the repeal.[26]

[23] Dasent, III, 352. The proclamation involved was *TRP* no. 378.
[24] SP 1/150/138-9 (*LP* 14[1] no. 775).
[25] Richard Grafton, *Chronicle of the History of England* (London, 1809), II, 506-7. The speech concluded with an admonition to return to their shires and 'to see good order and rule kept.'
[26] Norwich first recorded that proclamations were 'delivered to the sheriff to proclaim accordingly' in 1541. After that date the delivery of royal proclamations was consistently noted in the Mayors Court Book; however this probably only indicates better record keeping rather than the impact of the Statute of Proclamations. NNRO Mayors Court Book 1540-9, 85. Similar references are found on folios 48, 94, 463, 491.

Comments on lax enforcement are also found in other sources. Bishop Latimer, in a sermon before Edward VI on 12 April 1549, criticized justices of the peace for not doing their duties in enforcing the acts designed for the preservation of archery. He suggested that 'some sharp proclamation' ought to be sent to them.[27] Accusations of outright corruption by port officials were common. Some have already been mentioned. Others are found in a series of cases brought to the statutory court set up by the Statute of Proclamations.[28] At approximately the same time that Richard Rich made his speech accusing justices of the peace of not giving proclamations sufficient publicity, the officials of Bridgwater were accused before the Exchequer of not proclaiming a proclamation on export until six months after it had been sent out, and allowing illegal export during that period. Although the officials denied the charges, their accusers mentioned that they were prepared to bring witnesses to prove their accusations. Unfortunately the result of the case has not survived, but the evidence in the depositions suggests that the officials of Bridgwater were probably guilty.[29]

The most complete records of administrative enforcement have survived for those proclamations which were enforced by commissions often made up of justices of the peace and other local officials. In these cases we can at last describe in detail the response of local officials. Commissions were used for a variety of purposes. As has already been noted, they were used to enforce enclosure legislation. Henry VII also used a commission in June 1507 to inquire about violations of his feudal rights as well as infractions 'contra formam quorumdam statutorum actuum provisionum et proclamacionum.'[30] Commissions were most commonly used for carrying out the proclamations designed to supply the markets in times of dearth. The commissioners also submitted detailed reports of their activities to the central government. The extensiveness of the effort under Wolsey and its effectiveness at least for some areas has already been commented on in an earlier chapter. Less evidence survives to illustrate the work of other commissions in Henry VIII's reign, but that which is available again indicates that local officials were diligent in carrying out their duties.[31]

[27] George F. Corrie ed., *Sermons by Hugh Latimer* (Cambridge, 1844), 197.
[28] See below p. 285.   [29] E 111/38.
[30] C 66/605/15d. Commissions were also used in Edward VI's reign to enforce distraint of knighthood proclamations. *CPR Edward VI*, 1 (1547–8), 185–6.
[31] YCRO House Books, XIII, 27d. *TRP* no. 259 ordered a search for grain by commissioners in Norfolk and Suffolk. The King appointed special commissioners named in the proclamation for that purpose. A letter from one of those commissioners to the chief

ENFORCEMENT OF ROYAL PROCLAMATIONS

The council's extensive efforts to assure enforcement of the two proclamations ordering a search for grain in 1550[32] also resulted in good response. New Romney officials made a search and returned a report listing the quantities of grain found in various houses in the city a little over two weeks after the first proclamation was issued.[33] The Lincoln records do not mention the first proclamation, but on 6 November it was agreed in the council that the second proclamation would be proclaimed 'in several places at the market time, and after shall be speedily put in execution by the justices of peace of this city according to the sense of the same.'[34]

York and Shrewsbury records contain a good deal more information making it possible to describe the activities of the commissioners in considerable detail. Letters were sent on 12 October to the mayor, sheriffs and justices of peace of York ordering them to 'have a continual care and earnest respect to the inviolable observation of our said proclamation and the punishment of all offenders.' The same day the mayor and one of the aldermen received a special letter which stated that because the justices of the peace had at times been guilty of 'some slackness' they were to use whatever means they thought necessary to assure compliance.[35] City officials reacted on 19 October when the council assigned four men, including two aldermen and the sheriff, to go to Aynsty and to view the barns and other storage places and 'order the same according to the tenor of the said proclamation.' The second proclamation, which repeated the order that a search should be made for grain, was proclaimed on 20 October; but it was not until 21 November that aldermen were assigned to make searches in all places in the city in order to find how much grain was available 'according to the King's proclamation made for that purpose.' Two days later they received a letter addressed to the mayor and sheriffs of the city which complained that those with the 'greatest quantities of grain, butter and cheese' were not bringing them to market. It ordered that those

constable of the hundred of Hensted ordering him to make a 'book' listing all the towns in the hundred, the names of the people who had grain, the quantity of grain, how much they had sold, and to whom it was sold, is preserved in the Norfolk city archives. We do not know how the constable responded, but the letter at least shows that the commissioners attempted to carry out their tasks. NNRO Mayors Court Book 1540–9, 301. See above pp. 101ff for the work of Wolsey's commissions. Leadam, *Star Chamber*, II, 165–7 n. 2 has a description of the men in one of those commissions.

[32] The proclamations were *TRP* nos. 365 and 366. See above pp. 227ff.
[33] KRO NB/JB/4. [34] LCRO L/1/1/1/2/79.
[35] YCRO House Books, xx, 27. These are the two letters discussed above, p. 228. The first is simply recorded in the council records as having been sent, but the text is not included (Dasent, III, 135).

who refused to bring victuals to market should be put in the custody of the President of the Council of the North.[36] A search must have followed, because on 5 December the commissioners ordered officials of the wapentake of Bulmer to bring the available grain to market and to sell it at the prices 'by his highness' said commission limited.' At the same time the city must have complained to the council about 'scarcity of corn in the markets' because the council sent new orders to the commissioners which named thirteen 'townships assigned to the market at York.' The inhabitants of these areas were required to come to York on market days 'with such quantity of corn' as in the opinion of the commissioners 'may be spared.' Six days later the King and council wrote to the mayor, sheriffs and justices of the peace of the city and county of York rescinding the second proclamation. The letter praised the 'great diligence and obedience' of these officials 'in the accomplishment of our pleasure in the said proclamation.'[37]

There also seems to have been a great effort to carry out the instructions of the proclamations in Shropshire. On 6 November a letter was sent to the bailiffs of Shrewsbury from Sir Richard Brereton and Sir Robert Nedeham, who were the 'special persons' assigned to see that the justices of the peace carried out the proclamation in that county. It is not clear why they waited over a month to act, but the plan set up by them for carrying out the proclamation seems to have been quite effective. They appointed five men to cooperate with the bailiffs 'to give attendance at the market' and 'to see the said proclamation executed accordingly.' These men were also instructed to report those who were 'remiss, negligent and make default in the execution of the said proclamation.' The bailiffs and their associates did a very thorough job. They first made a survey of the available grain and then listed the amount of surplus grain each individual had been ordered to bring to market on a specific day. Lists for 22, 25, 26, 28, and 29 November survive in the city records. On 28 November the bailiffs received a letter from Richard Barewall and Thomas Cresset, who may have been the new 'special persons' appointed in the King's letter of 17 November. The letter stated that 'we have rated, taxed and appointed the persons subscribed to the markets of Shrewsbury weekly every Saturday the quantities of corn and grain and victual upon their names.' The bailiffs were told that they were to call the names of those people

[36] YCRO House Books, xx, 28d, 29, 31–2.
[37] YCRO House Books, xx, 32d–33, 36–36d.

'weekly in the open market.' Those who failed to bring in their allotment were to be reported 'like as in the said proclamation is commanded.' The letter included forty-five names together with the amount of wheat, cheese, oats, rye and barley they were to bring to market. The most anyone was required to bring was four bushels of grain; the average was one or two bushels. The final entry in the Shrewsbury records, dated 5 December, again listed the names of individuals and the quantities of grain they were to bring to market.[38]

The evidence above suggests that the bailiffs of Shrewsbury, their associates, and the city officials of York made a real effort to carry out an extremely difficult task. The bad harvest, the inflation, and the unreasonable prices set in the second proclamation must have made their action extremely unpopular with those who were ordered to bring grain to market. Revocation of the second proclamation may have aided them, for producers were no longer required to sell at such low prices, but it must still have been difficult to get them to part with their limited surplus of grain. We do not know whether the town officials of York and Shrewsbury were able to keep their markets supplied. However, if they failed, that failure was due to the impossible task they were asked to perform rather than any negligence on their part.

The valiant efforts of the bailiffs of Shrewsbury could lead one to conclude that, at least when commissions were used, local officials generally carried out the orders in proclamations diligently and efficiently. But this would be to misconstrue the evidence. The council used all the means at its command to assure that local officials obeyed the orders in the two proclamations. It is, in fact, difficult to document a more determined effort by the council in the entire early Tudor period. The series of letters, including the appointment of 'special persons' to oversee the work of justices of the peace, must have aided in assuring cooperation from enforcement officials. In addition, the officials of the cities discussed certainly had a greater interest in having their markets supplied than even the central government. One wonders if rural justices of the peace were as zealous in attending to their duties.[39] Probably all that can be concluded from the examples cited is that administrative enforcement could be very good if local officials were subject to enough pressure from the council and if local needs gave them good reasons to obey. Normally, local officials were not so diligent. Both the examples cited

[38] SCRO, Miscellaneous Documents, no. 2696. This is a thick packet of documents without any pagination, entitled 'Market Inspections.'
[39] The justices of the peace in Sussex found convenient excuses for not carrying out the search immediately. SP 10/11/10.

throughout this work and the lamentations in the proclamations reveal that at times they were extremely negligent, and even deliberately allowed the violation of proclamations for personal gain.

Judicial enforcement

Although the judicial enforcement procedures prescribed in individual proclamations have been discussed in previous chapters, it is worth reviewing certain highlights of that information before attempting to determine the effectiveness of those procedures. Very few proclamations mentioned specific courts; ninety-four percent of Henry VII's mentioned none. Although proclamations became more specific on this subject as the period progressed, eighty-three percent of Henry VIII's, seventy percent of Somerset's and sixty-four percent of Northumberland's still failed to state where offenders should be tried. It was once commonly believed that because proclamations could not be enforced in the ordinary courts of the land, the government had to rely on prerogative courts and especially the Court of Star Chamber.[40] However, the evidence from the proclamations does not substantiate this. Two proclamations referred to the 'council in Star Chamber,' but only one during the entire early Tudor period actually mentioned the 'Court of Star Chamber.'[41] Although two mentioned the Exchequer in the 1530s, proclamations never until after 1539 included the formula commonly found in penal statutes which allowed informers to sue by bill, plaint, information, or writ of debt in any court of record. While the Statute of Proclamations was in effect the government used the statutory court to deal with violations of those proclamations which it was especially anxious to have enforced effectively, but common law courts were also used at least three times.[42] Somerset relied largely

[40] Steele, xxivff, maintained that proclamations were enforced in the same way as statutes until the reign of Edward III. After that time the government relied more on the council and in the Tudor period most offenders against proclamations were tried in the Star Chamber for contempt. Adair, *EHR*, CXXVI, 44ff; Elton, *Tudor Constitution*, 22; Plucknet, *History of Common Law*, 183, all believed that proclamations could not be enforced in common law courts and that the government had to rely on prerogative courts. Professor Elton later revised his earlier opinion and noted that there was still a good deal of uncertainty about where proclamations were actually enforced. G. R. Elton, *England Under the Tudors*, 2nd ed. (London, 1974), 478.

[41] *TRP* nos. 118, 118.5 ('council in Star Chamber'); no. 365 ('Court of Star Chamber').

[42] *TRP* nos. 133, 134 (Exchequer). Nos. 231 and 242 specifically mentioned the statutory court and no. 197.5 probably did, but we do not have the full text. All other proclamations which cited the Statute of Proclamations could probably be enforced in the statutory court even though it was not mentioned. Nos. 218, 231 and 242 also cited common law courts.

on the council, but three proclamations mentioned or implied that offenses could be tried in any court of record and two implied local courts.[43] After Somerset's fall, the mention of specific courts became more common. One proclamation listed the Courts of Star Chamber, King's Bench and Common Pleas, as well as the Exchequer and quarter sessions. In addition three mentioned the Exchequer, two quarter sessions, two implied local courts and two specifically listed any court of record.[44]

Although local courts were seldom mentioned in proclamations, local officials were commonly instructed to execute the orders they contained. One might, therefore, expect to find most offenses against them tried in local courts, but their records do not bear this out. These records are, of course, very deficient – hardly any county quarter sessions material exists for the early Tudor period, and that for mayor's courts and courts leet is also as a rule rather incomplete. But even when the records are more than adequate there is little evidence that proclamations were enforced. Local courts often dealt with offenses that were violations of them but they were seldom identified as such. Leet courts and hundred courts, for example, punished people for breaking price control regulations, for playing at unlawful games, and for forestalling and regrating, as well as other minor crimes, but they seldom mentioned that the accused was violating a proclamation. It is probable that many of the minor offenses punished by these courts were in fact offenses against proclamations but the records do not state this.[45]

Mayoral court records are more useful, but although they often state that an offense was 'contrary to the statute' – even at times identifying the statute specifically – they seldom mention proclamations. The first action involving a proclamation that I was able to find in the extensive records of the Norfolk mayor's court, which cover almost the entire early Tudor period, took place in September 1544 when a Frenchman, John Shobells, was called before the mayor's court 'for that he made not suit to the King's majesty to be made denizen.' He was then ordered to leave the realm 'according to the

---

[43] *TRP* nos. 326, 336, 332, 292, 322.

[44] *TRP* nos. 357, 359, 361 (Exchequer), 374, 380 (quarter sessions); 378, 382.5 (local courts); 366, 380 (any court of record); 365 (Star Chamber, King's Bench, Common Pleas, Exchequer and quarter sessions).

[45] Colchester has an excellent set of leet and hundred court records for the entire early Tudor period. The only reference to a proclamation I was able to find concerned a certain John Borrow, who was fined 2s in October 1536 for selling wine in violation of the King's proclamation. BRC Translated Abstracts of Court Rolls, 28 and 29 Henry VIII, 4. Since the abstracts proved so unrewarding, I did not use the actual court rolls.

King's proclamation.'[46] The only other cases based on a proclamation were heard in 1551 when three individuals were punished for spreading rumors that the shilling was to be devalued again.[47]

The records of the mayor's court at York are a bit more rewarding, largely because they give more details. Some of the cases are particularly interesting because they reveal that the city officials went to a good deal of trouble to locate and punish offenders, although they do not seem to have punished them very severely. On 11 September 1551 the mayor of York reported that 'untrue and slanderous rumor within these three days was risen and spread abroad this city concerning a further abasing of testons contrary to his grace's proclamation.' He ordered an investigation which revealed that a certain John Barker had sent a letter to his brother-in-law, William Gibson, in which it was stated that testons had been 'cried down in London and will be at York tomorrow.' Gibson was ordered to appear and to bring the letter. In his testimony Gibson stated that he had given the letter to Robert Barker, one of the city officials, to read after he had received it. The court immediately committed Robert Barker to prison since 'having the said letter so delivered unto him to be read, it cannot be supposed but he had knowledge of the contents of the same.' It also tried to see that John Barker, the writer of the letter, would be punished. Since John Barker was not living in the city, a letter was sent to the Council of the North 'to the intent that they take such further order against the same John as seem to them to stand with equity and justice.' The city also sent a letter to the King's council, informing them of the action they had taken. Meanwhile Robert Barker was released from prison, but he was removed from his office and bound by recognizance to answer further when called. However, a month later all seems to have been forgiven, for Robert Barker was restored to his office on 15 October, and there is no evidence that William Gibson or John Barker were punished.[48] The whole affair reveals that city officials could expend a good deal of energy in the enforcement of a proclamation when the matter involved the interests of the city. The rumors were reported to have caused some 'inconvenience' in York and this was why the investigation was carried out. When it was learned that a city official was involved in an incident that could and possibly did cause some panic and confusion in the city, rapid action was taken against him.

[46] NNRO Mayors Court Book 1540–9, 243. *TRP* no. 234.
[47] NNRO Mayors Court Book 1549–55, 143, 145. *TRP* no. 378.
[48] YCRO House Books, xx, 74, 75, 75d, 78.

Furthermore, at least some effort was made to deal with the author of the rumor who was not within the jurisdiction of the city. All this reveals relatively good enforcement. It is not surprising that the city officials made a complete report to the King's council; they probably expected and deserved some commendation for their actions.

On another occasion the officials of York not only sent a report to the council but they received praise for their action and advice on how to proceed further in the matter. On 5 December 1548 they arrested and imprisoned a man named Nicholson who had 'made and set upon the minster door' a 'slanderous bill.' The city council informed Somerset of the incident. Within two weeks they received an answer praising their vigilance and telling them that Nicholson, 'who hath confessed his lewd demeanor contrary to the proclamation lately set forth against such seditious bills,' was to be set on the pillory with a paper describing his offense in order to deter other potential offenders. The contents of the 'slanderous bill' were not identified in the correspondence nor was the date of the proclamation mentioned; however, since the bill was posted on the cathedral door it may very well have involved a violation of the proclamation of 24 April 1548, which forbade the spreading of rumors stating that the King intended to tax baptisms and burials. If so, the penalty ordered by Somerset was not included in the proclamation, for it simply stated that offenders would suffer the King's 'displeasure and grievous imprisonment of such offender's body.'[49]

The use of an open public punishment to deter would-be offenders was not uncommon even when the proclamation did not provide for this type of penalty. In March 1552 the Court of Aldermen in London punished a number of people who had violated the proclamation enforcing the Lenten fast. The proclamation involved was probably the one now lost of February 1552, but since these proclamations often repeated one another verbatim from year to year, it is likely that the penalty threatened was fine and imprisonment. The Court of Aldermen, nevertheless, ordered that a group of people who 'had prepared a duck and caused it to be roasted minding to have taken it the same Friday contrary to the King's majesty's laws and proclamations' be set on horseback with the 'duck between them on a spit' and led through the major markets as a public example. Two days later two people who had sold two pigs during Lent 'contrary both to the laws of the realm and also the King's majesty's proclamation' together with the individuals who had

[49] YCRO House Books, xiv, 42-42d. *TRP* no. 303.

purchased the pigs were also sentenced to be taken through the market places of the city on horseback 'either of them having one of the said pigs hanging upon their breasts and the entrails of the same pigs severally set in garlands upon their heads in example terror and stay of other like offenders.'[50]

The cases mentioned above illustrate relatively effective enforcement by local courts, but they were the exception rather than the rule. Local court records, whether mayor, leet, or hundred courts, simply did not often identify the fact that they were dealing with cases involving proclamations. At times they used other terms to describe them,[51] but even if these cases are taken into consideration there are not many. City quarter session presentments and indictments also seldom cited an offense as being 'contra formam proclamacionis' even when the charge could have been based on a proclamation. Forestalling and regrating offenses were commonly called 'contra pacem' or 'contra formam statuti.' Vagabonds were also punished for violating statutes as were those who sold meat above the prices in the proclamation. I have only been able to find one example of a jury of presentment accusing a butcher of violating a proclamation. At the Colchester sessions in 1543 a butcher was accused of not selling 'his flesh according to the King's proclamation.'[52] Of course many proclamations simply ordered enforcement of statutes, and it may be that its issuance encouraged justices to pay more attention to enforcing statutes. There is scattered evidence that this was the case. The proclamations ordering enforcement of a number of statutes on unlawful games on 13 September 1538 were, for example, followed by a number of cases in the Norwich sessions dealing with offenses against those statutes. However, any statistically valid correlation between proclamations ordering enforcement of statutes and more vigilant enforcement of them cannot be established.[53]

Proclamations were at times cited in sessions indictments without actually providing the basis for the indictment. At the sessions in York in April 1539 an indictment was returned against a certain

[50] CLRO Rep. 12(2) 458, 460.
[51] KRO SaAc 3/247d where the proclamation on the Lenten fast is enforced but the offense is cited as being 'contrary to the ordinance of our sovereign lord the King.' CCRO CMB 13/48 where an offense against *TRP* no. 184 is referred to as a violation of the King's 'general restraint.' CLRO Rep. 9/40 where a proclamation on unlawful games is referred to as 'the King's most gracious placard.'
[52] BCR Abstracts of Court Rolls, 25 and 26 Henry VIII Roll 19, 19 January 1534.
[53] NNRO Quarter Sessions Minute Book, 30 Henry VIII, 159d.

Thomas Pratt for heresy. Pratt was accused of stating 'that God never bled all his blood for if he had bled all his blood then he could never have risen again from death to life.' Although Pratt seems to have been engaged in what must have been little more than relatively harmless idle speculation, he was accused of standing in breach of 'diversorum statutorum de heretico.' However, the indictment also added that the statement had been made in December after the King's proclamation had been issued. This may have been a reference to the proclamation of 16 November 1538 which included among its many clauses an order that no one was to 'reason, dispute or argue upon the said Holy and Blessed Sacrament nor of the mysteries thereof.' Although Pratt's statement did not deal directly with the sacrament, no other proclamation seems even remotely related to the charge. Whatever the explanation, a true bill was returned and Pratt's case was heard in the archbishop's court where it was again emphasized that the statement had been made 'in the month of December last past sithens the King's proclamation.' Pratt confessed that he had said the words and that he now recognized that they were contrary to the faith; he abjured and was pardoned. It is difficult to explain why it was felt necessary to cite the proclamation since it does not seem to have related directly to the statement, but seemingly those who drew up the indictment felt that the fact that the statement had been made after the proclamation was issued added to the seriousness of the offence.[54]

There are a few surviving examples of indictments and presentments in city quarter sessions that were based solely on a proclamation. The earliest example I have been able to find was at the Canterbury sessions of 12 December 1502. A jury of presentment accused four men of wearing the cognizance and badge of a lord 'contra proclamacionem' of the King. This was probably a reference to the proclamation of 10 March 1502 which forbade retainers. It simply ordered the enforcement of a number of earlier statutes so this case seemingly documents better enforcement of statutes as the result of a proclamation. The surprising thing is that the proclamation was used as the basis of the charge, for it added nothing to the earlier statutes.[55] Another case in the Canterbury session records is based on a proclamation alone but it is undated so it is difficult to determine which one was involved. The jury for the wards of

[54] Borthwick Institute of Historical Research, Cause Paper Files R VII G 265.
[55] CCL J/Q/302/3; *TRP* no. 50. A writ for publication of the proclamation was probably sent to Canterbury on 1 April.

Northgate and Burgate presented 'that all the butchers refuse divers money being silver and the King's coin contrary to the King's proclamation.'[56]

The most interesting case based solely on a proclamation is found in the Chester sessions for September 1550. It is particularly revealing because the accused was convicted and the penalty that was applied is noted in the margin. An indictment was brought against William Hope for attacking the sheriff's deputy with a dagger while he was seeking to attach Hope in a plea of debt. The proclamation Hope was accused of violating was probably a reissue of the one of 3 August 1547, which had threatened those who hurt or maimed the King's officers in the performance of their duties with loss of 'all their lands, goods, and chattels, and their bodies to be committed to perpetual prison.' Although Hope was clearly a local troublemaker who was constantly being accused of offenses in the sessions records, the court did not choose to apply the full penalties in the proclamation. A marginal note records that Hope was fined 20s for an offense which could have cost him all his possessions and resulted in perpetual imprisonment. This fine was more severe than the normal penalty given for assault with a weapon, but it was nevertheless surprisingly light, especially considering that Hope was a notorious offender. Although very little can be based on one case, it certainly reveals that the full penalties threatened in proclamations that had severe penalties were not always applied.[57]

Although county quarter sessions records for the early Tudor period have rarely survived, there are a few examples in those extant of cases that were also based solely on a proclamation. The most complete collection of early Tudor county quarter sessions records are those for the county of Norfolk.[58] A series of boxes containing indictments and presentments for the period 1532–53 offers an opportunity to determine whether there was an increased awareness of royal proclamations by juries of presentment or those making accusations to juries at any time during the early Tudor period. Although survivals are not uniform, it is nevertheless interesting that there were no indictments or presentments which even mentioned a proclamation until 1551. In that year five presentments

[56] CCL J/Q/335/1.
[57] CCRO MB15/18. Normal fines recorded in the Chester sessions for assault with a weapon ranged from 3s 4d to 6s 8d.
[58] Other collections do not contain any proclamations cases. J. C. J. Jeaffreson ed., *Middlesex County Records* (London, 1886); W. P. William ed., *Calendar of the Caernarvonshire Quarter Sessions Records*, 1, 1541–58 (Caernarvon, 1956).

stated that an offense had been 'contra formam proclamacionis.' All of them accused individuals of regrating grain. The offenses occurred between 12 September 1551 and 9 November 1551. They could have been based on either of two proclamations which forbade regrating; however, because the second, issued shortly before the presentments on 24 July 1551, simply ordered enforcement of old statutes, it is more likely that the presentments were based on the proclamation of 24 September 1550 which specifically mentioned that accusations could be brought 'before four justices of the peace of the shire where the offenses shall happen.'[59] All that survives are the presentments, so that one cannot determine if the alleged offenders were convicted or what punishment was meted out. It would be interesting if this evidence were available, for the penalties in the 1550 proclamation for regrating grain were a 'moiety of their goods, chattels, leases, and farms, for term of life, lives or years, or at will, which he or they all have to their own use.' The case is also significant because there was no specific statute which forbade the buying of grain in the market and reselling it until the following Parliament when a comprehensive statute on forestalling, regrating and engrossing was enacted.

This statute may have been the basis for an indictment the following year. Robert Fraye was accused of buying grain in the market on 12 January 1552 and reselling it on 10 March 1552, 'contra formam statuti et proclamacionis.'[60] Three other indictments in the same year also alleged offenses against proclamations and statutes. All accused individuals of regrating butter and cheese. The statute involved was probably 3 and 4 Edward VI c. 21. A proclamation of 24 July 1551 had ordered enforcement of that statute, but since it had not added any new penalties,[61] it is difficult to explain why the individual who brought the information to the jury chose to cite both the statute and the proclamation. True bills were returned on all of the cases based on the statute and the proclamation and on two of the earlier cases based on the proclamation alone, but no further information is available for any of them. Nevertheless, the sudden appearance in two years' time of nine cases that refer to a proclamation suggests that Northumberland's effort to get the ordinary

[59] *TRP* no. 365. None of the statutes cited in *TRP* no. 377 specifically forbade the buying of grain in the market to sell again. No. 365 did state this and all of the defendants were accused of this offense. NNRO County Sessions Rolls 153a–53 Box 3.

[60] The indictment probably came after Parliament ended its session in April 1552, but the offense occurred before the end of Parliament. NNRO County Sessions Rolls 1532–53 Box 3A. The statute was 5 and 6 Edward VI c. 14.

[61] *TRP* no. 377; NNRO County Sessions Rolls 1532–53 Box 3A.

courts of the land to deal with violations of proclamations may have met with some success. Unfortunately, the lack of county quarter sessions records makes it impossible to find additional documentation for this generalization.

Central court records are a good deal more complete than those of local courts. In fact, they are so voluminous that it was not possible to search all the available materials; therefore, since ten proclamations mentioned or implied enforcement in the Exchequer, I have concentrated on the Exchequer King's Remembrancer's Memoranda rolls.[62] These are particularly useful records because a complete set has survived and for once makes it possible to compare the total number of cases mentioning proclamations in the various periods. In addition, since it is usually possible to locate the result of the action, one can also determine how effective the enforcement procedure was.[63]

The Exchequer dealt with all matters involving the royal revenue; consequently any proclamation which provided for a forfeiture or fine to the King might have come before the court. However, cases involving proclamations did not commonly appear on the memoranda rolls until after 1539. The only exceptions to that rule were the prosecutions for distraint of knighthood. Henry VII issued four proclamations on that subject, and the last threatened those who failed to obey with a £200 fine. Sheriffs were ordered to certify to the Chancery by a specified date the names of those who had not carried out the order.[64] Although none of the proclamations mentioned the Exchequer, the court became very active in collecting the fines. After the names were presented to the Chancery by the sheriffs, the clerk of the Chancery began process against offenders in

---

[62] Sampling of King's Bench and Common Pleas plea rolls revealed no proclamations cases and only three proclamations even mentioned these courts. In addition there is no evidence that the King's Bench ever called up cases from quarter sessions involving a proclamation. I have gone through the entire file in the PRO classified KB 9 Ancient Indictments of the King's Bench, and found no references to proclamations. I have relied heavily on the work of Dr Guth, 'Exchequer Penal Law Enforcement' for the reign of Henry VII, and I used Leonard's 'Knights and Knighthood' for the distraint of knighthood cases, although I had found most of the evidence before I discovered this dissertation.

[63] I was unable to locate the result in a few cases even though the continuation of the case was noted on the roll. A great number of the actions broke off after the information. I have assumed in each of these cases that the action was dropped by the court. In many cases the informer who brought the information may have arrived at a private agreement with the accused and therefore did not pursue the prosecution further. This was a common practice in the Elizabethan period. Davies, *English Apprenticeship*, 62. For a description of Exchequer procedure, see Guth, 'Exchequer Penal Law Enforcement,' 82ff.

[64] *TRP* nos. 9, 48, 49, 53.

the Exchequer. If the fines were paid, or if the individual proved that he had taken up knighthood, the process was stopped. The crown pursued the matter with great energy in the latter part of the reign of Henry VII and in the early part of his son's. The Exchequer records include a file of names returned from the Chancery of men who had not taken up knighthood as well as a list of fines. In addition the process against them is often recorded on the memoranda rolls. The impressive number of names on the lists, the number of cases on the memoranda rolls, and the amount of the fines collected reveal that the government was both serious and successful in enforcing its feudal rights.[65]

Since fines for distraint of knighthood involved the enforcement of the King's feudal rights, they can be considered an exceptional case, and their appearance on the Exchequer rolls should not be particularly surprising. It is more important to discover how often other types of proclamations were enforced in the Exchequer, and how successful that effort was. Table 8 provides a summary of all the informations that appeared on the memoranda rolls during the early Tudor period and that cited offenses against proclamations. Excepted are those dealing with distraint of knighthood. The statistics clearly document an increase in activity at the end of the period. Over fifty percent of the cases were heard in the last three and a half years of the period. They also seem to indicate that the Statute of Proclamations may have had some effect on the enforcement of proclamations in the Exchequer. Proclamations were mentioned in informations only eleven times before 1539 and only two of these were based solely on a proclamation. Informations were most commonly brought by private individuals. The King's attorney general

[65] E 198/4/21 contains a list of 296 names compiled in 19 Henry VII from the returns of sheriffs. A similar roll for 24 Henry VII entitled 'process returned against diverse gentlemen for the order of knighthood' contains fifty-six names. E 198/4/23. The most impressive roll is dated 1 Henry VIII. It contains the names of 505 men. Names are listed by county and an estimate of the value of the land holding of each man is appended E 198/4/36. Another file, E 198/4/20, lists fines received by the clerk of the chancery during the latter part of the reign of Henry VII. Although the fines were generally small, not even approaching the £200 fine threatened in the last proclamation, there are an impressive number of fines. There are ninety-five fines ranging between £2 and £14 for 19 Henry VII alone. I have not tabulated the number of cases on the memoranda rolls, but they were most numerous in the reign of Henry VII and ceased entirely after Michaelmas 1514. Once the process had started the individual usually settled by paying his fine. More persistent offenders were turned over to the jurisdiction of the Council Learned in Law. After Cromwell came to power, a new procedure was introduced. Offenders were assessed by commissioners without having to appear and they paid directly to the sheriff. If they failed to pay they were summoned before Cromwell. Leonard, 'Knights and Knighthood,' 43ff.

Table 8. *Cases involving royal proclamations heard in the Exchequer 1485–1553*

	Period						
	1	2	3[a]	4	5[b]	6	Total
Offense against							
Proclamation only	1	0	1	6	6	7	21
Statute and proclamation	1	0	8	20	14	59	102
Total	2	0	9	26	20	66	123
Action begun by							
Attorney general	0	0	0	1	0	2	3
Other officials	2	0	0	10	3	4	19
Private individuals	0	0	9	15	17	60	101
Accusation							
Illegal export	2	0	9	21	14	54	100
Illegal import	0	0	0	3	0	0	3
Price control violation	0	0	0	0	0	6	6
Coinage offenses	0	0	0	0	0	6	6
Pulling, plucking, clipping	0	0	0	0	6	0	6
Not selling surplus corn	0	0	0	1	0	0	1
Other	0	0	0	1	0	0	1
Successful prosecutions	1	0	0	11	1	17	30

[a] Cases in Trinity Term 31 Henry VIII were included in period 3, while Michaelmas term was included in period 4.
[b] Cases in Michaelmas 3 Edward VI were included in period 6.

was responsible for beginning actions only three times. With the exception of the last part of the reign of Henry VIII, other crown officials or local officials were not particularly active in initiating prosecutions. Illegal export of grain was by far the most common accusation. Most of these informations accused defendants of violating both statutes and proclamations, but a few were based solely on a proclamation. Prosecutions were most successful in two periods. It can be established that over forty-two percent of the actions resulted in a fine or forfeiture in period four, while approximately twenty-five percent of the considerably larger number of prosecutions in period six were successful.

More interesting information can be gleaned from a careful study of the cases. Of the 1804 actions based on penal laws in the reign of Henry VII, only two cited royal proclamations.[66] The first was based on both a statute and a proclamation. James Slaughter, deputy searcher at Great Yarmouth, maintained that

[66] Guth, 'Exchequer Penal Law Enforcement,' 188.

three merchants had shipped wheat and candles to Burgundy in violation of a proclamation and a statute enacted in 5 and 6 Richard II. Both are difficult to trace. The offense took place on 13 December 1492, so that it predates the proclamation of 18 September 1493 forbidding trade with Burgundy; however, there may have been an earlier proclamation on that subject which has been lost. It may also be that the proclamation referred to was that of 19 September 1491, forbidding unlicensed export of grain.[67] The statute may have been 5 Richard II st. 1 c. 2, which forbade departure from the realm without license by anyone except 'great men of the realm and true and notable merchants, and the King's soldiers'; but it is also possible that Slaughter confused his regnal years and meant 17 Richard II c. 7, which gave license to export grain but stated that the council could restrain export 'when they shall think best for the profit of the realm.' Whatever the explanation, Slaughter was not successful. The case continued until Hilary 1496, when one of the defendants appeared through his attorney and pleaded not guilty. The King's attorney stated that he knew the plea to be true and the case was dismissed.[68]

The second case is more interesting, because the charge was based solely on a proclamation, and the prosecution was successful. William Richard, deputy searcher at Bristol, accused William Sewell of attempting to export wheat to Burgundy on 28 February 1505. Richard had seized the wheat and he accused Sewell of acting 'contra formam quarundam proclamacionum et restrictionum ac prohibicionum dicti domini Regis.' When the defendant did not appear in Michaelmas 1505, the wheat was declared forfeit and Richard received half its value, 5s, to share with John Whitington, the searcher at Bristol.[69] Once again it is difficult to trace the proclamation. It may have been either of the two mentioned earlier, or an unfound one; however, the importance of the case is that the accusation was based solely on a proclamation, and the barons awarded the forfeiture solely on the strength of that accusation. Although one would prefer more evidence, it suggests that at least in isolated cases, as early as the reign of Henry VII, the ordinary courts of the land did punish violations of proclamations. The lack

---

[67] Dr Guth prefers the former explanation because the information emphasized that shipment was being made to an area under the rule of the Duke of Burgundy. The proclamations are *TRP* nos. 26 and 33.
[68] E 159/269 Hilary, xxxid.
[69] E 159/383 Trinity, xxxiiid. The two cases are discussed in Guth, 'Exchequer Penal Law Enforcement,' 189–91.

of definition probably left broad leeway to the judges, because it had not been stated that proclamations could not be enforced in the Exchequer or for that matter any common law court. However, no clear precedents were established during the reign of Henry VII because the proclamation seldom mentioned courts, and the law courts rarely dealt with cases alleging violations of them.[70]

With the exception of a few cases dealing with distraint of knighthood early in the reign of Henry VIII, I have not been able to find any actions on the memoranda rolls that mentioned proclamations until Easter term 32 Henry VIII. In that term six informations alleged violations of proclamations. This must have been connected with the renewed emphasis on the enforcement of export legislation which began at that time. The proclamation involved was probably an unfound one forbidding unlicensed export, for although the only extant proclamation on that subject, issued at approximately the time of the informations, forbade all export, some defendants presented a successful defense by claiming that they had a license. All but one of the actions also alleged that the shipments had been made without paying customs in violation of a statute. The single exception also stated that customs had not been paid, but the formal charge did not mention a statute.[71] All of the actions were initiated by informers and none of them was successful. The court ordered the appearance of the defendants in each case, but they either denied the charges or claimed that they had a license.

Informations did not again mention proclamations until Trinity term 31 Henry VIII, when three unsuccessful actions maintained that individuals had exported grain without paying customs in violation of a statute, a restraint and a proclamation. All of the alleged offenses took place while the Parliament which enacted the Statute of Proclamations was in session in June 1539.[72] However, the Statute of Proclamations did not result in a sudden increase in the number of cases based on proclamations. Only three more informations accused individuals of violating proclamations in the next two years. The first was introduced by that notorious professional informer, George Whelplay, who said he had seized a ship exporting coin in violation of a statute and a proclamation. When the defendant

[70] Dr Guth also believes 'there was no reason for thinking that the Exchequer or King's Bench jurisdictions were somehow precluded' from dealing with proclamations. 'Henry VII's proclamations never specified judicial jurisdiction leaving that an open-ended matter.' *Ibid.* 194.

[71] E 159/311 Easter, xlviii. The other cases are found in *ibid.* xxxiii, xlviii, L, Ld, Li. The statute was 3 Henry VII, c. 8. The only extant proclamation is *TRP* no. 134, issued on 7 September 1531.   [72] E 159/318 Trinity, i, id, iii.

failed to appear the coin was declared forfeit and Whelplay was awarded a share of the forfeiture. A second successful prosecution alleged illegal export of wheat and tanned hides, also in violation of a statute and a proclamation. The third case was based solely on a proclamation. Richard Byrde accused Richard Holden of buying grain even though he had sufficient for his household. However, either they settled the issue out of court or the barons did not think there was sufficient evidence to summon the defendant; the case breaks off after the information.[73]

There was a significant increase in the number of actions based on proclamations after that of 16 February 1541 forbade unlicensed export of victuals. The lucrative rewards promised to informers (including a share of the items exported, the ship in which the export had taken place, and the goods and chattels of the exporters) may have stimulated the increase, because nineteen informations alleged violations of proclamations forbidding unlicensed export in the five years following its issuance.[74] Of course, one cannot be certain that all of the actions were based on it, but one of them stated specifically that the proclamation was made by virtue of an act of Parliament. This was probably a reference to the fact that the February 1541 proclamation was based on the Statute of Proclamations.[75] Furthermore, successful litigants were often rewarded with a share of the ship as well as of the goods being exported, which also suggests that the action was based on this proclamation.[76] The vast majority of these informations were based on both a statute and a proclamation; however, two cited only a proclamation. In both cases the court took action. One ended in a successful prosecution and the other resulted in the defendant's acquittal after a jury trial.[77] A good

[73] E 159/318 Michaelmas, viiid; E 159/319 Easter, ii, Trinity, xxii. All three proclamations are difficult to trace. Whelplay's information was either based on an unfound proclamation or *TRP* no. 133, which was issued eight years earlier on 18 July 1531. A proclamation forbidding export of tanned hides was issued on 14 October 1538, but it did not mention the Exchequer (*TRP* no. 184). The last action must have been based on an unfound proclamation. The only extant proclamation which would apply was issued in November 1535 and was certainly intended only as a temporary measure (*TRP* no. 151).

[74] *TRP* no. 197.6. Three of the four other actions which referred to proclamations were probably based on no. 224 forbidding unlicensed imports from France. E 159/324 Hilary, ii, iid; E 159/325 Michaelmas, xv. The fourth was based on 24 Henry VIII c. 1 and an unfound proclamation forbidding the sale of unsealed leather. E 159/323 Michaelmas, xxi.   [75] E 159/324 Hilary, Lxxix.

[76] Examples are E 159/321 Hilary, Lxxxiii, Michaelmas, iiid; E 159/323 Michaelmas, iiid. I have not been able to find an example of informers being awarded a share of the defendants' goods and chattels.

[77] E 159/322 Hilary, x, xx. In the successful case the informer had seized the ship and the defendants did not appear, so the informer was awarded a share of both the goods and the proceeds from the sale of the ship.

number of the actions were initiated by port officials and one case was started by the attorney general, William Whorwood, possibly because a port official was accused of corruption.[78] Professional informers were also very active. Henry Sayer, who was active both in the conciliar court set up by the Statute of Proclamations and in the Exchequer, introduced one information, and Baldwin Smith, another professional informer whose name often appears on the court rolls, introduced two others.[79]

The number of cases referring to proclamations in the period 1539–47 is impressive when compared to the eleven cases in the previous half century. But in light of the vast number of actions citing violations of statutes in the same period, even this increase did not constitute any threat to the primacy of statute-based informations in the Exchequer.[80] While it may be that the Statute of Proclamations and the rich rewards available to successful litigants by virtue of the proclamation forbidding unlicensed export encouraged informers to cite it in their information, the statistics do not reveal a radical change in Exchequer actions as a result of the statute. Port officials were probably also more aware of the possibility of using proclamations as the basis for an accusation because the enforcement clauses of a number of them now specifically mentioned the Exchequer. Finally, the clause in the Statute of Proclamations ordering that proclamations be obeyed as statutes may have clarified what was probably a doubtful point earlier. If proclamations were to be obeyed 'as though they were made by act of Parliament,' surely they could also be enforced in the same way that those acts were. Even though the statute said nothing about enforcement in the Exchequer, it can be presumed that this was implied.

The repeal of the Statute of Proclamations did not, however, result in a decline in the number of actions citing proclamations. During the approximately twenty-two months between December 1547 and the fall of Somerset, seventeen informations mentioned proclamations. All but six of them cited both statutes and proclamations. The six exceptions were introduced by the same man, John Samon, a leatherseller. They all accused individuals of violating a proclamation of 31 March 1547. This was the one which added

[78] E 159/320 Easter, xxviii.
[79] E 159/323 Easter, ix; E 159/334 Hilary, ii, Michaelmas, ix.
[80] By rough count there were at least fifty-one cases in Easter term 32 Henry VIII, alleging illegal export without paying customs based on a statute (E 159/319 Easter). In comparison there were only twenty-six cases in the entire period 1539–47 which even mentioned a proclamation.

the names of a number of counties to 37 Henry VIII c. 15, which limited the purchase of wool to merchants of the Staple in specific counties named in the statute. Only its last paragraph, which forbade pulling, plucking and clipping of wool fells, added new regulations without previous statutory authority. Samon seemingly recognized this, for the six actions, all of which accused individuals of violating this portion of the proclamation, were based solely on the proclamation. The court took action in four of the cases and ordered the defendants to appear. The defendants or their attorneys appeared in each case and after denying the charges asked for dismissal. Three actions were dismissed after the initial answer, but one continued into the reign of Mary, when the attorney general finally accepted the plea and the case was dismissed.[81] Although Samon was unsuccessful in every case, the court had responded to an information based only on a proclamation even after the Statute of Proclamations was repealed. However, the proclamation had been issued before the repeal and in each case the charges were finally dropped. Therefore we are left with inadequate evidence for determining whether the position of proclamations in the Exchequer was changed as a result of the repeal of the Statute of Proclamations. However, it is likely that after 1547 it was again unclear if the proclamations fell under the jurisdiction of the Exchequer. Even the government may have been uncertain, because only three of Somerset's proclamations ordered enforcement in common law courts. One was specifically based on a statute and the other two were coinage proclamations which may simply have been using the normal methods of enforcement for this type of proclamation.[82]

Northumberland was equally cautious in his use of common law courts to enforce proclamations which were not specifically based on statutory authority or simply repeated statutory prohibitions. As has been pointed out, he relied more heavily on informers and the ordinary courts, but his proclamations seldom made new regulations. Since six proclamations mentioned the Exchequer or any court of record,[83] it should not be surprising that there was

[81] E 159/327 Easter, ivd, vd, vi, vid, vii, viid; *TRP* no. 278.

[82] *TRP* 336 was based on 25 Henry VIII c. 2. No. 326 forbade buying and selling of coins above the prices in the proclamation and allowed informers to sue 'in any of the King's majesty's courts, by bill, action of debt, or information as in such cases heretofore hath been accustomed.' No. 322 penalized subjects with fine and forfeiture for exchanging testons above the value in the proclamation and allowed suit in any court of record. Both might have been based on 25 Edward III c. 12 st. 5, which forbade taking of profit on exchanges. See above Chapter 8 n. 69.

[83] *TRP* nos. 357, 359, 361, 365, 366, 380.

a great increase in the number of actions in the Exchequer which cited proclamations. But because these proclamations were inevitably based on statutes, the informations normally also stated that the actions were contrary to statutes. The vast majority dealt with illegal export. These cases need little further comment except to point out that successful prosecutions were not as common as they had been in Henry VIII's reign. Only seven of the sixty-six cases I was able to find were based solely on a proclamation. Five accused individuals of selling sheep or oxen above the prices in the proclamation of September 1551, which was based on the authority of 25 Henry VIII c. 2. Another information, which accused John Burwell of selling cheese above the price in the proclamation, actually began with a detailed summary of that statute and went on to state that the proclamation had been made by its authority. Different from the other cases, this information accused the defendant of action contrary to the proclamation and the statute.[84]

The other two informations which rested solely on a proclamation accused individuals of selling coins above the values set in the proclamation. One, brought by the attorney general, accused three men of selling gold coins at prices higher than those rated. Although the attorney general rested the information on the proclamation alone, another information in the same year, accusing individuals of the same offense, stated that the deed was contrary to the statute and proclamation.[85] The statute referred to may have been 25 Edward III st. 5 c. 12, which forbade the taking of profits on exchanges, but this is not made clear in the information. Other informations do state this specifically. On 3 June 1553 William Staples of London brought an information alleging the purchase of royals and angels at prices higher than those in a proclamation of 11 April 1549. The information cited the terms of 25 Edward III st. 5 c. 12 and 5 and 6 Edward VI c. 19, even though the second statute which forbade 'giving, receiving or paying' of more for coins than stated in the King's proclamations had not been enacted when the proclamation was issued. Staples based his charge on both the statutes and the proclamation. When the defendant did not appear he was awarded

[84] E 159/330 Michaelmas, xlviii. The other cases are *ibid.* xxxvi, xliii, xlv, xlvd, xlviid. *TRP* no. 380.
[85] The proclamation was probably *TRP* no. 367. The attorney general's case is E 159/330 Hilary, xxxviiid. The other case is *ibid.* Pasche, vid. Two informations in the following law term also accused individuals of selling gold coins above the prices in the proclamation but they maintained this was contrary to the statute and the proclamation. *Ibid.* Trinity, iiii, Michaelmas, ld.

half of the forfeiture, as provided for in the statute and proclamation.[86] None of the informations based solely on a proclamation was successful: there are no examples of successful prosecutions based on a proclamation alone in the reign of Edward VI.

Despite the vast increase in the number of informations citing proclamations, it is interesting that plaintiffs seldom relied on proclamations alone. They were probably added to statutes because at times the penalty in them was greater than that in the statute. It may also be that plaintiffs hoped to impress the barons with the seriousness of the offense by reminding them that both a statute and a proclamation had been violated. It must again be emphasized that the status of proclamations in ordinary courts simply was not clearly defined, and with rare exceptions their texts did not before 1539 encourage informers to resort to them. This probably explains the lack of informations citing proclamations before that date and the increase afterwards. It is also true that while the Statute of Proclamations was in force the government did not hesitate to encourage resort to common law courts even when the proclamation was based only on that statute. Somerset was more reluctant to do so, possibly because he preferred to use the council acting in a quasi-judicial fashion, or maybe because he realized that the jurisdiction of common law courts in proclamation cases was again unclear after the repeal of the Statute. Northumberland preferred to use informers and the ordinary courts, but since his proclamations seldom made new regulations, his use of common law courts to enforce proclamations does not help to answer questions about their status in those courts after the repeal of the statute. A good deal more evidence on the enforcement of royal proclamations might be acquired by a more thorough study of the memoranda rolls, but additional insights must await a really definitive study of Exchequer penal law enforcement for the reigns of Henry VIII and Edward VI similar to the work done by Dr Guth for Henry VII's reign.

The second major source providing evidence of the enforcement of royal proclamations by central courts are the records of the council. The council dealt with offenders against proclamations in two ways. Sometimes it acted in its administrative capacity as a board and punished individuals in a quasi-legal fashion without a formal trial. It also operated as a formal court when it sat as the Court of Star

---

[86] E 159/332 Trinity, i; *TRP* no. 326. An earlier case accused the defendant of violating no. 379, but, since the proclamation had no provision for informers to receive a share of the forfeiture, the plaintiff asked for a share according to the form of the statute. E 159/331 Trinity, vid.

Chamber with an established procedure and a defined jurisdiction.[87] Because a formal register was not initiated until August 1540, it is difficult to know the extent of the council's activity in enforcing proclamations in a quasi-judicial fashion. Although the council was mentioned in eleven proclamations before 1539 and presumably was involved in enforcing them, there is little evidence of such activity in the surviving records.[88] I have been able to find only one reference in the Liber Intrationum which might have involved a royal proclamation. On 10 November 1493 Rodner Catt and Peter Sericke were 'committed to the Fleet for taking upon the King's streams, ships and goods of certain Portugals and subjects of the King of Denmark contrary to leagues with them concluded.' This involved the violation of a proclamation issued seven days earlier, ordering punishment of piracy against England's allies, but the entry does not mention a proclamation.[89] There are three references to proclamations in the Ellesmere manuscripts before 1539. All must have involved violations of the proclamation of 22 June 1530 forbidding certain religious books and Bible translations. It ordered that offenders were to be reported to the council where they would be 'corrected and punished.' Individuals were 'corrected and punished' but the account reads as though the council acted in its capacity as a board rather than as a court.[90]

Although most of the administrative records of the council have been lost, a good many fragments of the records of the Court of Star Chamber have survived; a careful search of these records has uncovered only three cases involving proclamations which were definitely heard before 1539. In each of them the complaint came to the Star Chamber only after local officials had failed to enforce the

---

[87] See Elton, *Tudor Constitution*, 101–2, for council's judicial work as a board, and 158ff for its work as a court.

[88] *TRP* nos. 54, 59, 106, 118, 118.5, 129, 133, 142, 151, 158, 186.

[89] BM Hargrave 216/148; Bayne, *Select Cases*, 26; *TRP* no. 24. The Liber Intrationum contains extracts from the now lost registers of the council.

[90] The Ellesmere manuscripts are extracts from the Star Chamber books of orders and decrees made during the reign of Elizabeth. It may be that the punishments described in these cases were ordered by the Court of Star Chamber but they read more like punishment ordered by the council in its capacity as a board. On 25 October 1530 John Parsecke and others 'for having books against the King's proclamation' were 'judged to ride openly with papers in their own hands to throw the books into the fire' (HHL Ellesmere 2652/15). The case is also referred to in Ellesmere 6100 where it speaks of Semen, Tyndale, and others. A third reference in Ellesmere 436 on the same date is probably a different case since John Borstick was sent 'to the Tower for having books against the King's proclamation.' On 14 October John Coke was sent 'to the Fleet for having a New Testament contrary to the proclamation' (Ellesmere 2652/15). The proclamation was *TRP* no. 129.

proclamation. In addition, resistance to local officials or negligence on their part was an important concern in each of the bills. The earliest is dated January 1528. It was probably based on one of the proclamations in November 1527 designed to supply the market. James Newby was accused of not selling grain according to the King's proclamation and not obeying the bailiff when he was ordered to do so. He was accused before the commissioners but still would not obey. In addition he played at unlawful games and resisted all efforts at correction; therefore, the constable and bailiffs were forced to turn to the Star Chamber. Newby's answer, in which he simply denied all the accusations, has survived, but there is no evidence of the final result. The proclamations had provided that offenders were to be reported to the 'council in the Star Chamber,' consequently the town officials were following these instructions; however, they seemingly resorted to this only because they could not get Newby to obey, for they maintained that they could 'do to him the best and worst that they can for he sets not a stay by them all.'[91]

The following November the inhabitants of Yaxley and Holme accused Thomas Alward and Christopher Branston of engrossing and forestalling 'contrary to the King's proclamation.' The citizens maintained that they had complained to a justice of the peace, but he would take no action and threatened them with imprisonment if they molested the accused. Complaints at sessions also resulted in no action. Seemingly in desperation they appealed to Wolsey and asked him 'to set such directions according to the King's high pleasure and proclamations' that they would not starve.[92] A third bill was addressed to the Star Chamber probably early in 1531. The constable and bailiff of Taunton in Somerset accused John Combe of playing at unlawful games contrary to the King's proclamation. Efforts by town officials to enforce the proclamation were resisted. As a result other persons in the town had begun to ignore their authority, and good order could not be maintained. The defendant answered the bill by denying the charges. We do not have the court's decision, but depositions taken from witnesses seem to establish that the accusations were true. Again the Star Chamber seems to have been resorted to only because local officials could not cope with an

[91] St Ch 2/22/340; Leadam, *Star Chamber*, II, 168ff; *TRP* nos. 118, 118.5.
[92] Two bills have survived. The first reads like a simple complaint to Wolsey rather than a formal bill, but the second was phrased like a Star Chamber bill and included both the claim that poor men were being denied justice because of the power of overmighty subjects and that violence had been used. The second bill specifically requested that the accused be summoned to appear 'before Wolsey' and 'other the lords of the King's most honorable council.' St Ch 2/17/344; 2/23/104; Leadam, *Star Chamber*, II, 178ff.

overly powerful offender, and this was leading to a general breakdown of law and order.[93]

A fourth bill cannot be dated specifically. It was probably submitted after the enactment of the Statute of Proclamations, because it involved an offense committed in April 1539. Only the bill survives. It was brought by John Goodall, the energetic and tactless under-bailiff of Nicholas Shaxton, Bishop of Salisbury. It was part of a complex series of events that were intertwined with a jurisdictional dispute between the Bishop of Salisbury and the city officials of Salisbury.[94] Goodall accused the curate and priest of St Martins in Salisbury of encouraging idolatrous practices and failing to explain the true meaning of rites and ceremonies in violation of the proclamation of 16 November 1538. In addition they persuaded people not to eat eggs and cheese in Lent 'after your grace's proclamation concerning the same was published within the city of Sarum to the open and arrogant contempt also of your said proclamation.' The bill quoted at length from the section of the proclamation of 16 November dealing with ceremonies and idolatrous practices. It maintained that the priest at St Martins had refused to explain 'the true meaning and understanding of holy water, holy bread, creeping to the cross' and other ceremonies and had also allowed idolatrous practices the previous Easter.[95]

With the exception of the last bill, which was probably introduced after the passage of the Statute of Proclamations, the other bills were all either introduced by law enforcement officials who were unable to deal with offenders or they alleged that officials had failed to carry out their duties in enforcing the proclamations. There is nothing in any of the bills to suggest that offenses against proclamations were normally heard by the Court of Star Chamber. All that can be said is that in exceptional cases the Court of Star Chamber occasionally dealt with proclamations, but if the surviving records are at all representative of the total activity of the court, this was unusual.

A major change occurred after the Statute of Proclamations established a special conciliar court to deal with offenses against proclamations. The conciliar court was composed of twenty-six judges, including members of the privy council as well as lesser officials and heads of governmental departments. Thirteen members, including at least two of the most important officers of the realm, the lord chancellor, the lord treasurer, the lord president of the council,

[93] St Ch 2/18/307.
[94] Professor Elton has described these events in *Policy and Police*, 100ff, although he does not mention this bill.   [95] St Ch 2/16/91; *TRP* no. 186.

the lord privy seal, the lord chamberlain, the lord admiral, and the two chief justices were necessary for a quorum. The court was to sit 'in the Star Chamber at Westminster or elsewhere.' The chancellor and the lord privy seal with the assent of six of the court, upon information presented to them, could initiate process under the privy seal or the great seal. Accusations had to be brought within six months of the offense and the case had to be completed within eighteen months after the offense. The court could inflict imprisonment and fine and was empowered to diminish the penalties specified in the proclamations as it saw fit. The statute also stated that no offender would 'incur the danger and penalty' of a proclamation unless it has been proclaimed in his shire before the offense was committed.[96] The procedure of the court was revised four years later because according to the preamble of the amending act, the court had been extremely busy and it had proved difficult to achieve the quorum specified in the Statute of Proclamations within the time limit of eighteen months:

Divers and sundry informations have been given and had for the King against the same offenders before the said honorable council mentioned in the said act [Statute of Proclamations] according to the tenor and effect of the same act and the same informations after issue joined and witnesses published, have taken no effect, end, or perfect determination within the time limited by the same act, for and in default that there hath not been present so many of the King's said most honorable council as be limited and appointed by the same act; and so thereby offenders have been and be like hereafter to be unpunished, to the great encouraging of all such like offenders.[97]

The statute therefore provided that nine persons, including two of the important officials mentioned in the Statute of Proclamations, would be sufficient for a quorum. The closing sentence of the statute limited its duration to the life of Henry VIII.

Bills for at least fifteen cases which were heard by the court survive. They are easily recognizable from their unique address:

To the right honorable the Lord Archbishop Canterbury, the lord chancellor of England, the lord treasurer of England, the lord president of the King's most honorable council, the lord privy seal, the great chamberlain of England and other the King's most honorable council named and appointed by an act of Parliament made at Westminster the xxviiith day of April in the xxxi year of the reign of our sovereign lord

---

[96] 31 Henry VIII c. 8. What follows is largely a summary of my previously published work, 'The Enforcement of Royal Proclamations,' 205–31.

[97] 34 and 35 Henry VIII c. 23.

King Henry the Eighth for the hearing and determination of the contempts and offenses committed and done by any person or persons contrary to the King's highness' proclamations set forth, made and proclaimed by the King's highness and his most honorable council named in the said act or the most part of them by virtue of the said act.[98]

The bills followed a careful formula that specifically stated their reliance on the authority of the Statute of Proclamations. They quoted a portion of the statute as well as the proclamation upon which the accusation was based. Furthermore, they stated that the proclamation was based on the authority of the statute and that it was proclaimed in the defendant's county on a specific date before the offense took place. They then stated that the alleged offense was in violation of a proclamation. They ended by requesting that the defendant be subpoenaed to appear and answer the charges before 'your lordships'; however, one bill requested appearance before 'the King's Court of the Star Chamber.'[99]

Twelve of the fifteen bills alleged offenses against the proclamation of 16 February 1541 forbidding unlicensed exports. Two rested on the proclamation of 4 April 1542 prohibiting the stealing or keeping of hawks' eggs or the raising of certain kinds of hawks,[100] and the final bill charged violation of three proclamations.

Sebastian Danckered and Henry Pyntill were accused of shipping cheese and butter in violation of the proclamation of 7 January 1544 which temporarily forbade all export of a series of food items. The port officials of Ipswich and Colchester were also accused of collusion, possibly because it included a very severe fine of £100 for port officials who allowed illegal export. In addition a number of other persons were accused of violating a proclamation of 20 May 1541 which had modified the earlier one of 16 February to allow the victualling of Calais, but had warned that anyone who maintained he was going to ship to Calais and then went elsewhere would incur the penalties of the earlier proclamation.[101] Each of the proclamations carried an unusually severe penalty and promised a substantial reward to informers, probably to attract private prosecution. The

---

[98] St Ch 2/1/153. The remaining bills are found in 2/2/168; 2/2/170; 2/2/210; 2/17/195; 2/20/188; 2/23/7; 2/23/183; 2/23/208; 2/23/248; 2/23/310; 2/28/14; 2/28/24; 2/29/96; 2/29/175. Two other surviving cases may also have been addressed to the court. One is so badly mutilated that the full address is lost; 2/8/150 and the other consist of only a series of depositions which dealt with an offense against a proclamation 2/2/22.

[99] St Ch 2/28/24.

[100] *TRP* nos. 197.6 and 211. The proclamation is dated 16 April 1542 in *TRP* but this is probably the date when it was proclaimed. Both bills cite it as having been issued on 4 April.   [101] *TRP* nos. 197.6, 201, 225.

surviving bills confirm that they were successful. The King's attorney general, William Whorwood, was responsible for initiating process in only three cases. Three were introduced by John Mascy, searcher of Chester, but the remaining all came from private citizens, including individuals who were certainly professional informers.[102] The bills are difficult to date, but the offenses were always dated in the bills. Six occurred in 1541, seven in 1542 and one in each of the two following years. All but two stem from the period before the revision of the Statute of Proclamations; however, these two bills make it possible to make some comparisons with the earlier bills in order to try to determine if the enactment of 34 and 35 Henry VIII c. 23 improved the efficiency of the court. The bills, if the accusations were true, suggest some corruption among port officials. In three cases they were specifically accused of allowing illegal export, and in three other cases, although no specific charge was made in the bill, it is clear that, if the defendants were guilty, the port officials were implicated.[103]

Some of the cases survive in rather complete form. Answers are available in ten cases, replications in three and a rejoinder in one. The answers reveal that the defendants were very aware of the terms of the Statute of Proclamations. At times they based their defense on the specific wording of that statute. One defendant argued that the bill had not alleged 'that the said proclamation was made at four several market towns according to the tenor of the said Statute of Proclamations.' Another maintained that the offense had taken place before the proclamation was actually proclaimed in his county.[104] The most interesting answer was that given by Robert Vawdrey, deputy customer of Chester. He was accused by the attorney general of allowing illegal export of grain. He maintained that he did not have to answer because he was a deputy customer, and the proclamation named only customers, comptrollers and searchers, but said nothing about deputy customers. Therefore, Vawdrey maintained, 'he is not charged nor chargeable by the said proclamation for the same proclamation is to be taken and construed in like manner and form as a statute penal which ought not to be construed by any equity but directly according to the word in the same contained.' He went on to answer and to deny the charge, but his plea seems to have been taken seriously, because efforts were made in the interrogatories

---

[102] St Ch 2/2/168; 2/2/170; 2/2/210 for attorney general's bills. 2/24/310; 2/28/14; 2/28/24 for Mascy's bills. Henry Sayer and Baldwyn Smythe, both professional informers, were responsible for three of the actions.
[103] St Ch 2/22/217; 2/29/96; 2/29/175. [104] St Ch 2/23/248; 2/29/175.

to establish that even if he were a deputy customer, he still did the same work and had the same responsibilities as a customer.[105]

The replications and rejoinders usually failed to provide any new information, but one replication is interesting because it suggests that lack of a quorum may have been a common plea by defendants. John Hogges accused Thomas Isakke of keeping goshawks contrary to the King's proclamation. Isakke admitted keeping the hawks, but maintained that it had not been proclaimed in his vicinity and therefore he had no knowledge of it. Hogges argued in the replication that since Isakke had confessed keeping the hawks he should be awarded the decision, but possibly to meet a defense that the court lacked a quorum Hogges' replication stated that Isakke had made his confession in the court 'being fully furnished with such number of the King's most honorable council as be mentioned in the said act [Statute of Proclamations].'[106]

Depositions have also survived for some cases. In one case they were taken in the Court of Star Chamber. A note at the end reads: 'The said John Spodill came into the Court of Star Chamber' and depositions were taken by Thomas Eden, the clerk of the Star Chamber.[107] In three cases commissions were used to take depositions in the country. A commission of *dedimus potestatem* was employed in one post 1543 case, probably, as was not unusual in Star Chamber proceedings, to lighten the burden on the court. The commissioners were ordered to arrest the ship and goods seized and to call the parties before them, and if 'it shall appear to them the same corn to be forfeit' they were given full power to keep the ship to the King's use and to sell the corn. They were also instructed to make a report of their actions 'in this Court of Star Chamber.'[108] In one case the interrogatories reveal that the informer took seriously the penalty of forfeiture of all goods and chattels specified in the proclamation, because one of the questions he submitted was 'of what substance in goods, money, plate and other things is the said defendant worth.'[109]

Since results have not survived for most of the cases, it is difficult to determine how effective the court was, but it is at least possible to say something about the swiftness of its procedure by comparing the time elapsed between the last offense cited and the taking of the deposition in five cases where this information is available. Three of them were heard before the quorum of the court was changed and

[105] St Ch 2/2/211.
[106] St Ch 2/23/248.
[107] St Ch 2/19/209.
[108] St Ch 2/22/217.
[109] St Ch 2/29/96.

they moved relatively slowly. The longest period between the offense and the depositions was twenty-two months in one of the cases involving John Mascy. The offense took place in July 1542 and depositions were not taken until May 1544.[110] Another case citing an offense in July 1542 resulted in a commission being sent out in June 1543 and depositions being returned in October 1543. In this case there must have been almost a half year's delay between the bill and the commission. The offense took place in July 1542 and by the limitations imposed by the Statute of Proclamations information had to be brought by January 1543. Yet the commission was not sent out until at least five months after the last possible date for the bill, and the report did not come back until four months later.[111] The only case that moved relatively swiftly before the quorum for the court was amended was the attorney general's case against Robert Vawdrey. The offenses were committed in June and August of 1541 and depositions were taken on 4 July 1542, thirteen months after the first offense cited.[112] After the Statute of Proclamations was amended the procedure was more swift. John Lysse seized a ship which Symond Edwards was using for illegal exporting on 11 November 1543. The bills can be dated specifically, because the commission made reference to it. He submitted the bill on 29 November 1543. The commission was sent out the same day with orders to decide the issue and report back by 20 January 1544.[113] Baldwyn Smythe and Richard Barnes were not so fortunate, but possibly the blame rests on them for bringing such a complex case. In one bill they alleged a series of five offenses committed between 13 July 1544 and 12 September 1544 by seven different men. Depositions for the informers were taken in court on 29 February 1545 and those for two of the defendants are dated 23 April 1545, nine months after the date of the first offense.[114] None of this, of course, reveals the full time involved in the case, but it does suggest that the preamble to 34 and 35 Henry VIII c. 23 was not exaggerating when it maintained that it was difficult to secure convictions within the time limit of eighteen months, and that after the revision the court acted more swiftly.

It is more difficult to learn anything about the actual results of the cases or if the full penalties threatened in the proclamations were exacted. Some information on the second question can be obtained

[110] St Ch 2/2/174-6; 2/28/14.
[111] St Ch 2/29/96. This case spanned the period when 34 and 35 Henry VIII c. 23 was enacted. [112] St Ch 2/2/210-12.
[113] St Ch 2/22/217; 2/23/183. [114] St Ch 2/17/195; 2/19/209.

when it is possible to trace the careers of the defendants after the decision must have been given. John Mascy, the searcher of Chester, in addition to initiating action in three cases, was also accused by the attorney general in another case. He was either not convicted or the full penalty was not applied, for he was still searcher at Chester on 29 July 1546, four years after the alleged offense.[115] Robert Vawdrey, who had presented that clever defense, was certainly not ruined professionally even if he lost the case. In October 1545 he was made serjeant-at-law at Chester.[116] Finally, Sebastian Danckard and Giles Hostman, two of the merchants accused by Baldwyn Smythe and Richard Barnes of shipping butter and cheese in violation of the proclamation of 7 January 1544, were allowed by the council to convey cheese with the remainder of their license, because they had not been able to use the full amount specified as a result of the restraint imposed by the proclamation.[117] All of this implies that, if the men were convicted, the full penalties in the proclamation were not applied.

This is substantiated by the one case for which a decree is available as the result of a unique recording on the King's Remembrancer's Memoranda Rolls in the Exchequer which at last makes it possible to discuss a case in its entirety. Henry Sayer accused Peter Henryksen and Harmar Artson of illegal export of grain on 31 March 1541 in violation of the proclamation of 16 February 1541. The defendants maintained that the goods were bound for an English port and that they had signed an obligation with the customer of Lynn. In addition, they maintained that the shipment had been made before the proclamation was proclaimed at Lynn. The depositions for the defendants, which were taken by commissioners in the country and returned to the court on 4 July 1541, contained testimony from nine witnesses, most of whom maintained that the grain had been shipped before the proclamation had been proclaimed at Lynn. The depositions for Sayers attempted to establish that port officials had been bribed.[118] On 14 June 1543, after the defendants failed to appear at the final hearing, the decree was issued by 'the honorable court of Star Chamber.' The court decided against the defendants. Both the grain and the ships were declared forfeit. Sayer received £50 6s 11½d,

---

[115] Dasent, I, 499. The offense occurred on 18 August 1542 (St Ch 2/2/170). Mascy seemingly had a bad reputation. He was accused of misconduct on 17 October 1539 (SP 1/154/37) and on 7 June 1545 the inhabitants of Chester complained to the council that he had seized certain Spanish wines from a merchant and he was ordered by the privy council to restore them (Dasent, I, 184).
[116] *LP* 20[2] no. 706[21].
[117] Dasent, I, 509, 513.
[118] St Ch 2/29/175.

one quarter of the total forfeiture.[119] At least in this case, the court had proved a useful instrument for enforcing royal proclamations, and after a two-year wait the informer was handsomely rewarded for his efforts. Nevertheless, the full penalties of the proclamation had not been imposed, and despite the fact that the goods had been seized it took a long time before the decision was rendered. In fact, the decree was not given until twenty-three months after the offense, in violation of the time limit set by the Statute of Proclamations. One wonders if the defendants would have had more success if they had appeared at the final hearing and reminded the court of the limitation.

Although the surviving cases demonstrate a rather extensive use of the conciliar court, there is no evidence that this court functioned as a body separate from the Court of Star Chamber. One bill requested appearance before 'the King's Court of the Star Chamber.' Depositions were taken in the Court of Star Chamber by the clerk of the Star Chamber, and commissioners were ordered to report to the 'Court of Star Chamber.' Even the single surviving decree indicates that the decision was given by 'the honorable court of Star Chamber.' The procedure of the court was identical with Star Chamber procedure, with the single exception that it relied very heavily on the Statute of Proclamations for authority.[120] Thus the major impact of the Statute of Proclamations on enforcement seems to have been to involve the Court of Star Chamber more actively in enforcement. Nevertheless this was an important change, for, as has been shown, the Star Chamber does not seem to have been used in the enforcement of proclamations before 1539 except in rare cases. After the repeal of the statute, the Court of Star Chamber seems not again to have been used to hear cases alleging offenses against proclamations. Only one proclamation issued in Edward VI's reign provided for enforcement there. I have not found any proclamation cases in the

[119] E 159/322 Michaelmas, L.

[120] A series of other bills dealing with proclamations offenses did not begin with the formal address normally used in statutory court bills. George Whelplay brought twenty-three bills between 1541 and 1543 based on violations of proclamation of 16 February 1541 forbidding unlicensed export. None of them was addressed in the normal manner used for other proclamations cases. Rather all were addressed to the King as was normal for Star Chamber cases. They followed two set forms. Fifteen bills followed a short form in which the bill simply cited the proclamation and asked for a writ of appearance 'before the lords of your most honorable council at Westminster.' St Ch 2/27/63; 2/27/90; 2/27/32; 2/27/40; 2/27/42; 2/27/64; 2/27/87; 2/27/91; 2/27/118; 2/27/93 (six bills). Eight bills used a longer form which ended with a request that the accused be summoned to appear before 'your honorable council in Star Chamber.' St Ch 2/18/149; 2/27/80; 2/27/93 (six bills).

Star Chamber Proceedings for the reign of Edward VI after the repeal of the Statute of Proclamations. Evidence of more extensive use of the Court of Star Chamber comes primarily from the reigns of Elizabeth I and James I.[121] Although the overall effectiveness of the court especially before the quorum was revised is open to doubt, it was brought in by the government to deal with those proclamations which had proven particularly difficult to enforce in the past. Even though the evidence is very limited, at least on the basis of the two surviving cases one is led to believe that there was some improvement in the efficiency of the court after the quorum requirement was changed.

The council also punished offenders against proclamations in the quasi-legal manner after 1539. On 3 September 1540 four men were 'adjudged to be set on the pillory in several places' with 'papers on their heads declaring their offenses' for causing the 'price of victuals to be enhanced contrary to the King's highness' proclamation.'[122] In April 1543 the council was especially busy. On 4 April John Glover, that stubborn Barking fisherman, was imprisoned and ordered to be set on the pillory for disobeying the proclamation on Thames fishing.[123] On 7 April eight printers were imprisoned for printing books 'contrary to the proclamation made on that behalf.' They were in prison for two weeks and then released and bound by recognizance to 'make by writing a true declaration what number of books and ballads they have bought within these three years last past, and what they have sold in gross, and what merchants they knew to have brought into the realm any English books of ill matters.' They also had to agree to pay whatever fines 'shall be set upon their heads for such offense touching the printing of unlawful books contrary to the proclamation they have printed and sold since the time of the said proclamation.' Three days later twenty-four book sellers were also bound in recognizance in the same way, and a book seller was imprisoned 'for delivering of a certain erroneous book.'[124]

---

[121] One case involving illegal export of wool, brass and hides, contrary to 'laws, statutes and proclamations' was heard shortly before the repeal of the Statute of Proclamations. It came to the Star Chamber in a rather unusual way. The defendants were indicted in the Admiralty, but since the value of the goods could not be known 'without the confession of the said parties offenders upon due examinations,' the plaintiff requested that the Star Chamber direct a commission 'to examine the said offenders' (St Ch 3/1/46). See Youngs, 'Proclamations', 247ff for description of Star Chamber involvement in enforcement of proclamations in the reign of Elizabeth.

[122] Nicolas, VII, 29. This must be a reference to an unfound proclamation, Appendix B item no. 28.   [123] Dasent, I, 190.

[124] *Ibid.* 107, 117, 120. The proclamation may have been *TRP* no. 186, for they were to report their activities for the previous three years.

After these very busy months the council register is strangely silent on its activities in enforcing proclamations both for the remainder of the reign of Henry VIII and for his son's reign despite the numerous proclamations mentioning the council under Somerset.[125]

As has been pointed out, the inevitable problem in trying to answer any questions about the enforcement of royal proclamations is the inadequate state of some records combined with the immense volume of court records which have survived. Consequently, any conclusions must be tentative and subject to correction when a thorough study of penal law enforcement in the early Tudor period is available. However, at least some limited answers can be given to the questions posed at the beginning of this chapter. For example, it is clear that proclamations were enforced in a great variety of places at different times in the early Tudor period. They were certainly enforced in the Exchequer and Star Chamber although not commonly before 1539. They were also enforced on occasion in local courts and quarter sessions, and the council dealt with them in a quasi-legal way in its administrative capacity. But local officials and central courts gave very little attention to royal proclamations in comparison with their activities in enforcing statute and common law. At times when their own interests were involved, they could be very diligent in attending to the orders in proclamations, but unless we are willing to ignore the complaints in the proclamations and the admonitions to local officials it would seem that enforcement was at times totally inadequate. Sometimes this may have been due to the unrealistic legislation they were asked to enforce. But lack of concern and effort on the part of local officials must have also been an important reason for poor enforcement. It is seldom possible to document inadequate enforcement from court records, but the government certainly felt that improvement was needed especially in the late 1530s when the severe penalties in the proclamations for negligent officials suggest a growing exasperation with their inadequate efforts. However, for

[125] There are additional cases in the Ellesmere extracts that were probably heard by the Court of Star Chamber. One on 14 February 1542 involved Robert Danby, who was accused of transporting corn 'against the King's proclamation' (HHL Ellesmere 436). This is probably the same case which was addressed to the statutory court in the Star Chamber proceedings. St Ch 2/2/167. A second case involved Edward Baker, who was sent to the fleet 'for maintenance at the bar in a cause for conveying corn against the King's proclamations.' HHL Ellesmere 2652/15. A third dealt with keeping a hawk in violation of a proclamation. *Ibid.* The last two were probably based on *TRP* no. 270, regulating legal pleading. One reads 'Richard Strode to the Fleet for pleading his father's cause at the bar against the proclamation in that behalf' in October 1546 and the other on 29 April 1547 reads 'Humfrey Stuart to Wimbush for speaking at the bar contrary to the King's proclamation.' *Ibid.*

the present we are in no position to say whether law enforcement officials enforced common and statutory law more zealously than proclamations. The courts certainly paid more attention to other forms of legislation, but proclamations were not often used to make new regulations, and at least in the early part of the period they seldom specified judicial jurisdiction.

It is clear that the year 1539 was a major turning point in the enforcement of royal proclamations. The Statute of Proclamations not only set up a special court to deal with them, but it probably also encouraged prosecutions in the Exchequer. The conciliar court set up by the act appears never to have functioned as intended. The result was that the Court of Star Chamber was forced to deal with a sizable influx of proclamation cases. The repeal of the statute seems to have ended the practice of resort to the Court of Star Chamber, but the number of informations citing proclamations in the Exchequer increased especially during the second half of the reign of Edward VI. Most of these were based on both statutes and proclamations probably because of the emphasis in proclamation texts in the last years of Edward's reign and the effort of the government to have them enforced in the ordinary courts of the realm. The abortive effort to improve enforcement at the end of the reign by means of 'commissioners for consideration and execution of penal laws' suggests that this method was not entirely successful. But it is significant that the two major efforts in the early Tudor period to improve enforcement were probably the work of the two statesmen who most clearly recognized that royal proclamations were limited instruments and used them to uphold rather than to compete with Parliamentary legislation.

CONCLUSIONS

Matters of importance, however, relating to the sovereign or to the people are referred to the King's privy council, consisting as decreed by the late King Henry, of sixteen great personages; and whatever they decide there is published by edicts and proclamations which have the vigor and force of laws, provided they do not extend to capital punishment, or to the disinheritance of anyone; or that they be not in effect repugnant to the ancient statutes. Those who disregard these proclamations are imprisoned, but not for life, and the decrees remain in force at the King's pleasure, and during his reign.[1]

In 1551 Daniel Barbaro, the Venetian ambassador, wrote a remarkably accurate description of the authority of royal proclamations. By the date that he wrote he had the advantage of being able to draw upon the definitions which had been formulated during the reigns of the Tudor Kings. Even though the Statute of Proclamations was repealed three years earlier, he seems to have relied on it for his definition, probably because he felt that it provided the clearest statement. He was, of course, correct. The 1539 act both defined and limited the powers of royal proclamations in a way that finally made it possible to describe their legislative function in specific terms. Even though it was repealed within a decade after its enactment, it had a major impact in setting precedents that not only influenced Barbaro's description but which were also commonly cited in the Elizabethan and Stuart debates over royal proclamations.

Because of its importance in defining the authority of royal proclamations and providing for a new system of enforcement, the Statute of Proclamations deserves a good deal of attention. However, it is surprising that there has been so much furor about the alleged threat it or the original government bill posed to the legislative supremacy of Parliament. Although there were objections to the original bill, there is no evidence which would suggest that the government sought to acquire an unlimited power to legislate by royal proclamations. Tudor monarchs and their ministers never used

CSPV v no. 703, p. 341.

CONCLUSIONS

proclamations in a way that posed a major challenge to Parliament. Even Wolsey and Somerset, who had little patience with Parliament and who might have preferred to legislate by decree, did not use them consistently to enact new permanent legislation. Even to say that the Tudor Kings 'legislated' by proclamation would seem to involve a very broad definition of that term. Proclamations were 'law' in that they embodied rules binding on citizens and were enforced in the courts, but they were a very different kind of law from that enacted by statutes. They normally did not have the permanence associated with Parliamentary legislation, and they seldom made new regulations except on matters dealing with coinage. Even in this they were limited to setting values on coins and declaring what coins were legal tender. They were used to improve enforcement of old laws by introducing new enforcement procedures and penalties or by publicizing the King's desire to see those laws obeyed. They added to statutes, dispensed from them and even suspended them temporarily, but they normally did not compete with statutes or challenge the authority of Parliament. A history of penal law legislation based solely on proclamations would be a very slim volume indeed, and, as has been shown throughout this work, could not be written without constant reference to Parliamentary legislation. Furthermore, proclamations never even touched the common law and especially that portion of the law which was most important to Englishmen – the land law. They were, especially during the 1530s, often used as delegated legislation, and in that sense they were used in a very 'modern' way.[2] Although their authority was not clearly defined at the beginning of the early Tudor period, the broad limits of their power had been set down. These limits were generally accepted and seldom exceeded throughout the period.

Proclamations were limited instruments, but they were important to the smooth running of early Tudor government. In addition to their value as propaganda devices and for publicizing the King's commands, they served to aid in the enforcement of statutes both by the changes they sometimes introduced and by the threats to enforcement officials. Finally, they were also essential instruments for instituting temporary emergency solutions to deal with situations which could not wait for the next session of Parliament. The only real controversy which arose over proclamations in the entire period was the result of an effort to make them more effective instruments

---

[2] C. K. Allen, *Law in the Making*, 6th ed. (Oxford, 1959), 515ff.

for serving these purposes. But it is hard to conceive of the struggle over the Statute of Proclamations as a major constitutional crisis, as later historians have maintained. It was only in the Stuart period that the use of proclamations became a constitutional issue.[3] Later historians interpreting the Tudor period in terms of the conflicts of the Stuart period were responsible for giving the Statute of Proclamations a nefarious reputation which it ill deserved and for mistakenly associating the use of royal proclamations with government by decree and the legend of Tudor despotism.

It is difficult to conceive of contemporaries viewing proclamations as instruments of tyranny even while the Statute of Proclamations was in effect. They were often irritated by their contents. They even resisted or evaded the orders in them both passively and actively. But there is no evidence that they saw them as a threat to their ancient liberties. Furthermore, no Tudor government could have successfully used them in this fashion. The Thames fisherman, William Smith, was angered when in 1543 the King's proclamation threatened the traditional way of carrying on his livelihood, but he was not intimidated by the King's authority. One need only recall his response to the water bailey of London, when in an effort to enforce the proclamation on Thames fishing he threw Smith's fish overboard, to realize how far removed from the realities of Tudor life any effort to use royal proclamations as a weapon of despotism would have been:

The said Smith asked me where mine authority was saying I know you for none officer. I answered here is the King's proclamation for mine authority, is not this sufficient for this? He said no, bring a proclamation under My Lord Admiral's seal and I will obey it or else not. And then I commanded the same Smith in the King's name and my lord mayor's name to be before your lordship and masterships this Thursday at your court at the Guildhall to answer for his offences aforesaid. He answered me saying, and if my lord mayor have any more to do with me than I with him, let him come to me and if he will, for I cannot come tomorrow. I commanded him then to come on Sunday next or any other day at his best pleasure. He answered and said that he had other business to do. He would neither come on Sunday nor none other days.[4]

[3] On this see Cope, *American Journal of Legal History*, xv, 215–21. See also BM Harl. 6842/146, which lists a series of grievances against the use of proclamations in the reign of James I.   [4] CLRO Rep. 10/346.

APPENDIX A

TEXTS OF PROCLAMATIONS NOT INCLUDED IN HUGHES AND LARKIN

(The numbering system I have adopted is that used by Hughes and Larkin. In cases where some doubt exists I have appended an explanatory note justifying my acceptance of the text as a new proclamation.)

No. 135.5   Providing victual for London
(10 October 1531; CLRO Journals 13/285)

The kyng our soveraigne lord for many grete and dyverse consyderacions his grace specyally movyng wyllyng his Citie and chambre of London to be substancyally furnysshed and provyded of whete malte rye and all other grayne as well for the comoditie of the noble men of this his Realme and all other his subiectes repayryng to the same Citie specyally at this his parliament geveth full power licence and auctoritie to all and every person or persons within this his Realme as well within the liberties as without that wyll repare to the sayd Citie wyth any whete malte rye or other grayne for the vitaillyng of the same may at all tymes from hensforth at his or their liberties frely quyetly and peasably lede carry or conveye the same to the sayd Citie as well by lande as by water and further his highnes wyllyth and geveth straitly in commaundement to all Justice of Peace Shireffes mayres baylyffs constables Custumers comptrollers Serchers and their deputies and all other his graces officers ministres and subiects as well within the liberties as without to whome in this cace yt shall apperteigne that they and every of theym permite and suffre all and everysuche person or persons frely and quyetly without any manner let or interupcion of theym or any of theym to leade carrye and conveye all suche whete malte rye and other greyne to the seyd citi for the victaillyng of the same as they woll advoyd the kynges high displeasure any Acte proclamacion restraynte commaundement or provysyon heretofore had made or gyven to the contrarye vndre his grete Seale or otherwyse notwithstandyng provyded alwayes nevertheles that the Custumers comptrollers Serchers or one of theym in every porte haven or creke where any suche grayne or other vitaill shall fortune to be laden for that purpose shall take sufficient boundes of the owners or conveyors of the same grayne that they shall truely convey the same to the Citie aforseyd for the vituallyng therof and to none other place vpon payne of forfayture and god save the Kyng. Et hoc sub periculo incumbenti nullatenus ommittas Tunc ipso apud Westm x die octobr Anno R M vicesimo tercio.

APPENDIXES

No. 135.6 Proroguing parliament
(4 October 1532; CLRO Journals 13/348d)

Where as of late the kynge our soveraigne lord vpon sundry respects signyfied to be his pleasure towching the prorogation of his moost high courte of parliament vnto the xvi daye of Octobre nowe next comyng hys gracys pleasure ys that nowe vpon lyke Respects hys highnes hath appoynted that the same his highnes courte of parliament shalbe proroged from that day vntyll the iiijth daye of February nowe next comying to his palays of Westmynster and therefore his highnes wyllyth and comaundith that alle suche persones as owe to geve attendaunce at his saide courte of parlyament shall make their repaire and kepe their apparaunces at the said place and at the iiijth day of February aforesaid nowe appoynted accordyngly and god save the kyng.

No. 138.5 Distraining knighthood
(26 April 1533; Dur 3/78/3d. Text: same as *TRP* no. 48)

No. 174.5 Permitting exchanges and rechanges
(13 August 1537; CLRO Journals 14/41)

Albeit the Kynges most Royall maiestie lately signyfied to all and singuler his lovyng Subiects by his graces proclamacion vnder his greate Seale that noo persone or persones shuld make exchaunge nor rechaunge contrary to his lawes and statutes in that case provided / Yet nevertheles at the humble petycions of dyvers and sondry merchauntes his lovyng subiettes / his highnes of his excellent goodnes is contented and pleased that all and synguler marchaunttes aswell straungers as other his lovying subiects shall use their exchaunges and rechaunges as they dyd and vsed afore his saide proclamacion without interupcon of any persone vntyll the xx day of Octobre next comying his graces saide proclamacon not withstandynge / Provided alwaye that alle and every suche persone and persones whiche shall exchaunge or rechaunge doo make a true and Juste declaracion of the particularities of the somes by any of them exchaunged or rechaunged before his graces Counsaill in the Sterred Chambre on thissday the feaste of alle saynttes next comyng / to thentent that a fynall ordre and determynacion may be hadd and made by advice of his graces counsayll aswell for satisfacion of suche dueties as shall vpon their examynacions appere to be rightfully due to his highnes as for the manor and facion of using the said exchaunges hereafter; goven under his graces great seale the xiij day of August in the xxix yere of his moste noble reigne.

No. 191.5 Pricing wines
(10 November 1539; CLRO Journals 14/269-296d)

Where as yt ys ordeyned and provyded by statuyt that the prices of Gascoygne and frenche wynes shulde be lymtted and declared by the lord

APPENDIXES

Chauncellour of england lorde presydent of the kynges most honorable cownsayle lorde pryvye seale/ and other the Councellors of our sayd soveraigne lord specyfyed and declaryd yn the sayd statuyt as by the same statuyt made and establisshed yn the parlyament begonne and holden at Westminster the thyrde day of Novembre yn the xxith yere of the kynges most gracyous Reign and contynued by dyverse progracions/ more playnely appyeryth forasmoche as the sayd lordes and Counsaylers yn execuson of the sayd Acte have by theyr deliberate advyses taxed Lymyted assigned and appoynted the pryces of Gascoign and frenche wynes to be sold withyn thys hys realme that ys to saye eny tonne of the Best Gascoign wyne or frenche wyne to be solde after the rate and pryce of fower poundes sterlinge the tonne and not above and every pype hoggeshed ponchean teerse and other vessel of the same wyne to be solde for theyr quantyties after and accordyng to the same Rate and not above/ and for smalle and thynne wynes to be solde vnder the sayd Rate as the byers and sellers therof can agree/ The kynges most Royall maiestye therfore straytly chargeth and comaundeth all manner hys subiectes and others puttyng any manner gascoigne and frenche wynes to sale withyn thys his Realme/ that they no any of theym yn any manner of wyse by any crafte couyn or private agrement shall sell any manner of gascoign or frenche wynes above the sayd price and rate of fower poundes sterling the tonne/ and every pype hoggeshed ponchon tyers and other vessell of the same wynes to be sold for theyr quantyties after and accordyng to the same rate and not above/ And to sell the sayd small and thynne wynes vnder the sayd rate in manner and forme above specyfyed/ and not above/ vpon payne to forfait and pay suche penaltyies as be conteignyd and expressed yn the same act/ And moreouer hys high pleasure and commaundment also ys that all synguler mayers sheryffes/ baylyffes constables and other offycers to whome yt apperteignyth that they and every of theym with all dylygence cawse and see that thys hys proclamacion be put yn due execuson after the tenor of the same/ And also accordyng to an other Act of parlyament establissed yn the parlyament above rehersed ageynst suche as woll refuse to sell theyr wynes at prices taxed as ys aforesayd as they woll answer therto at theyr vttermost perylles Et hoc sub periculo incumbenti nullatenus ommittatis T me ipso apud Westm viii de Novembr Anno xxxi.

No. 197.7   A proclamation concernyne eatynge of whyte meates

(16 February 1541; KRO NR/ZPr 15; BM Harl. 7614/195)

(Text: Same as *TRP* no. 177 with exception of last sentence which is omitted in this proclamation)

No. 311.5   Limiting access to court because of plague

(August 1548; CLRO Journals 15/373-373d)

Forasmuche as the kinges Matie ys adverteysyd that thinfeccon of the comen plage daylye encreasythe in that his highnes Cytye of london and that dyvers and manye citezens and Inhabitaunttes of the same have daylye recourse in to the courtt for dyvers their affayers and singular busynes to the greate daunger of his moost royall personne and other his nobles and Lovinge servaunttes attendauntt vppon the same his highnes therfore by Thadvice of his moost entyerly belovyd vncle Edwarde duke of Somersett governor of his moost royall person and protector of all his Realms domynyons and Subiecttes and the resydue of his Mates counsell streightlye chargythe and commaundythe all and singular Thinhabitantes and all other his lovinge subiectes and Resydaunttes in the Cytye of London the Suburbes and libertyes of the same that none of them be so hardye as to repayer or comme into the court at Anye tyme on this syde the last day of this present monthe of August Vppon payne of his highnes displeasur and as they and everye of theym will awnser to the same at their vttermost perills God save the kynge.

No. 313.5 Prohibiting export of victual
(26 September 1548; CLRO Journals 15/382d)

(Hughes and Larkin list this as a draft of no. 315. Since it is unlikely that a draft would survive in the London records and since *TRP* no. 315 is also recorded in the London records [CLRO Journals 15/389], I have rejected this explanation and consider them separate proclamations. There are a number of minor differences between the two texts, but the central difference is that *TRP* no. 315 forbids export without licenses obtained 'after the date of this proclamation' thereby voiding all old licenses. This proclamation does not contain that phrase and thereby allows export under old licenses.)

Forasmuche as the Kinges most royall matie consideringe the highe prises of corne and other victualls the which of late ys rysen in dyvers places within his maties realmes dominions and the marches and confynes of the same hathe thought yt mete weyinge the wealthe and commodytye of his subiects to have a restrayt for a season for all manner of grayne and vyctual in all places within this realme of England/ His most excellent matie therfore with Thadvyse of his most derest vncle Edward duke of Somerset governor of his most royall person and protector of all his realmes and dominions and subiectes and other of his most honerable counsaille streightlye commaundythe all and everye his subiects that they nor enye of them after the publyshing of his proclamacion shall transporte or carye over the seas into anye owtwarde parties eny manner of greyne butter chese or other kind of victualls with owt his specill licence vnder the great seale of England to be had and obteynyd for the same (his maties townes of Calyes bullyon and other his piers beyond the seas onlye excepted) vppon payne not onlye to encurr all suche paynes as by the statutes and proclamacions ar provyded in this behallf and to forfeyt the greyne and victualls so conveyd but allso to be further punissyd by imprisonmenttes of their bodyes and other wyse to the tyrryble example of all others/

provydyd always that everye person transportinge eny manner of graynes or other kind of victualles vnto his maties sayd townes and other his pieries beyond the seases shall not onlye entre the same into the custumers books but shall with one sufficient surtye with hym be bounde by obligacon vnto the kinges matie to be taken by the customers and comptroller of the port or creke where the seyd greyne shall be shippyd in the double value of the seyd greyne or victualls to discharge the same at his seyd townes and other his pieries and not ells where/ and to bringe a true certyfycate with in four monthes next after from the kinges maties deputies of Callis or bullion and iiij other of his counsaile there at the least that the seyd grayne and other victualls so shippyd were ther dyschargyd accordingly provydyd allso that of his custums subsydies and other dutyes due unto his matie in this behalf be dulye awnseryd as apperteynythe/ provydyd also that this proclamacon shall contynue duringe the kinges pleasur and no longer.

No. 330.5 Regulating wool trade
(29 April 1549; Grafton 42–44v)

(This proclamation is similar to *TRP* no. 331 issued 18 May 1549. There are however significant differences in both the dating and the contents. *TRP* no. 331 contains two clauses which are not in the proclamation included in the Grafton collection. Either Grafton was incredibly careless or this is in fact a separate proclamation which was revised three weeks later by *TRP* no. 331.)

For asmuche as vpon the pitifull complainte made vnto the kynges maiestie by his louyng subiectes the clothiers of this his Realme it appereth that through the gredines of some persones, who perceiuyng that Wolles is so necessary for the kepyng of the multitude of his highnes subiectes from idlenes, that it cannot bee lacked, colourably made and named themselfes factors, for Marchauntes of the staple, and so haue of late daies used to buy and sell Wooles, for their singuler profite, not onely the price of the same Wolles is so aduaunced, that within short tyme, if it be not forseen, a greate nomber of his subiectes, shalbee destitute of liuyng, and driuen to suche misery, as is not tollerable in any good common wealth, but also that the Clothiers, cannot make Clothes of the iust bredth, length, content and goodnes, that is prescribed by the lawes and statutes of this his Realme, wherby, greate infamy hath in forrain nacions, growen to this Realme, and thesaied Clothes in some places have been burnte, to the greate losse of the Marchauntes, and in some places have been banished, and forboden to bee brought thether: his highnes consideryng the daungiers, that maie thereby ensue to this his realme, and mindyng the preuencion thereof, nothyng doubtyng, but suche as be his louyng, faithfull and obedient subiectes will willyngly do for the loue of the countrey that those that be eiuill, must be forced to do for feare, by theaduise of his moste entierly beloued uncle, Edward duke of Somerset, Gouernor of his royall persone, and Protector of all his realmes, dominions and subiectes, and the rest of his Maiesties priuie counsaill straightly willeth, chargeth and commaundeth, that from, and after the first daie of June next comnyng, no person upon pain of his maiesties displeasure and greuous imprisonment of his body, other then suche persons and their houshold seruauntes, as shall conuert thesame, onely into Yarne, Clothe, Hattes, Cappes, Girdelles, Worsted Stamin, Saie, Arras, Tapestrie, or any other kinde of thyng, to be wrought within this realme, and Marchantes of the Staple, and their houshold seruauntes, for the onely prouision of the said Staple, and for to be shipped onely to thesaied Staple, shall by hym or herself, or by any other, buye or bargain, or take promise of bargain, of any Wolles, beyng nowe unshorne, of the growyng of the Shires, or Counties of this realme, or of Wales, or any of theim. Also, his highness by the aduise aforesaied, straightly chargeth and comaundeth, that no persone, from, and after thesaied first daie of June, shall buye or bargain, for any Yarne, other then suche, or his or their householde seruauntes, as shall conuert the same into Clothes, Hattes, Cappes, Girdelles, Worstedes, Saies, Stamin, Arras, Tappastrie, or other thynges to bee bought within this realme, upon pain of his graces displeasure, and imprisonment of his body.

And for the better execucion hereof his highnes by the aduise aforesaied, straightly chargeth and commaundeth all and singuler Justices of Peace, Maiors, Sherifes and Bailifes not onely to se this Proclamacion truely executed, but also if any person, be iustly accused before hym or them, for contempnyng, or breakyng this Proclamacion, or any parte therof, thei shall commit suche persone to warde, there to remain without bayle or mainprise till the kynges maiesties, and his saied Counsailes pleasure shalbee further knownen.

APPENDIX B

ROYAL PROCLAMATIONS FOR WHICH NO TEXT HAS BEEN FOUND (1485–1553)

(1) After November 1485, Forbidding exchanges, C 66/562/11, not in Steele.
(2) 2 February 1486, A general pardon, Hall, *Chronicle*, 431, Steele no. 6a.
(3) 1487, Prohibiting trade with Empire, C 82/34, Steele no. 7b.
(4) 5 December 1496, Revising statutes on artificers and labourers, Kingsford, *Chronicles*, 212, Steele no. 24b.
(5) January 1497, Expelling Scots from realm, C 82/164, Steele no. 24c.
(6) Before August 1501, Distraint of knighthood, E 198/4/19, not in Steele.
(7) Early 1503, Distraint of knighthood, E 198/4/22, not in Steele.
(8) 9 July 1504, Trade treaty with Spain, Bayne, *Select Cases*, 37, not in Steele.
(9) 17 August 1508, Against resort to court (sweating sickness), James Gairdner, *Historia Regis Henrici Septimi* (London, 1858), 128, Steele no. 51a.
(10) 12 May 1509, Distraint of knighthood, E 198/4/27, not in Steele.
(11) Before November 1511, Proclamation against excess in apparel, *CSPV*, II, 138, Steele no. 57.
(12) 13 November 1511, Proclamation of Holy League, *CSPV*, II, 166, Steele no. 58.
(13) Before 12 June 1517, Proclamation on taking and refusing pennies, SP 1/232/27, not in Steele.
(14) Before 29 July 1531, Restricting export of grain, SP 1/66/193–4, not in Steele.
(15) 1532, Pricing wine, 24 Henry VIII c. 6, not in Steele.
(16) Before August 1533, Forbidding regrating and forestalling in Calais, SP 1/78/184, not in Steele.
(17) 26 April 1535, Distraint of knighthood, BM Harl. 41/13, not in Steele.
(18) Before 2 September 1535, Forbidding export of victuals, SP 1/96/72, not in Steele.
(19) 30 September 1535, Proclamation for corn, SP 1/97/68, not in Steele.
(20) 30 September 1535, Proclamation for clothiers, SP 1/97/68, not in Steele.
(21) 1537, Distraint of knighthood, E/101/521/28 m 8, not in Steele.
(22) Before 28 March 1537, Dispensing Lenten fast from white meats, SP 1/117/158, not in Steele.

APPENDIXES

(23) December 1537, False and clipped coin, BM Titus B 1/421, not in Steele.
(24) March 1538, Rumors and seditious words, SP 1/130/95, not in Steele.
(25) September 1538, Suspending statute on cloth manufacture, St Ch 2/23/115, not in Steele.
(26) 16 May 1539, Forbidding carrying of sword in King's presence, *LP* 14[1] no. 989, Steele no. 181.
(27) 31 August 1540, Molesting strangers leaving realm, Kaulek, *Correspondence*, 214, not in Steele.
(28) Before 3 September 1540, Pricing victuals, Nicholas, VII, 29, not in Steele.
(29) 20 October 1540, Against Londoners coming to court, Nicholas, VII, 68, Steele no. 184.
(30) 23 February 1541, Forbidding loading on Flemish ships, Kaulek, *Correspondence*, 274, not in Steele.
(31) November 1542, Excluding Scots from realm and sending them to row as slaves in galleys, BM Add. MS 32648/170d, Steele no. 225.
(32) 30 November 1546, Distraint of knighthood, BM Add. MS 34148/174–5, not in Steele.
(33) 15 February 1547. Distraint of knighthood, *CPR* Edward VI 1547–8, 184–5, not in Steele.
(34) 25 February 1550, Staying killing of flesh in Lent, CLRO Rep. 12(1)/201d, not in Steele.
(35) 22 August 1550, Prohibiting hunting and hawking at court, Dasent, III, 110, Steele no. 388.
(36) 28 August 1550, Limiting access to court because of plague, Dasent, III, 110, Steele no. 387.
(37) *c.* 11 July 1551, Gentlemen to return to homes for fear of plague, Strype, II(i), 491, Steele no. 401.
(38) 13 October 1551, Calling in testons and groats, Strype, II(i), 488, Steele no. 407.
(39) 14 December 1551, False rumors about the new coinage, BM Royal 18c xxiv, Steele no. 410.
(40) February 1552, Abstinence in Lent, Strype, II(ii), 214, not in Steele.
(41) August 1552, Limiting access to court because of plague, Strype, II(ii), 213, Steele no. 413.
(42) 5 October 1552, Enforcing statute on great horses, Dasent, IV, 137, Strype II(i), 592, Steele no. 415.
(43) 8 October 1552, Forbidding selling of great horses, Strype, II(i), 588, Steele no. 416.
(44) November 1552, Enforcing statute on tillage, Strype, II(ii), 15, Steele no. 418.

INDEX OF STATUTES CITED

3 Edward I. c.34 (rumors), 80 n.59
13 Edward I, cc.
   1–6 (Statute of Winchester), 89, 90 n.12
   47 (fishing), 196 n.60
12 Edward II, c.6 (price setting), 89 n.9
2 Edward III, c.6 (archery), 90 n.12
9 Edward III, st.2, c.3 (coinage), 243 n.130
10 Edward III, st.3 (sumptuary laws), 104 n.50
23 Edward III, cc.
   6 (price setting), 89 n.9
   st.3, c.2 (victuals), 89 n.9
25 Edward III, st.5, cc.
   12 (coinage), 75 n.42, 76 n.43, 222 n.69, 278
   13 (coinage), 77 n.48, 107 n.59
27 Edward III, st.2, c.23 (wool winding), 194
31 Edward III, st.2, c.3 (fish and wine), 44
34 Edward III, c.20 (grain export), 71 n.25
37 Edward III, c.8 (sumptuary laws), 104 n.50
2 Richard II, st.1, c.5 (rumors), 80 n.59
5 Richard II
   st.1, c.2 (coin export), 42 n.42, 76 n.43, 79 n.57, 128 n.118, 129, 148, 164, 273; c.4 (wine prices), 110
   st.2, c.5 (religion), 136 n.140, 207 n.24
7 Richard II, cc.
   5 (vagabonds), 80 n.61
   11 (wine prices), 110
12 Richard II, c.6 (archery), 89 n.9, 90 n.12
14 Richard II, c.7 (staple), 75
15 Richard II, c.7 (staple), 75
16 Richard II, c.5 (Statute of Praemunire), 134 n.135
17 Richard II, cc.
   1 (coinage), 243 n.130
   7 (grain export), 71 n.26, 273
   9 (fishing), 196 n.60

2 Henry IV, cc.
   5 (exchange), 76 n.43
   15 (religion), 133 n.131, 134 n.140
4 Henry IV, c.10 (coinage), 243 n.130
11 Henry IV, c.4 (archery), 90 n.12
2 Henry V, st.1, c.7 (religion), 133 n.131, 136 n.140, 207 n.24
4 Henry V, c.6 (coinage), 76 n.43, 77 n.48
2 Henry VI, cc.
   6 (exchange), 76
   9 (coinage), 76 n.43
6 Henry VI, c.3 (laborers), 44
8 Henry VI, c.17 (staple), 45, 60 n.4, 75
11 Henry VI, c.13 (staple), 45, 75
14 Henry VI, c.2 (staple), 45, 60 n.4, 75
15 Henry VI, c.2 (grain export), 71 n.27, 119
18 Henry VI, c.3 (export of butter and cheese), 45
20 Henry VI, c.6 (grain export), 71 n.28
23 Henry VI, c.5 (grain export), 71 n.28
17 Edward IV, cc.
   1 (exchange), 76 n.44, 128 n.118
   3 (archery), 90 n.12
22 Edward IV, c.4 (price of bows), 192 n.46
3 Henry VII, cc.
   2 (law enforcement), 89
   6 (exchange), 76 n.45
   8 (customs), 274 n.71
   13 (price of bows), 192 n.46
4 Henry VII, cc.
   12 (law enforcement), 79
   15 (fishing), 196 n.60
   16 (enclosure), 94 n.21
   18 (coinage), 76
   19 (enclosure), 94 n.21
   23 (coin export), 76 n.44, 128 n.118
7 Henry VII, cc.
   6 (vagabonds), 81 n.65
   7 (wine prices), 110 n.65
11 Henry VII, cc.
   2 (vagabonds), 81 n.63, 90

INDEX OF STATUTES CITED

11 Henry VII, cc. (cont.)
  22 (laborers), 81
  65 (treaty with France), 68 n.11
12 Henry VII, c.3 (laborers), 81
19 Henry VII, cc.
  5 (coinage), 60 n.5, 77 n.51
  12 (vagabonds), 81 n.63
  14 (retaining), 80
  27 (staple), 75 n.41
1 Henry VIII, c.13 (coin export), 128 n.118
3 Henry VIII, cc.
  1 (coin export), 129 n.118
  3 (unlawful games), 90
4 Henry VIII, c.19 (subsidy), 3
6 Henry VIII, cc.
  2 (unlawful games), 90
  5 (enclosure), 95
  13 (archery), 90
7 Henry VIII, c.1 (enclosure), 95 n.24
14 & 15 Henry VIII, cc.
  7 (handguns), 90-1
  12 (coinage), 105
21 Henry VIII, c.10 (export bell metal), 210
22 Henry VIII, c.12 (vagabonds), 60 n.7, 119 n.94, 195 n.57
23 Henry VIII, cc.
  7 (wine prices), 19, 45-6, 110-11, 178, 244
  17 (wool winding), 194 n.54
24 Henry VIII, cc.
  3 (meat prices), 46, 113 n.76, 116
  6 (wine prices), 45, 110
  13 (apparel), 117 n.88
25 Henry VIII, cc.
  1 (meat prices), 15 n.45, 19, 46, 60 n.7, 114-16, 178
  2 (export, pricing victuals), 37 n.24, 44 n.46, 46, 60 n.7, 120-1, 171, 179, 202, 204, 214-15, 229, 240, 277 n.82
  13 (enclosure), 96 n.24
  14 (religion), 136 n.140, 207 n.24
  17 (handguns), 147 n.170, 185
26 Henry VIII, cc.
  1 (Act of Supremacy), 140 n.150
  10 (export), 46, 121
27 Henry VIII, cc.
  9 (meat prices), 115 n.84
  12 (cloth manufacture), 9 n.22, 17, 19, 123 n.107, 127
  14 (export), 146 n.168, 179 n.4
  21 (tithes), 135 n.139
  26 (Wales), 47, 116
  63 (Calais), 47
28 Henry VIII, cc.
  3 (Wales), 47
  8 (wool winding), 194 n.54
  14 (wine prices), 45, 111 n.67
31 Henry VIII, cc.
  5 (Hampton Court Chase), 181 n.13
  8 (Statute of Proclamations), vii-viii, 5-6, 12 n.39, 14, 18, 31, 33, 37 n.24, 43-5, 47-53, 57, 60 n.5, 61, 63, 85-6, 112, 116, 140, 141 n.151, 145, 152-79, 181-7, 199-202, 204, 206-7, 215, 222-3, 247-8, 257-8, 262, 271, 274-7, 279, 282-3, 289, 290 n.121, 292-3, 295
  11 (Wales), 47
  12 (hawking), 182 n.15
  14 (Act of Six Articles), 140, 141 n.151, 154 n.2, 189 n.39, 207 n.24
32 Henry VIII, cc.
  11 (hawking), 182 n.15
  14 (export), 143
  16 (aliens), 50, 193 n.52
  26 (religion), 51
33 Henry VIII, cc.
  5 (stallions), 245 n.135
  6 (archery), 185
  11 (meat prices), 116 n.86
  15 (sanctuary), 8, 50, 187
  17 (vagabonds), 195 n.57
  18 (cloth manufacture), 127
34 & 35 Henry VIII, cc.
  1 (religion), 51, 188-91, 206, 207 n.24
  3 (fuel), 193
  7 (pricing wines), 19, 52, 111
  9 (export), 179 n.3
  23 (revising Statute of Proclamations), 37 n.24, 50, 175-7, 184, 283, 285, 287
  26 (Wales), 52
35 Henry VIII, c.5 (religion), 51, 207 n.24
37 Henry VIII, cc.
  12 (tithes), 51, 135 n.139
  15 (wool sales), 195, 201-2, 210-11, 277
  23 (wine prices), 52
1 Edward VI, cc.
  1 (religion), 207 n.24, 208 n.25, 209
  2 (religion), 207 n.24
  6 (wool spinners), 211
  12 (repeal of certain statutes, viii, 50, 52, 174-5, 200-1, 206 n.21, 207 n.24, 257, 277, 292
  14 (chantries), 207 n.24
2 & 3 Edward VI, cc.
  1 (Act of Uniformity), 210 n.31
  19 (religion), 208 n.26, 245
  36 (sheep), 216
3 & 4 Edward VI, cc.
  2 (cloth manufactor), 212 n.37, 223 n.70
  5 (unlawful assemblies), 52, 224 n.72
  21 (regrating), 269

INDEX OF STATUTES CITED

5 & 6 Edward VI, cc.
  5 (enclosure), 245 n.135
  6 (cloth manufacture), 212 n.37
  7 (buying and selling of wool), 52–3, 223 n.70, 243 n.127
  14 (forestalling, regrating, engrossing), 269 n.60
  17 (wine prices), 244 n.133
  19 (coins), 52–3, 214 n.44, 221 n.65, 243 n.127, 278

7 Edward VI, cc.
  5 (wine prices), 244 n.133
  6 (export of coin), 245 n.138
  11 (unlawful assemblies), 52

INDEX

Adair, E. R., 159–60, 161 n.30, 162, 177, 262 n.40
ale and beer vessels, 17
Alford, Edward, 155 n.8
aliens, 50, 142–3, 145–6, 187 n.31, 193; *see also* denizens
alliances and allies, 67–8, 82, 87 n.4
Alward, Thomas, 281
Anabaptists, 11, 135, 136 n.140, 137–9
angles, *see* coinage
Antwerp, 70, 129, 143
Anvers, fair of, 104 n.49
apparel, *see* clothing
archery, neglect of, 89–93, 108, 146–7, 258
armor, price of, 193; *see also* weapons and armor, pricing of
Armthorpe, 181 n.11, 181 n.14
army, maintenance of, 87 n.4, 88, 109 n.63, 181; order of, 66; pay of, 233 n.99; unemployed military personnel, 225; *see also* deserters; mustering; wages, for soldiers
Artson, Harmar, 288
assemblies, unlawful, 52, 66, 136, 217–20, 224
Attorney General, 271–2, 276, 278, 285
Audley, Thomas, 21–2, 116 n.87, 122, 124–5, 127, 130–1, 134, 144 n.162
Augmentations, court of, receivers of, 11; treasurer of, 201
Austria, 69
Aylmer, John, 154, 163, 169
Aynsty, 259

Bacon, Francis, 155, 173
Bacon, Matthew, 30 n.3
Bacon, Nathaniel, 155–6, 173
Bacon, Nicolas, 155, 173
Baker, Edward, 291 n.125
Baker, John, 241, 253 n.6
Bale, John, 189, 190 n.40
Barbaro, Daniel, ambassador of Venice, 293

Barewell, Richard, 260
Barker, John, 264
Barker, Robert, 264
Barking, 197, 290
barley, export of, 71; pricing of, 71, 119, 144, 202; sale of, 261
Barnes, Richard, 287–8
Barnes, Robert, 189
Basille (pseudonym), *see* Becon, Thomas
Beale, Robert, 19
bear-baiting, *see* London, bear-baiting in
Becket, Thomas, 138–9, 170
Becon, Thomas, 189
Bedford, 253
beggars, 80, 117, 119; *see also* vagabonds
Berkshire, 126, 195
Berthelet, Thomas, 21
Berwick, 191, 237; *see also* Lawson, George
Bible and Scripture, 133, 137–8, 140, 188–9, 191, 205, 208; Great Bible, 9, 188–9, 256
Bird, John, Bishop of Chester, 255
Blackheath, 66
Blackstone, William, 156
Boleyn, Ann, 134
Bonner, Edmund, Bishop of London, 144, 256
books, licensing of, 133, 136, 138, 156 n.9, 189, 234 n.100, 280, 290; of exports, 148; *see also* heretical books; printing
Bordeaux, 79, 130
Borrow, John, 263 n.45
Borstick, John, 280 n.90
Boston, 231
bows and arrows, prices of, 10–11, 192; *see also* archery
Boys, William, justice of the peace in Kent, 10, 192
branding, *see* penalties
Branston, Christopher, 281
Brereton, Sir Richard, 260
Bridgewater, 258
Bristol, 179 n.3, 273

INDEX

Brittany, 66; invasion of, 69
Brooke, Robert, 34, 35 n.19, 36 n.23
Bruges, fair of, 104 n.49; Treaty of, 88
building, *see* London, against increase of
Bullinger, Johann Heinrich, 133
Bulmer, 260
Burgate, 268
Burghley, Lord, 38 n.30
Burgundy, 69–70, 78, 273
Burnet, Gilbert, 156
Burwell, John, 278
Busch, Wilhelm, 70, 72 n.30
butchers, 115, 240, 241 n.121, 254, 266, 268; *see also* London, butchers of
butter, export of, 45, 203 n.12, 284, 288; forfeiture of, 151; hoarding of, 259; pricing of, 45, 214, 229–30, 232, 233 n.98, 236; regrating of, 269; shortage of, 241; surplus of, 103; *see also* London, pricing of butter
Byrde, Richard, 275

Calais, 191, 233 n.99, 237; exchange rates at, 76 n.46; exports to, 73 n.35, 119 n.97, 120, 144, 149, 150, 226; free market at, 18, 70, 83, 104; governing of, 47; religious troubles at, 171 n.54; repairs in, 89 n.10; staple at, 45, 60 n.4, 75, 202; victualing of, 15, 80, 180, 204 n.14, 284; wrecks at, 67
Cambridge, University of, 140
Canterbury, 251 n.3, 267; Archbishop of, 283; *see also* Cranmer, Thomas
carolus, *see* coinage
Catherine of Aragon, 134
Catt, Rodner, 280
Cecil, William, 219, 226, 227 n.82, 231–2
chamberlain, 283
chancellor, 7–8, 13, 20 n.62, 22, 24, 30, 41, 44, 49, 79, 83, 107, 110 n.66, 111 n.70, 115, 122, 135, 136, 148, 196–7, 226–7, 282–3
chancery, 96–8, 135 n.139, 175, 270–1; clerk of, 23, 26, 270, 271 n.65
Chapuys, Eustace, 22, 136 n.140, 143, 180, 187 n.31
Charles I, 181 n.11
Charles V, 22, 105 n.52, 141, 143–4, 155, 173 n.58, 179 n.4, 180
cheese, export of, 45, 203 n.12, 284, 288; forfeiture of, 151; hoarding of, 259; pricing of, 45, 214, 229–30, 232, 236, 240, 278; regrating of, 269; shortage of, 241; surplus of, 103; *see also* London, pricing of cheese
Chester, 8, 50, 187, 251 n.3, 268, 285, 288; *see also* Bird, John

Chichester, 253 n.6
churches, bringing horses and mules into, 244; fighting in, 244; clerics fighting in, 244 n.134
cinque ports, 88 n.8; warden of, 17, 102
clergy: benefit of, 145–6; *see also* churches; preaching; priests
cloth, duties on, 43; export of, 123, 125–6, 150 n.178; manufacturing of, 9, 17, 19, 122–4, 127, 130, 193–5, 202, 210, 212; markets for, 70; standards for, 212; trade in, 129–30, 212; *see also* clothiers; wool
clothiers, 10, 123–8, 130, 195; *see also* cloth
clothing, regulations on apparel, 89 n.9, 116–17, 146
Cobham, Lord, Mayor of Rochester, 150
coinage, 14, 38, 40, 59, 60 n.6, 75, 105, 107–8, 118 n.62, 225–6, 234–5, 237, 243, 246, 253, 268, 277 n.82, 278; angles, 105 n.51, 278; carolus, 106; clipping of, 76–8, 82; counterfeiting of, 76, 78, 212–14; crown of the double rose, 106; debasement and devaluation of, 76, 78, 105–8, 191–2, 212–14, 233, 235, 237–9, 243, 246, 252, 264; exchange of, 75–6, 105 n.53, 128–32, 213, 221, 222 n.69, 236–7, 243–5, 277 n.82, 278; export of, 41, 76, 106, 128–9, 213, 234 n.99, 236–7, 244–5, 274; florins, 106; foreign, 77–8, 105–6, 145 n.166; French, 233 n.99; george noble, 106; groats, 77, 105 n.51, 235, 237, 239, 243 n.128; Irish, 78, 88, 191; placks, 78; royals, 278; shilling, 25, 27, 235, 237–9, 252–3, 264; teston, 213–14, 222 n.69, 243, 264, 277 n.82; value of, 25, 27, 52–3, 105–6, 107 n.8, 107 n.57, 145 n.166, 192, 212–14, 221, 233 n.99, 235, 243–4, 246 n.140, 277 n.82, 278
Coke, Sir Edward, 30, 34–6, 38, 41, 108 n.61, 155, 181
Coke, John, 280 n.90
Colchester, 28, 251 n.3, 263 n.45, 266, 284
Combe, John, 281
Commissions of Oyer and Terminer, 88 n.7
common law, 32, 35–6, 39, 40 n.39, 43, 53, 61, 63, 66, 67 n.10, 76, 82–3, 154, 159, 171, 185, 214, 220, 223 n.70, 229, 262, 274, 277, 279
Common Pleas, court of, 41, 61, 184–5, 201 n.5, 228, 252 n.3, 263, 270 n.62
copyholds, 218
corn, 71–2, 101–3, 120, 122, 144, 149, 150–1, 171, 179, 203, 260; engrossing of, 100 n.36; licensing of, 72, 149; pricing of, 102; regrating of, 102 n.42, shortage of, 231, 260; *see also* grain

INDEX

Cornwall, 66, 241
Corson, Robert, 10
council, 21, 25, 31–3, 41, 42, 53 n.70, 65, 71, 78, 87, 104, 123 n.100, 126–9, 138, 140, 157, 171, 187 n.29, 198–9, 203 n.12, 204, 206–7, 210 n.32, 212–14, 217, 224, 233 n.99, 236, 240, 254, 257, 274; advice of, 1, 38, 45, 166, 234–5; advice and consent of, 193, 197, 223; council of the North, 264; council in Star Chamber, 88 n.7, 92, 100; orders and instructions of, 2 n.7, 113, 119, 245, 252–3; price setting by, 46, 111 n.70; role in enforcing proclamations, 63, 82, 97, 120, 122, 147, 158 n.20, 161, 166, 175, 179, 180–1, 209, 212 n.36, 226–8, 231, 241–2, 246–9, 259–61, 279–92; role in formulating proclamations 12, 16, 18–19, 139, 293; role in regulation of book trade, 188, 190 n.40
Coventry, 87 n.4, 252 n.3; *see also* Lee, Rowland
Coverdale, Miles, Bishop of Exeter, 137, 170, 189
Cox, Richard, 256 n.21
Cranmer, Thomas, Archbishop of Canterbury, 19, 134, 135 n.139, 139 n.147, 205–6, 208–9
Crayer, Philip, 150 n.177
Cresset, Thomas, 260
Croke, John, 22
Cromwell, Thomas, 10–16, 22 n.69, 25 n.80, 33, 60 n.7, 85–6, 96 n.24, 115–16, 119–22, 124–6, 128, 130–2, 134, 136, 254–5, 271 n.65; concern for statutory authority, 44–5, 47 n.56, 53, 59–60, 98, 111, 112–13, 118–19, 129 n.121, 153, 165, 167–8, 173–4, 178–9, 243; effort to improve enforcement of proclamations, 148–51, 170, 253; policy similar to Northumberland's, 200, 246; report of judicial decision on proclamations, 41–2, 158, 161, 163–5; role in formulating proclamations, 139
Cromwell, Thomas, grandson of above, 169
crossbow, 89–94, 146, 185, 186 n.26, 201 n.5
crown of the double rose, *see* coinage

Dalison, William, 37, 53, 54 n.71, 108, 246 n.140
Danby, Robert, 291 n.125
Danckered, Sebastian, 284, 288
Dartmouth, 75
Davies, Margaret G., 251, 256 n.22, 270 n.63

death, *see* penalties
de Ayala, Don Pedro, 65, 83
de la Pole, Edmund, Earl of Suffolk, 79
de la Pole, John, Earl of Lincoln, 66
de la Ware, Lord, 231
denizens, 187 n.31, 193, 263; *see also* aliens
Denmark, 68, 280
Derbyshire, 74 n.37
deserters, punishment of, 187 n.31
Dicey, Albert V., 157
Dixon, Richard W., 157
dogs, at court, 195 n.57; seizure of, 201 n.5
Doncaster, 181 n.11
Dorset, 88
Dudley, John, Earl of Warwick, and Duke of Northumberland, 15–16, 37, 53 n.70, 59, 62–3, 181 n.14, 200, 218, 224, 226–7, 227 n.82, 229–30, 233, 239, 242, 243, 246–7, 249, 262, 269, 277, 279
Durham, 23
duties, 43, 70, 110, 142, 145–6, 172, 274

East Anglia, 10, 103, 124, 144, 211
ecclesiastical and canon law, 32–3, 50–1, 128, 136 n.141, 148, 187, 190, 204, 207–9, 223; *see also* clergy; excommunication; heresy; heretical books; London, clergy of and tithes; pilgrimage; preaching; priests
Eden, Thomas, clerk of Star Chamber, 286
Edward I, 196
Edward III, 44, 90, 107, 194, 262 n.40
Edward IV, 72, 73 n.34, 76, 108, 290
Edward VI, 13, 16, 19–20, 26, 31, 52–3, 63, 98, 131, 156, 176, 200–6, 208, 211, 213–15, 217, 222–7, 230–1, 233 n.99, 234–5, 237–8, 241–6, 252, 253 n.5, 253 n.6, 254–5, 257–9, 265, 278–9, 289, 291–2
Edwards, Symond, 287
Egerton, Thomas, 33, 34 n.13, 37
Elizabeth I, 17 n.52, 21–2, 26, 30 n.3, 37–8, 40 n.39, 53, 169, 172 n.57, 251, 270 n.63, 280 n.90, 290
Ellesmere manuscripts, 280, 291 n.125
Elton, G. R., 1 n.2, 3, 18 n.56, 21 n.64, 33 n.12, 41 n.40, 45, 49 n.59, 96 n.24, 97 n.29, 113 n.76, 117 n.90, 118 n.59, 119 n.95, 121 n.102, 123 n.106, 126 n.112, 127 n.115, 128 n.117, 129 n.120, 129 n.121, 130 n.123, 132 n.130, 133 n.131, 133 n.132, 137 n.142, 139, 143 n.154, 145 n.164, 147 n.171, 151 n.183, 161–5, 168–9, 170 n.50, 174–5, 180 n.6, 215 n.47, 251 n.2, 253 n.5, 262 n.40, 280 n.87, 282 n.94
embargo, 25, 243–5, 172–3

INDEX

enclosure, *see* farms
English primer, 187
engrossing, *see* corn; farms; grain
Erasmus, Desiderius, 205
Essex, 101, 122, 126, 252; *see also* Waltham in Essex
Etaples, Treaty of, 68–70
exchanges, keepers of, 129–30; *see also* coinage
Exchequer, court of, 37, 120, 147–50, 150 n.77, 151, 179, 184–5, 202, 225–6, 241, 258, 262–3, 270–1, 274, 275 n.73, 276–9, 288, 291–2
excommunication, 244 n.134
Exeter, 22, 28, 218; *see also* Coverdale, Miles
exportation, 88, 148, 228; restraint of, 7, 17, 39, 43–4, 71–3, 103, 108, 143–5, 150 n.178, 179 n.4, 180, 202, 204, 226; unlicensed, 27, 37 n.24, 45, 60 n.7, 71, 103 n.47, 109 n.63, 146, 149, 150 n.178, 172, 179–80, 202, 226, 254, 258, 275–6, 278, 284–5, 287–8, 291 n.125; *see also* books; coinage; cloth; food; fuel; grain; gold; leather; metals; rye; silver; wool

false tales, 80, 136, 147, 187 n.31, 204–5, 218, 221, 223, 234–5, 237–9, 243, 246–7, 252–4, 264–5
farms, cultivation of, 245 n.135; enclosure of, 94 n.21, 95–8, 108, 214, 216–20, 223; engrossing of, 94–5, 236; *see also* Isle of Wight
fast, days of, 19; *see also* Lenten fast
Faversham, 251 n.3
feudal rights, of king, 67, 258, 271
fines, *see* penalties
Firth, John, 133, 189
fish, breeding of, 196; fisherman, 68 n.11, 208, 295; forestalling of, 100 n.36; pricing of, 111 n.70, 188 n.33, 196–7; selling of, 44; *see also* forestalling, of herring; Thames
Fish, Simon, 133
Fisher, John, Bishop of Rochester, 22–3, 136
Fitzherbert, Anthony, 34, 35 n.19, 41, 42–3
Fitzwilliam, Sir William, 47
Flanders, 11, 106, 143 n.155, 190 n.40, 192, 194, 253 n.6
florins, *see* coinage
food, export of, 121, 148, 284; pricing of, 37, 112 n.74, 255–6; regulation of meals, 104; shortage of, 226; *see also* barley; butter; cheese; corn; fish; grain; meat; oats; rye; wheat

foreign affairs, 38–40, 46, 57, 59, 67, 70–2, 84, 87, 104 n.49, 109 n.63, 141, 171–2; *see also* treaties
foreign travel, regulation of, 79
forestalling, of foreign merchandise, 110 n.36; of herring, 100 n.36; *see also* fish; grain; wine
forest laws, 40, 181, 221
Fortescue, Sir John, 31–3, 36 n.20
Fowey, 75 n.41
Fox, Richard, Bishop of Winchester 9–10
France, alliance against, 68 n.13, 105 n.52; coins of, 233 n.99; commodities from, 130; exports to, 120 n.99, 192; fisherman of 68 n.11; imports from, 38, 45–6, 275 n.74; king of, 141, 155; merchants travelling to, 13; peace treaty with, 29, 68–9, 201; war with, 69 n.18, 88, 99, 181, 186, 187 n.29, 187 n.31, 193 n.52; wines of, 110, 111 n.69
Francis I, 9, 141, 144, 154 n.3, 155, 173 n.58
Fraye, Robert, 269
fryd, 69
fuel, export of, 224, 227; *see also* London, fuel

games, unlawful, 81, 89–94, 146–7, 253 n.6, 263, 266, 281
Gardiner, Stephen, 43–4, 154–5, 157, 163, 171–3, 176, 204–6
Gascony, 87, 100 n.36, 110, 111 n.69
Gee, Henry, 137 n.143, 188 n.35
george noble, *see* coinage
Gibson, William, 264
Gloucester, 122
Glover, John, 197 n.65, 290
gold, export of, 147–8; *see also* coinage; metals
Goodall, John, 282
Gostwick, John, 149–50
Grafton, Richard, 4 n.10, 19, 211 n.34, 247, 257 n.25
grain, 17, 73, 88, 119, 121, 144–5, 180 n.6, 228, 230–1, 233, 259 n.31, 260–1, 269, 272, 275, 281, 288; engrossing of, 100, 102, 122, 238–9, 269, 281; export, licensed, 73, 103, 119–21, 144, 149, 203–4; export, unlicensed, 71–2, 83, 103 n.47, 117, 120–1, 149–50, 171, 179, 202, 229, 272–4, 285, 288; forestalling of, 100, 101 n.40, 102, 238–9, 263, 266, 269, 281; hoarding of, 10, 100–3, 121, 148, 185, 259; pricing of, 73, 99–100, 103, 122, 150, 185, 202–3, 203 n.12, 203 n.13, 229–30, 236, 261; regrating of, 100, 102–3, 122, 150, 230, 238–9, 263, 266,

311

INDEX

grain (*cont.*)
  269; searches for, 101–3, 108, 121, 149–50, 185, 228–9, 231, 258 n.31, 259, 261 n.39; shortage of, 7, 73, 94 n.21, 95, 99, 101, 120, 204, 214, 224 n.76, 226, 261; surplus of, 101 n.40, 102–3, 202, 260; *see also* barley; corn; London, scarcity of grain in; malt; oats; rye; wheat
Gras, Norman, S. B., 71–3, 103 n.47
great seal, 39, 42, 46, 49, 51–2, 69 n.19, 283
Great Yarmouth, 44, 272
Gresham, Richard, 9, 123 n.106, 126, 130–2
Grey, Lord, 219 n.59
Grimsby, 251 n.3
groats, *see* coinage
Guildford, Sir Edward, 102
Guildhall, 198, 295

Hales, John, 216
Hall, Edward, 91
Hampshire, 257
Hampton Court, 181
handguns, 89–94, 146, 147 n.170, 185–6, 201 n.5, 244
Hardy, William J., 137 n.143, 188 n.34
Harwich, 251 n.3
Hatfield Chase, 23, 181, 186
hawking, 11, 19, 24, 181–2, 284, 286, 291 n.125
Henley on Thames, 170
Henry VI, 44, 71
Henry VII, 5, 13–14, 28, 57, 59, 60, 64–73, 75–83, 85–6, 88–9, 94–5, 96 n.26, 97–8, 104–5, 109, 110 n.65, 118, 200, 262, 270–4, 279
Henry VIII, 1 n.3, 5, 14, 20–2, 24–5, 49, 57, 85, 88, 90, 118, 128 n.118, 165, 169, 177 n.68, 178, 181–5, 187 n.31, 189–91, 194–6, 199–200, 255, 258, 262; accused of tyranny, 154–7; appoints commission, 151; character, 159; concern about illegal export, 151, 180 n.61; death of, 174, 176; debasement of coinage, 107, 212, 233, 235, 243 n.129; enclosure legislation, 95, 97; first marriage, 135; given right to repeal export legislation, 121; injunctions of, 205; payment of debts, 201; price control legislation, 109, 112; proclamation on white meats, 28; proclamation on wool winding, 225; role in formulating proclamations, 11–12, 18, 137 n.142, 139; statutes on religion, 207
Henryksen, Peter, 288
Hensted, 259 n.31
Hereford, 232, 251 n.3

heresy, 49, 132–3, 135–40, 168 n.48, 174, 188–91, 204–5, 207 n.24, 208, 255–6, 267, 282; *see also* Anabaptists; heretical books; Lollardy
heretical books, prohibition of, 12, 51, 132–3, 137, 188–90, 256, 280
herring, *see* forestalling, of herring
hides, *see* leather and hides
Hill, Justice, 36
Hilter, Adolph, 163
Hoak, Dale, 15, 175 n.62, 207 n.23
Hobart, Henry, 37–8
Hodgkin, J. Eliot, 26 n.84
Hogges, John, 286
Holden, Richard, 275
Holdich, Robert, 124, 127
Holdsworth, William, 32 n. 7, 34–5, 55 n.2, 100 n.36, 159 n.22
Holme, 281
Holy Roman Empire, 68–9, 78, 82, 87 n.4, 109 n.63, 141, 155
'homilies', 205–6, 206 n.19, 209
Hope, William, 268
horses, 245 n.135; *see also* churches, bringing horses and mules into
Hostman, Giles, 288
Hughes, Paul, 1–4, 20 n.61, 21, 119 n.95, 140 n.150, 179 n.3
Hume, David, 156–8
hunting, 11, 210; of king's deer, 201, 222
Hurstfield, Joel, 86 n.3, 163–4, 165 n.45, 168
Husse, John, 144 n.163, 154, 157, 171 n.54
Hutton, John, 129, 130 n.122

importation, restriction of, 69 n.19; unlicensed, 187 n.31, 275 n.74; *see also* duties; wine
impressing, 195, 280, 291 n.125
indulgences, 136
inflation, 57; *see also* prices; coinage, debasement and devaluation
Innocent VIII, papal bull of, 66
inns, 91 n.13, 94, 110 n.64, 253 n.6
'Instructions for a Principal Secretary', 19
insurrection, 66, 109 n.63, 136–7, 210 n.33, 215, 218–20, 224, 234 n.100
Ipswich, 111 n.68, 170, 251 n.3, 284
Ireland, 78, 187 n.29, 233 n.99; *see also* coinage, Irish
Isakke, Thomas, 286
Isle of Wight, 94

jailers, 24 n.78
James I, 30, 37–8, 154, 155 n.8, 161, 163, 173, 290, 295
James V of Scotland, 20

312

INDEX

Johnson, John, 203, 237
Johnson, Otwell, 202, 203 n.13, 237
Jordan, W. K., 55 n.2, 174 n.61, 200, 204 n.15, 206 n.21, 210 n.33, 212 n.36, 213 n.41, 216 n.49, 218 n.56, 220 n.62, 222 n.68, 225 n.78, 227 n.82, 244 n.131, 246 n.139
Joy, George, 189
Julius II, 72
justices of the assize, 24 n.78, 79
justices of the peace, negligence of, 146, 196, 225, 240, 248, 250, 256–8, 261 n.39, 281; reports of, 95; to enforce proclmations, 50, 245, 269; to enforce statutes, 79–80, 92; to imprison offenders, 204–5, 208, 236, 238; to inquire about unlawful assemblies, 220; to make proclamations, 44; to search for impotent poor, 119; to see markets supplied, 99, 101–2, 185, 214, 228, 231; writs and letters directed to, 24 n.78, 113–14, 229, 232, 241, 253, 259–60

Kent, 23, 27, 99; *see also* Boys, William
kerseys, 125–8; *see also* clothiers; wool
Ket's rebellion, 217
King's Bench, court of, 63, 80, 88 n.7, 184–5, 227, 252 n.3, 263, 270 n.63, 284
King's Book, 51 n.64, 189–90, 206
king's officers, prohibition against maiming of, 8, 19, 145, 201, 268
knighthood, distraint of, 24, 67, 82–3, 258 n.30, 270–1, 274
Knightly, Sir Edmund, 34–5
Knox, John, 245

laborers, 89 n.10, 95; *see also* wages
Larkin, James, 1–4, 20 n.61, 21, 119 n.65, 140 n.150, 179 n.3
Latimer, Hugh, 258
Latin grammar, 187
Lawson, George, Treasurer of Berwick, 10
lead, 75; *see also* metals
Leadam, I. S., 72, 96 n.25, 96 n.26, 98 n.31, 259 n.31, 281 n.91, 281 n.92
leather and hides, export of, 146, 179, 210, 227, 254, 275, 290; pricing of, 210; restraint of, 224; sale of, 275 n.74
Lee, Rowland, Bishop of Coventry and Lichfield, 116 n.87
Leicester, 252 n.3
Leicestershire, 35, 254
Le Neve, Peter, 4 n.10
Lenten fast, 24, 28, 57, 128, 188 n.33, 208, 224, 245, 247, 254–5, 265–6, 282
Lichfield, *see* Lee, Rowland

Lincoln, 251 n.3, 254 n.11, 255, 259; *see also* de la Pole, John; Longland, John
Lincolnshire, 22–3, 136, 181 n.11
Lingard, John, 157
Lisle, Lord, 47, 120, 144, 150 n.178, 154, 171 n.54
Lollardy, 133 n.131
London, bear-baiting in, 190 n.43; brothels of, 190 n.43; building, against increase in, 38, 155 n.8; butchers of, 113–16, 114 n.79, 115 n.81, 115 n.85, 185 n.85, 241, 254; butter, pricing of in, 240; cheese, pricing of in, 240–1; circulation of books in, 243 n.100; city government of, 6, 17, 92, 94, 184, 191, 196–7, 201 n.4, 210 n.32, 236, 242, 253; clergy of and tithes, 51, 134–5; commissions of, 88 n.7; Corporation of, records, 251 n.3; Court of Aldermen, 6–7, 14, 22–3, 28, 94, 112 n.74, 114–15, 135 n.139, 184, 197–8, 201 n.4, 236, 254, 265; crossbows and handguns, prohibition against, 92, 94; fuel in, 193, 240; games, unlawful, 94; grain, pricing of in, 203–4; grain, scarcity of in, 100, 102; idle people in, 195; keepers of exchange in the Tower of London, 75; king's absence from, 19; king's service, lodging those in the, 210; mayor of, 6–7, 18, 23, 28, 112, 135, 183–4, 190 n.40, 196 n.60, 197–8, 241, 253; meat, pricing of in, 112–16, 113 n.76, 115 n.81, 184, 240, 242 n.126; military personnel and residence in, 225; plague in, 104; plays and interludes, prohibition of in, 8, 28, 191, 220 n.61, 254; poulterers of, 185 n.23; pricing in, 242, 254; proclaiming proclamations in, 27, 89 n.9; residence requirement and employment in, 224; sheriffs of, 28; sugar, pricing of in, 183; supplying of, 98–9, 121; vagabonds in, 17, 118, 119 n.95, 234, 255; *see also* Bonner, Edmund; Medway; Stokesley, John; Thames
London Bridge, 190 n.43, 196
Longland, John, Bishop of Lincoln, 3, 170, 254–5
lord admiral, 8, 196–9, 283, 295
lord chief justice, 145, 151–2, 166, 173, 283
lord privy seal, 7, 49, 196, 283
lords ordinaires, 107
Louis XII, 4 n.9
Low Countries, 104, 203; *see also* Flanders; Netherlands
Luther, Martin, 132
Lutherans, 143 n.155
Lynn, 27, 150 n.178, 288
Lysse, John, 287

313

INDEX

Magna Carta, 41 n.39
Maitland, Frederick, 158
malt, export of, 150, 203 n.13, 228; pricing of, 144, 228
Marillac, Charles D., 154, 157, 161
Marler, Anthony, 9, 188
martial law, 145 n.164
Mary I, 21, 35-6, 42-3, 54, 108, 246, 277
Mary of Hungary, 12, 190 n.40
Mary Tudor, 4 n.9
Mascy, John, 285, 287-8
Mason, Sir John, 232-3
Mawdysley, John, 150 n.178
Maximilian, 68-70
Maxwell-Lyte, H. C., 26
meat, forfeiture of, 191; pricing of, 7, 19, 46, 60 n.7, 109, 112-17, 148, 165, 184-5, 214-15, 218, 221, 240-2, 253 n.5, 253 n.6, 255, 278
Medway, 196
Merchant Adventurers, 18, 70, 83, 125, 129
Merriman, Roger B., 17, 41 n.40, 42 n.41, 86 n.2, 145 n.165, 158
metals, export of, 74-5, 147-8, 210; mining of, 73-4, 83; pricing of, 73
Middlesex, 195, 252 n.3
monastic property, confiscation of, 181
money, *see* coinage
monopoly, 39, 74, 186
Montmorency, 154
Mordewe, William, 230 n.89
More, Sir Thomas, 35, 98, 132, 141
Morre, Francis, 36 n.23
Morrice, James, 38-40, 107, 246 n.140
Muller, James, 43 n.45, 171 n.55, 171 n.56, 206 n.19, 206 n.20, 206 n.21
murder, *see* penalties
mustering, 23, 66-7, 67 n.11, 69, 69 n.18, 109 n.63, 141-2

navy, 187 n.31; *see also* impressing
Nedeham, Sir Robert, 260
Netherlands, 141-4; *see also* Low Countries
New Romney, 94, 251 n.3, 259
Newby, James, 281
Nice, Treaty of, 141
Norfolk, Duke of, 22, 41, 103, 141-2, 144, 158, 161, 163-4, 166, 180 n.6
Norfolk, 17, 101, 252 n.3, 258 n.31, 263, 268
Northamptonshire, 26, 35, 101
Northgate, 268
Northumberland, 10
Norwich, 99, 102, 150 n.178, 211, 224 n.76, 233 n.98, 251 n.3, 254, 257 n.26, 266; *see also* Mordewe, William

Nottingham, 251 n.3
Nottinghamshire, 102 n.40

oats, sale of, 261; *see also* grain
Ogilvie, Charles, 161
Oxford, 254; University of, 140
Oxfordshire, 195, 219 n.59, 254

Paget, Sir William, 190, 207 n.23, 256 n.21
papal bulls, 66, 133, 141
pardon, 66, 88 n.7, 89, 96, 139, 145-6, 210, 217, 219, 220 n.64, 224, 226, 267; papal, 136
Parliament, 42-3, 65-6, 78-81, 102, 166-8, 182-3, 193, 194 n.54, 292; authority of, 153-9, 293-4; coinage and exchange legislation in, 75-7, 105, 107-8, 129, 131-2; debate on statute of proclamations, 154-64, 170 n.54, 171-4; delegates powers to proclamations, 42-53, 110-11, 113-21; ecclesiastical legislation in, 133-4, 135 n.139, 141 n.151, 188-91; enclosure legislation in, 95-8, 216; fails to act on alien customs, 142-3; fails to act on Thames fishing, 198; fails to revise handgun legislation, 186 n.27; of 1539, 126-7, 274-5, 283; of 1547, 202-4, 206-8, 211; of 1548, 210, 216; of 1549, 223-4; of 1552, 239, 242-5, 248, 269; reformation parliament, 118, 123; repeals statute of proclamations, 52-3, 201, 206; revises statute of proclamations, 174-7, 184 n.19; treaty confirmed by, 68
Parsecke, John, 280 n.90
Paul III, 141
Paulet, William, 35
Pembrokeshire, 27
penalties, 61-3, 102, 134, 140, 170 n.54, 172 n.57, 194, 234, 245-6, 288-9; applied by justices of peace, 49; branding, 118, 244 n.134; death, 8, 48-9, 61, 65-6, 68, 78, 82, 93, 109 n.63, 135, 138, 145-6, 171, 189 n.37, 214, 217, 220-1, 223, 245; felony, 76; fine, 53, 67, 76-7, 80-3, 146, 184, 192-3, 202, 208, 214-15, 221 n.65, 225-6, 235-6, 238-44, 265, 268, 270-1, 277 n.82, 283-4, 290; forfeiture, 67, 70, 74, 138, 211-12, 214, 227-8, 235, 239, 243, 273, 275, 277 n.82, 286; imprisonment, 81, 103, 114, 122, 135, 189 n.27, 192-3, 197, 204, 207-9, 211, 213-14, 225-6, 235, 244, 265; in statutes, 79, 89, 91, 98, 100, 114; mutilation, 238, 244 n.134, 246; severe or harsh, 92, 122, 138, 140, 147, 173, 179-80, 182-3, 220-2, 228 n.83, 229-30, 240-1, 255, 269, 284; stocks or pillory, 80-1, 90, 118, 197,

314

INDEX

penalties (*cont.*)
    238–9, 253, 290; treason, 48, 154 n.3; whipping, 118–19, 136, 255 n.18
Percy, Henry, Earl of Northumberland, 66
Petre, William, 190
pillory, *see* penalties
piracy, 143–4, 220 n.64, 280; aiding of pirates, 220
placks, *see* coinage
plague, 187, 210 n.32, *see also* London, plague in
plays and interludes, prohibition of, 8, 28, 191, 220 n.61, 234
Pole, Reginald, 141
Pollard, A. F., 96 n.24, 108 n.62, 158–9, 159 n.21, 177
Pollard, John, 36 n.23
poor relief, 117–19, 119 n.95, 195; *see also* beggars
port officials, 148, 172, 179, 211, 253 n.6, 276; corruption of, 10, 180, 258, 276, 284–5, 288; *see also* cinque ports
Portsmouth, 88
Portugal, 150 n.178, 280
poultry, pricing of, 45, 112, 184, 185 n.23; *see also* London, poulterers of
Pratt, Thomas, 266
prayer book, pricing of, 210, 295
preaching, forbidding of, 209, 254–5; licensing of, 208–9
prerogativa regis, 67 n.10
pricing, 45–6, 72, 100, 112, 226–7, 231, 233, 235–6, 238–41, 244 n.133, 253, 263; *see also* armor; barley; bows and arrows; butter; cheese; coin; fish; food; grain; leather; London; meat; metals; poultry; prayer book; rye; sugar; weapons; wine; wheat
priests, reviling of, 206–7, 222 n.68; *see also* clergy
printing, 234, 246, 290; *see also* books; plays and interludes
privateering, 187 n.31
privy seal, 20–1, 42, 49, 283
proclamations, royal, authority of, 30–54, 293; collections of, 4 n.10; definition of, 1–2; enforcement of, 62–3, 82–3, 87, 147–51, 159–60, 162, 167–8, 170–3, 199, 222–3, 247–92; function and role, 57–60; number, 3–6; penalties for offenses against, 60–2, 81–2, 87, 145–7, 166, 220–2, 246; printing, 21–4; proclaiming of, 27–9; role of council in formulation, 12–8; seals and warrants for, 20–2, 26–7; statutes delegating authority to, 44–54, 109–17; subject matter of, 53–7, 86, 109; writs, 24; *see under individual subject*

proclamations (*cont.*)
    matter listings; *see also* Common Pleas, court of; council; Exchequer, court of; King's Bench, court of; penalties; Star Chamber, court of; 31 Henry VIII, c.8 (Statute of Proclamations)
prostitutes, 66 n.6; *see also* London, brothels of
purveyance, 66
Pyntill, Henry, 284

Rastell, John, 1
regrating, 100 n.36; *see also* butter; cheese; corn; grain
religious pensioners, 11, 201, 210 n.32
retaining, 79–80, 89 n.10, 267
Rich, Richard, 26, 257–8
Richard II, 41 n.40, 42, 71, 80, 164
Richard III, 65
Richard, William, 273
Ringley, Edward, Comptroller of Calais, 10
Roche, Abbey of, 181 n.11
Rochester, *see* Cobham, Lord; Fisher, John
Rolle, Henry, 30 n.3, 35
Roy, William, 133, 189
royals, *see* coinage
rumors, *see* false tales
Russell, Lord, 218
rye, export of, 228; price of, 202, 228, 233 n.98; sale of, 121, 261
Rye, Borough of, 252 n.3

St Germain, Christopher, 32–3
St Luke, Feast of, 188
St Mark, Feast of, 188
St Mary Magdalen, Feast of, 188
Salisbury, 282; bishop of, 36; *see also* Shaxton, Nicholas
Samon, John, 276–7
sanctuary, 8, 50, 145–6, 187
Sandwich, 231, 255
Sandys, William, 115
Sarum, 282
Saunders, Ambrose, 237
Sayer, Henry, 276, 285 n.102, 288
Schanz, George, 72, 109 n.64, 112 n.71
Scotland, 28, 68–9, 81, 88, 109 n.63, 141–2; *see also* James V of Scotland
Selby, Monastery of, 181 n.11
Selden, John, 156 n.9
Sericke, Peter, 280
servants, conduct of, 206; number of, 195
Sewall, William, 273
sewers, 147, 195
Shaxton, Nicholas, Bishop of Salisbury, 282
Sheeley, Edward, 231

315

INDEX

sheriff, 67, 69, 81–3, 98, 201 n.4, 207, 225, 231, 239, 241, 253, 257 n.56, 259–60, 268, 270, 271 n.65
shilling, see coinage
shire levy, see fryd
Shobells, John, 263
Shrewsbury, 90 n.11, 99 n.35, 115 n.82, 251 n.3, 259–61
Shrewsbury, Earl of, 252
Shropshire, 260
silver, export of, 147–8; see also coinage; metals
Simnel, Lambert, 66
Slaughter, James, 272–3
Smith, Baldwin, 276
Smith, Sir Thomas, 38, 107, 219
Smith, William, 197–8, 295
Smythe, Baldwyn, 285 n.102, 287–8
Somerset, Charles, 69
Somerset, Edward Seymour, Duke of, 6–7, 13–16, 43, 52, 57, 61, 63, 154, 165, 171, 174–6, 200–10, 212–14, 216, 217 n.49, 218–23, 222 n.68, 222–30, 241–2, 246–7, 249, 262–3, 265, 276–7, 279, 291, 294
Southampton, 60 n.4, 73, 74 n.37, 75 n.41, 83, 88, 105, 175 n.63, 252 n.3
Spain, 53 n.70, 68 n.13, 87 n.4, 131, 150 n.178; see also Chapuys, Eustache; de Ayala, Don Pedro: Van der Delft, François
Spencer, Sir William, 34–5
Stafford, 8, 187
Staffordshire, 101, 195
Stamfort, Justice, 37
Stanford, 41 n.39
Stantham, 34, 35 n.19
Staples, William, 278
Star Chamber, court of, 37, 63, 80, 82, 87, 88 n.7, 92, 100, 114, 130, 227, 252 n.3, 257, 262, 263, 279–84, 286, 288–92; clerk of, 286, 289
Stationer's Register, The, 24
Steele, Robert, 1, 4 n.11, 12, 20 n.61, 24 n.77, 26 n.83, 27 n.85, 32 n.7, 36 n.22, 55, 58, 63 n.9, 72 n.33, 77 n.48, 110 n.64, 158–9, 262 n.40
stocks, see penalties
Stokesley, John, Bishop of London, 136 n.141
Stone, Lawrence, 65 n.2, 86 n.3, 160–1
Strode, Richard, 291 n.125
Stuart, Humfrey, 291 n.125
Stubbs, William, 157–8
Suffolk, 126, 170, 241, 258 n.31
Suffolk, Duke of, 102
sugar, adulterating of, 183 n.18; pricing of, 18, 183

Surrey, 88
Surrey, Earl of, 105
Sussex, 231, 261 n.39
Sussex, Earl of, 241

Tanner, J. R., 160
Taunton, 281
taxation, 46, 53, 85, 156, 216, 265
Ten Articles, The, 137
teston, see coinage
Thames, regulation of fishing on, 7–8, 196–9, 255, 290, 295
tin, 75; see also metals
tithes, 254 n.11; see also London, clergy of and tithes
Tooley, Henry, 111 n.68
Tracy, Richard, 189
trade, 70–1, 74, 83, 129, 132 n.130, 194; prohibited, 142–5, 273; restricted, 69; unlicensed, 70; see also cloth; duties; exportation; grain; importation; leather
treasurer, 11, 44, 110 n.66, 111 n.70, 120, 282
treaty, 67–8, 70, 194; of peace with France, 29, 87 n.4, 187 n.31, 201, 224, 233 n.99; of peace with Scotland, 28, 109 n.63, 224; see also Bruges, Treaty of; Etaples, Treaty of; Nice, Treaty of
Turkey, 68
Turner, William, 189
Tyburn, 78 n.53
Tyndale, William, 133, 188–9, 280 n.90
Tyrrel, Thomas, parson of Gislingham, 170

vagabonds, 17, 60 n.7, 66 n.6, 80–2, 89 n.9, 94 n.21, 117–18, 119 n.95, 136, 146–7, 195, 219, 234, 255, 266
Van der Delft, François, Spanish ambassador, 175
Vaughan, Stephen, 129, 150–1
Vawdrey, Robert, 285, 287–8
Venice, 110; see also Barbaro, Daniel
Viner, Charles, 30 n.3, 35

wages, for laborers, 44, 81; for mariners, 187 n.31; for soldiers, 233 n.99; in ready money, 10
Wales, 8, 46, 47 n.56, 51–2, 116, 120, 191, 242 n.125
Walgrave, Sir William, J.P., 170
Waltham in Essex, 221–2
Warbeck, Peter, 69
Wards and Liveries, court of, 38 n.30
Warwick, Earl of, see Dudley, John
Warwickshire, 35
watches, keeping of, 88

INDEX

weapons, and armor, pricing of, 15, 192; assault with, 268; disturbing peace with, 80 n.62; in church, 244 n.134; near court, 210 n.134
Western rebellion, 217–18
Westminster, 25, 92, 100, 201 n.5, 283, 289 n.120
wheat, export of, 71, 150 n.178, 228, 253 n.6, 273, 275; pricing of, 71, 119, 171, 188 n.24, 202, 233 n.98; sale of, 261; shortage of, 231
Whelplay, George, 10, 180, 274, 275 n.73, 289 n.120
whipping, *see* penalties
Whitehall, 210 n.32
Whitington, John, 273
Whorwood, William, 276, 285
William the Conqueror, 109 n.63
Wimbush, 291 n.125
Winchester, 105; *see also* Fox, Richard
Winchester, Statute of, 89; proclaimed in London, 89 n.9
wine, empty casks, 88; forestalling of, 100 n.36; importation of, 38, 45–6, 87, 130; pricing of, 19, 51–2, 109–12, 145 n.166, 187, 244; seizure of, 288 n.115; selling of, 44, 263 n.45
Wolsey, Cardinal Thomas, Archbishop of York, 9, 14, 59, 85–9, 91–2, 94, 96–8, 101–6, 108–9, 112–13, 116, 165–6, 200, 216, 253 n.6, 258, 259 n.31, 281, 294
wool, 75, 122–3, 125–8, 193–5, 210, 212, 277; broggers and middlemen of, 201–2, 211; clipping of, 202, 211, 277; export of, 150 n.178, 194, 210–11, 227, 290 n.121; licensing of export, 45, 211; pricing of, 211; selling of, 52, 201–2, 243, 277; winding of, 194, 225; *see also* cloth
wrecks at sea, 67
Wriothesley, Charles, 18, 27 n.85, 29, 144, 154 n.2, 185 n.24, 189, 257
writs of attachment, 97
Wyar, John, 253
Wycliffe, John, 189

Yans, John, 92 n.16
Yarmouth, 150 n.178; *see also* Great Yarmouth
Yaxley, 281
Yelverton, Henry, 155 n.7
York, 16, 29, 69, 242 n.125, 251 n.3, 259–61, 264–6
Yorkshire, 23, 101; *see also* Hatfield Chase
Youngs, Frederic, 1, 2 n.6, 17 n.52, 18 n.53, 20 n.61, 21, 26 n.84, 290 n.121